D1064639

The
Eastern
Screech
Owl

Number Sixteen:
The W. L. Moody, Jr.,
Natural History
Series

Frederick R. Gehlbach

The Eastern Screech Owl

Life History,
Ecology, and
Behavior
in the Suburbs
and Countryside

Texas A&M
University Press
College Station

Library of Congress Cataloging-in-Publication Data

Gehlbach, Frederick R., 1935–
   The eastern screech owl: life history, ecology, and behavior in the sub-
urbs and countryside / Frederick R. Gehlbach, — 1st ed.
      p. cm. — (The W. L. Moody, Jr., natural history series ; no. 16)
   Includes bibliographical references (p.   ) and index.
   ISBN 0–89096–609–5 (acid-free paper)
      1. Eastern screech owl. 2. Eastern screech owl—Texas. 3. Urban
fauna—Texas. I. Title. II. Series.
QL696.S83G44 1994   94–11135
598.9′7—dc20   CIP

For Nancy,
who understands
the spirit of the owl.

Contents

Preface

This is my story about eastern screech owls in Central Texas. It is an ecological life history with observations of behavior, all linked to population dynamics. The tale focuses on comparisons between a suburban and a nearby rural population, studied concurrently so that I might discover peculiarities of the suburban birds in their modified surroundings. No similar study exists for any other creature in the New World. The tale is comprehensive, because I investigated what I thought might be major components of the screech owl's ecosystem. My aim is to estimate what is needed for the bird's successful coexistence with humanity.

I have written a somewhat personal narrative, so the story might be of interest to all who have not lost touch with their ancestral world. But I include quantitative detail sufficient to be relevant to ecologists and ornithologists, since the eastern screech owl has never been the object of focused long-term research. Consequently, much of its life history is unknown or inaccurately reported. I think it is wise as well as interesting to know one's neighbors better than this. My investigations have been those of a suburbanite curious about his left-over natural surroundings, and also the daily work of an academic ecologist.

Because many of the numbers I use may seem overwhelming and the statistics mysterious to amateur biologists, I recommend that you read right past them (though I include a brief introduction to procedures and have eliminated as many statistical symbols and values as possible to facilitate reading). The quantitative detail is meant mostly for professional scientists who want to see my claims substantiated. But everyone can use numbers for comparative purposes—to discover if their local birds do things in more or less the same way. Also, the many references to scientific literature can be ignored selectively or entirely if one simply wants to know what eastern screech owls do to make a living in Central Texas.

This story proceeds from 1967 through 1991—25 years—although the bulk of comparative study was 1976–87. Thus I have been able to follow several generations of screech owls and pinpoint the entire lives of many individuals. Proceeding with a trained eye, without haste, and with attention to detail facilitates discovery, but each new field season still offers surprises. Much remains to be learned, and I hope the following pages will stimulate a new generation of students to discover eastern screech owls, other native species, and themselves in their own cities and rural landscapes.

Owl Hollow
Nesting season, 1993

Acknowledgments

The field work could not have been accomplished without the cooperation of my friends and neighbors. Those who have tolerated me in their yards across all the years are Jerry and Mary Bush, Claudia and the late Dub Davis, and Beanie and the late Ray Graves. They deserve particular thanks.

Others not only permitted my nest boxes for many years but occasionally helped monitor them, as did the Bushes and Davises. They are Cris and Bob Baldridge, Alice and Tony Echelle, Jo and Elmer Fisher, Ann and Ed Gordon, Anita and Howard Rolf, Donna and Darrell Vodopich, and Flo and John Wise. John first showed me how to "fish" for male owls, something he discovered quite accidentally while practicing his casting late in the evening.

Additional neighbors with long-term patience are Helen Benedict and Andy Kovacs, Carol and Noley Bice, Sherry and Roy Craft, Yvonne and Danny Daniel, Ellen and Ray Deaver, Martell and Glenn Hilburn, Nan and Walter Holmes, Gene and the late Esther Jud, Aletha and Tom Keelen, Winnie Lind, Owen Lind, Pam and Don Moes, Ruth Schlecte, Pat and Willard Sledge, Sandra and Don Twitty, Ruth and the late Fred Williams, and the Waco Camp Fire Girls at Camp Val Verde.

My children, Gretchen and Mark, grew up with the owls and helped me from time to time, but my wife, Nancy, has been involved almost daily and hence read the manuscript with special perspicacity. She in particular is aware of the project's demands and the fun we all have had. My family deserves much credit.

I owe a special debt of gratitude to the late William J. Hamilton, Jr., who showed this callow undergraduate that studying a common creature in one's backyard could be as rewarding as searching for rarities in a far-off country. And I cannot forget patient correspondence by the late H. N. Southern, as I began to use nest boxes and could benefit from his pioneering experience with boxes and tawny owls in Wytham Wood.

My students, who helped for short periods, were Julie Bright, Chris Coody, Dave Dillon, Beth Eldridge, Joan Glass, Dave Jordan, Sally Hartfield, Jerry and Jim Kimmel, Jill Leverett, George Newman, Jeff Roberts, Mandeep Singh, John Spencer, and Beth Underwood. Also,

Dave Dillon and Jerry Bush made some nest boxes, and Rod Aydellote, Ann and Ed Gordon, and Curtis Williams supplied some photographs.

Among my colleagues at Baylor University, Bob Baldridge (nest-cavity symbioses), Steve Pearson (radiotelemetry), Ben Pierce (genetics), and Darrell Vodopich (computer technique) aided field and laboratory efforts. Sharon Conry transcribed my many taped field notes, and Darla Millsap typed this manuscript again and again with great interest and good cheer. Bob Baldridge, Chris Coody, colleague Erkki Korpimaki of Finland, and my graduate student Wendy Rosser read the whole manuscript, while colleague Joe Marshall, Jr., read chapter 7. All made many helpful suggestions.

I am grateful for the monetary assistance, released time from teaching, and two sabbaticals given by Baylor University in behalf of this study. Biology department chairmen Keith Hartberg and the late Floyd Davidson were particularly supportive.

Finally, for enriching my life by revealing theirs, and for their resilience in our urbanizing world, I thank 659 eastern screech owls.

The
Eastern
Screech
Owl

1. On Studying Screech Owls
An Introduction

One morning, a long time ago, a youngster rode his bicycle along a path through a wooded city park on his way to a softball game. In an oak grove he spotted three fledgling screech owls on a limb well over his head. The roost tree was a giant that could not be climbed, so he knocked each bird off the limb with his softball. After the intrigue of ultrasoft plumage, death-feigning, defiance, and the pain of extracting talons from fingers, all were placed on another perch for later observation. That afternoon the young owls were gone, but their mystery became a memory that followed me to a place where I could look more closely.

The eastern screech owl is certainly one of our most familiar birds, for it is widespread over the eastern half of North America in wooded environments with tree cavities, including suburbia. Central Texas, inhabited by the boldly marked race, *Otus asio hasbroucki* (Ridgeway), is no exception.[1] Screech owls are familiar because they are quite tolerant of human activity and nest in several kinds of artificial cavities like mailboxes, porch columns, and purple martin houses. Yet the birds are seldom studied. There is only one long-term investigation, but it was not designed to ask or answer questions particular to screech owls. Most of the relevant literature consists of such incidental observations.[2]

I began to watch eastern screech owls in central Ohio about 1945, in upstate New York beginning in 1953, and in southern Michigan six years later. Also, I was able to observe them and their cavity-using relatives in Texas, New Mexico, Arizona, and Mexico beginning 1951. I saw the Central Texas population for the first time in 1955 but did not start a close watch until 1967. A pair that nested in a neighbor's "squirrel box" sparked my interest in a truly thorough study that would detail life history while attempting to learn how suburban individuals got along relative to their rural counterparts. Then, as now, essentially nothing was known about the population ecology of any native bird in urban versus rural North America.[3]

Explorations, 1967–75

At the start I scattered nine nest boxes over 135 hectares (ha) of Woodway (suburban Waco), McLennan County, Texas, banded their occupants, and eventually secured life history information from these nests and others in nearby natural cavities.[4] Not only did I learn about the birds, I learned about myself—how to interpret screech owl activities with a minimum of observer bias.[5] Also, I wanted to discover the longevity and generation time of these permanent residents and, therefore, planned a meaningful long-term investigation. This was the exploratory period of 1967 through 1975, a time to learn by trial and error, eliminate mistakes, and formulate hypotheses based on personal experience.[6]

The early data on 28 successful nests is remembered relative to 31 others that were unsuccessful, sometimes because I inadvertently frightened the adults or exposed their nests to cultural (human) and natural predators. Simply changing my approach—for example, handling females differently depending on their nesting stage and personality, or approaching nests by different paths to avoid making trails for predators—increased the 47 percent rate of success to 65 percent in 171 suburban nests during 1976–91. This significant difference (P = 0.01) illustrates how inexperience can alter findings despite several years of presumed familiarity.

The explorations also showed that suburban screech owls breed no differently in nest boxes than in natural tree cavities, unlike boreal owls and some other secondary-cavity users; but both the screech and boreal owls choose boxes as readily as natural cavities for nesting.[7] Average annual use of five exploratory boxes and five closest, previously used cavities was similar and productivity as measured by fledglings/eggs was no different either.[8] Neither kind of site attracted a particular age class of owls (chapter 8); and even fox squirrels, the most frequent box users besides screech owls, occupied boxes and cavities about equally each year (61 and 55%, P = 0.18).

Nest boxes were made of outdoor plywood, pine, or cedar, which did not influence the owls' site selection or productivity.[8] They had floors of 225 square centimeters cm² (small), 400 cm² (medium), or 625 cm² (large), with four 0.5 cm drain holes and a 7-cm diameter entrance hole 25 cm above the floor. Each was painted dark brown outside and had a sloping lid, 3 cm above the entrance, hinged at the back to permit examination from the top with minimal disturbance. Rarely the inside floor was bare if European starlings had removed debris and not returned. Usually, however, dead vegetation was placed

Adult female (*left*) in suburban box and (*right*) close-up.

inside as nesting material by the starlings, Carolina wrens, tufted tit-mice, great-crested flycatchers, and fox squirrels, or me.

Because relatively few boxes were employed initially, only the floor area was altered to investigate its effect on choice of site and reproductive outcome, although the owls selected deep natural cavities (> 25 cm) with small entrances (< 15 cm) and large bottom areas (> 100 cm²).[8] Floor area seems to influence clutch size in other birds and perhaps nestling survival and fledging in my subjects, so I will say more about this (chapters 5, 6). In the eventual confirmatory study I dispersed the three wood types and sizes of boxes randomly and placed them 2.7–3.5 meters high on straight trees with trunk diameters equal to or larger than box width.

Early findings suggested that intensive study of a few dozen nest boxes would answer more questions more convincingly than the extensive use of hundreds of boxes plus cavities.[9] I wanted to spend sufficient time per nest recording details to avoid estimates of such things as nest success and to eliminate back-dating.[10] When I found that fundamentals like incubation time and vocal function had been incorrectly reported or were unknown, the intensive approach was mandated, although I continued monitoring natural cavities to track individual owls and assess total nesting density. Withal, I opted for small, controlled samples of many details rather than larger, more error-prone samples of fewer variables.

As I would keep detailed records of relatively few pairs, albeit over several generations, I decided against interfering with reproduction in any conservational or experimental manner. For instance, if a chick fell from a watched nest for any reason aside from my tinkering, I let it be. And there would be no experimental nest or owl manipulations, for example altering clutches or supplying additional food. There were two minor exceptions, however. Three orphaned owlets were trans-ferred into two broods for a look at adoption proceedings, which com-menced without incident, and two other broods were "seeded" with live and dead snake food to study an amazing new kind of symbiosis (chapter 6). These four nests are not considered henceforth.

The 59 original nests revealed the screech owl's basic lifestyle, in-cluding its long nesting season (figure 1.1). Major events in first nests of the year were timed for the third and fourth weeks of each month, March through May; but a distinctly later period of replacement nest-ing was evident, centered on the second and third weeks of April through June. This was my first notice that features of first nests dif-fered from those of renests, and I confirmed that the first-egg, first-chick, and first-fledgling events peaked at the same time in 1967–75 as during my 1976–87 confirmatory study. The exploratory period was to prove exemplary for later investigations.

Males were smaller than their mates, mostly monogamous, and pri-marily responsible for defending tree cavities and nest boxes used for dining, roosting, and nesting. This they did most vigorously, vocally, beginning in late January to mid-February about a month before egg-laying. Then too they began to court females with food directly and placed it in each "owned" cavity. Pairs sometimes roosted together and allopreened, which must be important to reproductive cohesion gener-ally, not just pair bonding, for I also saw adults engage in mutual preening with fledglings.

Males were also responsible for feeding their mates and delivering food for chicks until brooding ceased. Then females joined the hunting of small vertebrates, which gave way seasonally to invertebrates, al-though females seemed to be more involved in delivering food from mates to their nestlings and fledglings. Fledglings stayed with their par-ents for 8–13 weeks but dispersed from July into September coinciden-tally with renewed parental vocal activity, different from that of the early spring.

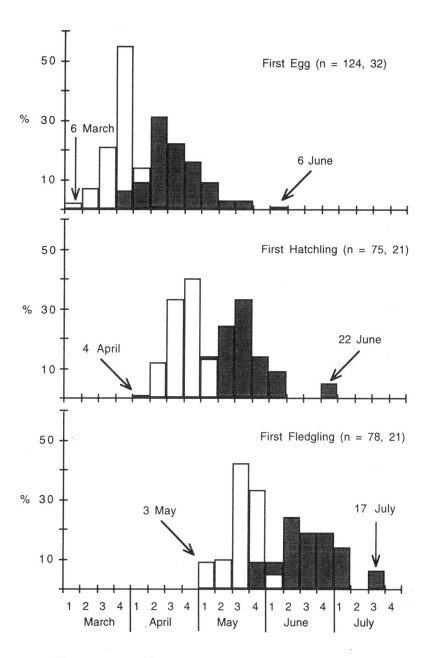

Figure 1.1.   Weekly appearance of major events in first nests of the year (clear columns) and replacement nests (shaded columns), 1967–87. Extreme dates are indicated. Suburban and rural data are combined here but see chapters 5 and 6 for differences. Sample size is number of first nests and then replacement nests. Note the 4.5-month nesting season with major events a month apart. Weekly events were the same, statistically, in both exploratory and confirmatory periods.

Lost clutches were replaced with fewer eggs, and females were the primary chick and fledgling defenders. It seemed that most unsuccessful females disappeared during or after their first nesting attempt and among the survivors, a select few were superior breeders. Their offspring were only a kilometer (km) or two from natal areas and sometimes just 10–12 months of age as breeding adults. Of course there were disappointments like my oldest bird, a 14-year, 2-month-old female, apparently poisoned along with the rest of her family in 1990. But mostly there were exciting discoveries such as the first instance of a female altering her own completed clutch size.

To learn about behavioral development, five owlets were hand-raised to independence. The first two downy chicks with closed eyes were recovered from a cut natural-cavity tree, and two more were hatched from four abandoned eggs, caused by my inexperience. A fifth downy chick with a badly deformed leg was raised to the flying, self-feeding stage but disappeared before its natal dispersal. And four adults with various minor afflictions were kept for a few days to weeks, affording the chance to compare their behavior toward me as an enemy versus the hand-raised birds' acceptance of me as just a "fellow owl."

At first I tacitly assumed that all eastern screech owls were a common entity, a subtle form of human prejudice. But quickly I found that their individualities, including sizes and plumages, were as distinct as the countenances and clothing of humans. Some owls were fierce and defiant, others simply fractious, regardless of how many times they were caught; while a similar proportion were calm and passive in responding to me. A number remained aggressive throughout their lives, but most learned about the handling and changed their attitudes toward (became habituated to) my inevitable prying.

The behavioral differences suggested that reproduction might be altered by the frequency of my nest checks, so two protocols were tested in the last four exploratory years after I knew who comprised the nesting population. Two box nests were monitored every five days and paired with two others occupied by same-age females of similar temperament observed every ten days during incubation each year. Another matched pair was treated likewise during the nestling period. Since I found no significant differences in incubation period and percentage hatch, corrected for clutch size, or in fledging weight and percent of fledged chicks, corrected for brood size, the five-day regime was selected as providing potentially more information (a few chicks were weighed every 2–3 days to record growth rate).[11]

Radiotelemetry may permit one to learn more about movements and home ranges than is possible visually, and I tried it. Two suburban males were captured, one outfitted with a backpack, the other with a tail-mounted transmitter, and both were kept for a week's observations in an outdoor flight cage. Then, with the help of assistants, one was released in its home area and watched simultaneously with its caged partner and a third free-flying suburban male. After two weeks, the transmittered birds were captured and changed places for a second two-week field and laboratory period. Both encumbered birds lost more weight, as did transmittered boreal owls, and moved more often over a wider area than the free individual and others observed previously (see also chapters 6, 9). Because of these biases, I gave up radio-telemetry.[12]

Still another approach was to census the suburban nesting population by driving a 3-kilometer (km) route at dusk, stopping every 400 meters (m), playing a one-minute tape of the pair-contact song (monotonic trill), and listening for responses. Unfortunately, environmental modifications such as wind, rain, moonlight, and cultural noise were so numerous that not enough samples could be obtained in one breeding season to control these variables.[13] By walking 3 km in a suburban ravine (Woodway), I eliminated the hubbub, noted song frequency and attenuation, found nests, and confirmed the lineal extent of home ranges. But the best estimate of nesting density was simply to find essentially all nesting pairs, and I did.

Five rural nest boxes were operated for the first time in 1975. Two were used for nesting but several days after the first suburban boxes were occupied. One rural clutch was eaten by a black ratsnake and not replaced, at least where I could find it, while the other was destroyed by human vandals but replaced by the owls in a third box. Those nestlings fledged but at a smaller size than owlets in two successful suburban nests. Was the breeding biology and perhaps population result in rural owls that different? Just their productivity (fledglings/eggs) was 38 percent by contrast to 57 percent coincidentally in suburbia.

To substantiate the apparent distinctions, I devised a confirmatory study that would assess four generations of about three years each at the suburban and rural locales. Twenty nest boxes of all three sizes would be scattered over 270 hectares (ha), in and around which all natural-cavity nests would be monitored. Logistical explorations in 1974–75 determined plot size, and average number of suitable natural cavities per suburban home range determined the nest-box sample (one natural site per 13.5 ha × 0.259 or one per 3.5 ha of green space, table 1.1). Besides clarifying aspects of life history that might be advantageous in cities, I would compare at least 12 years of concurrent population dynamics to verify the presumed population differences.

Table 1.1. Cultural features of screech owl habitat in Woodway and Harris Creek, 1987. Data are mean ± one standard deviation and (n) of houses and lots. Note that the younger suburb (Harris Creek) has more green space.

Features	Woodway (211)	Harris Creek (84)	P
House length (m)	20.8 ± 2.5	28.1 ± 7.5	=0.001
Distance between houses (m)	9.4 ± 3.4	31.0 ± 17.0	<0.001
Green space per hectare (%)	25.9 ± 6.5	62.8 ± 9.7	<0.001

Confirmatory Study, 1976–91

My primary suburban study area is in Woodway, which has 508 human residents/km^2 (figure 1.2).[14] This plot sits on the Balcones Escarpment, a hilly region at 150–200 m elevation, and includes 35 ha of seminatural ravines. Juniper (cedar)-oak woodland is the common vegetation type joining riparian forest in ravines. Nest boxes are in the front or back yards of interested folks; and, despite the necessary bias of a cooperative landowner in placing them, are broadly dispersed, averaging 311 ± 152 m apart. However, because people move I must relocate or temporarily remove some boxes which vary between 16 and 20 per year. Tree-cavity nest sites in the 270 ha and a 2-km wide survey zone around it are 17–24 each year, depending on storms, cutting, filling, and natural rotting that eliminate the trees or their cavities. Essentially all the natural sites are known.[15]

The survey zone is mostly for monitoring normal fledgling dispersal and adults that forsake nest sites inside the plot for nearby alternatives. An equal area surrounds my rural study plot (figure 1.2). But not all of those perimeter zones is suitable woodland. The landscape is a patchwork of woodlots of different ages, stringers of trees along creeks, city developments, pastures, and farms. Banded and unmarked screech owls nest in only about 20 percent of each perimeter, entirely in habitat contiguous with that of the plots. Here also I can appraise nesting density without boxes to compare with the density inside plots.

Southwestward 8 km from Woodway and 20 m lower in elevation is Harris Creek, a 45-ha bedroom community with a human density equivalent of 402 persons/km^2. This suburb is in former cedar elm-dominated riparian forest. Here five boxes per year are also in yards of the flat 30-ha wooded portion of the site, their density about like that in Woodway. Although I have made no explicit attempt to locate natural cavity nests, I censused two; and others are within the 2-km survey

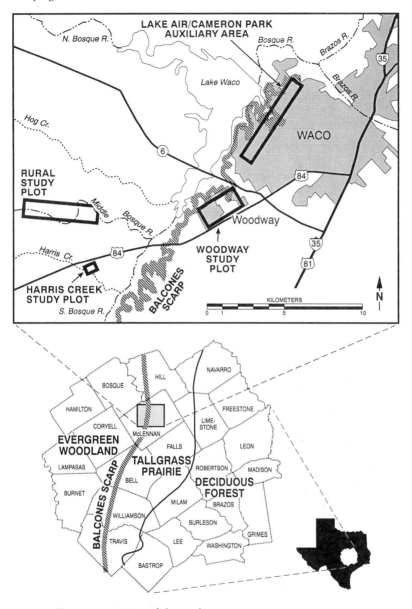

Figure 1.2.   Map of the study area, 1976–91.

radius of my rural plot on the north (figure 1.2). The Harris Creek plot was added in 1979, since this bedroom community was only ten years old and in a rural setting. By contrast, Woodway was 30 years old at that time and located on the southwestern edge of a 100,000-person urban complex (figure 1.2).

Indeed, Harris Creek and Woodway are different developments, based on ten street transects in Woodway and six in Harris Creek (table 1.1). Dwellings are larger and 3.3 times farther apart at Harris Creek. Despite the lack of green belt ravines, Harris Creek has more green space (vegetation) due to its much larger yards. It is only 37.2 percent built on and paved over compared to 74.1 percent in the outside-ravine area of Woodway, and the latter is not unlike cities in general.[16] Also, Harris Creek is cooler and drier, like my rural plot, but its yard vegetation matches Woodway's in most respects (discussed in chapter 2).

Harris Creek is of special interest, because its screech owls might have life history features intermediate between those of older Woodway and others typical of my rural site, presumably closest to the ancestral condition. Certainly I have no intention of comparing population size and flux because of the small sample. Moreover, I want to see if any Woodway or rural owls exchange with Harris Creek; and, to study further such long-distance movements, operate another five to eight nest boxes annually in the Lake Air and Cameron Park suburbs 2.5–6.5 km northeast of Woodway. The local landscape suggests that young birds might move northeast-southwest along the wooded Balcones Scarp (figure 1.2).

My rural study plot is a lineal area at 150 m elevation, half flat riparian forest and half rolling juniper-oak woodland, between Speegleville Road and Camp Val Verde along the floodplain and adjacent hills of the Middle Bosque River. This area has less than one human resident per square kilometer and is 7 km west of the Woodway plot and 3 km north of Harris Creek (figure 1.2). The trial run of 1975 was at nearby Hog Creek but excessive vandalism forced the change in 1976, and I continued to move, remove, and repair boxes which numbered 11–20 per nesting season and were distributed as in suburbia, 318 ± 169 m apart. Some 24–31 tree-cavity nest sites per year were in the plot and its 2-km survey zone, most of which were located by 1981 according to my discovery-rate curve. This plot was discontinued after the 1987 nesting season, when enough data had been obtained to satisfy the four-generation comparison with suburbia.

In late December through early March I visit all nest boxes about every two weeks and walk the Woodway ravines at night to monitor singing and hence impending reproduction. Males inside or close to cavities by late February, replaced by their mates in mid-March, are strong evidence of nesting, so I often find the first egg within a day of laying. Tolerant females are followed daily until their clutch is complete and then checked at five-day intervals until hatching. Males within a few meters of the nest each afternoon certify that all is well. When they move closer, the first egg has hatched. Chicks are also monitored every five days, and when they begin to look out of the entrance hole, I am reminded that fledging is just a few days away (appendix 1).

After the owlets leave I try to keep up with the mobile families as long as possible, usually a week or two. About the time fledglings begin to feed themselves, following any screech owl is difficult, so the field work slows down considerably for the last half of each year. There is increased flying about and vocalizing associated with natal dispersal; but all screech owls are molting then, so observations of individuals with unique plumage or my color markings becomes difficult. Even so, secreted owls are found for me by mobbing songbirds, and I periodically check the habitual roost sites anyway.

Regular daytime assessments include counting, measuring, and weighing nest occupants and other contents between 1300 and 1600 hours (CDT). The tail tips of adults are dipped in different colors of aniline dyes to distinguish them at a distance, and nestlings are spot-dyed while too small to retain aluminum leg bands (less than about 50 grams). Healthy chicks are never deserted, as eggs sometimes are; so the manipulation of flighty females is scheduled during brooding. Nighttime observations from sunset to around 2200 hours and near dawn for an hour or two start with incubation and number two to three per week upon hatching. I select suburban pairs, because of their habituation to humans, and sit against a tree or house about 15 m from their nests. Street, porch, or patio lights provide adequate illumination.

My basic field equipment includes a ladder, notebook and pencil, tape recorder, camera, binoculars, measuring tape and ruler, calipers, spring scales, dyes, sacks, vials, pans, forceps, pliers, and the aluminum bands. Sometimes I have employed a mist net or ground traps, light meter, starlight scope, and an electronic thermometer and hydrometer with leads inside and outside the nest to record microclimate. This baggage could be reduced to just the ladder, notebook or tape recorder, and banding equipment in 1988 after I had recorded enough life history detail. Only individuals, their nest efforts, results, and annual nesting densities were noted thereafter.

Of course eastern screech owls are but a single link in a living "chain-link fence," an ecosystem of climate, vegetation, prey, predators, competitors—a fence without beginning or end as far as I can see. So I selected weather, woody plants, other animals, and especially food supplies to assay at the primary study sites or nearby. Predation by the owls was seen many times, on them never; but indirect evidence at nests provided information on mortality, and carcasses from city streets and elsewhere were examined. Avian depredations could only be guessed at, since barred or great-horned owls nested in or near the plots each year, but I had learned the signs of other vertebrate predators or competitors and occasionally found them in the nest boxes.

Statistical Concerns

Due to the interdependence of variables in the ecosystem context, random sampling is difficult though it is a requisite for statistical analysis. Being fully aware of sampling error, including pseudoreplication, I have done my best to eliminate the common problems. Nevertheless, attempts to draw patterns and deduce processes in the data may be confounded by complex interrelationships. Consider, for instance, that repeated breeding by a particular screech owl may be either replicate or sequential data for comparison with other long-lived individuals, but each annual effort is modified by concurrent environmental conditions, and even the year each bird hatched may affect its subsequent performance by getting it off to a good or bad start (chapter 8).

While the confirmatory study seems to validate repeated patterns or trends, they could be chance occurrences. To find out, it is necessary to subject the data to various statistical analyses which establish the probability (P) that any particular finding is fortuitous. For instance, $P = 0.001$ means that only once in a thousand events is it likely that the result is accidental, and $P = 0.05$ means five times in one hundred, the conventional minimum acceptance of significance.[17] Occasionally I ascribe tentative meaning to something with a probability of error greater than five percent ($P > 0.05$) but ten percent ($P = 0.10$) or less ($P < 0.10$), if I think that sample size (n) is the cause of nonsignificance (NS).

Hereafter, details from just the confirmatory period are used unless stated otherwise, and those years contributing data are given for clarification. But the information is not always confirmatory in the statistical sense. Confirmatory statistics verify patterns or relationships, while exploratory statistics are used to seek them.[18] Much of what follows is exploratory, since I did no experiments to control the many variables I found. However, variables can be controlled statistically. For example, if I find that body weight and birth year both distinguish breeding success (exploration), I can combine them in one analysis to learn if and how they might be independently or interactively influential (confirmation).

Mostly I have repeated measurements of things like owl weight or counts of features such as roost sites. The data are continuously variable, like weight, or categorical, like roosts in evergreen versus deciduous trees, and each set requires different statistical procedures. I may have several weights of several birds and want to know if the individuals differ according to their average (mean, x̄) weights. This involves univariate statistics. But usually I also have age, clutch size, and other information on the same owls. If individualities are of concern, not just body weight, the multiple characteristics are used together, and multivariate statistics are necessary.

Regarding the categorical information, comparisons are made with an expectation of occurrence based on my own experience or someone else's. I may ask if there is a pattern to start with or if the pattern I observe differs from others. The kind of question always determines the statistical procedure, whether the data are categorical or continuous. Nonparametric statistics are necessary for the categorical data as opposed to the parametric tests I use to answer questions about owl weight or lifestyle. Also, nonparametric techniques are necessary for any continuous data that do not approximate a bell-shaped or normal curve on a graph, but I can transform (normalize) such data with logarithms or arcsines in order to use the more versatile parametric procedures.

Averages are a good way to pinpoint patterns, many of which may be adaptations. I can also distinguish among owls on the basis of their relative variations—their lifetime weight changes, for example. This is more likely to disclose the opportunity for natural selection.[19] Therefore, I usually provide averages with (plus and minus) their standard deviations (e.g. 10.2 ±3.7). The latter is a measure of variation in the data so both patterns and processes may be estimated simultaneously. Because very different kinds of attributes may be illustrative in a group context, coefficients of variation (CV) may be given instead. These are simply standard deviations divided by means that allow a standard basis of comparison. Variance ratios provide probability values for distinguishing two samples according to the variation of single features, while covariance analysis does the same for more samples and features per sample.

My univariate parametric techniques that test averages are the student's t-test or analysis of variance (ANOVA, sometimes followed by a Least Significant Difference [LSD] test), and often-used nonparametric substitutes are the Wilcoxon two-sample or rank-sum tests plus the Mann-Whitney and Friedman tests. Chi-square tests are applied to category frequencies like roosts in evergreen versus deciduous trees in winter versus spring, except that Fisher's Exact test is substituted if samples are small. Multivariate analysis of variance (MANOVA), a parametric method, is used when multiple features might distinguish patterns, sometimes after they are discovered with another multivariate procedure called principal components analysis (PCA). The field-guide attributes of those patterns may be discovered with discriminant function analysis (DFA), a third multivariate test.

Correlation demonstrates the extent of covariation between parameters like body weight and food, and linear regression indicates how much weight is gained or lost per unit food. Cause and effect is not shown with these tools, in fact cannot be illustrated without experimentation, but they can indicate relationships or trends and thus suggest processes. I use the Pearson correlation (r) for normally distributed data and Spearman rank correlation (r_s) for non-normal data. The coefficient of determination (r^2) is the amount of variation in the probable dependent feature (e.g., weight) explained by the presumed independent or causative feature (e.g., food). Multiple stepwise regression (MSR) is a favorite approach, because it considers a dependent variable simultaneously related to two or more independent variables and sorts out the variation due to each.

Whenever I discover an apparently meaningful correlation, I run both linear and various curvilinear ($2-7°$ polynomial) regressions to find the highest significant r^2 (logistic regressions are used with categorical data). That is the one displayed in figures or mentioned with its coefficient of determination and probability of error in the text. If not stated otherwise, the pattern is linear; that is, the "tightest" relationship is one of straight-line positive or negative change in the dependent variable with every unit change in the independent variable. Also, I sometimes transformed data to investigate linearity, since most environmental factors seem to exert linear pressure on the owls, but with one exception (figure 10.1), the original data are summarized in text and figures.

After most field work was finished for the year, usually in late July, I added that year's data to one or several of over 400 mainframe computer files. These I analyzed if new or reanalyzed in one or more of the above-mentioned ways, constantly looking for new patterns and testing old ones with the additional data. Whenever the owls gave me a new idea, particularly during the first half of the year, I did some trial runs on my personal computer; and, if they seemed promising, created the appropriate mainframe files. But, despite my six decades of owl watching, discoveries continue. The life and times of the eastern screech owl are only beginning to unfold.

What Follows

So this book is a kind of treasure map, not a blueprint, to the events and population consequences of reproduction by eastern screech owls. Reproduction is, after all, the essence of continued life, the epitome of existence. Everything the owls do is geared to it, either directly as in laying eggs and fledging owlets, or indirectly as in the choosing of food, mates, and nest sites. Population maintenance or change results from these and other features of life history. Thus, the comparative reproduction and population dynamics of suburban and rural screech owls are major themes. I shall try to explain why the eastern screech owl is the most familiar member of its family in suburban North America.[20]

This focus requires comparisons with other birds in and out of suburbia, especially cavity-nesting owls. Fortunately there are relevant studies of four such owls: the barn, boreal (Tengmalm's), tawny, and Ural. Both barn and tawny owls commonly nest in cities, so information on their lifestyles and coincidental population ecologies is of special interest. But neither species' population, nor that of any other raptorial bird, has been studied concurrently in the city and countryside; and I must do the best I can with information from disparate sources.

Each chapter opens on a personal note. I have always tried to use both intuition and rationale, and these introductory thoughts are intended to convey my emotional plus intellectual attachment to my subject. Like many naturalists, I operate on an egalitarian basis, having a sense of neutral kinship with all life.[21] Specific methods may then be described or general questions posed before a chapter is subdivided into topics that progress from beginnings to endings in life history or from simple to more complex subjects. A summary called "the essentials" concludes chapters 1–9 but not 10, itself a different kind of summary (see below).

Endnotes are employed primarily to cite relevant literature through 1992 with a few later references. They provide selected readings about owls, other birds (particularly raptors), and concepts. Endnotes also include further descriptive details and occasional ancillary observations. The appendices give individual or exemplary observations, since the chapters are synthetic renderings with only occasional case studies. Appendix I is perhaps most important in this regard, as it is a compilation of representative field notes selected to illustrate topics covered in chapters 2–7. Common and scientific names of species and higher taxa are given alphabetically in appendix X.

The chapters comprise four groups based on their primary subject matter, although many topics must be discussed in more than one chapter because of the manifold relationships. Chapters 2 and 3 are strongly environmental but describe important uses of resources by the owls. Essential life history, weighted toward suburbia but focused on the suburban-rural contrast, is presented in chapters 4–7, and chapters 8 and 9 concern breeding success and its consequences for population structure and dynamics. Chapter 10 focuses my thoughts on suburbanization of the eastern screech owl and is a recapitulation of the book's major theme, including a prescription for further study.

The Essentials

Between 1967 and 1975 a few nest boxes and natural-cavity nests provided enough information on eastern screech owls to instigate an intensive investigation of suburban versus rural nesting populations. About 20 nest boxes could be used in study plots in each environment to afford data on the life histories of four generations over 12–16 years. Comparative reproduction and hence population dynamics would be the major themes. Natural cavity nests could be ignored, except to furnish data on overall nesting density and the whereabouts of banded individuals, because they do not differ appreciably from nests in boxes. A perimeter-survey zone around each plot would permit checks on density and dispersal. In this exploratory period, investigative bias was gradually reduced to a minimum and working hypotheses were formed.

Major study plots of 270 ha were set up 7 km apart in 1976 and assayed concurrently through 1987. The suburban study extended through 1991. A smaller secondary area in a younger suburb and a nearby larger area furnish additional details of life history but are not used for population analysis. The early explorations had revealed proper ways to investigate major reproductive features such as first-egg date, clutch size, hatching, and fledging but also the necessity of measuring weather, food supply, predators, and competitors. Regular preseason censuses and nest-season observations were made, the latter in the afternoon at every known nest and at night at selected nests. No estimates or reconstructions of life history data were permitted in this confirmatory period of study.

2. Landscapes
The Owls Select Habitat

From Dallas south through Waco to Austin and San Antonio, through rolling land cut by rocky rivers and along the eastern Edwards Plateau, runs the Balcones or White Rock Escarpment, high above flatter former prairies. The chalky limestones of this scarp and its deep ravines, its cities, and remnant woodlands contrast markedly with deep soils, reservoirs, and agriculture below. Surviving streams are flanked by regrown riverside forests crossing the once diverse prairies that have become monocultural simplicity. And the suburbs nibble away at scarp woodlands and the people attracted to them in the first place. Little heritage landscape remains.

The Balcones Scarp is the great divide but not a particularly strong barrier. Tree-dependent birds like the eastern screech owl once had to follow riparian forest across tallgrass prairie that was the strongest obstacle to dispersal between the forests of East Texas and Central Texas woodlands.[1] Westward was a narrower midgrass prairie and then additional woodlands of the Edwards Plateau (Lampasas Cutplain). Scarp woodland mingled with riparian forest in the study area and was home to screech owls years ago, much as it is now. Yet there must be fewer owls today, because there is only half as much wooded habitat. Even farmland has been cut in half. An elevenfold increase in cityscapes caused the change (figure 2.1).

This change is important, because the Woodway study plot is warmer, wetter, and has less temperature and moisture flux than the rural plot and even Harris Creek (appendix II). Woodway is a pronounced heat island.[2] The rural–Harris Creek resemblance is surprising, since mean values are similar but seasonal flux is less at Harris Creek. This bedroom community may be too small to generate its own heat island but sufficiently productive of cultural heat to moderate seasonal changes. Nevertheless, Harris Creek is somewhat intermediate, and Woodway is so different from the countryside that my attempts to link weather with screech owl dynamics will concern Woodway for the most part (table 2.1).

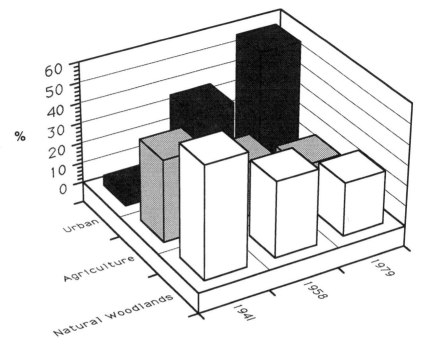

Figure 2.1. Changes in major landscape types of the Woodway study area, based on aerial photographs (data from McAtee, 1980). Note the decline in wooded habitat and farmland compared to the increase in urban space over time (P < 0.001).

Climate and Weather

Since local patterns of temperature and moisture also differ dramatically during three major events in the screech owl's annual cycle, it is informative to describe long-term atmospheric character (climate) and day-to-day changes (weather) in terms of these events (table 2.1). The first is nesting, the March–June period in which egg-laying and chick rearing are definitive. This season is mild with reference to the annual average temperature (19°C) and has the most rainfall which must stimulate food production.[3] Moreover, year-to-year temperature and moisture flux are reduced significantly at this time. It is the most favorable part of the owl's year.

Next is the July–October period of dependent fledglings and their dispersal (table 2.1). This season is hot and dry with slightly more annual temperature variation but twice the moisture flux of the nesting season. Similarly, there is more annual variation in both temperature

Table 2.1. Climatic attributes of three distinct seasons in the eastern screech owl's year, shown by averages and percent coefficients of variation at Woodway in 1967–87 (MANOVA, P <0.001).

Attributes	Nesting March–June	Fledgling Dispersal July–October	Winter November–February
Mean air temperature (°C)	21.1 (2.6%)	26.1 (3.2%)	9.9 (4.2%)
Total precipitation (cm)	34.0 (25.5%)	22.1 (53.9%)	19.8 (32.4%)

and moisture over winter, November–February, surely the time of greatest physical stress on both the young and old birds due to the cold and dry conditions. I found only one significant climatic trend during 1976–89, and it occurred in winter; precipitation increased 1.0 cm per year (P = 0.008).

Suburbia averages 239 (±14) freeze-free days each year, based on the Woodway data in 1967–91. March 18 (±17 days) is the average last day of freezing weather in the nesting season, and it may be significant that most egg-laying does not commence until a few days later (chapter 5). November 14 (±8 days) is the average first freeze of the winter period, and it could be important that most fledglings settle on their home ranges before then (chapter 6). The number of cold fronts that drop nighttime temperatures below about 10°C and thus reduce the availability of insect food doubles between October and November.

While few weather records were set in the confirmatory period, two are noteworthy because they came at normally stressful times. The fledgling season experienced a 42-day sequence of 38°C (100°F) or hotter in July–August, 1980, when only about two weeks of such heat is typical. Yet the owls seem not to have suffered greatly. On the other hand, five days of continuous subfreezing temperatures in December, 1983, when all surface water was ice, appear to have had serious consequences (chapter 4), contrary to what might be expected of urban birds buffered by culturally heated cities.[4] Normally, any period of more than 24 hours below freezing is unusual and more than tree days is practically unheard of in my study area.

Microthermal gradients are also worth observing, because they may help to explain activity patterns of the owls. For instance, a suburban ridge above a 22-m deep ravine is hotter and more variable than the ravine, which receives cold air drainage at night (appendix II). Also, the ground is cooler than air in the daytime and summer but warmer at night and in winter, its reduced variation due to its insulating layer of dead leaves. Mean minimum temperatures pinpoint the microclimates and seasonality better than mean maximums, since they are 1.5–5.5 times more variable and show greater differences, for example between the air and ground and the ridge versus ravine air. Furthermore, minimums happen at night when screech owls are most active, so I will pay special attention to them.

Woody Vegetation

Historically, the study area was a landscape mosaic with evergreen tree islands (motts) of live oak and Ashe juniper in grassland on each side of the Balcones Scarp. Toward the scarp edge, grassland gradually disappeared in the increasingly shallow soil, replaced by open evergreen-deciduous woodland that added Shumard and scalybark oaks, cedar elm, and white ash. In ravines the woods merged with a closed-canopy, streamside forest of cedar and American elms, sugarberry, eastern red cedar, red mulberry, and bur oak as major species. Today, however, most trees are second-growth replacements.[5]

The presettlement forest grew away from the scarp along permanent waterways, adding other trees like American sycamore, pecan, black walnut, and green ash, but cedar elm and sugarberry are current codominants in the regrown vegetation. Even so, screech owls nest in most woodlots provided with at least one tree large enough to have the requisite cavity (trees about 20 cm in diameter at cavity level).[6] Apparently the birds are linearly arranged along suitable riparian corridors and in the linear woods of the Balcones Scarp, based on fledgling dispersal as well as adult distribution (chapter 6).

Of course, knowledge of the historical landscape serves primarily for its appreciation relative to the current culturally modified conditions. Native trees remain in suburban yards, although they are a selected subset of the natural array. Large individuals of large species are favored, particularly oaks and pecans. If not already present, they are planted. Live and Shumard oaks are first choices, scalybark oak and cedar elm are appreciated, and white ash and large red cedar are tolerated. But sugarberry and Ashe juniper often are removed and replaced by fast-growing exotics like Arizona ash and white mulberry. Thus, there is no change in species diversity from the original but a tendency for fewer trees with less canopy coverage, more of which is evergreen (appendix III).

The most dramatic distinction between yard and rural vegetation resides in the shrub layer beneath the tree canopy, for suburbanites remove "brush" in favor of manicured exotics. Asian privet, boxwood, and holly replace native thicket-growers like coralberry, skunkbush, and roughleaf dogwood. Consequently, shrub diversity is higher in yards, though its height is halved and density reduced by over 50 percent compared to the rural landscape and those few suburban lots that folks like me have kept partly natural (appendix III). Suburbia is very open, park- or savanna-like, compared to the often brushy second-growth woodland and forest of the countryside.[7]

Nesting Environments

The first thing I wanted to know was how my nest boxes represented the cultural and rural environments by comparison with natural nest-cavity sites, as that might affect their use. After all, I tried to place them as naturally as possible, albeit to accommodate my 2-m ladder and 1.8-m height. Also the suburban sites are 3–38 m from houses by design to provide a certain initial contrast to rural conditions (appendix III). And many are in clear view of a house window and/or near a porch or similar night-light that permits observations. I did not avoid particular exposures disfavored by some cavity nesters, since the eastern screech and other owls have no directional preferences.[8]

For appraisal of the nesting landscapes and site usage, notes were made at 15 suburban and nine rural boxes with a minimum five-year record of deployment and at each closest natural-cavity site.[9] I used 75-m transects, randomly aligned through the nest tree and at 15-m points along them recorded the identify of, distance to, diameter and height of the nearest canopy tree and shrub in each of four quarters. Canopy coverage and its evergreen fraction comprising species like live oak, Ashe juniper, and red cedar were measured along the entire transect. Also, I noted diameter of the nest tree; its distance to the nearest house, permanent water, and to the closest alternative nest site; plus box or cavity floor area and height above ground.

After computing synthetic variables like species diversity and density, nine vegetational features of each transect were submitted to principal components analysis (appendix III). This procedure sorted the nest sites in bi-dimensional space, constructed from the nine features, and explained 61 percent of the variation in my data (figure 2.2A). The main result is that certain suburban yards differ from others and from rural sites in having fewer larger trees. These I call open yards to contrast them with the more heavily wooded yards that cluster close to wooded rural settings (figure 2.2A). Both wooded yards and rural environments also have denser, larger shrubs.

More importantly, however, nest-box vegetation is nearly indistinguishable from that around natural nest cavities (figure 2.2A). Greater species diversity seems to denote the box setting but actually separates

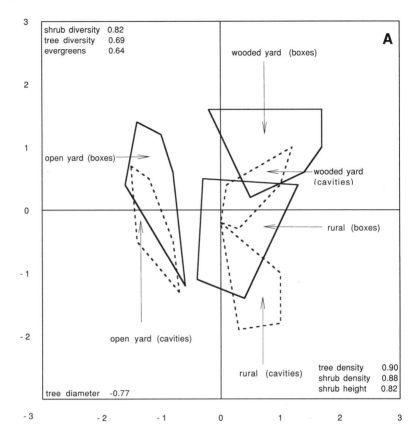

Figure 2.2A. Principal components graph of 24 nest-box sites and the closest 24 natural-cavity sites, derived from nine features of woody vegetation structure. Outside plotted points of the same type are joined by solid (nest-box) or dashed (natural-cavity) lines. Correlation coefficients of significant features with the graph axes are shown (horizontal axis = 39%, vertical axis = an additional 22% of variation in the data). Note that open-yard sites are distinguished from wooded-yard and rural sites by having fewer larger trees, while the wooded sites have more smaller trees and more taller shrubs. Also note that nest-box and natural-cavity sites are almost indistinguishable within the same environments.

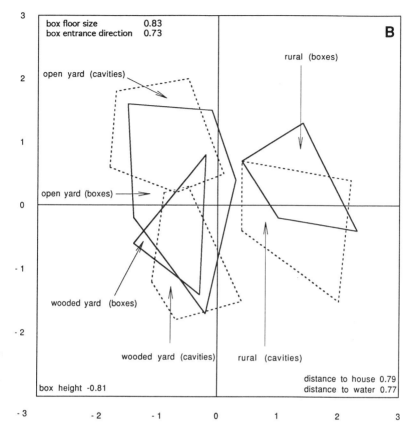

2.2B Similar graph but derived from six physical features of the
nest-box (solid lines) and natural-cavity (dashed lines) sites. Correlation coefficients of significant features with the graph axes are shown
(horizontal axis = 33% , vertical axis = an additional 27% of variation in the data). Note that both open and wooded-yard sites of both
the nest-box and natural-cavity groups cluster together, separate
from all rural sites on the basis of greater distance to the nearest
house and permanent water in the rural environment.

wooded yards from rural sites more strongly. In fact, a multivariate
analysis of variance of the box versus cavity transects, using the nine
vegetational features, shows no distinctions, whereas one of just the
three suggested landscape types verifies their existence (P < 0.001).
Thus, natural-cavity and nest-box sites do not differ within landscapes,
only between them, and all structural features except tree height, diversity, and evergreenness are good field-guide characteristics (appendix
III).

Representative nest-box and natural-cavity sites: (*top left*) cedar elm in C. W. Davis's open suburban yard; (*center left*) Shumard oak in author's wooded suburban yard; (*bottom left*) natural cavity in broken (trimmed) live oak limb, open suburban yard; (*above*) cedar elm on the rural study plot.

While native shrubs are mostly gone from suburbs, native trees are not and they also define the three kinds of nesting landscapes in a second MANOVA (P < 0.01). Dissimilarities arise only from unique local dominance. For instance, cedar elm is the frontrunner in the countryside, because it is an invader as well as canopy dominant in the mostly second-growth forest. And live oak predominates in open yards because it is highly favored by humans, hence building sites with large individuals are selected and other trees are removed to show off the big oaks. The most even representation of tree species is in wooded yards, which have the highest diversity for this reason (appendix III).

All natural nest cavities were rotted hollow areas in tree trunks (12), broken trunks (8), or limb stubs (4), sometimes enlarged by fox squirrels; the largest local woodpecker, the red-bellied, does not drill a large enough cavity. Most were in cedar elms (44%) as were the most nest boxes (54%), and the frequencies of cavities and boxes were similar among seven leading canopy trees (NS, appendix III). Cavity- and box-tree diameters differed among the study environments (P < 0.01) but were alike within environments (NS, two-way ANOVA). However, 24 natural-cavity trees were larger than their nearest neighbors in the canopy (41.9 ± 20.8 versus 33.2 ± 9.6 cm diameter at 1.4 m; P < 0.001).

In analyzing nest sites by means of the six physical variables, a second principal components analysis arranged the transects; and it too explains most of the variation in two-dimensional space (figure 2.2B). But it suggests only a single group of suburban boxes and cavities, separate from the rural ones on the basis of proximity to the nearest house and permanent water. That rural box sites are relatively isolated is part of the study design, but I did not know about rural cavities and had not anticipated the difference in accessibility of water. A MA-NOVA of the two clusters of transects in figure 2B substantiates their separateness (P < 0.001), and all but box/cavity height and floor area distinguish them (appendix III).

I reconsidered what parameters best define any nest sites by combining the six vegetational and four physical features that were significant in separate analyses. I wanted to know if the three kinds of nesting environments remained distinct and which features were the leading descriptors. I employed discriminant function analysis, the jackknifed procedure of which correctly classified 57 percent (open yards), 67 percent (rural), and 83 percent (wooded yards) of all transects. The hierarchy of significant features was, first to last: distance to nearest house, shrub density, tree density, canopy height, and nest-tree diameter (P < 0.05).

Nest-Site Selection

Male eastern screech owls may advertise and defend two to three nest boxes and natural cavities per season, 109 m apart on average (appendix III). But their vocal signals (monotonic trills) occur a mean maximum distance of only 9.5 ± 5.3 m from cavities in five wooded yards compared to 20.6 ± 11.2 m away in seven open yards (P = 0.008), surely because of differences in tree density (appendix III). Thus, individual nesting territories are isolated patches occupying but 12.2–18.8 percent of the average distance between adjacent territories. Such suites of potential nest sites may be called polyterritories as in the boreal owl.[10] The alternatives are important, since failed first nests are not infrequent, and the owls usually switch sites for replacement nesting (chapters 5, 8).

Among 17 suburban females, whose lives were fully documented by 1989 and who had the opportunity to choose among sites for first nests in three to seven successive years, five (29%) changed sites 2.3 ± 0.7 times. The number of switches they made, year to year, did not correlate with their lifespans (r = 0.39, NS). And the number made to natural cavities (38%) and other boxes (20%), relative to the times they reused original locations (42% of 26 nests), did not differ statistically from the number of concurrently available unused sites.[11] But people often remove "unsightly" natural-cavity trees, fill the holes with cement, or prune the cavity-containing snags from them, so there were fewer alternative nest sites in suburbia than in the rural plot (2.9 ± 1.4 versus 5.5 ± 2.8 cavities plus boxes per nesting pair, 1981–87; P < 0.001).

Considering all nesting pairs, annual use of available boxes was similar in the suburban and rural plots, 1976–87 ($70.5 \pm 20.1\%$ versus $61.4 \pm 23.4\%$, respectively; NS), and year-to-year turnover rates were equal ($24 \pm 7\%$ versus $24 \pm 12\%$) though not coincidental ($r_s = -0.20$, NS).[12] Most boxes were used one year by individual females, the maximum sequential use being six years in suburbia and five on the rural plot. These two patterns of occupancy were not significantly different either.

With respect to their availability over all years, boxes in open yards were used about like those in wooded yards (75% versus 70% respectively, NS), as were boxes on Woodway's warmer ridges versus cooler ravines (75%, 67%, NS). Also, Woodway and Harris Creek boxes were chosen similarly in 1979–91 (65%, 79%, NS). But high population density probably affected nest site selection by forcing owls into the predation-prone wooded-yard sites. Relative to unused sites, more nest boxes in wooded yards were occupied at densities above than below the 1976–91 median nesting density of 15 pairs (86.7% versus 54.2% use), whereas that was not true of the safer open-yard boxes (75.0% versus 65.8%, P < 0.001; see also chapters 5, 6, 9).

Also based on availability, the different-sized nest boxes were occupied by all pairs about equally and no differently in the suburban versus rural landscapes (NS). Curiously, though, large boxes were chosen more often for replacement nests than first nests in the same year (38% of 42 renests versus 17% of 95 original nests, P $= 0.01$). Perhaps this is because they are cooler in the later hotter weather (see chapter 6). In any case, the data validate my exploratory ideas that nest boxes are quasinatural cavities, and eastern screech owls are quite catholic in their nest-site selection. Thus, they resemble other secondary-cavity nesters but not the boreal owl which prefers smaller boxes.[13]

Yet four (10%) of my original 40 nest boxes and at least seven (13%) apparently suitable natural cavities were never used. If large-scale landscape factors did not account for selectivity, perhaps screech owls perceived certain details. I needed to try a different approach. The median percentage use of the 24-box sample was 69, so I divided boxes into high- and low-use groups accordingly and analyzed their differences in another discriminant function analysis, using the five features that identify the three kinds of nesting landscapes. Amazingly, 89 percent of the high-use boxes and 70 percent of the low-use group were correctly classified in the jackknifed procedure, based entirely on distance to the nearest house (P < 0.001) and shrub density (P = 0.02).

Boxes closest to houses and in the midst of fewer shrubs were in the high-use group, so I wondered if human activity plus an open understory deters predators and competitors, making a site safer and hence more acceptable. This idea was easily tested, for I knew how many nesting attempts were successful or failed due to predation or desertion. Broken and missing eggs, missing nestlings too small to fledge, and nestling remains (rarely adults) are signs of predation. Disturbed box-bottom debris and muddy footprints on the outside are other clues. Conversely, abandoned eggs are not broken, nor is the litter below them disarranged, and live chicks are never deserted.

To investigate I plotted (regressed) average productivity (fledglings/ eggs) against house distance and shrub density in my sample of 24 boxes. Variation in success rates is determined by distance ($r^2 = 0.38$, P = 0.001), not independently by density (r^2 added = 0.11, NS) because the two features are correlated and explain much the same thing (r = 0.49, P = 0.01). Distant boxes among the most shrubs suffer most and, of course, all of them are rural. Human neighbors must be advantageous to my suburban birds as they are to a number of other urban species.[14]

Other studies record that boreal owls and some other birds prefer new nest boxes.[15] In Norway pine martens are most likely to depredate boreal owl nests in old boxes which they have learned to patrol. Does a similar pattern exist among my subjects in Central Texas? Probably not, for incidence of predation does not increase with box age in suburbia ($r_s = 0.05$, NS) and actually declines with age in the rural setting ($r_s = -0.64$, P = 0.02), 1976–87. More importantly, there is no correlation between percent use of the boxes and their age ($r_s = -0.09$, −0.13, NS; respectively), so there is no obvious selection on this basis.

But compared to older, experienced birds, eastern screech owls nesting for the first time must not know about safe or unsafe sites, so the apparent lack of discretion may be naivety. Such owls potentially unfamiliar with the environment comprise about half the nesting females (chapter 9). Compared to the very few recruited fledglings (6.1%), newcomers are essentially all immigrant yearlings who are least likely to know about predatory and competitory foci, since they were not raised in the area. Therefore, it is not particularly surprising that box use and age are unrelated in both my study populations (chapter 8).

What about the older owls, presumably the best judges of safety? Do they discriminate? Yes, indeed, and immigrants do not by comparison. Following any level of breeding success, 67 percent (n = 30) of the suburban females and 82 percent (9) of their rural counterparts reused the same sites the next year; whereas, after failure, 77 percent (10) and 70 percent (7) of the respective users were immigrant females (P < 0.001). Moreover, there was no difference in reuse after predation versus desertion (P > 0.45). Certainly these long-lived birds recollect prior success if not actual safety.

Furthermore, older owls are more likely to habituate to disturbances because of their exposure (see also chapter 5). In suburbia only 21 percent (8) abandoned eggs compared to 79 percent (30) of the newcomers, whereas the incidence of predation was equal in both age classes (50% each of 16, P = 0.03). On the rural plot all cases of abandonment by known-age females (6) were attributable to immigrants (P = 0.04). Two examples of tolerance, possibly through habituation, are a two-year-old female who bred successfully 14 m from my house under construction—even watched the workmen occasionally—and a successful three-year-old who sat tight on her eggs as tree trimmers with power saws worked in her nest tree and fed the limbs to a power grinder 10 m away.[16]

Besides proximity to a house, lower shrub density distinguished high-use boxes and was correlated with more successful nests per box (r = 0.59, P = 0.002). But I suggest that open sites are selected because they facilitate flying and hunting as much as the repulsion or avoidance of competitors and predators.[17] Screech owls do not fly above the tree canopy and rarely through its upper half. More commonly they fly among lower branches which lack the many twig obstacles of the upper canopy. Most commonly, though, they travel beneath the canopy above the shrub-sapling layer or about 2–3 m above ground. And in suburbia they can make even lower traverses across open yards and streets, where shrub plantings are the most widely spaced.

Since natural cavities, nest boxes, and favored perches are mostly at canopy level, the owls have developed an unusual flight pattern that avoids impediments and disguises entrances and exits. When departing a cavity or the foliage, the birds drop quickly, then proceed straightaway, and when approaching a cavity or canopy site, they rise abruptly at the end of their excursion. This makes it difficult to see their origin and destination. Clearly, they know perches and flight lines which they follow like we follow paths on the ground. The U-flight behavior is well known among other woodland species, including boreal and flammulated owls, which also select open nesting habitat.[18]

It is significant that lower shrub density, not lower shrub height, distinguishes high-use boxes, because density varies considerably more than height among nesting landscapes and thick shrubs may hide prey and predators more effectively than tall shrubs (appendix III). Screech owls catch most food on the ground within about 100 m of the nest, so fewer and widely spaced shrubs should afford easier hunting as sparse vegetation apparently does for tawny owls (chapter 3). Also, competitors and predators ought to be scarcer—due to fewer hiding places— or easier to locate and repulse in sparse shrubbery.[19]

Yet only in the rural setting are sparser shrubs an apparent advantage. Correlations (r_s) of shrub density with percent desertion plus predation are 0.83 (P = 0.005) for the nine rural boxes but only 0.13 (NS) for the 15 suburban ones. Possibly suburban housing alone suffices to deter predation, or suburban shrubbery is below some threshold density that hides enemies effectively. Based on 95 percent limits of variation in the density of wooded yards (maximum 2,907/ha) and rural plot (minimum 3,083/ha), around 3,000 shrubs per hectare could be that threshold (appendix III). On the other hand, the patchy plantings of suburbia might leave enough open space, regardless of overall density, to facilitate the avoidance and repulsion of enemies.

Roost-Site Choices

I found 293 adult screech owls roosting individually during the day, often in more than one location, and discovered pairs together in six nest boxes, thrice in winter and otherwise while the female incubated or brooded. Most of the owls in foliage were on branches, twigs, or vines (96%), the few others in shrubs or at the base of a limb next to a tree trunk. Gray and rufous individuals did not differ in this regard.[20] Fifty-three screech owls were 3.8 ± 1.3 m high in the lower to mid-canopy, no different in height from 31 others in cavities and boxes at 3.1 ± 0.5 m. (NS). The birds in foliage perched higher in taller trees (r_s = 0.91, P < 0.001), as northern saw-whet owls do.[21]

Differences among the foliage roosts suggested further evaluation, and 600 trees recorded in the 30 suburban transects at nest sites provided a good measure of availability. Unfortunately, too few observations of rural roosting outside the nesting season were made for comparison with suburbia. Just as with nest-site selection from the array of natural and cultural opportunities, I want to know if eastern screech owls make certain choices for roosting. If so, do these places change seasonally as the foliage cover changes and hence concealment and protection vary, by contrast to the unchanging boxes and cavities? During 1976 to 1991 the native deciduous tree canopy was 90 percent closed by April 16 (± 7 days) and 90 percent open, except for Shumard oaks, by November 28 (± 8 days).

Deciduous trees lacking suitable cavities comprise 71 percent of the

Adult male in (*left*) typical foliage roost in a deciduous holly, and (*right*) less common roost on a branch next to the trunk of a Shumard oak.

600-tree sample, evergreens without cavities only 24 percent, and nest- or roost-cavity plus box trees a mere 5 percent. Thus, it is striking that the owls prefer cavity or box roosts over deciduous or evergreen foliage (45% of the roosts in figure 2.3). This is true also in Virginia.[22] Further, they choose evergreens instead of deciduous trees when not using cavities or boxes (P < 0.001). Better concealment from enemies and protection from inclement weather are obvious advantages of these choices.

Seventy-seven percent of 131 winter roosts were in cavities or boxes, whereas 80 percent of 152 were in foliage during the nesting season (P < 0.001). In March, as females began their pre-laying occupation of boxes and during incubation that month, 90 percent of the foliage roosts of 20 males were in evergreens compared to only 45 percent of 44 during April incubation (P = 0.001). Among the principal evergreens available by virtue of their abundance around nests, junipers (cedars) were selected over live oaks (P = 0.009). I suspect that juniper foliage is denser and more protective.

Thermoregulation is probably the chief factor in roost-site selection, as it seems to be for spotted owls.[23] This is most evident in winter. Percentage occupation of boxes in December, 1976–88, corresponded to mean air temperature the preceding week (r_s = −0.67, P = 0.03), not the week's total precipitation (r_s = −0.26, NS). But in January, when average air temperatures were colder (6.3° vs. 8.6°C, P = 0.04) and more continuously so (CVs = 8.2 vs. 11.7%), there were no such relationships (r_s < −0.41, NS), because the same birds occupied the boxes more often.

The coincidental roosting habits of three suburban males, 0.2–0.6 km apart in November–February, are exemplary. I knew their whereabouts on 86 days, most (70.9%) of which were in nest boxes at mean minimum air temperatures of 4.9 ± 1.3 °C. Conversely, in warmer weather (9.2 ± 1.6 °C, P = 0.006), they all used nearby juniper roosts or could not be found. Since environmental parameters were similar for the three on the same 34 days, I regressed the box use or not of each male (logistically) on mean minimum temperature, rainfall, and fox-squirrel occupation of the boxes. Low temperature explained 16–22 percent of the daily variation (P < 0.002), high rainfall another 13–17 percent of box roosting (P < 0.01), and preemptive use by squirrels a final 7–10 percent (P < 0.04).

Another suburban male and his mate caught my attention one winter, since they sunned in separate southwest-facing natural cavities of the same bare cedar elm in January and February. Each bird's presence or absence in the cavity entrance at 1300–1400 hrs was regressed on concurrent air temperature, wind speed, percent cloud cover, and intensity of precipitation over 21 nonconsecutive days. The male was observed 54 percent of the time, the female 45 percent.[24] Air temperature was the only significant correlate but just for the male (r = 0.60, P < 0.001), indicating that he appeared more often with warmer weather.

Winter use of the suburban nest boxes was primarily by males, which numbered 15.5 ± 6.1 annually, 1976–89, relative to only 5.1 ± 2.9 females (P < 0.001). Yet when one sex was present, the other was usually in the nearest cavity (r_s = 0.77, P = 0.001), although there were differences among years (P = 0.001), possibly related to mean winter temperature for males (r_s = −0.49, P = 0.07) but not females (r_s = 0.26, NS). Total precipitation was not a factor (r_s < 0.19, NS). Because males are smaller with more skin surface area per unit volume than females, I expect them to lose heat more readily, hence being more responsive to cold and more likely to roost in the boxes. But they are also nest-site guardians and could be present for this reason, since 64.7 ± 8.7 percent used their winter-roost boxes for nesting each year.

Later I shall postulate why males are the smaller sex. For now, however, let me propose that they are less influenced by winter food shortages than females, since they require less food, but are more susceptible

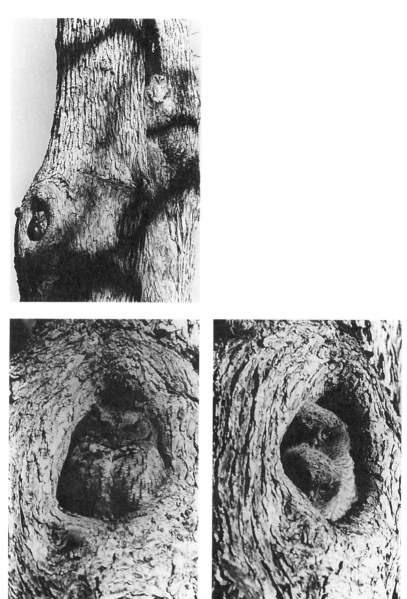

Top: Adult pair sunning in suburban cedar elm cavities in January; gray male in eventual nest cavity on lower left, rufous female upper right. *Bottom left:* The male with closed eyes and erect breast feathers. *Bottom right:* The pair's four-week-old nestlings.

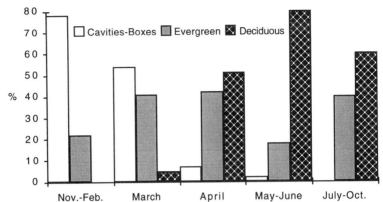

Figure 2.3   Monthly changes in roost-site selection by 93 adult screech owls, 1976–89. Note the preference for natural cavities or nest boxes in winter, the subsequent shift to evergreen tree foliage, and finally to deciduous foliage during the April–June part of nesting. Compared to availability of the three kinds of roosts, these choices are significant (P < 0.001).

to energy (heat) loss because of their larger skin-surface area.[25] Females, on the other hand, should be more mobile due to their larger size. Therefore, it makes sense that the males remain at nest sites, use them for protection from the cold, and serve the reproductive function as nest-site defenders; while females leave temporarily and thus reduce intraspecific competition for food and shelter.[26]

Male residency and female movement away in winter are also known in boreal and Ural owls, but the female boreals make nomadic journeys or migrations. The few (35% of 52) suburban females I located away from defended nest sites were all within 0.5 km. In substantiation of my idea of reduced food competition, the annual percentage of absent females, 1976–86, is correlated with reduced bird-mammal foods (r_s = 0.88, P < 0.001), whereas that is not true for males (r_s = 0.13, NS). Because boxes and natural nesting-roosting cavities were more abundant than the owls themselves, I doubt that males remain chiefly to guard scarce nest sites as proposed for boreal owls.[27]

From winter into the nesting season there is a major shift from cavity-box roosts to evergreens and then deciduous foliage (figure 2.3). Deciduous trees are most abundant, so of course they are most likely to be used around nests. Yet egg-laying begins in March, whereas the final shift of nest-attending males does not occur until April when deciduous leaves are fully developed and thus furnish protection. The western screech owl makes a similar shift.[28] Unlike the choices among evergreens used in the earlier colder weather, I could not discover any preferences for particular deciduous species or leaf types and believe that temperatures are too mild for heat conservation to be important after March (cf. table 2.1).

Beginning in April, cooling and protection from strong wind may determine roost-site selection, as the air warms and screech owls are more active hunters in behalf of their families (chapter 6). I seldom saw the birds switch roosts during a winter day (7% of 131 cases) whereas such switching was the rule in the nesting season (82% of 152, $P <$ 0.001). I think this is because deciduous-foliage roosts afford so little protection. In addition, males are increasingly attentive as nesting progresses, so roost switching seems to be tied as strongly to reproductive demands as to individual protection (chapter 6).

The Essentials

The study area, dominated by the high Balcones Escarpment, was half wooded historically. Today it is half urban and only a quarter wooded screech owl habitat. A heat island characterizes Waco's urban climate, including my primary study plot, but not the secondary suburban site surrounded by farmland. Climatically, the screech owl's year is divided into a mild, wet nesting season (March–June), hot, dry fledgling dispersal period (July–October), and a cold, dry winter (November–February). Egg-laying usually follows the last spring freeze, and fledglings normally settle on winter ranges before the first freeze of winter. During this study, weather records were set with the longest period of 38°C or hotter and longest freezing period.

Screech owls inhabit streamside and upland locales, using both deciduous forest and evergreen-deciduous woodland regardless of area as long as cavity trees or cultural substitutes are present. The cavity trees are damaged larger-than-average individuals of all dominant species. Suburban habitat is either an open-yard or wooded-yard variant of the natural; the former has fewer larger trees, while the latter is more like the rural landscape with denser smaller trees of more different species. Both have few short shrubs in plantings compared to the brushier natural (rural) condition. Within each type, nest-box and natural-cavity sites are nearly identical vegetationally, but the suburban boxes and cavities are closer to houses and permanent water.

Two or more nest boxes or cavities and their immediate surroundings are advertised by male screech owls. However, there are fewer available nest sites in suburbia than in the rural plot, because damaged hence unsightly cavity trees are pruned or cut down. Older, experienced owls do switch sites after one is unsuccessful, but the birds generally do not select among the three sizes or different ages of boxes for nesting. Nor do they choose particular nest-site environments except for those closest to houses amidst sparse shrub cover. These are selected apparently because they suffer less predation and offer better subcanopy flying and hunting space. Annual use of the nest boxes and turnover rates among them do not differ between suburbia and the rural environment.

Use of boxes and natural cavities or foliage for roosting is even more selective. Cavities and boxes are preferred, especially in winter by males who occupy them particularly in cold weather and sun on the warmer days. Most males also nest in the same spots. A third of the females move away from their usual nesting areas in relation to reduced winter food supplies, which reduces intraspecific competition. That the smaller, less food-stressed males remain, while the larger, more-mobile females move, makes sense in terms of body size and heat conservation; so it follows that males have evolved the role of nest-site defender. The owls prefer denser evergreens over other tree roosts in winter because they offer better protection against cold. But they shift into the more abundant deciduous-foliage roosts after the tree canopy closes in April.

3. Food Supplies and Predation
Why Owls Are Mobbed

I dozed off listening to a screech owl trilling, katydids rasping, and June bugs buzzing about my patio and dreamed of the bird's home range, an area of 20 residences supporting 3.6 kilograms of edible birds in the nesting season—house sparrows, cardinals, bluejays, and the like. The male owl removed 2.6 kilograms, but the last kilo tripled during breeding that spring. Had the surplus satisfied the owls? The family of five needed about 255 grams of food each day over a two-month period or 15.3 kilos, but the birds they consumed would have sustained them only a week and a half. I roused briefly to find the katydids and June bugs gone and, satisfied, slumbered on.

Dissecting pellets to learn what eastern screech owls eat is less informative than watching predation directly, so hunting forays were observed in suburbia at judiciously selected nests. I saw 165 in their entirety. Small prey such as insects usually were consumed immediately, while the larger vertebrates were stashed in cavities and nest boxes. Some of these were beheaded and partly eaten before storage, which lasted 1–5 days in winter but only a day or two during nesting. Rather than caching surpluses as a buffer against food shortage, a popular belief about this behavior, my subjects cached regularly and in only eight percent of 152 larders, which I checked daily, neglected to eat what they had stored.[1]

Furthermore, their caches corresponded to food demand but only through the brooding phase of nesting, even though food supplies continued to increase and diversify for weeks afterward (see below). To study foods and predation without concurrent analysis of supply is like noting nest and roost sites without assessing their availability—ecologically unrevealing. So I designated permanent study plots for assays of the terrestrial vertebrates I knew the owls ate. Other short-term investigations, such as light-trapping nocturnal insects, were conducted too. Since birds were the favored vertebrate prey, as they are elsewhere, I paid especially close attention to them.[2]

Inside my principal suburban plot (Woodway) a 6.1-ha subplot was marked to include one branch of a seminatural ravine and adjacent culture on both sides. Initially set up for trial runs in 1967, the birds of this area were trapped, netted, banded, and marked on a map weekly,

November–June, 1976–91. This subplot was also hunted by two pairs of screech owls and housed one or two nesting pairs each year. Concurrently in 1976–87, I mapped all birds in a 6.1-ha area of the rural plot which contained one nesting pair of owls. (Summer resident birds were only 2–13% of the total avifauna and were so seldom eaten by screech owls that I mostly ignore them; see appendix IV).

On the southern edge of the suburban 2-km perimeter zone I located a 1-ha, 70-trap grid for the capture, marking, release, and recapture of small rodents and shrews. This was a tallgrass prairie remnant 50 m from the nearest pair of screech owls. The grid was censused on two to four consecutive afternoons in November, February, and June, 1967–91. And on the northern periphery in 20 ha of open woods with a pair of owls, I established a 1-ha plot for censusing small snakes in the same years. Market flat rocks on the ground were turned and replaced and the snakes marked, released, and recaptured beneath them biweekly in the morning from mid-March to mid-June.

The rodent and snake data could be used for a general assessment of food supply, even though no counts were made inside the suburban plot, because short-term exploratory trapping and rock-turning in suburbia suggested that there were no profound differences. This was not true for birds, however (appendix V). Also, as comparative measures of food supply, density (individuals of the censused vertebrates/unit area) and biomass (mean density $\times$ mean live weight) provided somewhat different explanations, because the two features were uncorrelated (r < 0.23, NS).

The Food Niche

Among the wide variety of vertebrates cached in nest boxes and natural cavities, birds constituted the striking majority—48 (rural) and 65 (suburban) percent by density and 57 (rural) and 80 (suburban) percent by biomass (appendix IV). Compared to all other stored vertebrates, birds appeared 1.7 times more often per species, and among 19 species common to both suburban and rural larders, there were many more bodies in the suburban depots (10.4 $\pm$ 13.4 versus 1.7 $\pm$ 1.2, P < 0.001). A similar emphasis on birds as food in cities, by contrast to mammals in the countryside, characterizes tawny and long-eared owls.[3]

What kinds of birds are eaten? Both the suburban and rural owls killed permanent-resident species and passage-migrant plus seasonal-resident species about equally (18 versus 21), but they stored about twice as many permanent-resident bodies (P < 0.001). This happened despite the seasonal species being 2.8 times more abundant (appendix

Hunting female (*top*) attracted to our bird-banding in December flies (*bottom left*) to Ann Gordon's head and (*bottom right*) to the ground near a trapped northern cardinal. Intent on securing food, the habituated owl is unconcerned with the human activity. (Ann and Ed Gordon photos)

V), and it is contrary to the situation in northern Ohio, where screech owls cache 1.8 times more migrants plus seasonal residents. I think my owls have greater access to permanent residents, since they are available year-round, especially in suburbia with its significantly larger bird populations (appendix V).[4]

To examine this contention further, I regressed the number of stored bodies of 22 species in suburbia on average weight, density, annual variation in density, and the average number of weeks per year that species was present. Indeed, the latter feature does determine "cacheability," (r^2 = 0.35, P = 0.01), although screech owls also choose larger species (r^2 added = 0.08, P = 0.06). Repeating the analysis with 17 species in the rural landscape revealed no significant relationships. Instead, the rural owls stored more other kinds of terrestrial vertebrates, relative to their suburban cousins (P = 0.05), and rural owls in northern Ohio did too (P = 0.01).[4]

My rural population apparently substituted mammals and reptiles for the comparatively scarce birds in their environment. Bird density was only 31 percent of that in suburbia (appendix V). Average densities and year-to-year flux (CVs) among the 22 birds occurring in both rural and suburban plots were parallel (r_s > 0.69, P < 0.001), as expected, since the two areas are close and have an 88 percent species similarity. But those densities and even biomasses, overall and individually among the shared species, are significantly greater in suburbia (appendix V). The milder suburban climate and fund of insect food that increases into the nesting season (see below), plus bird baths and feeders, must make the difference.

But there are additional aspects of selectivity besides abundance, especially the prospect that larger prey is stored, because it maximizes energy return per unit of delivery energy.[5] Certainly, boreal owls select larger prey species as do other raptors.[6] So I compared the number of stored bodies in five weight categories with the average available per category among the 22 species of birds common to both study plots.[7] The choice of large prey is striking (figure 3.1). Flight loads of less than 41 grams or about 25 percent of adult male weight usually are rejected for caching. Not surprisingly, they are below the minimum daily food requirement of my captives at around 25°C. A 50-gram (g) load like a mockingbird is 25–31 (winter) to 29–33 (spring) percent of adult weight, a usual nightly meal.

Foremost selections in the 41–60-gram class of avian prey are the Inca dove, northern cardinal, and northern mockingbird, three of the top food species (appendix IV). All are abundant in both suburban and rural settings and no more or less numerous in larders, relative to

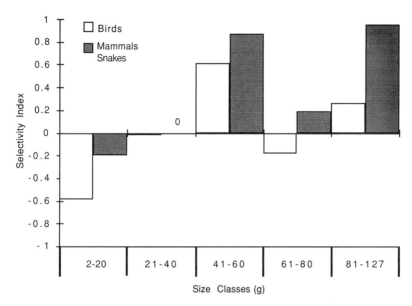

Figure 3.1. Selectivity of terrestrial vertebrates stored in cavities and nest boxes, 1976–87. Bird data are from species in common to the suburban and rural study plots. The selectivity index relates the production of food stored to that currently available. Note that few small and many large-size bodies are stored. Differences between utilization and supply are significant for the birds and for mammals plus small snakes (P < 0.001 in both categories).

their average densities, than four other leading birds (NS). But Inca doves and cardinals are almost entirely ground foragers, and mockers feed there much of the time. The ground surface habit may increase vulnerability, since 94 percent of 18 primary ground-feeders on the two study plots were eaten compared to only 27 percent of 33 primary foliage-feeders (P < 0.001).

Bluejays and common grackles are predominant prey in the 81–127-g category and two more of the leading food species. They also feed on the ground. Additionally, however, both flock noisily in large numbers, and grackles as well as the oft-eaten cedar waxwings form dense flocks that feed on geometrid caterpillars in late March through early April in the defoliated tree canopy. This renders them conspicuous, certainly, and perhaps vulnerable. Three pairs of bluejays plus one each of cardinals and mourning doves nested 2–13 m from screech owl nests and lost their chicks plus one or both adults to the owls each time.

Are these open nesters taken more readily than the better-protected cavity nesters? And what about the vulnerable nestlings and fledglings or adult males versus females, since males tend to be more fearless in my experience.[8] Actually, the first two aspects make no difference, but there is a distinct tendency for male culpability. Eleven open and seven cavity nesters are among the stored food (NS) and nestlings-fledglings comprise only 20 percent of the spring larders, but males of the obviously dimorphic house sparrow, cardinal, and common grackle total 64 percent (P = 0.07). Similarly, boreal owls take only 18 percent nestlings and fledglings and, along with tawny owls, kill a majority of male prey.[9]

Small mammals and snakes were cached in about equal numbers relative to supplies in the rural plot, so I combined them for an additional look at body-size selectivity. The picture is generally the same as for birds (figure 3.1). Fewer small and more large bodies were cached, though in different proportions than birds in the same weight categories (P < 0.001). However, it is important to add that subadults of the larger mammals were chosen, since only postnestling eastern cottontails and mostly (78%) juvenile rats represent the large-size categories.

Brown and black rats, almost exclusively urban, dominated the suburban caches of small mammals; whereas hispid cotton rats, the commonest native rodents, were most prominent in the rural caches (P = 0.001). The largest bodies were 90–100 g, similar to the largest usual avian prey (bluejays and common grackles). Yet parts of some rats, mourning doves, northern flickers, and great-tailed grackles suggested that much larger individuals are killed, cut up, and flown to the storage depots. My captive adult screech owls of both sexes could fly up from the ground with a 90-gram bluejay but not a 120-gram coturnix quail.

As for small vertebrate prey, 71 percent in the 2–20-g range were ectotherms (fish, amphibians, reptiles), and 71 percent of these were snakes, previously unknown as such important food.[10] The largest was a 60-cm-long rough-green snake, but most (94%) were small burrowing species that should be inaccessible to screech owls. I believe that these blind, flathead, ground, and rough earth snakes are caught primarily after heavy rains flush them to the ground surface, based on the strong positive correlation between numbers of cached blind snakes and amount of previous rainfall.[11] Lawn watering may accomplish the same thing, accounting for the large numbers of these species plus June beetles, earthworms, and cicadas stored in suburban nests (appendix IV, chapter 6).

But the small-prey fraction in figure 3.1 does not represent invertebrates, which constituted 76 percent of all observed food deliveries at nests as noted below. Crayfish, moths, and beetles were the leading taxa cached, amounting to 59 percent of all stored invertebrates (P < 0.001). They were also the three major taxa delivered to nestlings in New York, where only 48 percent of all items were invertebrates.[12] Some crayfish, dragonfly naiads, and transforming frogs were caught like fish in shallow water at my backyard pond.[13] These were cached in dry as well as wet weather, but earthworms were stored only during rainy periods, when I saw them picked up from wet streets.

Of additional interest is the screech owl's lack of hesitation in catching and eating animals with repellent secretions or various physical defenses. Among invertebrates, carabid beetles, oriental roaches, reduviid bugs, and millipedes possess particularly (to me) noxious chemical repellents. All serpents do too, especially blind, rough earth, lined, garter, ribbon, and brown snakes. Blind snakes can repel predatory snakes but apparently not screech owls.[14] Judging from crayfish with claws, spiny horned lizards, and other armaments represented among stored prey, screech owls are not easily deterred.

Invertebrates as a group and the five vertebrate classes did not differ significantly in cache representation year-to-year, although there were consistent differences among the taxa with birds predominating throughout 1976–87 (P < 0.001, two-way ANOVA). Nor were the annual numbers of stored birds, rodents, and small snakes related to their supplies (r < −0.38, NS) in the manner of rodents in boreal owl larders.[15] Instead, the number of items and biomasses of 177 caches were larger relative to lower mean minimum temperatures (r^2 > 0.57, P < 0.001) and nesting stage (r^2 added > 0.35, P = 0.04, MSRs; table 3.1). Caching is a behavioral adjustment to food demand (see also chapter 6).

Because population cycles were detected in some vertebrate prey, I wondered if screech owls switch food types temporarily in the manner of boreal, eagle, Eurasian pygmy, tawny, and Ural owls.[16] Bird for mammal substitutions are reported, but screech owls may do just the opposite, since they seem to specialize on birds. Thus, I looked for changes in proportions of cached birds versus mammals and vertebrates versus invertebrates in the three- and four-year intervals that delimit local rodent and songbird cycles, based on my study-plot findings. Significant switches were lacking, however.

Just how broad is the screech owl's food niche? Generally, it is broader among the suburban individuals (26.9) than their country cousins (18.7), although the overlap is 66 percent.[17] Such an urban-rural difference characterizes the long-eared and tawny owls too.[18] Ex-

Table 3.1. Seasonal composition of food caches in combined suburban and rural samples, 1976–87. Data are mean ± one standard deviation and sample size (n). Since checks were about equally frequent during each phase of nesting, sample sizes are roughly
proportionate to cache frequencies. Note that during brooding,
when food demand is highest, caches are more numerous, larger,
and richer in species content but no different in biomass or potential energy content (MANOVA, P <0.001; asterisks indicate significantly different means in LSD tests).

Feature (P)	Winter (51)	Incubation (29)	Brooding (62)	Postbrooding (35)
Items (= 0.01)	1.2 ± 0.4	1.9 ± 0.8	3.9 ± 3.0*	0.9 ± 1.0
Species (< 0.001)	1.2 ± 0.4	1.3 ± 0.5	2.3 ± 0.8*	1.0 ± 0.8
Biomass, g (= 0.03)	64.9 ± 41.4	34.2 ± 20.2	51.6 ± 42.3	23.6 ± 19.7*

cept for the low overlap involving mammals (0.40), caused by caching
exotic rodents in suburbia and native ones in the country, food-type
overlaps are 0.64–0.91, further illustrating similarities in the two populations. While it is reasonable, therefore, to combine them for additional comparisons, I reemphasize that the suburban owls inhabit a
land of plenty, here indicated by their diverse larders.

Screech owls in northern Ohio did not cache insects but only crayfish
and leeches among invertebrates, so I compared them with my birds
after omitting invertebrates except crayfish from the Texas ledger.[19]
Sixty-nine species were stored in Ohio, 72 in Texas, resulting in a
slightly broader food niche in Texas (18.0 versus 16.6). Niche overlap
is low (0.31), which may reflect changes in abundance and the general
decrease in animal species, and hence alternative foods, from south to
north. Even so, the Ohio population did not focus on a few species as
might be expected from forced specialization. The top three birds, for
example, comprised 32 percent of all those stored, the top three mammals 85 percent, scarcely different from Texas (39 and 76%, respectively; NS).

Finnish boreal owls have a much narrower food niche (4.4) based
on only 40 species of stored endotherms.[20] They live much farther
north, of course, with access to correspondingly fewer food species
than in Ohio or Texas. Yet the proportion of top three mammal species
(80%) does not differ statistically from that in the two screech owl
populations. Rather, those boreal owls concentrate more heavily on

three leading birds (59%, P < 0.001). Their bird-food niche is narrower, therefore, only 5.5 versus 14.2 for the Ohio and Texas screech owls, and only 1.3 times broader than their mammal-food niche compared to 3.7 times broader in the combined screech owls.

Food Type Seasonality

November through June trends in the average monthly densities of all edible suburban and rural birds were so similar ($r_s = 0.74$, P = 0.03), that I averaged the data for seasonal assessments. Winter residents comprised 81.4 ± 7.3 percent of the avifauna through March (46.2 ± 10.6 birds/ha) but were replaced by passage migrants as the April–May dominants (40.5 ± 4.9 percent of 40.1 ± 7.4 birds/ha) and permanent residents in June (75% of 26.3/ha). The seasonal decline in overall density was occasioned by the strong drop in winter residents (b = −5.2, P = 0.05), because passage migrants were present only momentarily (b = 2.2, NS), and permanent residents actually increased (b = 2.3, P = .006).

This increase plus their consistent availability must contribute to permanent residents being the only group cached selectively each month between November and June (selectivity index = 0.38 to 0.52 monthly compared with −0.05 to −0.72 for the other groups). Their month-to-month variation in density (CV) was just 56 percent by contrast to 79 percent for winter residents and 143 percent for the migrants. Furthermore, in comparing the seasonal selectivity of permanent resident birds versus mammals, the only other food supply censused in February (25.4 ± 10.5/ha) and June (60.2 ± 14.9/ha), permanent residents were chosen in an unequivocal manner (SI = 73 versus −51% mammals in winter, and 71 versus −58% in spring).

Whether I considered these birds alone or all prey types together, there were no significant differences between suburbia and the rural situation in the proportions of winter versus nesting-season storage. Thus, caches from the two environments could be combined to reveal that their average size tripled from winter into nesting, particularly during the brooding of chicks, when males had to supply their offspring in addition to mates (table 3.1). Afterwards, when females roosted outside the nest cavity, caching dropped dramatically because they joined the hunt and ate outside, and insects became the staple, immediately eaten food. Similar nesting-phase seasonality was found in Finnish boreal owls.[21]

Although number of stored items increased into the brooding phase, biomass of the larder did not change significantly until postbrooding, when it declined (table 3.1). Then, ectotherms began to replace the larger endotherms (birds, mammals). Birds, for example, declined from 72 percent of winter caches and 64 percent of those during incubation to only 25 percent in the postbrooding phase, while invertebrates and the ectothermic vertebrates together rose from less than 5 to 26 percent. Birds certainly dominated winter caches but in relation to mammals, more (68%) were stored while nesting; whereas mammals were stored mostly in winter (61%, P < 0.001). This was also true for the screech owls in northern Ohio but not Tennessee, where there were no seasonal distinctions.[22]

Ectotherms appeared in larders almost entirely in the nesting season (95%), unlike in Ohio and Tennessee, where they were more evenly distributed. Winter records were surprising enough that I quickly noticed they coincided with mild rainy weather which must trigger activity and accessibility of these prey. A third of the stored Rio Grande leopard frogs were taken at times that I heard their breeding choruses. Most fish appeared early too, before brooding and the high water of spring rains (closest sources were 90–600 m from nest cavities). Conversely, I saw many terrestrial animals picked up within 90 m of the same nests during brooding and postbrooding. The owls hunt close by if they can, and a seasonal relay of prey types may facilitate this.

A principal components analysis of six major prey types stored during incubation, brooding, and postbrooding depicts the relay (figure 3.2) I count prey per type and nests in each phase each week to obtain information on the 16-week nesting season. Along the horizontal axis of figure 2, incubation in March and early April lacks any prey-type correlate and separates from postbrooding correlated with caches dominated by permanent-resident birds, invertebrates, and ectothermic vertebrates in late May and June. Segregated vertically is the late-April to early May cluster of brooding dates, accompanied by migratory-bird and mammal foods.

The average food niche width is 3.1 during ten weeks of incubation records and much the same (3.2) during nine weeks of brooding data but falls to 2.7 in nine additional weeks of postbrooding. Throughout, the temporal niche of permanent-resident birds as food is 6.7 compared to 6.4 for winter residents and 4.0 for passage migrants. Mammal (8.7) and invertebrate (6.9) niches are even broader. Nevertheless, the three overlapping phases of nesting are distinct in terms of associated food types (P < 0.001) and temporal patterns of the six major types are also (P < 0.001, two-way ANOVA).

Since birds are such important storage items, I took a final look at their selection, this time on a weekly basis during nesting and with reference to the total of cached individuals (figure 3.3). Just the winter

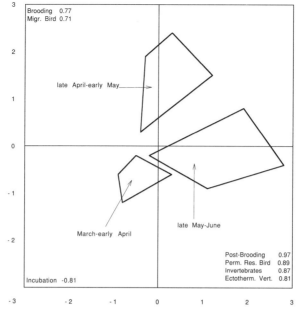

Figure 3.2. Seasonal shifts in the kinds of prey cached during nesting, derived from a principal components analysis of weekly counts of prey-types and nests between the second week of March and first week of July, 1976–87 (suburban and rural plots combined). Outside plotted points for the incubation, brooding, and post-brooding phases are joined and approximate time intervals indicated. Correlation coefficients of significant features with the graph axes are shown (horizontal axis = 53%, vertical axis = an additional 20% of variation in the data). Note that each phase of nesting is clearly distinguished, either by different associated food-types or their absence in the case of incubation.

and permanent residents are chosen, but selection of the former is minor (mean SIs = -37.7 and 19.9, respectively, P < 0.001). These are mostly the flock and ground-feeding juncos and sparrows plus cedar waxwings whose combined annual numbers fluctuate with mean minimum air temperature (r = -0.70, P = 0.02, 1976–87). Permanent residents provide a more stable food supply, concurrently unaffected by temperature (r = 0.12, NS).

Selection of permanent residents in late March and early April seems to offset the rejection of winter residents (figure 3.3). The two groups trade places again in mid-April but show parallel trends in late April and early May, as the total of cached birds peaks. Winter residents decline in March because local representatives move north, but are re-

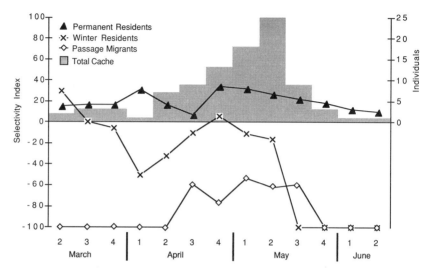

Figure 3.3   Selectivity of birds stored as food in active nests, 1976–
87, in the suburban and rural plots combined. The selectivity index
relates the proportion of food stored to that concurrently available.
Note that just the winter and permanent residents are chosen but
only the latter with any degree of consistency. Spearman rank correlation coefficients of each group's selectivity index with the total cache
of birds over the 13-week period are: passage migrants 0.67 (P =
0.01), permanent residents 0.50 (P = 0.08), and winter residents
0.14 (NS).

inforced temporarily by an April influx of more southerly individuals
also northward bound. Meanwhile, permanent residents become secretive during their April nesting and do not "reappear" until late that
month accompanied by demanding offspring. Besides their consistent
numbers, I think the April-May conspicuousness of parent-offspring
feeding fosters vulnerability.

Why are passage migrants usually rejected, even though they domi-
nate the avifauna in the late April-early May peak of migration and
screech owl nesting? The answer is quite simple theoretically. Passage
migrants arrive in pulses, coincident with south winds that they ride
northward and ensuing cold fronts that stop them in screech owl home
ranges. Some years the requisite winds bring more, other years fewer,
migratory flocks (P < 0.001, 1976–87). Furthermore, most passage
migrants are canopy foragers. Probably owls do not develop a search
image for sporadic birds that concentrate in a seldom-used stratum.[23]

Like the vertebrates, insects also appear in relays, and their observed importance in the diet of nestling and fledgling owls necessitated some estimate of seasonality and utilization. Therefore, in 1987 and 1988 students and I operated concurrent light traps 12 hours (one night) each week from late April to early June in Woodway, Harris Creek, and the rural plot. All known food taxa were assessed. Mostly these were scarab beetles (46%) and noctuid moths (43%), the same insect groups the owls caught and cached most often (see below and appendix IV). Surprisingly, densities and biomasses of all the potential prey did not differ significantly among the three sites or between years.

However, both measures increased weekly each year in both suburban plots ($r_s > 0.89$, $P < 0.01$) but tended to decrease in the rural plot ($r_s < -0.50$, NS). Scarabs alone increased in both suburbs ($r_s > 0.75$, $P < 0.05$) and declined in the rural setting ($r_s > -0.82$, $P < 0.02$), while moths showed no significant trends ($r_s < 0.61$, NS). These differences could be important, for instance, to survival of newly independent fledglings, whose initial clumsy predatory attempts are on insects on the ground (chapter 6). Many scarabs first emerge from and subsequently hide on the ground, especially the June bugs that screech owls eat and suburban folks cultivate in their watered and fertilized lawns.

Scarabs were twice as abundant per week in suburbia, moths 2.5 times more common in the rural plot; but the beetles may furnish more energy per unit capture, since they weight 3.5 times more on average (appendix IV). In fact, beetle biomass prevails overall ($P = 0.05$), but the suburban and rural environments are no different in this regard. Interestingly, food deliveries at four suburban nests spanning the same seven weeks of 1987 and 1988 revealed that moths were captured 1.4 times more often, although the harvest of beetle biomass was 2.4 times greater.

Interspecific Competition

Not only is suburbia comparatively rich in food, but the suburban screech owls have fewer avian predators to share it with. Species that ate many of the same items and nested on the Woodway study plot in 1976–87 were single pairs of barred or great-horned owls and broad-winged hawks plus two to three pairs each of chuck-will's -widows and American crows. At the same time single pairs of great-horned and barred owls, a pair of red-tailed or red-shouldered hawks, two additional pairs of "chucks" and one or two more pairs of crows nested on the rural plot.

Consuming biomass—the total weight of nesting adults of all predators—included 12–20 pairs of suburban or 2–6 of rural screech owls and averaged 10.2 kg in suburbia and 11.5 kg in the countryside. Since the seasonal biomass of vertebrates available to screech owls can be estimated as 321 and 115 kg per 270-ha study plot, respectively (appendix V), food per kilogram of avian predator could have been three times more abundant in suburbia.

Suburbia retained its owls in winter, lost the broad-wings and chucks, and gained 4–6 crows and 1–2 sharp-shinned or Cooper's hawks; while the rural plot housed 1–2 red-tails with the owls, lost its red-shouldered hawks and its chucks, and gained 1–2 accipiters plus 2–5 crows. Then consuming biomass averaged 10.8 and 12.5 kg, and bird-mammal prey averaged 447 and 189 kg, respectively; so a 2.8-fold advantange remained in suburbia.

During an average year, screech owl biomass exceeded that of potential avian competitors by a factor of about 1.2 in suburbia. Conversely, the consuming biomass of other species was about ten times that of screech owls at the rural site, in part because screech owls avoided the more numerous larger owls—their own predators—and hence were less abundant (chapter 9). The suburban combination of more food with less demand from potential competitors and fewer predators is advantageous to say the least.

Predatory Tactics

The eastern screech owl is a sit-and-wait predator, based on 291 (165 complete) suburban hunts 2–140 m from nests.[24] Fifty-nine percent of these were by males, whose tactics were like those of females but with three important differences. First, males transferred prey to females for eating (11%) or delivery to nestlings (89%), never the reverse. In the postbrooding phase, when both adults hunted, the males of 29 pairs transferred 19.5 ± 13.9 percent of the time, although there were considerable differences among pairs, ranging from 4 to 32 percent ($P <$ 0.001). In general, however, the more male captures, the more transfers were made ($r = 0.86$, $P < 0.001$).

Pairs and partners also differed extensively in their hunting intensity. Examples of average prey captures per hour at dusk during postbrooding are 16.0 for one male and 4.3 for his mate compared to 35.2 and 34.3, respectively, in a second pair (n = 5 nights/pair, P = 0.002 among 29; P = 0.03 between sexes in a two-way ANOVA). Overall, these males caught 1.6 items per female catch, while male boreal owls delivered 37.8 times more prey than their mates. Like the male boreals, I found that male screech owls brought in more large prey than did females, simply because they caught comparatively more vertebrates than insects during the coincidental hunts of both sexes (12% versus 1% vertebrates by females of 57 items: P = 0.01).[25]

Since males seem to work harder, I wonder if food transfer to their mates for delivery to nestlings saves them some flight energy. After all, the males have done essentially all hunting during incubation and brooding, so they should know best where to find food and hence continue to do the most provisioning. Conserving energy might be important, therefore. Conversely, females ought to reduce their hunting and stay closer to the nest for defensive purposes; food transfers for their own use as well as for delivery to nestlings should promote this behavior. I think the basic division of reproductive labor indicated early in nesting continues throughout, is based on sexual size dimorphism, and is adaptive (see chapters 4–6).

Males also tended to make longer flights ($\bar{x}$ 38.2 versus 29.1 m) between more waiting perches ($\bar{x}$ 3.6 versus 2.1) per hunting foray, although the differences are not statistically significant. Flights in open and wooded yards did not differ either but were longer than the 17-m average hunting flights of the boreal owl (P = 0.05). Too, the screech owl's hunting perches, usually in the lowermost tree canopy, are higher than the boreal's (2.6 ± 0.5 m vs. 1.7 m, P = 0.03).[26] Longer flights and higher perches might reflect the screech owl's more open habitat in suburbia, compared to the boreal's birch and conifer forests, but they could also relate to more extensive above-ground foraging.

Screech owls caught 66 percent of 165 prey items on the ground and 34 percent above it compared to 80 and 20 percent, respectively, for the boreal owl. However these differences are insignificant. Nor are sex-related differences apparent in my birds. Above-ground foraging sites were mostly foliage, flowers, and tree trunks. A few aerial captures seemed to result from fly-catching with the bill, though most were accomplished with the feet. Screech owls also hover-glean foliage and flowers, appearing to catch some insects after flushing them with wing beats like the elf and common barn owls do.[27]

Pair members usually hunt in different directions (69% of 291 forays), as in long-eared owls, but both occasionally make repeated trips to and from concentrations of invertebrates such as emerging cicadas and earthworms on a recently watered lawn or moths and beetles attracted to lights.[28] One pair, for instance, hunted entirely separately despite a flourescent bug trap, 45 m from the nest, that the female used almost exclusively. Both members of another pair made 30 percent of their hunts at number three of six frequently used perches one spring but switched 64 percent of the time to perch number two the next nesting season (P < 0.001). I think it likely that some sit-and-wait perches are selected on the basis of recent success.

The owls change perches if their quarry escapes or nothing appears in 1.2 ± 0.4 minutes (n = 43), similar to the boreal owl's average patience of 1.8 ± 1.1 minutes (n = 9, NS). In terms of optimal foraging, it seems that screech owls tend to fly sooner, probably because their insect prey is denser than the rodent prey of boreal owls and hence likely to be assessed (intercepted) more quickly if a perch is profitable. But the average waiting times are no different statistically, so perhaps the screech owl's is a compromise between waiting a little while for insects and longer for vertebrates.

On 72 hunts with escaped or captured foods that I verified, only 17 percent of 63 insects but 44 percent of 9 vertebrates were lost, even after short chases (P = 0.08). Those insects might be more profitable prey, except that their estimated average weight (0.25 g) and hence harvest of biomass (13 g) was much less than estimated vertebrate averages (8 g, 40 g). Three times more vertebrate biomass was taken, but biomass gain/lost ratios were 4.7 for insects and only 1.2 for vertebrates, so insects were four times more worthwhile on just this basis. If less energy was spent pursuing them, insectivory might be even more profitable.

Total capture success was 78 percent on those 72 hunts, very much like 81 percent for the insectivorous flammulated owl, but somewhat higher than 56–69 percent in the mostly insectivorous American kestrel.[29] By contrast, capture efficiencies are 27 and 33 percent, respectively, for the rodent-eating Ural and great-gray owls. These values and a 38.2 percent average for other vertebrate-eating birds suggest that hunting insects is quite efficient but, of course, must be measured against the energy savings of making fewer hunting trips if vertebrates are the primary quarry.[30]

Of 165 catches I could identify to type, 76 percent were insects. Their seasonality substantiates that of the invertebrate caches, mostly insects depicted in figure 3.2, since most (82%) were taken during post-brooding; whereas most vertebrates were captured earlier (61%, P < 0.001). Moreover, the hierarchy of moths (45%), beetles (28%), crickets (16%), caterpillars (6%), and roaches (4%) resembles that of these same groups in suburban caches (r_s = 0.81, P = 0.10). Other verified catches included snakes (15%), birds (7%), earthworms, two lizards, and a mouse.

Eight of the ten snakes, a lizard (ground skink), one earthworm, and a third of the beetles and camel crickets were beneath 1–5 cm of leaf litter into which screech owls dived after hovering over the spot or

Adult male delivers (*left*) crayfish to a nest box and (*right*) caterpillar to a prey-delivery perch; note the right-leg band. (Curtis Williams photos)

making a "beeline" flight from a waiting perch. Some leaves were clutched in these as well as cases of missed prey. Similar dives were made on two house sparrows and one chipping sparrow feeding in conspecific flocks of 5–11 birds in open yards. These were by male owls, roosting near active nests, to the closest perimeter sparrows. Each was successful with less than 20 seconds spent in the killing process of biting the head and neck.

Perch-to-prey strikes averaged 6.1 ± 3.4 m (n = 62), similar to the estimated 4.5-m dives of the boreal owl. Always they were straight-line or nearly so by contrast to U-flights between waiting perches (see chapter 2). The shortest ones were 2–3-m drops from perches and nest holes onto invertebrates immediately below. The other basic technique of hovering a half-meter or less near hidden or inactive prey was also followed by a sudden drop or surge toward the quarry. Hovers lasted less than ten seconds, and airborne insects were not pursued, but the owls sometimes walked surprisingly fast or hopped about after missed animals on the ground.

All vertebrate prey was taken with the feet and killed or disabled on the ground, where all that I saw were encountered. After being carried to a habitual killing-plucking perch in one foot or the beak, some

Table 3.2 Initial evening activity times in the suburban nesting season. Data are mean ± one standard deviation of minutes before and after (−) sunset for 19 pairs in April–May, 1976–89 (n = 5 each per nesting phase). One- and two-way ANOVAs indicate differences among pairs (P < 0.001) and the statistical distinctions given below. Note that males depart day roosts earlier than do females and both sexes leave earlier as nesting progresses; also, males begin earlier food deliveries late in nesting.

		Nesting Phases		
Activity/Sexes	Incubation	Brooding	Postbrooding	P
Day-roost departure				
Males	4.5 ± 7.7	17.4 ± 9.0	36.2 ± 4.3	< 0.001
Females	−17.7 ± 9.6	10.8 ± 18.3	15.3 ± 6.0	< 0.001
(P)	(< 0.001)	(NS)	(< 0.001)	
First food delivery				
Males		−19.7 ± 8.2	−12.0 ± 6.3	= 0.001

birds, snakes, and even large insects were bitten again. Small items were held up to the beak in a foot. Bird wing and especially tail feathers were sometimes plucked but often not until the carcass reached the nest. Next the owls used a customary prey-delivery perch from which transfers and deliveries were made, but occasionally they flew directly to the nest with prey held by the head or neck in their beaks. Plucking perches were at least 7 m from nests, delivery perches within 3 m, and aerial routes between them were straight-line and habitual.

Hunting Periodicity

In December-February, 11 suburban males entered their nest-box roosts 18.7 ± 6.7 minutes before sunrise and then looked out for several minutes. They exited 15.2 ± 4.1 minutes following sunset after looking from the holes 26.9 ± 15.7 minutes. Thus, they left about a half hour later than from tree roosts during nesting (P < 0.001, table 3.2). Over seven days in late January-early February the rufous female of a pair that roosted together looked out first, but her gray mate left the box 3–24 minutes before she did. What was the stimulus for departure? Among the 11 males, exit times were not related to food supply or air temperature (r < 0.29, NS) but were earlier under cloudy skies (r_s > −0.57, P < 0.001) suggesting that ambient light was involved.[31]

I took light readings at one male's roost box at sunset and departure for 24 days in January-February and found that his nightly activity was keyed to 0.65 ± 0.27 foot candles of light, regardless of sky cover, which was significantly less light than the 1.5 (cloudy) to 5.7 (clear) foot candles at sunset (P < 0.001).[32] While nesting in April-May, the same male roosted in a deciduous tree only 3 m away and on 17 days his departures were at 1.98 ± 1.07 foot candles of light, hence under brighter conditions than in winter (P < 0.001). This activity too was unaffected by cloudiness and surely related to an increased demand for food.

Apparently, the first nest visit each evening was just for "reassurance," whether by the attending male or postbrooding female, for no food was delivered. Males with incubating mates left their roosts just before sunset but stepped up their departures significantly as nesting progressed (table 3.2). The first food deliveries were earlier too, the time strongly and negatively dependent on the supply of bird and mammal food (r^2 = 0.94, P < 0.001), not air temperature or cloudiness (r^2 added < 0.09, NS, in a MSR; n = 29). While more food perhaps excited earlier activity, it did not insure quicker hunting success, because roost departure and first food-delivery times were uncorrelated (r = −0.12, NS).

Sometimes females were fed initially during their nightly recesses from nest duty, which began about 20 minutes after the males became active (see also chapters 5, 6). Their departures also were earlier as nesting continued, increasing an average of 1.2 minutes daily (P = 0.003), about like the males' 1.3-minute average (P < 0.001). Before leaving they always looked around from the nest-cavity entrance, 11.2 ± 7.2 minutes during incubation but only 3.7 ± 3.3 minutes while brooding (n = 8 each, P = 0.01). Seemingly more intent on leaving earlier in the brooding phase, females switched from after- to before-sunset exits, so their times varied widely (table 3.2).

Shorter nights with a consequent reduction in hunting time later in the season and increased nestling demand are both implicated in the trends toward earlier roost departures and food deliveries (table 3.2). Screech owls are crepuscular to be sure, but males with nestlings foraged in broad daylight on three percent of the 291 hunts; and one even bathed at 1003–1010 hours after delivering a bird despite being mobbed. Exemplary daytime kills were the above-mentioned sparrows at 0845, 1612, and 1750 hours, a fledgling bluejay delivered at 1630, and Texas spiny lizards at 0900 and 1430. On the other hand, an American robin was cached about 1530 on a cloudy February day as robins by the hundreds foraged around the roost.

It could be important to evening hunting success that eight suburban males left their tree roosts 32.9 ± 9.5 minutes before the first calling chuck-will's-widows in their home ranges. Thus, they had a headstart on the only other nocturnal bird that might compete with them for flying insects (and small birds?). But cardinals, bluejays, and mockingbirds were still active, and they scolded and often mobbed the owls as late as 6.1 ± 4.9 minutes after sunset (n = 10). Too, mobbing occurred as early as 11–17 minutes before sunrise (n = 3). This could impede hunting but only momentarily. I watched two foraging male owls fly at but not strike late-mobbing bluejays, which caused the jays to leave immediately. I never saw such behavior from roosting owls that were mobbed.

After hatching at my sample of 19 suburban nests, food deliveries each night were distinctly bimodal with the major peak at dusk. They dropped from an average of 19.2 to 10.2 per 15 minutes in the first hour, declining at every nest (r_s = −0.20 to −1.0, n = 7–9 nights/nest). Early hunting was apparently sufficient, although variation in brood sizes and types of prey obscured absolute differences among the 15-minute intervals (P = 0.08; see chapter 6). Hourly deliveries went from 60.7 ± 14.1 to only 14.3 ± 11.1 near 2100 (P < 0.001) and were practically nil around 2200. Two to three hours before sunrise was a secondary burst of feeding, again lasting 1–2 hours, but I did not enumerate it.

On average, Finnish boreal owls begin to deliver food 78 minutes later than my screech owls during incubation and 54 minutes later in the nestling period.[33] Both species have nearly the same egg and nestling periods, centered on April and May respectively, but nights are shorter further north; owls may be forced to hunt longer at northern latitudes. In fact, that seems to be the case. My birds have a 3–4-hour bimodal activity period, while screech owls in New York appear to hunt 5–7 hours in unimodal fashion.[34] Boreal owls hunt 4–5 hours daily; and their northern populations, plus those of Eurasian pygmy, tawny, and perhaps Ural owls, have a unimodal rhythm compared to the bimodality of conspecific southern populations.[35]

The crepuscular hunting of diverse food supplies should allow the Texas screech owls and southern populations of other owls to utilize a combination of diurnal (birds, insects, lizards) and nocturnal (mammals, other insects, snakes) prey. They should finish dusk and dawn hunting quickly by contrast to northern owls with fewer prey species, each perhaps active longer. This hypothesis is validated by the predominance of birds relative to mammals, broader food niches, and shorter activity peaks focused near dusk and dawn in the southern populations of several owls in addition to the eastern screech.

Mobbing

However, crepuscular hunting exposes a bird predator to its prey, and songbirds mob without hesitation in the dim light as I have noted. This seems unusual, perhaps because no one has tried to find repeated patterns in natural mobbing behavior. Experimentalists have been at work but without the benefit of knowing the reciprocal relationships of mobber and "mobbee." [36] After watching 134 mobs of roosting, nesting, and hunting screech owls and their empty perches and nest cavities in suburbia, I have little doubt that the primary functional significance of mobbing is as predator-warning, not predator-deterring behavior.

Only 13 percent of the studied mobs occurred during fledgling dispersal and another 38 percent in winter, the latter a time of less frequent bird-eating. Conversely, the significant majority were during the nesting season (49%, P < 0.001), when most birds are killed. This was my first clue. Other studies of screech owls show a similar nesting peak but no secondary period of winter mobbing, probably because they concern northern populations that eat relatively more mammals than birds in winter (see above). [37] My second clue was that permanent residents engaged in 82 percent of the mobs, migrants and seasonal residents in only 17 percent, a significant difference relative to their numbers and hence availability to mob (P < 0.001).

Other signals included that fact that permanent residents mobbed more often during nesting (60%) than in the other two seasons (P < 0.001), while for migrants and seasonal residents there was no significant seasonal difference (appendix VI). Also, fledgling screech owls seldom were mobbed and when they were, mobbing intensity seemed reduced. Finally, seven natives among the leading mobbers, all permanent residents, mobbed more often relative to their numbers than the exotic house sparrow and European starling (P = 0.04). Jeopardy and evolutionary-ecological experience may be the factors involved.

The next step was to look at specific relations between mobbing frequency and jeopardy, the latter measured as number of times the species was killed and cached. For all 31 birds that mobbed, there is a slight correlation (r = 0.34, P = 0.05), but the relationship is much stronger for 17 natives (r = 0.63, P = 0.006). Thus, it seems that species in danger mob with a frequency corresponding to their degree of danger, while others may be mere crowd followers. It certainly is adaptive to match the warning effort to the likelihood of predation, which explains why natives having the longest histories of coping with screech owls are the strongest mobbers. Now I understand why passage migrants, "here today, gone tomorrow," are minor participants (appendix VI).

If all of this is true, the predator-warning effort should extend to persistence in mixed-species mobs, where certain species may be facilitators and others just followers. For six permanent residents I could determine participation in 6–15 mixed mobs per species and thus figure the hierarchy of persistence as (most) bluejay, northern cardinal, northern mockingbird, Carolina wren, tufted titmouse, to Carolina chickadee (least). This sequence is also correlated with the number of bodies per species in screech owl larders ($r_s = 0.83$, $P = 0.04$), reaffirming that mobbing intensity is linked to liability.

Bluejays, by far, are leaders in this respect (appendix VI). Perhaps they are facilitators, since only 55 percent of their mobbing occurs in mixed-species flocks, which is significantly less than the 80 percent of other native residents ($P = 0.01$). Titmice and chickadees are the second and third leading mobbers but not as bold, almost always (90%) associating with other mobbers. Alternatively, jays may be more perspicacious and not need another's warnings to alert them to screech owls. This is suggested because they mobbed empty nest and roost sites 2.8 times more often than did the total of titmice, chickadees, Bewick's and Carolina wrens, and starlings—all cavity users unlike jays, and the only other empty-site mobbers ($P < 0.001$).[38]

Throughout the winter season, 36 owls being mobbed were in cavities and evergreen tree roosts about equally (53 vs. 47%) but were hassled more often in the trees where they could be seen ($P = 0.02$).[39] Mobbing frequency was no different in evergreen versus deciduous-tree roosts. The visual stimulus of an owl in a tree makes the mobbing of vacant sites all the more remarkable, and bluejays recognized these signs of owls up to 240 days after sites were vacated. But because male owls periodically revisit each cavity they defend, the alert jays may be restimulated.

Nonetheless, the birds have memory of former danger and knowledge that any large cavity is hazardous. I learned this serendipitously by removing decrepit nest boxes after owlets fledged, replacing them six to eight months later, and seeing bluejays, titmice, and chickadees mob the empty new boxes within 30 minutes. And I was really startled to watch these same species take about the same length of time to mob new boxes at entirely new sites. This shows that a suitably large cavity, albeit artificial and novel for that reason alone, is recognized. Mobbers do not need any past or present evidence of an owl. Why then do small songbirds sometimes nest in my screech-owl boxes (see chapter 1)? Are they naive individuals who did not learn from an earlier cavity-mobbing experience? I think so.[40]

Since birds are utilized as food less often as nesting progresses, I thought that mobbing might decline accordingly. At five suburban nests, I recorded the number of mobs by jays, cardinals, wrens, titmice, and chickadees during incubation, brooding, and postbrooding. After standardizing the data by number of days per phase per nest and averaging the results, I found that I was wrong. Mobbing increased in all species except the uneaten chickadee (r_s = 0.50–1.0). The female owl's presence outside the nest cavity during postbrooding must be the additional stimulus, since songbirds must then be wary of two hunters instead of just one.

The owl's responses also demonstrate that mobbing serves to warn of danger and occasionally remove it from the immediate vicinity, not to drive the predator out of its familiar hunting range. In only 41 percent of the 134 mobs did owls move (NS). They never flew more than 90 m and then only between known tree roosts (69%) or into cavities (31%). But jays moved them 52 percent of the time, other songbirds without associated jays only 28 percent (P = 0.10); and only the jays or American crows drove them into cavities or followed departing owls to alternate refuges, initiating new foci of harassment.

The Essentials

Among vertebrate prey, birds are eaten most often, particularly while the owls nest and especially by suburban individuals. Permanent residents are selected over seasonal residents and passage migrants, primarily because of their consistent availability, and suburbia offers many more individuals of the same species than does the countryside, even though the two avifaunas are structured similarly. For storage in cavities large species are selected, especially those that satisfy the owls' daily food needs of 25–33 percent of their body weight. Ground-feeding and flocking species plus males are especially vulnerable. Mammals and reptiles are also cached, but the former include mostly subadults of the larger species like cottontails and brown rats. Snakes, including several burrowing species, are important food items after rainfall or lawn watering flushes them to the ground surface.

Based on visual observations, though, invertebrates constitute the majority of food with crayfish, moths, and beetles leading the list. These smaller quarry are more likely to be eaten immediately than stored and are mostly utilized later in nesting, when birds are killed less frequently. Invertebrates are scarce items in the winter, when relatively more mammals are cached. A seasonal relay of prey types is indicated. Species are not avoided because of repellent secretions or physical defenses, nor do the cached taxa correspond to annual supply, even when rodent and songbird population cycles are considered. The suburban food niche is broader than the rural niche but very similar in species utilization. Local screech owls eat a more diverse array of taxa than their northern cousins.

Stored food increases in variety and weight from winter through the brooding phase of nesting and then declines, as females join their mates in hunting and roosting outside the nest cavity. Relatively more insects, eaten immediately, account for this; and they increase seasonally in suburbia, not in the rural environment, although general numbers and biomasses are nearly the same. Moths are caught most often, but beetles furnish more biomass; and all insects return more energy per predatory attempt than vertebrates, because they are missed less often. The capture efficiency of insectivory is greater than that of vertebrate-eating in owls and birds generally. Among nesting screech owls, postbrooding females catch fewer vertebrates and fewer prey items overall than their mates, who transfer some food to them for delivery to nestlings and thus save flight energy. This too may allow females to remain near their nests for defense.

Two-thirds of all prey are caught on the ground or in shallow water and one-third in foliage or at flowers after a short straight-line dive from a sit-and-wait perch, usually in the lower quarter of the tree canopy. Occasionally the owls hover over apparently hidden quarry a few seconds before plunging and may flush insects for fly-catching in foliage. Most captures are with the feet, but prey may be transferred to the beak for delivery. Habitual killing-plucking and delivery perches are used. Males tend to make slightly more and longer flights and use more perches per hunting foray than their mates. These perches are based on prior success and employed only a minute or two. Productive and hence favored ones vary year-to-year.

Roosting individuals look about for a few minutes before leaving to hunt and are active earlier as nesting progresses. Light levels seem to control the roost departures, although nesting birds often hunt successfully in broad daylight. Food deliveries are earlier later in the season, when food is more abundant, and are most frequent at the start of nightly hunting. They drop off rapidly but resume again near dawn in the characteristic bimodal activity pattern of southern populations by contrast to unimodal activity in northern populations of owls. Early evening hunting may reduce food competition with chuck-will's-widows but exposes screech owls to mobbing by songbirds. In general, though, the suburban owls have more food and fewer potential competitors for it.

Since mobbing frequency and persistence are positively correlated with vulnerability among the mobbers and mobbing takes place at vacated roosts and nests plus newly placed nest boxes, it is clearly predator-warning behavior adapted to relative endangerment. Experience with an owl is not needed; songbird mobbers seem to know about cavity configuration as indicative of the predator. They may need to learn this, since some species sometimes nest in screech owl boxes and are eaten. Moreover, mobbed owls usually stay put unless bluejays or crows are involved and then are only temporarily displaced, not put out of their usual hunting range.

4 Adult Weight, Coloration, and Molt

Basic Constraints

Twenty centimeters of snow overnight and −15°C are sufficient to bring Central Texas culture to a standstill. The woods are quite; noise is muffled by the snow. Like dawn, this is a peaceful time to be out. And screech owls are ensconced, so I can practice heft, the art of sexing them by simply holding their warm bodies in my bare hands. A female and her smaller mate occupy the same next box, sheltered against today's cold, snug amidst dry leaves from last year's fox squirrel nest and a cache of house sparrows and cedar waxwings. Three days later the male, whose plumage I recognize, enjoys the morning sun, perched in the box entrance, and squints at my passage through the melting snow.

By handling hundreds of eastern screech owls over the years, including many at different seasons and over several years, I learned to sex most individuals by weight. During the exploratory years, winter data were substantiated with spring recaptures of incubating-brooding females and their food-delivering mates. The males never developed bare breast patches or covered eggs or nestlings. Also I measured wings, bills, and tarsi but found that the extra handling meant those individuals often deserted their roosts and nests. Others simply weighed to the nearest gram in a dark bag did not, so I stopped measuring body parts in the exploratory period.[1]

Early in the study I found that yearlings were smaller than older owls, especially the females, but only because that age class includes comparatively small one-time breeders that soon disappear (chapter 8).[2] Among the survivors year-to-year differences in average breeding weight could not be found, although there is a tendency for weight increase in the first three years (chapter 8). Older female boreal owls are also slightly heavier than yearlings, especially at "poor" nest sites.[3] But site does not influence weight in my subjects, probably because they continue to use successful nest sites, unlike boreal owls.[4] There are two additional aspects of body weight (mass) exemplified by female screech owls: mass is partly inherited (chapter 8) and no different in the suburban and rural environments (table 4.1).

Males were weighed less often, since they were harder to catch, and I recaptured just one between fledging and its first complete molt in its

65

Table 4.1. Weights in grams of adult eastern screech owls, 1976–86. Data are mean ± one standard deviation and (sample size) derived from the means of two- to seven-year-olds recaptured at least twice per season or stage of nesting. Color and paired versus unpaired male comparisons involve owls in the same season and year. Note the sexual differences and seasonal plus nesting-stage decline in weights (P < 0.001) but no significant difference between suburban and rural birds (nested ANOVA of the sexes by site, season, and stage). Colormorph and paired versus unpaired differences are also insignificant.

Comparisons	Males	Females
Winter (November–February)	163.0 ± 13.2 (24)	196.1 ± 17.2 (22)
Suburban	166.3 ± 17.7 (18)	192.4 ± 16.5 (18)
Rural	160.6 ± 7.9 (5)	197.3 ± 7.4 (4)
Gray	166.8 ± 12.6 (5)	217.6 ± 9.5 (3)
Rufous	170.0 (1)	224 (1)
Spring (March–June)	152.3 ± 11.5 (13)	173.9 ± 11.6 (25)
Paired suburban	151.7 ± 6.4 (7)	—
Unpaired suburban	158.1 ± 4.8 (7)	—
Incubating suburban	—	179.5 ± 10.5 (20)
Incubating rural	—	180.6 ± 9.9 (10)
Brooding suburban	—	168.8 ± 9.6 (29)
Brooding rural	—	167.7 ± 8.1 (11)
Gray	—	178.6 ± 12.2 (18)
Rufous	—	179.9 ± 10.6 (5)

second summer. It was subadult size in January at age eight months (149 g, cf. table 4.1). Information on 10–11-month-old females suggests that they attain near-adult weight between their first winter and first nesting season. Five in their first winter averaged 173.6 ± 8.3 g, less than 22 older females (P < 0.001), but during subsequent brooding were no different at 171.2 ± 5.3 g (cf. table 1). Since most yearlings of both sexes nest, they should have reached adult mass, if that benefits breeding performance as it is known to do in the boreal and Ural owls and many other birds.[5]

The Size Dimorphism Question

Like most raptors, the eastern screech owls of Central Texas exhibit reversed, sexual size dimorphism (table 4.1). Mated individuals, caught together in my next boxes, are illustrative: a 179-g female and

158-g male in late winter (February 1), a 194-g female about to lay eggs and her 142-g mate (March 10), and a 161-g female with downy chicks plus 138-g male. Thus, the females remain larger than males despite profound, seasonal changes (table 4.1). Altogether, females average 33 g (20%) heavier in winter and 22 g (14%) heavier while nesting. The 17 percent average is comparable to 16 percent in an Ohio population and 20 percent among other North American owls.[6]

Furthermore, female hawks and eagles are even larger, averaging 34 percent heavier than males among North American species. Few students of raptor biology can resist comment on such unusual dimorphism, since males usually are the larger sex among other birds and mammals. But many observations are unconvincing because they lack detailed empirical knowledge.[7] Perhaps my screech owls can provide new insights, so I offer hypotheses on the causes and evolutionary directions of reversed size dimorphism that are examined here or in other chapters. Some of my ideas are borrowed, though expressed in a new context, and all are based on exploratory experiences tested with the confirmatory data.[8]

Hypotheses: Males catch and deliver essentially all food for their mates during incubation and brooding, including the supply of nestling food. They even catch more food than females when the latter hunt after brooding. Hence their small size permits energy savings and enhances their role as nest-site defender in the pre-laying period (chapter 2) and major provisioner of the reproductive effort (chapter 3).[9] Moreover, nesting males take mostly insects, which is most efficient energetically, since these small animals are the most abundant and easily dispatched prey (chapter 3).[10] All of this satisfies females and nestling demands and hence promotes breeding success; so perhaps mated males are smaller than unmated ones and pairs with the most sexual size discrepancy experience the greatest reproductive success.

More hypotheses: Females choose mates on the basis of more proffered food and suitable nesting cavities during courtship, so they must be the selective cause of small male size.[11] But they are the larger sex because larger females lay more and larger eggs and incubate them more successfully (chapter 5). Also a large body can withstand temporary food shortages better due to its large storage capacity and small skin-surface to body-volume ratio, hence reduced heat loss. Thus, larger females are not so prone to abandon eggs or starve downy chicks when their mates cannot deliver food, for example during rainy weather.[12] Large, well-fed females may even distribute food among and brood nestlings so as to prevent cannibalism; and this, like the other aspects of large size, augments breeding success and recruitment of offspring into the breeding population (chapters 6, 8).

Furthermore, females are most closely associated with eggs and nestlings, as males are often away hunting, so the females are the most frequent and most vigorous nest guards. Large females should be able to intimidate potential predators better and strike them harder than small males could, simply because of their mass. In fact, females do most physical and even vocal defending of nests (chapters 5–7). After brooding ceases and females roost outside the next cavity because the growing chicks require extra space, the females roost closest to recently fledged owlets, the pair's major energy investments, because of their role as primary defenders of the reproductive effort (chapters 3, 6).[13]

But females cannot be too large, or they will be unable to enter potential nesting cavities selected and defended by their mates. Small cavities with small entrances should be more numerous than large cavities, since there are more small trees and small cavity drillers (woodpeckers) than larger ones. More importantly, however, small cavities should be safest as well as most available for screech owls, relative to the cavity requirements of larger predators and competitors like the barred and common barn owls, ringtails, raccoons, Virginia opossums, and fox squirrels of Central Texas. Thus, females must be able to utilize relatively small cavities, and female size divergence is constrained.[14]

Weight Dynamics

From winter to winter, 1976–86, individual adult females showed slightly more weight flux than males. Average coefficients of variation were 6.5 for 22 females and 5.1 for 24 males. Though not different statistically, I suspect the somewhat greater variation among females was due to their temporary emigration from familiar nesting ranges (chapter 2). Perhaps they were more food-stressed than males, although apparently not to the degree of nomadic-migratory female boreal owls.[15]

Just how important is food availability, together with variation in weather, as a determinant of the annual weight flux? For winter males in Woodway, 1976–86, I ran a multiple, stepwise regression of mean weight on winter precipitation, mean minimum air temperature, resident bird plus small rodent density, and wintering finch density to learn about potential cause and effect. And I did the same for both winter and incubating-brooding females after modifying the data appropriate to season and adding male weight as a fifth possible explanatory factor, since males begin to court their mates with food by early February (chapter 7).

Indeed, the supply of resident birds and small rodents had the primary, positive influence on both sexes in winter ($r^2 > 0.57$, $P < 0.02$). Mean minimum air temperature was next in the causal hierarchy with a negative effect ($r^2 > 0.27$, $P < 0.05$). This is probably because winter finch numbers are negatively determined by air temperature (chapter 3). Dark-eyed juncos, white-throated sparrows, and their kin are most abundant when it is coldest, so I was not surprised that finch density positively influenced the owls' winter weights when temperature was dropped from the analysis (r^2 added = 0.48, $P = 0.007$). In fact, 84 to 90 percent of the weight flux of both sexes was explained by food supplies and minimum temperature ($P < 0.001$). Males contributed nothing significant to females at this time of year.

However, nesting males positively affected their mates' incubation-brooding weight (r^2 added = 0.26, $P = 0.03$) in addition to the stronger positive influence of more food ($r^2 = 0.51$, $P = 0.01$). When I controlled for the variation in food supply in an analysis of covariance, heavier males accounted for 40 percent of the variation in female weight. Mean weights of these nesting females were 168 to 183 grams annually and 87 percent of the variation was explained by resident food plus male weight ($P < 0.001$). Thus, by contrast to the winter situation, nesting females depend heavily, though perhaps not entirely, on well-fed males to deliver food.

Importance of the male's role as food provider was further indicated by his weight flux, relative to that of the female, as nesting began. In winter, coefficients of weight variation were 8.1 and 8.8 percent, respectively (cf. table 4.1). In spring, the male coefficient was 7.6 percent, but the female value dropped to 6.7 percent. While nesting, however, paired males exhibited a 4.2 percent coefficient, less than the 5.8 percent of their incubating-brooding mates. Interestingly, these paired individuals had a 1.4-fold larger coefficient of weight variation than unpaired males at 3.0 percent, although their average weight was essentially the same (table 4.1).

The winter to spring drop in weight of both sexes is significant ($P < 0.001$) by contrast to insignificant weight variation among years in the same 13 males and 25 females (two-way ANOVA). The seasonal change may increase flying and hence predatory efficiency, contributing to breeding success among males.[16] Paired males lost about twice the weight of their unpaired counterparts (table 1). This must mirror female and brood-feeding requirements and may permit these nesting individuals to be more effective hunters. Concurrently, females lost slightly more weight, but the 11 percent loss of both sexes combined equals the winter to spring loss in Ohio screech owls.[17]

The greatest drop in female weight, a 6.7 percent average in suburbia and 8.5 percent in the rural population, occurs from winter through incubation. Surely this relates to egg deposition, but average clutch weight (70.3 grams) is 36 percent of average female winter weight, so most of the loss is offset by courtship (production) feeding. Brooding females lose an additional 5.9 (suburbia) to 7.1 (rural) percent of their incubation weight because of nestling demand, suggested by the parallel between female loss and combined nestling weight gain ($r = -0.61$, $P < 0.001$, $n = 26$).[18] The greater weight loss of rural females must be due to comparatively sparse food supplies in that environment (see chapter 3).

Most females slowly lose weight during the six weeks of incubation and brooding, but some fluctuate, and a few even experience a net weight gain. Two cases illustrate the most common patterns: on April 2 an incubating owl weighted 177 grams; on the 22nd with one egg and three chicks totaling 63 grams, she was 163 grams; and on the 27th, brooding four chicks at 120 grams, she had dropped to 159 grams. Another female at 183 grams covered three chicks totaling 89 grams on April 10; on the 22nd she weight 168 grams when the owlets totaled 277 grams. However, when brooding ceased on the 29th, this bird was 174 grams so had begun to regain weight.

Among 24 pairs, reweighed at least twice during incubation-brooding, the net weight change of females was determined largely by average male weight ($r^2 = 0.49$, $P < 0.001$). Heavier males reduced the loss or effected a gain; the variation ranged from -19 grams (-10%) to 7 grams (4%). But another significant fraction of the flux was due to female pre-incubation size (r^2 added $= 0.30$, $P = 0.003$, MSR). Heavier females remained that way. Furthermore, by comparison to male weight (r^2 added $= 0.6$, NS), female pre-incubation weight was the only explanation of the average size difference in these nesting pairs ($r^2 = 0.64$, $P < 0.001$).

Breeding success is always the final consideration, and I found that females who lost the least weight while nesting ($r^2 = 0.47$, $P < 0.001$) and were larger to begin with (r^2 added $= 0.06$, $P = 0.01$, $n = 24$) lost the fewest eggs and chicks. Fundamentally, they fledged the most owlets and produced the most population recruits (chapters 6,8). Since they were provisioned by apparently well-fed mates, who should be most likely to feed them sufficiently, the principal influence of a heavier male is not surprising. But the female's prenesting contribution to weight maintenance was unexpected and later found to have a strong genetic component besides its primary link to food availability (chapter 8). Withal, my suggestions that paired males are smaller than unpaired ones and that sexual size difference contributes to breeding success are not supported.[19]

Yet the hypothesis that males are the smaller sex because their size requires less food energy and facilitates hunting is attractive when male versus female wing loading is considered. Wing loading or body weight supported by wing surface area was less among eight nesting males compared to their mates (32.6 ± 0.8 versus 41.0 ± 1.2 g/cm^2, P = 0.01).[20] Thus males carry 20 percent less weight per square unit of wing area, and ought to be more efficient hunters accordingly. They should catch and transport somewhat larger prey or more prey per unit time than females, and they do both (chapter 3). For example, a male carrying a 27-gram house sparrow has the flight energy demand of his mate toting a 22-gram dark-eyed junco, and the male's extra food just might avert starvation of his last-hatched nestling.

How much weight loss or flux is stressful to the adult owls I cannot say, but females that experienced the most lifetime flux, based on weights recorded in the same week over at least three years, did not fledge fewer owlets (r = 0.36, NS) or die sooner (r = 0.26, NS, n = 20). I did record 36 and 38 percent weight losses apparently caused by winter starvation, but they are like the 30 to 40 percent losses of other starved owls.[21] The first case was a 21-month-old, gray female that weighed 182 grams the day before the longest subfreezing period in local history (December, 1983). She was dead at 113 grams 19 days later, having lost 3.6 grams per day. This was 18 times the average weight loss of surviving females that winter. And the second owl, a rufous male found dead but supple two weeks later, was only 104 grams or 59 grams below average winter male weight (table 4.1).

Color Polymorphism

The rufous (red) phenotype interests me, since its comparatively bright color seems to contradict the species' cryptic plumage, its tree-bark mimicry. When confronted by an intruder, the eastern screech owl's feather patterns and behavior, including slim posture, squinted eyes, and erect "ear" tufts, enhance its blend into live or dead wood. Both rufous and gray owls behave in like manner, and they both roost next to a tree trunk, if not in a cavity or thick vegetation, which augments the camouflage. Gray individuals are quite difficult to see, whereas the rufous ones stand out, especially on a sunny day. How can they survive?

Perhaps they don't, by contrast to gray, for the rufous morph was comparatively scarce in my study area. I located but one rufous × rufous nesting pair, the male of which was the only rufous territory

Adult male in (*left*) cryptic posture and (*right*) relaxed position.

holder among 59 nesting males through 1989. The female died in an electrical storm, but this male obtained a gray mate, nested the next two years in the same box, and had two rufous and two gray offspring. Then he disappeared during or after a colder than average winter. Only two other rufous males are known to me including the starved bird that also perished in extreme cold. Compared to gray individuals, rufous screech owls are unfit in such weather, as reported in northern Ohio; and the smaller males may be more severely affected because of their comparatively unfavorable skin surface to body volume ratio.[22]

Rufous females certainly were more numerous than rufous males locally, as I recorded eight nesting individuals contemporary with 48 gray ones relative to the single rufous and 58 gray males (P = 0.03).[23] Four of the rufous females raised broods successfully, one in four successive years with the same gray mate in the same next box. All rufous × gray matings produced essentially equal numbers of rufous and gray nestlings, which is consistent with the concept of a single, dominant, rufous gene (table 4.2). The best evidence, though, is the fact that gray × gray pairs only have gray offspring; and a gray female, whose mother was rufous and father gray, mated with a gray male and fledged three

Table 4.2. Frequency of rufous and gray (including brown) colormorphs among nesting pairs and their nestlings at suburban and rural sites, 1976–87. Note that rufous is equally common among adults and their offspring (NS) and only rufous adults produce rufous nestlings.

| | Nestling Colormorphs | | | | |
| | Observed | | Expected | | |
Adult Colormorphs (Pairs)	Rufous	Gray	Rufous	Gray	P
Rufous × rufous (1)	3	0	3	0[a]	NS
Rufous × gray (7)	11	10	8.5	8.5[b]	NS
Gray × gray (74)	0	224	0	224	

a. RR × RR = 3:0 phenotype ratio; PR × Rr = 2.3:0.7 ratio.
b. Rr (rufous) × rr (gray) phenotypes.

gray youngsters. Thus, gray plumage represents the homozygous recessive genotype, while rufous owls are either homozygous dominant or heterozygous.[24]

Unfortunately for the concept of simple dominance, 26 percent of 82 adult screech owls were various shades of brown. In fact, one was gray with brown wings and tail. The intermediate plumages were so variable as to defy categorization and could not be detected among feathered nestlings. In my view they are impossible to trace phenotypically, and I am forced to ignore them while recognizing the potential of a multiple allelic system wherein rufous dominates brown which dominates gray. Throughout this study, the brownish birds were grouped with gray ones, which they most closely resemble, particularly as late nestlings and fledglings.

In both my study plots, 1976–91, rufous individuals averaged only 7.3 ± 3.0 percent of the population compared to 36 percent throughout eastern North America. Is this a local or perhaps regional phenomenon? Upon further examination of their frequency, I noted that rufous individuals constitute 56–72 percent of each population at midlatitudes from Arkansas to Georgia, Virginia, and northeastward to coastal New York. North and south of this zone, rufous owls comprise 55 percent or less of each local sample, and the mid-latitudinal distinction is significant.[25]

Since the rufous morph appears ill adapted to cold, and the extent of cold weather varies greatly over the species' broad range, a multiple regression of percent rufous in each regional population on various climatic feathers of that region might be illuminating.[26] After all, the rufous birds should be most abundant in the South, not at mid-latitudes, if cold is the only selective influence. So I assembled 12 temperature and moisture variables for 28 populations, ran the regression, and found that rufous increased primarily in response to more total precipitation (r^2 = 0.43, P = 0.008), but also fewer subfreezing days (r^2 added = 0.19, P = 0.03) and higher humidity (r^2 added = 0.12, P = 0.05).

Is it possible that rufous screech owls are more difficult to see in the limited light of cloudy weather associated with precipitation? Do they gain a special cryptic advantage in rainy climates, particularly those of cities?[27] Red light is weak and quickly filtered out at night, when the stronger wavelengths of blue light predominate, so most vertebrate eyes are comparatively blue-sensitive at night and red-sensitive in the daylight. It would appear that the same is true during cloudy weather; because, to my eyes, the rufous owls are most difficult to see on cloudy days.

But why the higher humidity connection? Because red light energy is so weak, it is readily scattered by water vapor, so rufous may be more cryptic where the humidity is high. However, this does not explain the rarity of rufous birds from East Texas through Louisiana to Florida, where the relatively humidity is quite high.[28] The red-scatter effect is also caused by dust particles, which should make rufous less visible at the drier, dustier, western edge of the species' range. But red pigments do not confer the structural stability of gray (darker) pigments, so rufous feathers may be more easily abraded, hence selected against by the dust.[29] Thus, I have additional explanations for the rarity of rufous in my study area and throughout the Great Plains.

Precipitation and cloudiness are not correlated on a continental scale (r = −0.09, NS, n = 28), so I had to make the case that each independently might benefit rufous screech owls. First I analyzed average annual precipitation and sky cover in the northern and southern areas, where gray screech owls predominate, compared to the mid-latitudinal region with its majority of rufous individuals. Precipitation averages 1.7 times more in the land of rufous owls than in the north, but the mid-latitudinal and southern regions are equivalent. Furthermore, sky cover does not differ among the three areas, though it seems to decrease southward.[30]

Persistence of rainy and cloudy weather ought to be of greater importance to the rufous birds, because the eastern screech owl is a permanent resident throughout its range. If rufous is cryptic in reduced light, then this phenotype's survival is most likely where light is limited

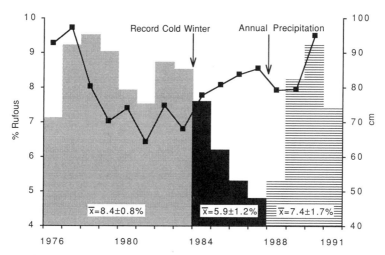

Figure 4.1. Four-year running average fraction of rufous individuals among nesting adults in the combined suburban and rural populations (suburban only in 1973–74 and 1988–91). Note the eight-year period of relative stability (gray columns) in which rufous parallels the running average annual precipitation; the four-year decline after the record cold of December, 1983 (dark columns), wherein rufous diverges from the precipitation trend; and the apparent recovery period that follows (lined columns). Percent rufous in the stability period differs from that during the decline (P = 0.01).

most often. Again, I used the precipitation and sky cover data from the three geographic areas but this time analyzed coefficients of monthly variation. Both climatic features are least variable only in the area of the most rufous owls, from Arkansas to Georgia and northeastward to Virginia and coastal New York.[30]

Next a temporal investigation was needed to support the spatially determined link between rufous plumage and mild winters plus warm and wet or cloudy weather. Information was available for seventeen consecutive years on a transect in Illinois-Wisconsin, plus 14 years in my confirmatory study, and the rufous fraction of both populations responded positively and significantly to increased precipitation, as predicted. However, a higher annual percentage of rufous was determined by warmer January temperature in the Midwest, whereas the previous year's total rainfall told most of the story in warmer, drier, Central Texas.[31] Here, nonetheless, cold may have had a significant, negative impact (figure 4.1).

Perhaps our winters are not severe often enough, although a trend after the record freeze of December, 1983, suggests that rufous owls may be cold-limited even this far south (figure 4.1). Beginning with this particular winter, rufous birds began an unprecedented, four-year decline from an above-average 8.4 percent of the nesting population to 6.7 percent in the spring of 1984. The next winter was slightly colder than average, and rufous dropped to 4.8 percent by spring, 1985, and then to 4.5 (1986) and 4.2 (1987) percent following more colder-than-average winters. This trend paralleled one at Austin, Texas 167 km to the south.[32]

The loss was particularly evident at Harris Creek, where rufous averaged 23.3 ± 3.6 percent between 1979 and 1983 but declined significantly to 16.1 ± 2.5 percent (P = 0.01). Concurrently, rufous individuals in Woodway, never as frequent as at Harris Creek, went from 3.2 to 0.8 percent. In the recovery period of 1988–91 (figure 4.1), rufous was only 15.3 ± 2.4 percent at Harris Creek but had increased to 5.7 percent in Woodway. Of comparable interest is the fact that in northern Ohio rufous birds declined from 25.4 ± 1.5 percent in the seven years before the severe winter of 1951–52 to 13.3 ± 3.2 percent in the 21 years afterward, hence they too did not recover fully (P = 0.001).[33]

Why rufous is so much more common at Harris Creek I am not sure, since that site is cooler and drier than Woodway. But its nesting females averaged 5.7 grams heavier than Woodway's in 1979–86 (P = 0.03)though not consistently year-to-year (NS, two-way ANOVA). Their average nesting weight rose 0.2 grams compared to 1.8 grams in Woodway after the big freeze. Although I could compare only 13 rufous and gray birds at Harris Creek with 24 contemporaneous individuals in Woodway, I am inclined to think that greater mass at Harris Creek is at least part of the answer.

Overall, rufous was more frequent and much more constant in suburbia than in the countryside (8.3 ± 3.9% vs. 1.4 ± 3.8%, P = 0.01). Because suburbia is warmer, wetter, and climatically more stable than the rural environment, I am not surprised. The city owls are buffered against cold though not immune to extremes, obviously. Also, the rufous morph may benefit from increased cloudiness, associated with the increased rainfall and its decreased variability in suburbia, since the red-filtered light of such weather could promote their camouflage. The rufous morph is preadapted to city life in my opinion; and, in nature, must be favored during warm-wet years, while gray is better adapted to cool-dry years in climatic cycles—an example of balanced polymorphism.[34]

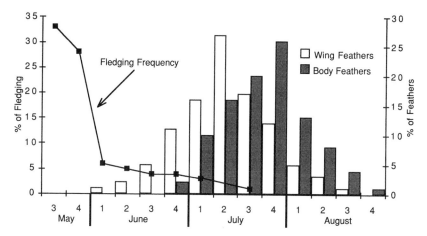

Figure 4.2.   Weekly frequency of molted wing (n = 261) and body
(n = 109) feathers of adults in relation to the fledging of owlets in
suburbia, 1976–89. Note that the annual molt peaks in July, mostly
after the nestling period, and that wing feathers are shed before body
feathers (P = 0.005).

Annual Molt

I also paid close attention to feather structure and the annual molt of
nesting screech owls, because they were clues to age of individuals first
captured as adults. Yearlings had broader (more rounded), fault-barred
primaries that were molted during their second summer.[35] Then they
grew more pointed, nonfaulted primary feathers. Thus, I could age
unbanded yearlings but not older birds, unless they had been found as
juveniles or yearling adults. Occasionally a June-nesting female shed a
primary or two in her nest cavity, but most information on lost feathers
came from those retrieved serendipitously in suburban yards and
woods.

Flight feathers did not begin to drop until the first week of June,
two weeks after the average fledging date (May 18) of suburban first
nests (figure 4.2). Then parental flying and food-catching ability may
wane, because of the shed feathers, about the time fledglings start to
fly well enough to make their first clumsy attempts to catch insects
(chapter 6).[36] But owlets from replacement nests in suburbia fledged
on June 20 on average and, therefore, might have been more disadvantaged by molting parents. This is suggested by the significantly lower
weights of those renest owlets (chapter 6). Molt-impaired flying could

select against second broods and late nesting in general (but see chapter 9).

The annual molt of all feathers peaks as fledglings begin their natal dispersal in late July (chapter 6). Contour feathers are shed significantly later than the more crucial primaries and secondaries (figure 4.2). A similar pattern typifies the long-eared, tawny, and Ural owls.[37] Yet the screech owl peak is four weeks after most renest owlets fledge, so those that survive are semi-independent and relatively less affected by their parents' flying ability. Withal, most molting seems timed to follow the adult requirement for feeding offspring and precede their dispersal, when adults are busy evicting owlets from polyterritories and hence benefit from nonimpaired flying (see also chapters 6, 7).

The Essentials

Female screech owls average 17 percent heavier than their mates, and the larger ones lay more, larger eggs and lose less weight while nesting, hence fledge more offspring. They are more successful, probably because they can store more energy to withstand temporary food shortages, so they are less likely to abandon eggs or starve chicks. Also, their size must enhance physical defense of the nest—potentially important in that males are away hunting much of the time. Conversely, the smaller male size is advantageous in hunting, the primary male responsibility, and males should be more effective than females catching the more abundant, smaller prey, and should demand less food themselves, hence deliver more to the nest effort. Males carry 20 percent less weight per unit wing area than females, which may increase hunting efficiency.

Winter weight flux among females exceeds that among males, possibly because females move out of the nesting area during times of reduced food supplies. This weight variation is tied closely to food and minimum temperature, which affects food (winter resident birds are more numerous under colder conditions). But while nesting, female weight depends mostly upon male weight; the heavier females are supplied by heavier males, whose weight flux exceeds that of unpaired males, presumably because of the demands of nesting. Yet most females lose weight steadily during incubation and brooding. Suburban individuals lose 13 percent from winter through brooding, whereas rural females lose 16 percent, most likely due to there being less food in the countryside. Two birds that starved to death in an unusually cold winter lost 36 and 38 percent.

Rufous screech owls average only 7.5 percent of the local population. Colormorph ratios among parents and nestlings suggest that a single, dominant, rufous gene is selected against by abnormally cold weather but selected for in cloudy climates, because red light is most difficult to see when the light intensity is reduced. Geographically, rufous is the most abundant morph at mid-latitudes, where winters are mild and cloudiness is most consistent, month to month. In the local population, rufous increases following rainy years but decreased after the very cold winter of 1983–84. Rufous is more abundant and less variable, year to year, in suburbia, presumably because of its comparatively warm, wet, stable climate. The reduced surface area/volume advantage of large size may counteract temperature and explain why more females than males are rufous.

Breeding adults begin their annual molt of wing feathers in early June, just as their dependent fledglings start to feed themselves. Body feathers are lost slightly later. The molt peaks in late July, just as most youngsters begin their dispersal and adults renew their defense of permanent nest sites. Thus, molting is timed to follow feeding demands by offspring and precede territorial defense by the adults. As such, any late nesting may be disadvantageous, because molting presumably contributes to less effective flying and food-catching as suggested by the smaller weights of renest fledglings compared to those from first nests in suburbia.

5 Eggs and Incubation:
Perilous Times

When the winter is foulest, between Christmas and Valentine's Day, male screech owls reoccupy their permanent nest sites, though they sometimes roost elsewhere for a few days to a week or so. And when trout lilies bloom and leaf-shuffling robins promise spring, the males may leave their cavities to fox squirrels for a while. But by St. Patrick's Day, in the time of greening rain and wild plum perfume, females arrive if they have not been there already, and spend a few quiet days before their first eggs are laid. Incubation requires the full month of tree canopy development, complete by mid-April, so successful first nests have to make it through April Fool's Day.

In March, when the females remain in my nest boxes all day, egg-laying is imminent. At first both members of the pair or just the male roosts inside or within about 10 m of the chosen site (see chapter 6). Then the females stays inside, usually alone, 5.7 ± 1.9 (n = 21) days before laying. Elf, boreal, and spotted owls exhibit similar behavior, which must conserve energy for egg production and limit if not prevent extra-pair copulation.[1] This pre-laying inactivity differs little from incubation in that the female screech owl leaves the box for a short time only each day, normally at dusk, and her mate usually feeds her outside the nest. Otherwise he remains close, often in the same roost(s) he uses during incubation, and maintains vocal contact with monotonic trills.

Originally, I thought pre-laying females might stay inside longer if air temperatures were cold, food was scarce, or the nesting population was dense. I reasoned that they would conserve energy for egg-laying better in a cavity and command that site more effectively, if there was considerable demand for cavities. But over ten years I found no convincing correlations between average annual pre-laying occupancy in days and winter temperature, food, date of the first egg, or owl density ($r < 0.58$, NS). Rather, longer pre-laying occupancy may avert interspecific competitors, because it is related to the number of nest boxes simultaneously used by squirrels or starlings ($r = 0.71$, P = 0.003).

Fox squirrels, especially, but also European starlings are major competitors for the use of nest cavities in suburbia, though the squirrels usually leave in April unless very rainy weather prevails. They and an occasional opossum or ringtail may use my boxes for winter shelter.

Table 5.1. First egg dates at the suburban and rural study sites, studied concurrently, in 1979–87. Data are mean ± one standard deviation and (sample size). Note that there is no difference between the
two suburban sites, but the rural average is 5.6 days later in first
nests (P = 0.001), and 13.4 days later in replacement nests (renests,
P = 0.02).[a]

Study Sites	First Nests	Renests
Suburban		
Woodway	March 22.2 ± 6.4 (57)	April 15.7 ± 11.1 (19)
Harris Creek	March 21.4 ± 6.7 (18)	April 14.8 ± 12.3 (9)
Rural	March 27.4 ± 6.6 (22)	April 28.6 ± 18.9 (6)

a. Earliest first-nest eggs: March 6 suburban, March 11 rural.
Latest renest eggs: May 25 suburban, June 6 rural.

Great-crested flycatchers, Carolina wrens, and tufted titmice rarely
nest in them, but squirrels and starlings are a very different story. Once,
for example, a pair of owls waited five days about 5 m from a nest box
with a litter of squirrels until they left. Over this interval the female
dumped two eggs on the ground beneath her day roost, although she
eventually laid five more in the box and fledged three owlets.

The Start of Nesting

The first suburban egg of the year was laid on March 21 on average,
whereas in the countryside the average date was March 27 (table 5.1).
This rural date is significantly later as is true of rural versus urban nests
of other birds including tawny owls.[2] Moreover, at least two-thirds of
the rural nests follow the average date of the last spring freeze (March
18); whereas suburban nests span it more evenly, perhaps because of
suburban warmth. Yet there is no statistical difference in first egg dates
between my two suburban study sites, even though Woodway is
warmer than Harris Creek, and none between the open and wooded-
yard or ravine and ridgetop environments. Suburbia may induce earlier
nesting through warmer temperatures but also additional food supplies, since supplemental food is known to advance laying date in several populations of owls and hawks.[3]

    To find out, I regressed average annual, first-egg date in 1976–88 on
the January to mid-March food supply and also mean minimum air
temperature, total precipitation, and densities of the owls and their

cavity competitors in suburbia. Only minimum temperature was a significant predictor, a negative influence, on egg date (r^2 = 0.50, P = 0.006), although I soon discovered it also predicted size of the food supply in the same negative way (r^2 = 0.52, P = 0.005). Thus, suburban owls lay their first eggs earlier when nighttime temperatures are warmer, because energy for maintenance versus reproduction favors the latter, even though less food energy may be available. This same effect of warm weather is known in the tawny owl but not the boreal owl, whose initial eggs are also laid in late March and early April.[4]

Perhaps suburban food is not so important, year to year, because it is relatively invariable. Of course the January to mid-March food supply includes about 80 percent winter-resident birds, but suburban screech owls eat mostly permanent-resident birds at that time (chapter 3). Furthermore, it is the strictly winter birds that are so negatively affected by warm weather. Because permanent residents are not influenced in this manner, I am not surprised that they are less variable annually, hence more often available and utilized as food than the winter residents (chapter 3).

But food could be relatively more important in years when nesting begins usually early, since food types are less diverse and the important invertebrates and reptiles less available hence less utilized early in the season (see chapter 3). When the year's first egg was earlier, 1976–91, suburban first nests started over a longer stretch of time (r_s = −0.81, P < 0.001).[5] This suggests increased environmental differences, possibly in food or microclimate, among nest sites. On average, 15.6 ± 6.0 days elapsed between the beginning and end of first-nest starts in suburbia. In 1976 and 1986 laying started on March 14 on average and was significantly early (P < 0.05; cf. table 5.1); January to mid-March mean minimum temperatures were higher than in any other year, but food supplies were not exceptional.

For some birds early nesting means larger clutches produced by larger, older females, but this is not completely true of eastern screech owls.[6] Neither in suburbia (r = 0.06, NS, n = 69) nor in the countryside (r = −0.24, NS, n = 20) did first-egg date correlate with completed clutch size among first nest attempts. Nor was it correlated with female weight in either environment (r < 0.13, NS), although related to age in suburbia (chapter 8). Similarly, the first egg dates of replacement nests had no bearing on their clutch sizes or relation to their producers (r < 0.26, NS). Events at the start of nesting apparently are not very important compared to the fate of eggs, as I soon learned.

Replacement Nests

If eastern screech owls lose their first clutches, they are replaced, usually only once (89% of 47) and in a different cavity (66%), but up to four times in one exceptional case.[7] Over 13 years, replacement nesting (renesting) was inversely related to the number of successful first nests in suburbia (r = −0.80, P = 0.001), indicating that the birds did not nest again unless their prior attempt was thwarted. I have no observations of second broods and just one of the replacement of lost chicks. Renesting involved 27.1 ± 9.6 percent of suburban pairs and 37.7 ± 12.3 percent of rural pairs each year (NS); although I believe the rural value is too low, because it was easier for those owls to escape notice in natural cavities (chapter 2). The ones I did find began renesting two weeks later than their suburban relatives (table 5.1).

Most renesting pairs had lost partial clutches (figure 5.1), but more of these were in suburbia (60.9% of 46), whereas more full clutches disappeared in the countryside (77.8% of 18, P < 0.001). Rural populations of Ural owls also lost more complete clutches but tawny owls did not.[8] However, unlike a variety of other birds including raptors, whose egg desertion and predation increases as the season progresses, my subjects experienced relatively more clutch loss near the beginning of nesting (figure 5.1).[9] Even so, there was no significant difference in the weekly incidence of lost versus successful clutches in suburbia and the rural environment.

Desertion was the frequent cause of loss in tawny owls and the suburban screech owls (73.9% of 46 clutches) by contrast to predation on my rural population (83.3% of 18, P = 0.005). Moreover, suburban desertion happened primarily in open-yard nests (71%), predation largely in the wooded-yard nests that are most like the rural situation (76%, P = 0.001). Cultural disturbances like children, pets, and tree trimmers, added to native and exotic nest competitors, overshadow the few predators that brave open space and hubbub in suburbia. So it is no wonder that the city owls lost proportionately fewer eggs annually (26.2 ± 15.4% vs. 60.3 ± 33.7%, P = 0.009), hence saved reproductive energy and got started with replacement clutches so much earlier than their rural counterparts.

Eleven females that I followed closely after they lost partial clutches waited 11.1 ± 4.7 days before re-laying, whereas eight that lost full clutches took longer (24.6 ± 13.2 days, P = 0.005).[10] Such a difference is expected in view of the greater time and energy lost in full clutches. Three additional females lost mates, abandoned partial clutches, acquired new mates, and renested in 19, 22, and 23 days. One suburban

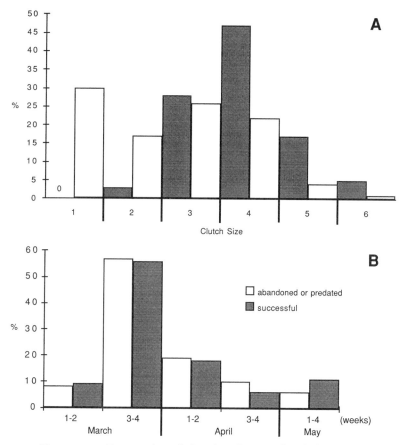

Figure 5.1. Frequencies of abandoned or predated clutches compared to successful ones in the suburban and rural study plots, 1976–87 (n = 82, 94, respectively). A. Relative to their size, more small and incomplete clutches fail (P < 0.001). B. According to the week in which they were initiated, there is no significant difference between the unsuccessful and successful clutches.

example laid her first egg on March 13 though her mate was killed by a car the previous night. She abandoned that egg on the 19th, remated about the 22nd, and renested April 4. In recognition of her resiliency, I must add that she had already lost a mate in mid-February, so was twice widowed, yet eventually fledged three owlets from three eggs.

Nevertheless, mate loss is inconsequential compared to predators and competitors, because it accounts for only five percent of all

Young Virginia opossum, an egg predator, in nest box.

egg mortality compared to 89 percent attributable to other animals.[11] Ringtails, opossums, raccoons, and black ratsnakes were involved in 11 of 31 (85%) identifiable predator impacts in the countryside by contrast to only 15 of 33 (45%) in suburbia. Conversely, fox squirrel and starling depredations were 2 (15%) and 18 (55%) in these two environments, respectively (P = 0.01). It is obvious that different suites of predators and competitors operate primarily in different places.

Both squirrels and starlings evict egg-laying screech owls, but the owls displace only starlings. This hierarchy must depend on the fact that fox squirrels are 3.5 times heavier than screech owls which, in turn, are 3.5 times heavier than starlings. Yet the owls were successful in only two of six contentions with starlings, undoubtedly because a pair normally renested but once a year, whereas starlings made 4.2 ± 1.3 (n = 44) nest attempts per box (I discovered starling persistence at ten eastern-bluebird boxes by removing all nests with eggs each year for three years). But I can only guess that individual starlings persist over particular owls, since I did not mark the former to see if more than one pair was involved.

Table 5.2. Completed clutch size in both suburban and rural populations in relation to progression of the nesting season and the temporal relation between first and replacement nests, 1976–89. Note that four-egg clutches predominate through the first week of April, while the three-egg clutches of replacement nests (renests) are commonest later; hence average clutch size declines throughout nesting (b = −0.01, P = 0.05) although not significantly within first and replacement nest periods.

Starting Dates	Mean ± SD (clutches)	% of Eggs in Clutches					Total (% in Renests)
		2	3	4	5	6	
March 6–14	4.0 ± 0.4 (11)		9	82	9		44 (0)
15–21	3.9 ± 0.7 (18)		26	46	28		70 (0)
22–31	4.1 ± 0.9 (52)	3	13	49	21	14	210 (0)
April 1–7	3.6 ± 0.7 (17)		39	45	16		62 (11)
8–14	3.5 ± 0.8 (12)	4	48	36	12		42 (81)
15–21	3.6 ± 0.8 (7)		48	32	20		25 (100)
April 22–June 6	3.2 ± 0.4 (9)		72	18			29 (100)

I still wondered about the relative influence of weather, because at least two cases of abandoned eggs were coincidental with prolonged heavy rain or unusually late below-freezing nights. So the annual number of lost clutches in suburbia, 1976–87, was regressed on mean minimum temperature and total rainfall, March–May, plus the current vertebrate food supply and incidence of squirrel-starling disturbance. The latter produced the primary effect (r^2 = 0.57, P = 0.01), which decreased during the nesting season (chapter 9). This puts renests at lesser risk than first nests (see below). Colder temperatures also increased the failures (r^2 added = 0.34, P = 0.04, MSR) but are less likely later in the spring.

Clutches

During 1979–87 the Woodway (n = 39), Harris Creek (22), and rural (24) owls produced similar clutches (3.8 ± 0.7 eggs, NS) which, however, differed among years (P = 0.03, two-way ANOVA).[12] Four eggs per clutch was the early-season mode, typical of first nesting attempts, whereas three-egg clutches prevailed by the second week of April as replacement nesting became common (table 5.2). Thus a seasonal decline in clutch size, supposedly found in other owls and a variety of birds, is due to smaller replacement clutches among my subjects (table

5.2).[13] Extreme clutch sizes in my study populations were two eggs, even in first nests, and six eggs. However, two females increased their outputs to seven eggs after incubating six-egg clutches with infertile eggs that they removed.

Because of such egg disposal and occasional replacement in 29 of 82 (35%) successful nests, I determined clutch size as eggs incubated together for at least 27 days, the minimum incubation period (see below). All removals involved one to three presumably dead eggs; but only four of 25 (16%) single removals were replaced, probably because most eggs were dumped after the others had hatched. Twice I saw females carry eggs in their open mouths away from nests at the start of their nightly recesses from brooding. Although the number of dead eggs in the 82 clutches (0.7 ± 0.8) was not related to clutch size (r = 0.15, NS), removals were more frequent in clutches of four to five (86% of 21) than two to three (25% of 8, P = 0.004) and from small nest boxes (91% of 11) more often than medium and large boxes (55% of 18, P = 0.04). This suggests crowding as the removal stimulus.

The influence of environment on suburban clutch size was assayed in a multiple stepwise regression of annual average size on nesting density, late winter (January–February) and early spring (March–April) vertebrate food, mean minimum temperature, and total precipitation, 1976–88. I did this separately for first and renest clutches, because they are distinct (table 5.2). More nesting owls might mean less food together with more strife over nest sites, hence smaller clutches. More food should counter this, but winter food ought to affect first clutches mostly, unless offset by cold temperatures. Spring food should largely influence renest clutches, and precipitation might enhance food production, increasing insect numbers for example.

In fact, the only significant influence on first clutches was winter precipitation (r^2 = 0.42, P = 0.02). Simply stated, more winter water meant more first-clutch eggs. Because 95 percent of these were laid between March 9 and April 5, it was interesting to discover how far in advance precipitation might affect clutch size; and January had the most influence on total winter precipitation (r^2 = 0.30, P = 0.06). On the other hand, renest clutches were enhanced primarily by more winter food (r^2 = 0.59, P = 0.003), and 95 percent of these eggs were laid April 5–27, when most winter-resident birds remained in the area. Spring rain had an additional, positive effect (r^2 added = 0.36, P = 0.04), and April was more influential than March in this regard (r^2 = 0.36, P = 0.03).

Just how winter precipitation, mostly rain, stimulates food production in this cold season, and thus promotes egg production two months later, is somewhat mysterious but perhaps linked to the rain-stimulated availability of ectothermic prey (chapters 3, 6). Also, it seems that April rain is too coincidental with renesting to have any serious consequences (see table 5.1). Yet it is intuitively pleasing that winter rain affects only first clutches, while spring rain influences renests, and both factors are positive. Seasonal precipitation is known to influence clutch size in other birds, but the specific mechanisms are unknown.[14]

I can summarize the influence of environmental flux on clutch size by regressing the annual means of all clutches on January through May rainfall and bird-mammal food in suburbia, 1976–88. Total rainfall is the primary, positive factor (r^2 = 0.41, P = 0.01). However, food is almost equally important (r^2 added = 0.36, P = 0.03), because it is uncorrelated with rainfall (r = −0.01, NS) and, therefore, separately influential. Probably most endothermic prey are little influenced by precipitation in contrast to ectotherms (chapters 3, 6). That more food promotes larger clutches is well known among birds, including several owls, but no one seems to have studied the concurrent effect of precipitation.[15]

Suburban clutches in 1976–79 were significantly larger (4.5 ± 0.2 eggs) than in 1980–83 (3.9 ± 0.3) and 1984–87 (3.6 ± 0.3), and accompanied by 1.5 times more rain and 2.3 times more food (P < 0.02). However, I see that the variation in clutch size among females over those years was exceeded by clutch-size variation among nest boxes during the same time (CV = 17.1 versus 22.4%, respectively; P = 0.06). This suggests that individual breeders or local resources were more important than the annual environmental flux. Unfortunately, it was impractical to monitor rainfall and food at each nest site, but I do know characteristics of their female users.[16]

For instance, female mass is a possible determinant of clutch size; and, indeed, the average size of first-nest clutches of 67 suburban breeders was slightly influenced by nesting weight (r^2 = 0.18, P = 0.001). Age, too, might influence clutch size, as it does in boreal owls and other birds.[17] But older females are also heavier (chapter 8), so it is not surprising that one of the two factors is redundant. Among 27 long-lived females, age is the only significant influent (r^2 = 0.23, P = 0.10), probably because increased breeding experience is linear, while nesting weight fluctuates with the annual vagaries of food and weather. Older, larger females tend to lay more eggs earlier in the season, but their year-to-year increases are insignificant (chapter 8), most likely because of strong environmental influences (figure 5.2).

Finally, clutch size may be related to cavity size, essentially an environmental constant. Some birds, including the boreal owl, lay more

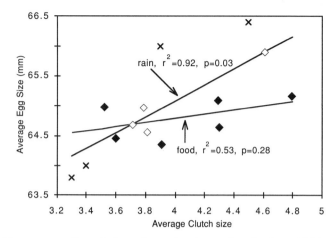

Figure 5.2. Covariation of egg size (mean length plus width) and clutch size in suburbia, 1976–89 (r = 0.68, P = 0.003). Note that four years with high January–May rainfall may promote egg size (hollow diamonds, 6.7–9.6 cm rain, x̄ of all years = 6.3 cm). Six other years with plentiful food in the same season could enhance clutch size instead (solid diamonds, 90–132 prey/ha, x̄ of all years = 88.5/ha), although the two regression coefficients are not significantly different. Xs are years in which both food and rain were above average (upper two) or below average (lower two) in January–May.

eggs in larger cavities, but others do not.[18] While I began the exploratory study using three different sizes of nest boxes, I quickly found that eastern screech owls were not significantly affected, either in 93 first or in 36 replacement nestings (two-way ANOVA). The smaller replacement clutches (P < 0.001) might be slightly influenced by floor area (r = 0.32, P = 0.05), but I consider this inconsequential, since the coefficient of determination (r^2) is only 10 percent, and renest eggs are comparatively few, hence should be less constrained by smaller cavities than by food supply.

In larger nest boxes apparently the male boreal owls store more food, which stimulates egg production; but the cavity size–clutch size relationship is slight (r^2 = 0.10) and obtains only when food is substantial.[18] Is the same true of screech owls? I think not. In six years of above-average winter–spring food there was no correlation between the sizes of caches and box floor area or between total or renest clutch sizes and nest-box floor area (r_s < 0.12, NS). While the birds tended to use more larger boxes in high-food years during 1976–88 (r_s = 0.76,

P = 0.02) and certainly laid larger clutches then, there was no obvious functional relation between the boxes and clutches.

Egg Size

Compared to counting eggs by gently probing beneath incubating females, measuring eggs is trickier. They must be extracted and replaced under tolerant females before the birds are frightened and leave them to chill. Relatively few females were subjected to egg measuring, and they were all long-lived birds habituated to my tinkering (see below). I carefully pulled eggs out, one by one, or set the females aside for a minute or two. By virtue of their proximity, I knew most suburban females better than rural females so extracted fewer rural eggs. But those I did measure were the same size as suburban eggs (table 5.3).

Egg length and width are correlated (r = 0.57, P < 0.001, 129 df), so I can add them as a convenient measure of egg size. This parameter is strongly correlated with egg weight (r = 0.87, P < 0.001), but the variation in length alone explains weight (r^2 = 0.59, P < 0.001; r^2 added for width = 0.01, NS). Similarly, mean egg size in 36 clutches is strongly related to female incubation weight in the spring (r = 0.84, P < 0.001) with mean length more responsive to female weight than mean width (r^2 = 0.86 and 0.45, respectively, P < 0.001). Larger females may lay larger eggs more readily (r^2 = 0.71, P < 0.001) than more eggs (r^2 added = 0.18, NS), but large eggs are usually found in large clutches (r = 0.56, P = 0.04).

There is an additional clue to the covariation of egg and clutch size. The same environmental factors that increase clutch size in suburbia also promote egg size and in the same hierarchical fashion (r^2 = 0.43, P < 0.001, for rainfall; and r^2 added = 0.24, P = 0.04, for food, 1976–87). But rain seems to promote egg size primarily, while food could be the chief influence on clutch. Of course I can only conjecture, since the sample sizes for excessive rain and food separately are so small (figure 5.2). Larger eggs in larger clutches of heavier females during high-food years also characterize the Ural owl but not the boreal owl.[19]

Accordingly, I expected the 1976–79 eggs to be bigger than later eggs, and they were (table 5.3).[20] Moreover, first-nest eggs were larger than renest eggs. Of confirmatory interest are two clutches laid sequentially in the same nest box by the two mates of a polygynous male. The first nest of four eggs was started on March 22; the second, a renest of three eggs, was initiated three weeks later when the second female displaced the first and incubated both sets unsuccessfully. Eggs of the first clutch averaged 1.5 mm longer (P = 0.01) and 1.3 g heavier (P = 0.01) but only 0.2 mm wider (NS). Since the oviduct is a tube, I under-

Table 5.3. Egg dimensions in different time periods, nesting attempts, and study sites. Data are mean ± one standard deviation derived from clutch means. Two-way ANOVAs analyze the contribu-
tions among females and years, nest attempts, and study sites
(asterisks = P < 0.05 of each time period from LSD tests; within
category variation is insignificant. Note that egg lengths and
weights distinguish time periods and first nests from replacement
nests, but that suburban and rural eggs are the same size.

Samples (n of clutches)	Length (mm)	Width (mm)	Weight (g)
Suburban			
1976–79 (24)	35.7 ± 1.1	30.0 ± 0.8	18.8 ± 1.9
1980–83 (20)	34.2 ± 1.1	29.7 ± 0.6	17.6 ± 1.3
1984–87 (22)	34.8 ± 1.0	29.9 ± 0.7	18.2 ± 0.9
(P)	(< 0.001)*	(NS)	(= 0.01)*
Contemporaneous suburban			
First nests (26)	35.2 ± 0.9	30.1 ± 0.6	18.5 ± 1.1
Renests (22)	34.5 ± 0.7	29.7 ± 0.9	17.1 ± 1.3
(P)	(= 0.04)	(NS)	(< 0.001)
Contemporaneous			
Suburban (22)	34.6 ± 1.3	29.8 ± 0.7	—
Rural (5)	34.2 ± 1.4	29.5 ± 0.6	none weighed
(P)	(NS)	(NS)	—

stand why egg length increases more readily than width—why increased length and hence weight are the essential indicators of larger
eggs.

Because some birds lay larger or smaller subsequent eggs, depending
on clutch size, I compared the lengths and weights of first- versus last-
laid eggs in 61 clutches of three, four, and five, 1976–87. But I found
no significant differences between eggs or among clutches.[21] Larger
clutches were 1.2 to 1.5 times heavier and, despite the fact that they
came from heavier individuals, might require a greater investment of
reproductive energy. Therefore, I divided clutch weight by female
weight. The mean percentages are 30.6 ± 1.4 (n = 23) for three eggs,
41.7 ± 2.8 (n = 26) for four, and 49.3 ± 1.4 (n = 12) for five, a
significant difference (P < 0.001) Thus, my hypothesis is valid.

Do eastern screech owls put more or less energy into egg-laying than
other owls? Because small, cavity-nesting species lay relatively more,
larger eggs than big open nesters, I utilize comparative information
only on the boreal, burrowing, elf, flammulated, Eurasian pygmy, and

Table 5.4. Number of days between the laying of sequential eggs in suburbia. Data are mean ± one standard deviation and (sample size). Only egg-interval differs significantly in a two-way ANOVA comparing first nests and renests (P < 0.001). Just the fourth and fifth eggs are laid farther apart than eggs two and three in first nests, but eggs three and four are farther apart in replacement nests than in first nests (P < 0.05 LSD test).

| | | Eggs | | |
Nests	1 and 2	2 and 3	3 and 4	4 and 5
First	1.1 ± 0.3 (29)	1.2 ± 0.4 (27)	1.6 ± 0.5 (18)	2.1 ± 0.6 (9)
Replacement	1.1 ± 0.3 (10)	1.5 ± 0.7 (11)	1.8 ± 0.7 (8)	

northern saw-whet owls (chapter 10).[22] My birds' average egg (18.2 g) is 10.1 percent of average female incubation weight (179.5 g), and not significantly different from the 11.3 ± 3.9 percent of the six other species. Likewise, the screech owl's average clutch of 3.9 eggs (71.0 g) is a 39.5 percent effort, essentially the same as the other species' 44.6 ± 7.8 percent (NS). Apparently screech owls are not exceptional in the energy they allocate to reproduction.

Egg-Laying Interval

Conventional wisdom maintains that raptorial birds lay eggs at least two days apart, so I am surprised to discover that eastern screech owls are unconventional.[23] Their first three eggs in first nests may be produced in three to four days (table 5.4). Beyond the third egg, however, longer intervals begin, and the only six-egg clutch I monitored closely required nine days to complete. The two-day-plus interval begins earlier, after the second egg in renests, presumably because less food is available to make later eggs as suggested by the fewer, smaller eggs of renests. This too is conventional "wisdom."

But food actually becomes more diverse and more abundant as nesting progresses (chapter 3). Other students, observing this in other birds, have also wondered why replacement clutches and eggs are smaller. Since females lose weight during their first incubation, some suggest they are energetically stressed before renesting.[24] Why then do they not wait and acquire enough energy to match their first nest attempt? There is no greater egg loss among renests, hence no energy savings in the screech owl's lesser second effort (see below), yet 17 females renested at their first incubation weight rather than their original, prenesting weight (172.4 ± 10.9 g versus 174.9 ± 10.5 g, respectively, NS).

Perhaps insufficient time remains in the nesting season, so screech owls are obliged to replace losses as quickly as possible, even if a sacrifice in energy investment is necessary. This may be one reason why incubation usually begins immediately, lost chicks are seldom replaced, second broods are not attempted, and no renests are tried after the first week of June (energetic constraint of the annual molt is a second reason, chapter 4).[25] Any later nest, if successful, would put newly independent owlets into October environments characterized by more cold weather and less food, because each egg plus chick requires about 4.5 months of parental care from the start of incubation to fledgling dispersal (chapters 5, 6). Getting started with reproduction after early June could be selectively disadvantageous, because young owls could starve to death.

Incubation

In 52 nests of three to six eggs each, incubation usually began the day the first egg was laid (63%, P < 0.001). Sometimes (25%) this egg was unattended, and incubation started with the second egg. Rarely (12%) did it start with the third egg and never later. Study sites and nesting attempts did not differ in this regard, which is the mode among hawks and owls. Once started, however intermittent, incubation lasted 30.3 ± 1.8 days for 78 first eggs, 1976–88, with no statistical differences between suburban and rural, open and wooded yards, or first and replacement clutches. This differs from the usual literature report of 26 days, but I found that no egg hatched in less than 27 or more than 34 days. Even the smaller saw-whet owl incubates for 27–29 (x̄ 27.3) days and the boreal owl for 26–32 (x̄ 29.2) days.[26]

Average annual incubation times were 29 to 31 days in 1976 through 1988. Longer periods were not related to rainfall (r = 0.26, NS) but to higher mean air temperatures in April, the month when most incubation occurs (r = 0.59, P = 0.04). This seems illogical, if one expects warmer air to augment female body temperature and perhaps shorten the incubation of large clutches in which proportionately fewer eggs fit together beneath the female. But my observations indicate that female screech owls are less attentive at air temperatures above about 30°C, presumably to cool eggs and themselves. They either sit beside the clutch or on only part of it, perhaps rotating eggs beneath the body. Rarely, they even perch in the nest-box entrance for short periods on warm afternoons.

As expected, then, among 78 clutches larger ones required longer to

Incubating females: (*left*) typical posture with laterally spread breast feathers; (*right*) sitting beside a four-egg clutch on a hot afternoon. Note the polyphemus moth wing indicative of a food item.

incubate (r = 0.61, P < 0.001), I assume because more time is needed to shuffle eggs to and from the incubation patch. Only so many can be covered simultaneously; and a larger body is no advantage, as it just lays more, larger eggs. But longer incubation exposes large clutches to the possibility of disturbance and predation longer, a potential disadvantage. Do such clutches suffer greater mortality? No, just the opposite; only 20% of 60 four-egg clutches and 17% of 18 five-egg clutches were lost compared to 42% of 38 complete three-egg clutches (P = 0.03).

I noticed four behavioral responses to my initial encounter with incubating females, whereas their mates were impassive or flew away as I climbed trees and opened nest boxes (males never incubated). Most females flew (41% of 114), but almost as many (38%) stayed on or beside their eggs with compressed body feathers, squinted eyes, and erect ear tufts. Others (21%) kicked eggs from under themselves.[27] Their plumage was erect, eyes open, and they bill-clapped, often striking with talons while lying on their back, or they quickly hunkered down and became quiescent. Did some death-feign? Sitting versus fighting are passive versus active defenses, respectively, while flying is escape behavior. Because both defenses were more frequent than escape (67%, P < 0.001), eggs certainly are protected, and females are entirely responsible for their safety.

That responsibility apparently increases and the defense changes from active to passive with age. Yearling females tended to fly (49% of

Incubating female in subdued threat posture.

70), whereas older birds usually sat tight (70% of 44; P = 0.003). The yearlings also fought more often (27%) than older owls (11%, P = 0.04), suggesting that the switch to passive defense may be learned. The two age groups were distinct with respect to all three responses (P < 0.001), but 19 females did not differ significantly between ages two and three in their frequencies of passive versus active defense.

Clearly, the yearling breeding experience is sufficient to learn passive defense with its obvious energy savings and hence reduced cost of reproduction.[28] But this must be advantageous only in relation to benign disturbances, the presumed majority of perturbations in suburbia. Sitting may actually increase female mortality in the predator-prone rural environment, which is why most yearlings fly instinctively before they learn to sit. Other small cavity-nesting owls usually fly as well.[29] Even a few of my long-lived suburban females always flew, regardless of repeated contact; and one learned to do so at the sound of my car, inevitably exiting her nest box as I parked at the curb the first time each year despite an eight-month overwinter period of no behavioral reinforcement. If I drove a different car, though, she stayed inside the box.

Incubating females normally leave their eggs anyway each evening to defecate, be fed by their mates, and sometimes drink and bathe (see also chapter 3). On nine nights in late April three first-nesting individuals left 21.9 ± 8.6 minutes after sunset and remained away 17.8 ± 8.9 minutes, while a third, renesting female stayed out 12.7 ± 4.0 (n = 5) minutes in May. Comparable data on the nightly recess of successful female tawny owls is 7–23 minutes within 29–70 minutes of sunset.[30] Before leaving, female screech owls look out of the nest hole a while, hence the April birds were actually off their eggs 27.6 ± 7.3 minutes. This recess time decreased as incubation progressed (r = −0.87, P < 0.001), perhaps because females have more invested in late-stage eggs and are less inclined to leave them unprotected (chapter 3).

Hatching Efficiency

This term is simply the number of owlets hatched relative to the number of eggs laid, a potential benefit/cost evaluation. Resulting values are 59.4 percent in suburbia and 39.0 percent in the countryside or 55.3 percent overall. While the rural birds are less efficient than suburban ones (P = 0.03), they are like some populations of barn owls (39.5%), and the tawny owl (52.2%) about matches the overall value. However, among cavity nesters generally, barn, boreal, elf, flammulated, little, saw-whet, tawny, and Ural owls are more efficient, averaging 73.6 ± 13.2 percent (P = 0.006).[31]

Hatching efficiency has two different components: survivability, the proportion of eggs that survive disturbances and predation long enough to hatch; and hatchability, the remaining fraction that actually hatch. Survivability relates mostly to external threats like storms and predators, while hatchability is internally mediated through infertility and inattentiveness. The two components are quite different (table 5.5), hence must be considered separately, and clutch efficiency should be the product of the two. Unfortunately, no one seems to have done this previously; either they have figured one component without the other or just divided total hatchlings by total eggs, thereby losing comparative information.[32]

Predation and desertion cost my rural owls many more eggs annually (see above) and 1.8 times more overall than their suburban cousins (table 5.5). By contrast to suburban losses of only 30 percent and similar losses in populations of boreal, tawny, hawk, and flammulated owls (30 ± 10%), the 55 percent fatality of rural eggs was outstanding.[33] Yet, compared to suburbia, the rural population was no more or less successful hatching its surviving eggs, which underscores the different and more critical role of survivability in nature as opposed to culture. Even so, suburban owls lost more eggs from first nests in open yards because of chilling through exposure due to disturbances (table 5.5). And they lost more in 1980–83, an unusual circumstance that will be considered again.

About the survivability of different clutch sizes, I recall that mostly

Table 5.5. Egg survivability after losses to desertion plus predation and the hatchability of surviving eggs in successful clutches, 1976–87. Mean survivability (67.1%) is less than mean hatchability (81.8%, P = 0.01). Note the relatively low survivability in the rural population, suburban first nests, open-yard nests, and those in 1980–83, and the more uniform hatchability of remaining eggs despite environmental differences.

Places and Times	All Nests Total Eggs		Successful Nests Surviving Eggs		Hatchlings
Suburban	468		329 (70%)		278 (84%)
Rural	118		53 (45%)		46 (87%)
(P)		(< 0.001)		(NS)	
Suburban					
First nests	362		246 (68%)		213 (86%)
Replacement nests	106		83 (78%)		65 (78%)
(P)		(0.04)		(0.07)	
Open yards	255		168 (66%)		131 (78%)
Wooded yards	213		161 (76%)		129 (80%)
(P)		(0.02)		(NS)	
1976–79	107		74 (69%)		60 (81%)
1980–83	142		77 (54%)		65 (84%)
1984–87	131		104 (79%)		82 (79%)
(P)		(< 0.001)		(NS)	

partial clutches were lost (figure 5.1) and among the full clutches, three eggs were lost about twice as often as four or five eggs (see above). Reasons for these findings are two, I believe: first, female owls most readily desert clutches in which they have the least investment of time and energy, and these are the partial or small clutches; second, the smaller, complete clutches more often are those of yearlings, who are flightier than older birds (see above and chapter 8). But the important outcome is that the greater energetic cost of large clutches may be offset by their increased survivability (benefit).

Hatchability did not differ over the study period or between nest attempts and plots, though it tended to be higher in first nests (table 5.5). Employing all suburban and rural data, therefore, I calculate 84 percent, a value slightly below 90 percent in the boreal and flammulated owls and the 88.7 percent average of cavity-nesting birds in general.[34] Even clutch size did not affect hatchability; all five sizes were similar, and clutches of three, four, and five each produced the 84 per-

Table 5.6. Frequencies of hatchlings in relation to clutch sizes of successful suburban and rural nests, 1976–89. Note that broods of three and four are most frequent in their respective clutches (P < 0.02), and that hatching efficiency does not differ significantly among the five clutch sizes, hence total hatchlings/eggs = 84.5%.

| Hatchlings | Successful Clutch Sizes | | | | |
	Two	Three	Four	Five	Six
One	1	2	3		
Two	2	7	5		
Three		14	10	4	1
Four			28	4	1
Five				7	1
Six					1
Hatchlings/eggs =	5/6	58/69	155/180	63/75	18/24
	(83%)	(84%)	(84%)	(84%)	(75%)

cent figure despite their different seasonality (tables 5.2, 5.6). Of special interest is the fact that the usual first-nest clutch of four eggs and renest clutch of three (table 5.2) were the only ones in which all eggs usually hatched (table 5.6).

Hidden in this general picture are three suburban females that hatched only 43–61 percent of their eggs, whereas nine others with the same four- to five-year lifespans hatched 80–100 percent. Because they tossed out some unhatched eggs before I checked them, I can only guess from five infertile ones (among the 20 examined) that there could be a fertility problem related to pesticide poisoning or possible inbreeding (chapter 8). Overall, however, hatchability must be related to weather, as the annual fraction of unhatched suburban eggs is higher in cooler (r^2 = 0.51, P = 0.01) and wetter (r^2 added = 0.11, P = 0.03, MSR) nesting seasons, probably because females are less attentive when fed less due to the unfavorable conditions.

I also thought that female mass (weight), nest-box floor area, incubation time, and laying date might have some individual influence, so I regressed the percentage hatch in 33 successful suburban, first nests with four eggs on these parameters (note that clutch size, nesting attempt, and environment were controlled). But there were no significant relationships. Thus, predation, desertion and weather are the only known limitations on hatchlings; and three- and four-egg clutches are primary hatchling producers, although two-and five-egg clutches are equally hatchable alternatives in case of food limitations or excesses, respectively.

The Essentials

Several arboreal mammals and suburban starlings are important competitors or predators insofar as screech owl nest sites and eggs are concerned. The owls occupy cavities before laying apparently to deter these animals, although their first eggs may be delayed by cold weather. The birds renest at least once if their first eggs are disturbed or destroyed, but renest clutches and eggs are smaller than those in first nests and are laid at greater intervals by energetically depleted females. Time seems to be a major constraint; females may not be able to take the time necessary to produce another large clutch of large eggs, because this could put their newly independent owlets at a selective disadvantage in fall environments characterized by increasing cold weather and declining food supplies.

Four eggs is the usual first clutch, three eggs the typical replacement clutch, and both clutch and egg size are determined by food supply and rainfall, which presumably augments food. Larger females lay more, larger eggs but not necessarily in larger cavities. Dead eggs from large clutches or small cavities are often removed but only rarely replaced. Thirty days is the mean incubation time for first eggs, which are usually incubated immediately and protected by females who seemingly learn that passive defense is a feasible alternative to fighting or flying in response to me as a disturbance factor. Although four- and five-egg clutches are energetically more expensive than three-egg clutches, their survivability is greater and hatchability the same, so there is an apparent tradeoff in efficiency.

Suburban eggs and clutches are the same size as rural ones but laid earlier in the spring, presumably because of warmer city temperatures. First egg dates bear no relation to female or clutch size. Desertion is the major cause of suburban egg loss, whereas rural eggs are most prone to predation. Also, predation is more frequent in wooded-yard suburbia, while desertion is the chief cause of egg loss in open yards. Rural screech owls suffer nearly twice as much egg mortality before hatching, but no more or less afterward. In general, then, the suburban population begins its nesting season with proportionately more hatchlings, a head start in annual reproduction.

Survivability of eggs is different from hatchability, each contributing independently to hatching efficiency (hatchlings eggs). Survivability is that proportion of eggs that survive predation or desertion, while hatchability is the remainder that actually hatch. Although the rural owls are less efficient than suburban ones, because of lower survivability, they are similar to at least the barn owl in this regard and to the suburban population in hatchability. Overall, eastern screech owls are similar to tawny owls but less efficient than several other cavity-nesting owls.

6   Chicks and Fledglings
Greater Investments

As a teacher I share the fruits of research while doing it and want to show my students what live screech owls are about, not just recite the statistics of their accomplishments. But one time of great significance, when reproduction culminates, is the time of final examinations and summer departures for both students and owls. The end of nesting comes too late for hands-on experiences in learning. By fall and the students' return, owlets catch crickets and earthworms on city streets, their kingdom's no-animals land. Flattened, lifeless birds are poor in-structors then, though human fledglings can still learn about that most dangerous time of life, the juvenile dispersal period.

Male roosting behavior is a very good clue to major happenings at the nest, so hatching, brooding, and fledging may be determined by watching males in their tree-foliage roosts (see also chapter 2). Unfor-tunately, though, I cannot keep daily track of more than one or two suburban males each year. Yet prior experience plus more limited knowledge of all nesting males each season permits assessments of main events in nestling life. Of course the chicks themselves and their mothers are fundamental sources of information, but it is quite pos-sible to know a lot without disturbing them, simply by observing males on their roosts.

Exploratory observations suggested that males move closer to their nests nearer sunset and hatching time, perhaps drawn by female and chick activity (hunger?). Seventeen suburban males, checked twice be-tween dawn and noon and twice more before dusk most days of the nesting period, provided daily and nesting-phase data amenable to two-way analysis of variance (n = 72–104/bird). First, though, I needed to check roost distances among them, as both open and wooded yards were represented. While there were no statistically sig-nificant differences, individuals in wooded yards averaged 1.8 m closer to nests, presumably because the denser trees afforded more potential roosts (r = −0.54, P = 0.07, for mean distance of 3–8 males/site versus tree density at 13 box sites, 1976–90).

The males roosted 5.6 ± 3.4 m away from nests during incubation but moved progressively closer within several days of hatching (r_s > 0.89, P < 0.01, for mean distance per day vs. 5–7 days per owl). Significantly close roosts characterized the day of first hatch through the brooding phase (4.1 ± 1.7 m), after which the males moved away somewhat (5.1 ± 2.4 m; P = 0.01). Also, these birds averaged 0.6 m closer to nests in the afternoon than in the morning (P = 0.04), regardless of nesting phase (NS). Male attentiveness and possible responsiveness to demands for food are indicated, I believe.

This is especially remarkable in that the 17 owls used up to four (1.8 ± 0.8) habitual roosts each day, depending on exposure to sunshine and wind as well as nesting events (the few individuals routed by mobbing returned to a familiar roost the same day, chapter 3). My repeated watches under the full gamut of weather conditions revealed that some sites were more shaded, shielded from heavy rain, or protected from strong north or south winds. I could classify roost trees according to owl biases and checked them personally by standing shirtless under roosts during heavy rains, cold north winds, and hot afternoon sunshine with and without strong wind.

Eleven males that moved among two or three deciduous and evergreen roosts on clear days with slight breezes selected greater shade in the afternoon (P < 0.01). And nine that moved during any strong wind chose protected leeward sites (P < 0.05). For instance, one midafternoon I watched a male fly from one Shumard oak affording more shelter from strong, prefrontal south wind to another 20 m away and better shielded form the cold north wind that blew in at 1330 hours. Heavy rain had no general displacement effect, as illustrated by a male that sat in a deciduous holly thicket throughout a 4-cm, 10-minute downpour.

Roost distances of rural males were not remeasured, but ten individuals averaged a bit farther from nests, though not significantly so, than 26 contemporaneous suburban males (5.8 ± 3.0 vs. 5.1 ± 2.9 m). However, 23 postbrooding females, roosting outside suburban boxes for the first time, were farther away than their mates seen simultaneously (5.6 ± 3.2 vs. 3.9 ± 2.8 m, P = 0.05). Newly emerged females are more skittish than males, which are habituated to customary occurrences around nests; and they appear to select roosts in denser foliage, even in the same tree.

Hatching

Upon the chicks' hatching, males suddenly depart their day roosts earlier, which is another clear signal of this change in life history (see also chapter 3). The difference between the last night before the first chick hatches and the next night in ten instances among four males that used the same nest site was 6.9 ± 3.7 minutes. By contrast, their night-to-night differences during the last week of incubation averaged only 3.1

± 2.9 minutes (n = 32, P = 0.03). The close approach of roosting males plus their earlier exists allowed me to find 76 wet suburban hatchlings and seven others on the rural plot.

Average hatching dates for first chicks in first nests were April 21.4 ± 6.6 days (n = 58) in suburbia and April 26.9 ± 5.9 (10) on the rural plot (P = 0.03). Considering that nesting begins 5.6 days earlier on average in suburbia and incubation is the same in both study plots, the 5.5-day earlier hatching time is not surprising. Although hatching at 31 nests in open yards averaged 1.5 days earlier than at 27 nests in wooded yards, and 15 on ridges 2.6 days earlier than 17 in ravines, these differences are not significant. Nor is the half-day difference between Woodway and Harris Creek meaningful. Chicks in 15 suburban replacement nests hatched May 19.5 ± 17.1, practically a month after first nests.

Just-hatched chicks were found between 0900 and 1730 hours (see also appendix VII; I did not check for hatches at night). All were wet, some with attached egg fragments, but 16 suburban hatchlings dried within two hours. Four times I chanced upon mothers nibbling pieces of eggshell, as they straddled hatchlings, and I suspect they assist the hatching process. Mothers also carried eggshell out of nests on their posthatch respites from brooding; I watched this 22 times and found shell pieces 2–65 m from nests. Twice, half-shells from hatched eggs enclosed portions of other eggs and apparently killed them, so the removal of eggshells is very advantageous.

Since the first two or three eggs of a clutch may be laid at almost daily intervals and incubation usually begins with the first egg, I want to learn about the possibility of coincidental hatching. Among 55 suburban clutches of three to six eggs, no chicks hatched within 24 hours of one another in 34 (61.8%); the first two arrived within this time frame in 13 (23.6%); and, interestingly—considering the paradigm of staggered laying and hatching in raptors—there were eight (14.5%) instances of three hatchlings within 24 hours. This does not surprise me, though, for the frequencies of incubation starting with the first, second, or third egg closely match these for coincidental hatching (see chapter 5). The first two chicks may hatch together in boreal, elf, flammulated and tawny owls as well.[1]

Of further interest is a decline in mean hatching interval among two to six siblings of 48 suburban broods over the ten-week hatching period (r = −0.38, P = 0.01). I rather expected late-nesting females to begin incubation sooner, hence increase the interval, because of the relatively short time for raising chicks to independence (chapters 4, 5). Even when controlling for brood size, which increases the mean hatch-

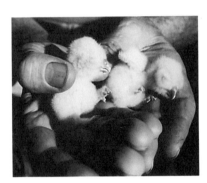

Downy hatchlings in a brood of staggered ages and sizes hatched over five days. *Left:* Day-old siblings; note their closed eyes and egg teeth. *Right:* Nancy Gehlbach holds the last-hatched (runty) owlet.

ing interval by 1.4 days for each additional chick ($r^2 = 0.34$, $P <$ 0.001), mean hatching date remains an influence (r^2 added $= 0.11$, $P = 0.02$). This casts doubt on the concept that asynchronous hatching hastens development of older chicks at the expense of younger ones. Instead, I think it permits adequate feeding of all nestlings, since younger ones require less food and catch up to the older ones near fledging time (see below).[2]

Eighty-three wet hatchlings weighed 11–15 (13.2 ± 1.1) g except for one 8-g runt that died, the last in a brood of five. Weight differences between study plots, suburban sites, first and replacement nests, and among different-size broods are insignificant. But, as in other raptors, including the boreal and tawny owls, there is a significant intrabrood distinction ($P = 0.02$).[3] Seventeen first chicks averaged 13.8 ± 1.2 g, no different from 13 second siblings (13.1 ± 1.1 g) but heavier than 17 later ones (12.7 + 1.0 g) in broods of three and four. Similarly, second chicks also differed from later ones, while third and fourth owlets were essentially alike (NS).

Larger hatchlings came from larger eggs, especially longer ones, according to my multiple stepwise regression of hatching weight on egg length (r^2 = 0.64, P < 0.001) and width (r^2 added = 0.11, P = 0.01). As with the eggs, hatchlings in 1980–83 were smaller than others during 1976–87 (P = 0.05; see chapter 5). Therefore, any survival value attached to hatchling size must originate when eggs are made. Average size at hatching was slightly if at all related to average size at fledging in 59 individuals (r = 0.23, P = 0.08).

Hatchling weight represents 11.2 percent of fledging weight compared to the boreal owl's 7.3 percent, hawk owl's 7.8 percent and flammulated's 13.8 percent as examples of variation among small and midsize hole nesters[4] Moreover, hatchlings are 11.8 ± 1.4 percent of fledging size in the countryside but only 10.9 ± 1.3 percent in suburbia (P = 0.06), so any head start attributable to larger size should be more important in the more natural rural environment. And hatchlings are 6.7–8.8 percent of adult size, similar to 5.1–7.9 percent in the boreal owl and 6.1 percent in the hawk owl but unlike the larger (11.4–14.2%) hatchlings of flammulated owls.

Brooding and Nest Microclimate

For 10.5 ± 3.9 days after the first hatch, 37 females brooded their downy nestlings. Thus, brooding covers 38.5 (suburban) to 40.2 (rural) percent of the average nestling periods in each environment (table 6.1) and is similar to the 35.0 percent average of four other hole-nesting birds compared to 53.6 percent for five open nesters.[5] When brooding ceased as a regular daytime activity, the oldest two to three chicks among four to six averaged 75.9 ± 14.6 g (n = 31) and could thermoregulate; their eyes were open, feathers had appeared, and they no longer shivered if uncovered (appendix VII).[6] But 15 youngest siblings were only 45.3 ± 14.1 g, hence smaller (P < 0.001). Since they usually survive, older chicks and the nest microclimate must keep them warm.

Normally, brooding females take a recess of 18.4 ± 7.6 (n = 16) minutes from the nest cavity at dusk and occasionally also near dawn, like their 17.8-minute average absence during incubation (chapter 5). Also, on hot afternoons females sit beside nestlings, peer from cavities, or even exit completely. Brooding averages a week shorter in replacement nests than first nests, perhaps because the later broods are smaller and the weather warmer (table 6.2).To find out I regressed number of brood days on brood, nest-box, and female size, plus mean maximum and minimum air temperatures and learned that only the mean maximum temperature is explanatory (r^2 = 0.62, P < 0.001). The brooding phase is shorter, indeed, when the air is warmer.

High nest-cavity temperatures in the late spring, during most re-

Table 6.1. Concurrent nestling and fledgling features of successful
broods in suburban and rural environments, 1979–87. Data are mean
± one standard deviation derived from brood means and (sample
size). Note that owlets from first nests in Woodway grow faster to a
larger size but do not fledge earlier because they spend more nestling
time than first-nest rural owlets, while Harris Creek and the renest
broods are mostly intermediate (the one-way ANOVA of fledging date
compares only first nests; in a MANOVA of the other features among
the four samples, P < 0001; asterisks = P < 0.05 in LSD tests).

| | Suburban | | | Rural | |
| | Woodway | | Harris Creek | | |
Features	First Nests (32)	Renests (12)	First Nests (14)	First Nests (11)	P
Growth to					
asymptote (g/day)	4.9±0.6*	4.2±0.2	5.0±0.7*	4.2±0.3	< 0.001
Peak wt (g)	124.8±6.8*	118.7±6.4	115.5±10.4	111.4±6.4	< 0.001
Brood size	3.4±1.0	2.7±1.1	3.4±1.0	3.3±1.0	NS
Fledging wt (g)	122.9±7.4*	118.0±5.7*	114.6±10.7	109.3±7.3	< 0.001
Nestling days	27.7±1.8	27.6±1.8	27.0±1.6	26.0±0.7*	= 0.06
Fledging date					
(May or *June*)	18.3±5.5	20.5±14.0	17.6±8.6	20.7±4.5	NS
Fledglings	2.9±1.0	2.5±1.2	2.9±0.7	2.9±1.1	NS

placement nesting, must obviate the need to brood (appendix II). Actually, the mean maximum temperature of renests (32.7°C) was like that
associated with eight panting or gular-fluttering, heat-stressed chicks
(32.9 ± 1.2°C). By contrast, the eight highest nest temperatures of
sleeping chicks were lower (31.3 ± 1.1°C, P = 0.03). I never saw an
adult owl pant or gular-flutter in undisturbed natural conditions, indicating that they thermoregulate effectively by switching among foliage
and cavity roosts.[7] Surely adult females adjust brooding, as they do
incubation, to suit the thermal circumstances (see chapter 5).

Females often return to their nestlings after brooding ceases, if the
weather suddenly turns cold or unusually rainy, whereas males rarely
take refuge in the nest cavity after egg-laying (chapter 2). This suggests
that females may reinstate brooding temporarily. For example, in late
April–early May, 1991, six neighboring suburban nests had outside-
roosting females for two to five days during 28–32°C midday tempera-

Table 6.2. Daytime brooding of nestlings, beginning with the first hatch, and the thermal environment of suburban first nests and replacement nests, 1977–84. Data are mean ± one standard deviation plus (sample size) from one to three nests per year. Note that brooding is longer and involves greater weight gain among more nestlings in the cooler first-nest period.

Features	First Nests (25)	Replacements (12)	P
Brooding			
Number of days	12.6 ± 2.3	5.8 ± 1.9	< 0.001
Brood size	3.7 ± 0.9	2.9 ± 1.2	= 0.03
Chick weight gain (g)	75.6 ± 21.9	30.7 ± 14.2	< 0.001
Nest temperature at 0700–2100 hrs (°C)			
Maximum	29.6 ± 2.6	32.7 ± 1.3	= 0.008
Minimum	21.8 ± 3.7	27.7 ± 1.9	= 0.001
Air temperature over 24 hrs (°C)			
Maximum	27.1 ± 1.9	33.2 ± 2.3	< 0.001
Minimum	15.8 ± 1.7	19.3 ± 4.6	= 0.002

tures until a cold front dropped the highs to 16–18°C. When I rechecked nests in the afternoon of the first cool day, females covered all chicks with spread wings in the four broods with youngest chicks below the thermoregulatory minimum of about 75 g and 11 days of age.

One spring I placed thermometers and hydrometers in single small, medium, and large nest boxes housing concurrent broods of four in wooded suburban yards. The nest debris below each brood and air 30 cm below each box were monitored at 0900, 1300, 1700, and 2100 hours for 12 days of brooding and postbrooding plus 12 more days after all chicks fledged. Because I thought the owls' presence might alter their cavity microclimate but be mediated by cavity size and time of day, differences between interior and outside temperatures and relative humidities were subjected to three-way analyses of variance.[8]

In occupied boxes, debris in the large one averaged 3.8°C cooler than in the small box, though 3.0° warmer than the air, with the medium-size box exactly intermediate (P < 0.001). Time was influential too, as nest material averaged 3.3 and 3.9°C warmer in the morning and evening, respectively, but only 2.7° warmer in the afternoon (P = 0.02). And there was a significant interaction between box size and time (P = 0.03), because the large box had a more stable thermal regime than the small one. Final evidence that owlets and their mothers

Female trying to brood three-week-old chicks during a cold spell.

alter conditions was the 3.2 ± 0.8°C nest-minus-air temperature during use compared to −0.4 ± 0.6°C afterward (P < 0.001).

Relative humidity differences also varied significantly between the
nestling and postfledging periods (P = 0.006) and during the day (P <
0.001), averaging 6.3 percent higher in the nest than outside in the
morning and 11.5 percent higher later, compared to only 2.4 and 8.2
percent higher after fledging. But I detected no significant differences
due to box size. Humidity averaged 9.9 ± 3.5 percent higher in occupied boxes, whereas the vacated nest-minus-air difference was 5.8 ±
3.1 percent (P = 0.01). Obviously, the owls both heated and humidi-
fied their nesting cavity.

That they also stabilized the environment is indicated by significantly
reduced variation in temperature and humidity inside relative to concurrent ambient conditions (P < 0.05). Coefficients of variation for
temperature ranged from 12.0 (large box) to 16.2 (small) compared
with 14.6–23.9 percent outside, and for humidity these values were
7.5(large)–12.6(small) inside and 12.1–21.1 outside. Since a large box
affords the least variable plus coolest microclimate, I understand why
it might be chosen for replacement nesting (chapter 2). Surely high
humidity in any box or cavity helps to stabilize its temperature, which
remains comparatively high in the cool morning and evening hours and

presumably also at night. Thus, body temperature and metabolism can be sustained in the critical period before thermoregulation.

Parental Responsibilities

Throughout brooding, males bring food to their mates in the cavity or outside it during the evening recess. Afterward, females receive food outside though sometimes in the cavity entrance. But if females are away, their mates deliver directly to the nest, dropping items in the entrance or giving them to chicks large enough to reach toward the entrance or perch in it. The males provide whole or headless bodies, never smaller fragments, while females dismember large bodies for distribution among the brood until the last week of nestling life. These sex roles are typical among both owls and hawks.[9]

The difference in food handling affects reproductive success in opposing ways. It allows males maximum hunting time, as they must be the most knowledgeable and efficient hunters, and females maximum time at the nest to brood, defend, and feed chicks (chapters 4, 5). This is beneficial, I believe, and if the male dies a new one is acquired from among the unpaired, mostly yearling males (chapter 5). However, if the female is lost before nestlings are old enough to thermoregulate and dismember food items—at 10–12 days and 65–80 g minimum— they too may succumb. I have no record of a replacement female.

At one suburban nest, for instance, 22, 34, and 42 g chicks were brooded amidst a cache of moths and small snakes when their mother disappeared. Five days later only the two oldest (37, 52 g) remained, surrounded by uneaten insects and a snake. Within another five days the middle chick died, although the oldest fledged at 99 g after a prolonged nestling period of 32 days. Meanwhile, at another suburban nest a female brooded four nestlings averaging 39 g alongside cached reptiles, when her mate was killed on the street. Then the cache was consumed and smallest chick (21 g) cannibalized during the four days until a new male brought in a snake and insects.[10] The three remaining owlets fledged in 26–27 days.

These contrasting situations underscore the indispensable role of the female early in the nestling period. However, this changes as shown by two other suburban broods of older, larger chicks. When a brood averaging 123 g lost its mother to a car, the smallest (112 g) chick died in five days and the other four lost 7–14 g (5–11% of body weight) but fledged later at an average 114 g. At the same time a 106 g brood of five that retained both parents gained 3–7 g (3–6%) and all fledged eventually at an average 117 g. There were too few nests to verify my notion of female versus male differences in dispensability related to nestling development, but I find it curious that the sex roles are so stereotyped when this may jeopardize breeding success.[11]

I was able to assess male provisioning by counting and weighing cached food and enumerating feeding trips during visits to each of six successful suburban nests with original long-lived pairs, April 20–May 29, 1988. Two broods of two, two of three, and two of four were watched from first hatch to first fledge (all chicks fledged). All were visited in the same six afternoons, and also observed two hours per evening, beginning with the first feed, five to seven times in random rotation. This sample, though small, was designed in advance to reduce vagaries in food availability (chapter 3) and adult experience (chapter 8).

At each site, weight and number of stored bodies declined during the nestling period (r > −0.43, P < 0.02), which corresponded to an increase in brood weight (r > −0.42, P < 0.02) without relation to brood size. But weight change of the chicks was the strongest determinant and a positive influence on both cache weight and size in separate multiple stepwise regressions of the whole data set (r^2 > 0.23, P < 0.005). Thus, provisions were sufficient without being tailored to brood size.[12] Fifty-one (items) and 54 (weight) percent of variation in the cache could be explained by nestling weight change, then date, and finally total weight of the broods (P < 0.001).

Although caching declined as owlets grew, number of feeding trips increased from 2.4 ± 1.9 per hour in nestling-week one (brooding) to 5.1 ± 4.5 in week three (postbrooding; P = 0.03) and began earlier in the evening (P < 0.001; see chapter 3). Similar increases are known in other owls including the boreal, flammulated, hawk, long-eared, and Ural.[13] My watches certified that a few, large, endothermic prey like birds gave way to more, small, ectotherms like insects and reptiles. Also, feeding declined from 4.9 ± 3.8 trips in the first 30 minutes to 1.7 ± 2.2 in the last 30 each night (P = 0.01) and did so despite the brood-size and seasonal differences (NS, three-way ANOVA). This drop characterizes other small owls but not large ones that deliver large prey less frequently.[14]

Regarding my screech owls, I think larger and hence fewer prey at the beginning of the nestling period are determined by the earlier (cool) season and can be stored and used periodically by mothers and owlets, when the females cannot hunt because they must brood and feed helpless nestlings. Too, the large items are most likely to last a while. Later, as the weather warms and insects plus reptiles become available, more feeding trips are necessitated, since each item is smaller; but post-

Female delivers oriental roach to four-week-old chicks during a cold spell. (Ann Gordon photos)

brooding females can help with the hunt, and the older, larger nestlings can manipulate the smaller items without assistance (appendix VII). Then the increased food demand precludes any major build-up of cached items.

Growth and Death

Eight-three nestlings from 20 suburban and three rural broods of one to six, weighed every two to three days upon hatching, attained their asymptotic weight in 20.0 ± 0.8 days (figure 6.1A). This time also characterizes the western screech, boreal, and saw-whet owls. During subsequent weight flux in 184 of my subjects, the peak was attained in 20–25 days as determined by growth rate ($2° r^2 = 0.37$, P < 0.001) and was linearly related to fledging weight (r = 0.96, P < 0.001), a significantly lower value (117.5 ± 11.2 vs. 119.8 ± 11.4 g, P < 0.001). Similarly, western screech and boreal owls lose body mass before fledging.[15]

Nevertheless, growth and nestling mass vary according to the environment (table 6.1). Whether calculated from the records of individuals or the means of broods, 118 chicks from Woodway grew faster than 29 rural chicks, while 37 from Harris Creek were also distinctly suburban. Peak nestling and fledging weights were greater in Woodway than in the rural plot and intermediate at Harris Creek. Less late-season food in the rural environment must contribute to reduced growth, as the rural and suburban clutch sizes are similar, indicating sufficient early-season food (chapters 3, 5). But why the difference at Harris Creek? Perhaps it is because those chicks fledge sooner (table 6.1).

Aside from locale, important influences on faster growth and larger mass include first nests of the year by contrast to replacement nests (table 6.1), older compared to yearling mothers (n = 71 vs. 78, P < 0.05), smaller rather than larger broods (n = 13, 15, 85, 71 in broods of 1–4; P < 0.02), earlier compared to later hatchlings (n = 60, 54, 47, 20; P < 0.001), and cohort membership with 1980–83 having the lowest and 1987 the highest growth rates and weights (n = 8–17 per year; P < 0.02). Since eggs and hatchlings from the early 1980s were also smaller, that time must have been relatively stressful; and I will be interested to learn of its consequences for population dynamics.

Generally, however, first-hatched owlets in the smallest, earliest broods of experienced suburban females have the most growth potential. How does this affect their siblings? Only two offspring per brood are necessary for maintenance of the suburban population (chapter 9). Any tawny owl nestlings after the first two are considered extras, as they grow more slowly and have a higher death rate.[16] Is this true of eastern screech owls? Looking at the growth rate and fledging weight of first plus second (n = 54) versus third plus fourth (43) chicks in suburban broods of four to six, I do find differences. Mean rate (P = 0.07) and especially weight (P < 0.001) are greater for those earliest two siblings, though influenced by brood size (P < 0.06, two-way ANOVAs).

Because food deliveries are unadjusted to number of nestlings, I am not surprised at the brood-size effect. Largest broods ought to experience the most body-size discrepancy early in the nestling period, when oldest and hence largest owlets have a head start. Indeed so. Subtracting the youngest chick's weight from that of the oldest (brood of two) or mean of all older siblings in first suburban nests without runts gives mean differences of 11.3 g in nine broods of two, 16.5 g in 11 broods of three, and 24.7 g in 12 of four at 5–10 days of age. At fledging, though, mean differences are only 4.4, 5.2, and 9.5 g, respectively; and both brood size (P = 0.001) and nestling age (P < 0.001) are significant influences.

Perhaps there is intrabrood competition with the oldest, largest chick influencing the weight discrepancy. Or is the youngest one's small mass, hence its hatching interval, more critical? Multiple stepwise regressions of the 5–10-day mean weight difference among chicks on weight of the oldest and brood size, then on weight of the youngest and the brood, indicate that the youngest chick's mass is more important (r^2 = 0.66, P < 0.001) than brood size (r^2 added = 0.11, P < 0.001). Mass of the oldest owlet is insignificant. At 15–20 days of age, influence of the youngest declines (r^2 = 0.60, P < 0.001) and drops even farther at fledging (r^2 = 0.35, P < 0.001), when brood size disappears as a determining factor. Thus, sibling competition seems unimportant.

Even the influence of hatching interval decreases during growth because of the leavening affect of sexual size dimorphism.[17] A male chick's initial size advantage should be offset by subsequent female owlets growing larger, while first-hatched females might maintain their size edge only until matched by later female siblings. Among oldest owlets half ought to remain larger (be females) than second-oldest (male) siblings, assuming a 50:50 sex ratio, and this is true in 45 successful suburban and rural broods (80 of 144 owlets, NS). Furthermore, 330 nestlings from 87 broods of all kinds in 1976–91 included just 1.04 presumed males per presumed female, judged by weight at fledging; and 19 of these captured as breeding adults were the sex predicted by fledging size.[18]

Youngest-sibling deaths occurred in only 14 (20.3%) of 69 suburban broods and 4 (33.3%) of 12 rural ones unaffected by environmental agents like storms and predation (NS). Adding three more broods in which older chicks died gives an overall figure of 25 percent, statistically similar to rates for flammulated owls (27.3%) and tawnies (31.5–36.9%). Corresponding values are lower for elf (7.1%) and Ural owls (2.7–4.3%; P = 0.002) and higher in the open-nesting long-eared owl (59.0%; P = 0.006).[19] This kind of mortality averages 19.2 percent among the seven samples of cavity nesters, which is low compared to the long-eared owl and similar hawks.[20] Are open nesters more thermally stressed, hence more easily starved and prone to brood reductions?

The partial-brood losses I recorded jumped from only five percent in 18 broods of one to two nestlings to 16 percent in 25 broods of three and 39 percent in 41 larger broods of all kinds. Tawny owls also tend to lose chicks from their larger broods.[21] Regressing life or death of the youngest chicks on the potential causative variables in table 6.3 indicates that initial brood size is the major influent (r^2 = 0.26, P = 0.001), although that chick's weight at less than 10 days of age (r^2 added = 0.11, P = 0.01) and brood crowdedness (r^2 added = 0.05, P = 0.05) are involved as well. Larger, more crowded broods with much smaller chicks (runts) are most likely to experience loss, and their slow growth may be an additional factor (table 6.3).

Yet I noticed that older females might make a difference in the fate of runts (table 6.3); so I regressed percentage of surviving chicks on female age, initial brood size, and nest-box area simultaneously, using data from 68 suburban and rural nests. Brood size remains most important and negative (r^2 = 0.12, P = 0.01), but age contributes positively albeit slightly to survival (r^2 added = 0.06, P = 0.05). Females might learn to mediate nestling squabbles that lead to fratricide through brooding behavior, because seven brooded runts survived and only two were cannibalized compared to four nonbrooded survivors and nine victims (P = 0.04). Experienced females do improve their fledglings-to-nestlings ratio (chapter 8).

Three distinct kinds of nestling mortality were likely. Small last hatchlings that gained weight or not but disappeared in less than 15 days, usually leaving some bodily trace, suffered probable fratricide (siblicide) or infanticide and invariable cannibalism in broods with significant weight discrepancy among siblings (figures 6.1C, 6.2).[22] Others that gained weight more slowly than their siblings and then lost it usually survived longer than ten days but starved to death, although only three of six were cannibalized (figures 6.1D, 6.2). A third group of

Table 6.3. Suburban and rural broods of two to six nestlings 5–10 days old without runts (youngest chick measured) compared with others having runts that live or die, 1976–87. Data are mean ± one standard deviation and (sample size). Runts are last-hatched chicks from ultimate eggs appearing later than the average interval after penultimate eggs. Note that broods lacking runts are smaller and less crowded with less weight differences between the older siblings and youngest chick, whereas those in which runts die experience slower growth than the others (MANOVA, P < 0.001; asterisks = P < 0.05 in LSD tests).

Feature	No Runt (32)	Runt Lives (23)	Runt Dies (17)	P
Runt or youngest weight (g)	28.7 ± 11.2*	17.7 ± 4.5	17.4 ± 5.9	< 0.001
Initial brood size	2.9 ± 0.7*	3.8 ± 0.8	4.0 ± 0.7	< 0.001
All siblings-runt or youngest (g)	53.1 ± 42.7*	92.1 ± 34.1	101.2 ± 37.7	< 0.001
Brood weight/box floor (g/cm^2)	0.3 ± 0.2*	0.5 ± 0.2	0.5 ± 0.2	= 0.004
Sibling growth rate (g/day)	4.4 ± 0.5	4.5 ± 0.6	4.0 ± 0.6*	= 0.06
Nest-box floor area (cm^2)	390.2 ± 157.6	330.5 ± 110.2	347.6 ± 154.1	NS
Female age (years)	1.9 ± 1.5	2.2 ± 1.4	1.9 ± 1.1	NS

owlets also gained weight and survived beyond ten days but apparently suffocated, since they were trampled and sat upon in the smallest nest boxes. None were eaten, however.

Frequencies of these mortalities among 25 certain cases are 64 percent fratricide plus infanticide, 24 percent starvation, and 12 percent suffocation without any obvious distinction between study plots. Also, there is no statistical difference in the incidences of cannibalism, though it is twice as high in the rural environment (31.2% of 16 nests versus 15.6% of 109 in suburbia). Whether in suburbia alone or both plots together, neither total deaths nor any of the three mortality types can be linked with food supply or even temperature, rainfall, and population density on an annual basis, suggesting that the internal factors identified above are primarily responsible.

Can staggered hatching that leads to size disparity among nestlings,

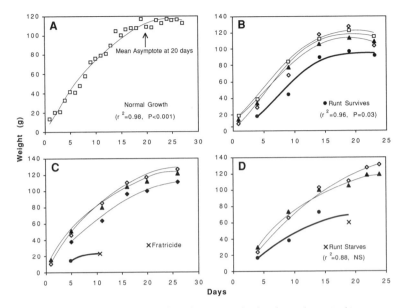

Figure 6.1.   Patterns of nestling growth, death, and survival in representative suburban and rural nests, 1976–87. A. Calculated growth
curve of 73 suburban and 10 rural chicks from hatching at 13 g to
fledging at 118 g on day 27 (overlapping and duplicate data points
omitted for clarity). Note weight flux after the asymptote. B. Suburban brood in which the runt survives but fledges are below-average
weight. C. Another suburban brood in which the runt is presumably
killed and certainly eaten by its siblings and/or parents. D. Suburban
brood in which the runt starves to death and is cannibalized. Note
that runts are usually late-hatched and/or small chicks whose survival
depends on normal albeit delayed growth.

cannibalism, and brood reduction be an adaptive adjustment to food
scarcity?[23] I doubt it, because cannibalism is not advantageous; non-
cannibal broods produce breeding adults as frequently as concurrent
cannibal broods (29.3% of 41 versus 25.0% of 12, respectively; NS).
Moreover, 38 percent of screech owl nests hatch two to three chicks
coincidentally, not asynchronously, and their food supply diversifies
seasonally (see above and chapter 3). Fratricide in particular could be
accidental at times, arising when plentiful food fosters large clutches
and broods (chapter 5), hence youngest chicks are comparatively runty
and more crowded with less chance to escape siblings in the scramble
for food.[24]

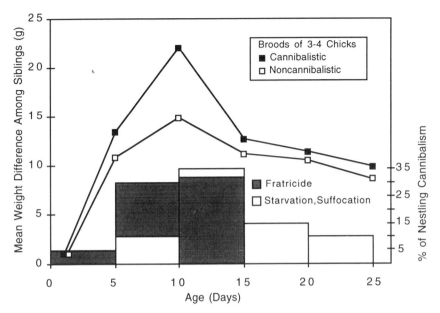

Figure 6.2. Body mass disparity among siblings in contemporaneous suburban broods of three to four and its relationship to the frequency of fratricide (siblicide) plus infanticide and starvation and suffocation during the nestling period, 1976–88. The two disparity patterns differ, especially at the 10-day interval (P = 0.02). Frequencies of the two types of mortality resulting in cannibalism are different (P = 0.03) and siblicide is more strongly concurrent with increasing disparity in mass than starvation and suffocation ($r_s > 0.82$, P < 0.10, compared to $r_s > -0.02$, P > 0.10).

Nevertheless, the slow growth of cannibalistic broods and occasional starvation imply food shortages subsequent to excesses that initially promoted large clutches and broods. In fact, 15 (75.0%) of 20 broods lacking food stores were cannibalistic compared to only 7 (38.9%) of 18 with stored food (P = 0.02). All runts died on the rural plot, which is relatively food-poor, while almost as many survived (16) as died (17) concurrently in suburbia. Probably because the mortality was so local, my general assessment of food and the other environmental factors could not predict it. Annually, only 10.3 ± 8.5 percent of suburban broods and 12.7 ± 19.1 percent of the rural ones registered partial losses (NS).

By contrast to this attrition, which also includes rare deaths from fly parasitism (1), drowning in the nest cavity (1), and falls from it (2), predators eliminated entire broods.[25] The partial losses as fractions of available chicks per year were no different in suburbia and the countryside (9.1 ± 7.7 versus 3.5 ± 6.5%, respectively; NS), but rural predators eliminated proportionately ten times more chicks each year during 1976–87 (17.5 ± 3.6 versus 1.8 ± 6.2% in suburbia; P = 0.007). Once in both study plots ringtails were certain predators; in the rural plot a black ratsnake and in suburbia a juvenile Virginia opossum were implicated.

All suburban predation occurred at wooded-yard nests in ravines, similar to the concentration of egg predation there (chapter 5), whereas cannibalism happened everywhere. Wooded sites surely favor the known arboreal predators, so it is not surprising that the owls tend to avoid them (chapter 9). Interestingly, predation throughout suburbia was less frequent when food was more abundant (r_s = −0.68, P = 0.02), suggesting that predators were diverted by alternate prey; and the owl population was also larger then, hence occupied the dangerous wooded-yard sites at a time when predation pressure was reduced (chapter 9). In the rural plot, however, the predation-food relationship did not hold (r_s = −0.12, NS), possibly because of less food generally or less restriction on predators in the absence of human activity.

Annually, total nestling mortality amounted to 14.2 ± 9.6 percent in suburbia and 20.0 ± 23.6 percent in the countryside, an insignificant difference. Yet over the whole comparative study proportionately fewer suburban nestlings were lost by contrast to rural ones, so nestlings generally are safer in the city (table 6.4). Interestingly, the rural mean is like the 19.5 ± 20.5 percent annual mortality of chicks over 12 years of a tawny owl population in rural England, and the total loss (28%) also like the tawny's (NS).[26] Similar total losses characterize boreal (12.3–23.7%) and flammulated (25.0%) owls but not the Ural owl (2.3–4.3%) among other cavity nesters.[27]

Nest-Cavity Symbioses

Only three (3.6%) of suburban and rural nestlings died, while 80 siblings fledged from nests housing one or more live Texas blind snakes in 1975–1991. This contrasts with 28 deaths (10.0%) and 253 fledglings from nests lacking the live snakes in the same period (P = 0.04), so I think that live-in blind snakes benefit nestling screech owls by eating and thus reducing numbers of fly maggots and ant larvae that compete with them for stored food.[28] The live blind snakes sequester in nest debris up to at least 15 days and are uninjured, except for superficial scarring related to their capture; whereas all other vertebrate prey, including eight species of snakes, are dead (appendix IV).

Table 6.4. Fledging efficiency in suburbia and the countryside, 1976–87. Note that there are more fledglings relative to lost nestlings in suburbia, especially in replacement nests, but fewer in 1980–83.

Places and Times	Total Nestlings	Fledglings (%)	P
Suburban	208	180 (86)	
Rural	61	44 (72)	= 0.008
Suburban			
First nests	161	136 (84)	
Replacement nests	50	48 (96)	= 0.03
Open yards	89	80 (90)	
Wooded yards	107	90 (84)	NS
1976–79	62	58 (93)	
1980–83	68	51 (75)	
1984–87	78	72 (92)	= 0.001

Four times I watched adult screech owls bring in live blind snakes, coiled in their bills instead of dangling like the carcasses of other snakes. Certainly the blind snake's writhing defensive behavior and smooth cylindrical body, smeared with repellent secretions, make it difficult to kill. But the owls do try to kill the snakes, as I saw one unsuccessful attempt and an apparently successful one. Dropping them alive into nest cavities can be nothing more than thwarted feeding behavior. The delivered snakes subsist on fly and ant larvae and pupae, based on their stomach contents. However, deprived of renewed food sources at fledging time, they must crawl out of nest cavities back to their usual underground habitat. In six unmanipulated instances live individuals disappeared from nest boxes two to seven days after fledging.

Though recovered from only nine of 20 suburban boxes and two of 20 in the rural plot, blind snakes were more frequent in suburbia (P = 0.01). Here, regular lawn watering must bring them to the ground surface more often than irregular rainfall, making them accessible (chapter 3). Twenty-seven times I found 1–15 together in a box but only during nestling periods between April 25 and June 24 (May 21.7 ± 11.2 days). The suburban sites did not fledge more owlets relative to their numbers of blind snakes (r_s = 0.24, NS) but did fledge more per hatchling than nine nearest-neighbor sites lacking blind snakes (95.5 ± 6.3% versus 89.1 ± 11.6%, P = 0.03). Was this because of faster growth to more equable sizes which reduced mortality?

To investigate I located nine broods with live-in blind snakes, the same number of nestlings, same-age females, and at least half the same nestling period as 11 broods without snakes. The mean weight difference among nestlings at their maximum was about equal in both groups (10.7 ± 3.6 g and 10.5 ± 7.5 g, NS). But the mean difference in growth rate was less with blind snakes present (0.5 ± 0.3 g/day versus 0.8 ± 0.3 g/day, P = 0.05) and, in the symbiotic broods, determined only by growth rate of the youngest chick (r^2 = 0.66, P < 0.001). Since faster growth is generally related to less size difference among siblings (table 6.3), the youngest chicks caught up to their brood mates quickly, and mortality was averted.

Is faster growth related to more cached food, or is food available longer because blind snakes eat the competing insects? Of course the blind snakes themselves could indicate more food deliveries, although average biomasses of stored foods were no different in the two groups (41.1 ± 21.2 g and 37.8 ± 18.5 g, NS). Unfortunately, I lack sufficient records of cache duration for these groups, though stored bodies ordinarily last but one to two days during nesting (chapter 3). But field notes remind me that in four of the broods with live-in blind snakes, caches persisted at least five days, so I am inclined to think that blind snakes benefit nestling owls by eating insects that would otherwise increase rates of cache decomposition.

Among the 16 families of insect decomposers and others in screech owl nests are ants, including wood ants that tunnel in my plywood boxes and natural nest cavities but do not interact directly with owls. Also, beginning in the mid-1980s, exotic fire ants replaced the occasional native fire and army ants that raided insects in vacated nest boxes but apparently not occupied boxes.[29] Acrobat ants, though, live in occupied boxes and cavities. Their brood (larvae, pupae) is housed in damp nest debris or on the nestlings' fecal piles in nest-box corners if the air is dry or in surrounding wood otherwise. They sting and spray me but not the owls and bite pieces out of food caches, removing these to their brood, often out of reach of the owls.

Cotton rat, house sparrow, inland silversides, and various insect carcasses are among the cached items that slowly disappeared under the onslaught of acrobatic ants, fly maggots, and other decomposers. Thirteen such instances, both suburban and rural, occurred April 22 through June 6, mostly (76.9%) during the nestling period when the most food is stored (chapter 3). Such symbiont competition with the owls for stored food could be severe, if Texas blind snakes did not reduce the numbers of at least some insect competitors, and my limited observations suggest they do. Of six nests with one blind snake and repeated food caches watched specifically over the last 10–15 nesting days in 1989–91, half had no observable maggots or ants by fledging time, although all had them at the beginning.

But there is a possible tradeoff in the owl-snake-ant symbiotic "triangle." Although the snakes are beneficial in removing ant brood, acrobat ants may protect the owls by attacking potential predators. If ants are indeed displaced by blind snake predation on their brood, the protection disappears. Which is more important, reducing or eliminating ant competition for cached food or cohabitation by the ants and hence their protection? Right now I cannot say, but I have noticed that flammulated and western screech owls are also apparently protected by cavity-cohabiting ants that do not disturb their owlets.

Even so, acrobat ants and blind snakes do not live in all screech owl nest cavities, and the snakes are intended food, since 9 (13.1%) of 69 were found dead, 2 having been partly consumed. Because they are obtainable largely near fledging time and mostly in wet weather, the blind-snake benefit to nestling survival is adventitious as is the apparent benefit from ants, in my opinion. If more fledglings from broods with live-in blind snakes or acrobat ants meant more population recruits, symbiosis would be selectively advantageous; but only 6 (10.7%) of 56 symbiotic fledglings became breeding adults, very similar to 8 (12.9%, NS) of 62 without symbionts in the same cohorts.

Fledglings

Seventy-nine oldest chicks spent 24–32 (27.5 ± 1.8) days in the nest, like the chicks of seven other cavity-nesting owls (28.3 ± 4.0 days) by contrast with four open nesters (22.5 ± 5.5 days, P = 0.09).[30] Crowding may be a slight influence, though, for the oldest chicks in 52 first nests fledged a bit sooner from smaller nest boxes (r = 0.41, P = 0.003). Conversely, those in 17 replacement nests in each of the same years did not fledge earlier (r = 0.13, NS), probably because they came from smaller broods that tended to occupy larger nest boxes and hence were less crowded (table 6.1 and see above). The nestling periods of these first and replacement broods did not differ significantly.

Greater exposure to predators may also stimulate earlier fledging, for my rural subjects spent less nestling time (table 6.1), as did 29 oldest owlets in wooded versus 40 in open suburban yards (P = 0.005). In fact the rural nestling period is somewhat negatively skewed (−0.14) by contrast to the positively skewed suburban period (0.52).

Thus, rural chicks from first nests shorten their stay in the cavity, gaining on the 5.5-day earlier start by suburban cohorts, and fledge only 2.4 days later on average (table 6.1). I think it is highly problematical that suburban screech owls have a seasonal advantage, therefore.

A multiple stepwise regression revealed that the nestling period of 66 oldest chicks from both study plots was determined partly by brood size ($r^2 = 0.22$, $P < 0.001$) and mean growth rate (r^2 added $= 0.08$, $P = 0.03$). These owlets fledged sooner from larger, faster-growing broods regardless of their hatching date and crowding (r^2 added, NS). Yet only 30 percent of the variation is explained, because windy rainy weather, nearby predators, and human disturbance delay fledging. Among seven closely watched suburban nests in 1988, for instance, only one rather than the expected four to five fledged within the 26–29 day range predicted from the long-term mean ± standard deviation of nestling period. Stormy weather was the deterrent.

Fledging is stimulated by parents withholding some food and even removing stored food from the nest, if any remains, beginning about midway in the last nestling week. This is most prevalent after the first chick leaves (62.8% of 70 cases vs. 27.3% of 44 before fledging; $P < 0.001$), when parental attention is focused more on fledglings than remaining nestlings as in the boreal owl.[31] Also, owlets may be induced to leave the nest with low-volume monotonic trills (chapter 7). Trilling adults, usually females, may have food or not but sit in habitual food-delivery perches where they are watched by the owlets who look out and food-beg from the cavity entrance two to five days before fledging.

At this time 77 suburban owlets lost weight in proportion to brood size ($r = 0.82$, $P < 0.001$), not their maximum weight ($r = 0.19$, NS), substantiating the effect of withholding food. This could be instead of or in addition to water loss or diverting energy to feather development, as suggested for other birds.[32] Moreover, the weight loss in 1976–87 depended directly on population density ($r^2 = 0.96$, $P < 0.001$), not food availability ($r^2 = 0.25$, NS), possibly because high density caused interference with feeding among nesting pairs, whose home ranges overlap more at such a time (chapter 9) Weight losses per nestling ranged from 0.2 ± 0.3-g (n = 21) to 5.2 ± 4.5 g (37) per year.

Surely the prefledging weight loss reduces an owlet's wing loading which facilitates its flying and hence survival. However, newly fledged screech owls cannot fly and are only 68.6 percent of average adult size—similar to the cavity-nesting tawny (72.0%) and hawk (77.9%) owls that cannot fly either upon fledging. Conversely, the smaller boreal, Eurasian pygmy, and elf owls fly from their nest cavities as fledglings yet are significantly larger in proportion to average adult size

(96.2 ± 4.5% versus 72.8 ± 4.7%, P = 0.03).[33] It seems, therefore, that reduced size at fledging is inconsequential to flying ability. Perhaps it is a matter of leaving as quickly as possible, thereby reducing the risk of being trapped in a cavity by predators or flooding rains.

Oldest chicks from first nests usually left toward the end of the third week in May at each study site, although I recorded one very early exit at a natural cavity on February 11 (table 6.1). Wooded versus open yards and ridges versus ravines made no statistical difference. Replacement nests depended so much on the vagaries of egg desertion or destruction (chapter 5) that they fledged oldest owlets over 2.5 times the seasonal span of first nests in suburbia (table 6.1). By fledging as late as July 17, perhaps even July 24 in one instance, some renests left dependent owlets possibly hampered by molting parents and practically no time beyond the ten-week fledgling-dependency period for dispersal before unfavorable weather in October (see below). Such late nesting must be selected against through high juvenile mortality (chapters 4, 5, 8).

Of 29 fledges in suburbia, 22 occurred 28.5 ± 24.7 minutes after sunset and six in the next hour, although I missed at least three later in the night; and one owlet fledged at 1630 hours. Owlets left in hatching order (r = 0.69, P < 0.001, n = 83); and five broods of two needed only 1.7 ± 0.5 days to vacate their cavity compared with 3.2 ± 1.5 days for 11 broods of three and 4.4 ± 1.4 days for 10 broods of four (P < 0.001). Similarly, boreal owls from broods of two to four fledge in hatching order over 2.3–4.0 days.[34] The screech owlets climb into their nest tree directly or jump-flap to the ground or a close tree limb. On the ground they hesitate but a few minutes before walking or jump-flapping to the nearest tree which is climbed with beak, feet, and flapping wings.

Most youngsters came from the common broods of three and four, but all originated with equal probability in any brood that was at least partly successful (table 6.5).Thus, as in the clutch size–hatching relationship, no particular reproductive unit appears to be most productive. Adding unsuccessful broods to the fledglings/nestlings efficiency gives an overall efficiency of 83.3 percent for 1976–87, like the 81.2 ± 12.2 percent average of barn, boreal, elf, flammulated, little, saw-whet, tawny, and Ural owls.[35] But fledging efficiency on the rural plot (72.2%) was significantly lower than in suburbia (85.5%, table 6.4), and rural tawny (76.2%) and some boreal owls (76.8%) are almost as low.

Curiously, suburban replacement nests produced relatively more fledglings per nestling than first nests, so fledgling production remained high throughout the nesting season (tables 6.4, 6.6).[36] Ordi-

Just-fledged siblings. Compare cross-banded breast plumage with the vertical streaking of adult in chapter 4 photos.

Table 6.5. Frequencies of fledglings in relation to brood sizes of successful suburban and rural nests, 1976–91. Note that number of fledglings usually equals brood size in the common broods of two to four and fledging efficiency (fledglings/nestlings = 91.3% overall) does not differ statistically among all sizes of broods.

Fledglings	One	Two	Successful Brood Sizes Three	Four	Five	Six
One	10	2	1	1		
Two		18	3	3	1	
Three			34	10	1	
Four				37	2	
Five					3	1
Six						2
Fledglings/nestlings		38/40 (95%)	109/117 (93%)	185/204 (91%)	28/35 (80%)	17/18 (94%)

narily, late-nesting pairs of raptors are less productive although perhaps not among Ural owls.[37] This may not be just an urban phenomenon either, because 77.8 percent of nine renest chicks fledged compared to 65.3 percent of 41 from first nests on the rural plot (NS). Perhaps the seasonal increase in food supplies promotes later fledging success, although it certainly does not enhance growth and fledgling size (table 6.1). Late-season declines in predation, fratricide, and starvation seem to be more important (chapter 9).

Despite sustained production, time and space made a difference in fledgling size and its consequent potential for first-year survival (chapter 8). For example, 34 rural owlets averaged 110.4 ± 9.1 g compared to 115 concurrent suburban owlets at 118.6 ± 10.9 g (P < 0.001). Since average fledging size is a negative linear function of brood size (b = −4.5, P < 0.001), only broods of three and four were used in comparing 79 Woodway owlets, which averaged 9.8 g heavier than 40 from Harris Creek, in turn 4.2 g heavier than 37 rural contemporaries (P < 0.001). The Harris Creek population also has an intermediate environment (chapters 1, 2) and nestling period (table 6.1).

Although suburban owlets from broods of three and four fledged at similar sizes in all habitats (NS), 82 from first nests averaged 7.5 g heavier than 29 from replacement nests in the same years (P < 0.001). And all were significantly smaller in the "lean" years of 1980–83 (LSD tests, P = 0.04). Because of such fundamental differences among cohorts, I investigated annual determinants of average fledging size in all

Table 6.6. Fledglings from successful suburban and rural nests according to fledging dates, 1976–89. Note the absence of any trend in average number over time (b = −0.08, NS) and statistical similarity of broods of four versus those of three as fledgling producers regardless of the season and nesting circumstance.

| Dates | Mean ± SD (broods) | Percent Fledglings from Broods of | | | | | | Total (% in Renests) |
		1	2	3	4	5	6	
May 3–7	3.2 ± 0.7 (8)		8	46	46			26 (0)
8–15	2.6 ± 0.9 (11)	4	21	27	48			29 (0)
16–21	3.2 ± 1.1 (26)	2	7	24	43	17	7	83 (0)
22–31	3.1 ± 1.0 (25)		9	15	54	22		78 (13)
June 1–15	2.6 ± 1.2 (9)	13		35	52			23 (69)
16–30	2.6 ± 1.3 (7)		17	39	44			18 (100)
July 1–17	2.8 ± 1.3 (5)	8	14	21	57			14 (100)

suburban broods over 1976–88 and found average growth rate (r^2 = 0.63, P = 0.01) plus perhaps hatching weight (r^2 added = 0.13, P = 0.07) to be important in a multiple stepwise regression. Brood size, nestling period, and fledging date were not implicated.

I am somewhat surprised that the year-to-year flux in growth rate is positively and more strongly influenced by nestling-season rainfall than by food supply (r^2 = 0.45 vs. 0.36, P < 0.03), since copious rain interferes with the feeding of nestling boreal and tawny owls, sometimes contributing to mortality of the tawnies.[38] But rain does not deter screech owls with chicks except momentarily (chapter 7). Instead, wet ground and humid air stimulate earthworm, insect, amphibian, and reptile activity which must foster predatory opportunity, leading to more food deliveries, enhanced growth, and larger size.

At the bottom of the ledger is the apparent tradeoff between fledgling number and body mass, which favors size as regards breeding success and recruitment into the breeding population (chapter 8). Nests produced few large or more small fledglings but more of larger size in suburbia (see also above). During 1979–87 all nests in Woodway averaged 2.0 ± 1.6 fledglings (n = 71), while Harris Creek produced 1.7 ± 1.5 (23), and the rural plot only 1.2 ± 1.5 (36; P = 0.01) without annual differences (NS, two-way ANOVA).[39] Open versus wooded-yard and ridge versus ravine sites were similar (NS). Thus Harris Creek, the younger suburb, has a third intermediate reproductive feature, suggesting that the suburbanization of eastern screech owls is a process related to age and growth of the city.

Dispersal

Despite fledging over several days, siblings tend to congregate, especially during their first two weeks out of the nest. New fledglings roost in open and sometimes precarious places like the ground (2.6% of 69), low shrubs (4.3%), and swaying tree tops (56.2%) but soon select the lower to mid-canopy within a few meters of one another and the female parent. Among 23 suburban broods watched most nights for one to three weeks, females always roosted closer to fledglings than males, as in Kentucky; whereas the males stayed closer to any remaining nestlings.[40] Both adults fed all owlets but tended to neglect nestlings (see above).

In contrast to their behavior during incubation and the early nestling period, males sometimes attacked me as I climbed to fourth-week nestlings and new fledglings; but females did so almost invariably, even those earlier habituated to handling and nest examinations (chapter 5). Starting when nestlings peer from their cavity and through the time fledglings roost in close proximity, females are given to vocal alarm and physical defense of closely approached offspring (chapter 7). A few simply make passes, but most hit me solidly on the head and upper body with open talons and do so repeatedly while I am within about a meter of owlets. Some do not allow me within a few meters of the nest or roost tree, and I have watched them treat domestic cats, raccoons, an opossum and even a benign eastern cottontail the same way.

Two to three days after fledging, owlets begin to make short weak flights toward incoming and outgoing adults, often following each other. Fist-week movements averaged 9.6 ± 4.9 m per night yet took the 23 broods only 29.5 ± 22.8 m away from their nests because of much circling and doubling back depending on directions the adult flew (only once did a fledgling enter its nest box but only momentarily; none used cavities for roosting or natal cavities for breeding). The owlets fly about 10 m across canopy gaps in three to five days and can keep up with their parents in the second postfledging week. By the end of that week 11 broods moved 104.2 ± 52.2 m beyond their first-week destinations (P < 0.001).

Beginning 9–14 days after fledging, owlets tried to catch June bugs, cicada nymphs, and camel crickets after staring at them with much orientational bobbing and weaving (see also appendix VII). These youngsters flew only a few meters to the ground, landed clumsily, sometimes flap-hopped or ran after insects, and were successful on

Fledgling in threat posture.

only five of 21 (41.7%) occasions compared to the 78 percent efficiency of adults (chapter 3). In three to four weeks, however, the owlets of nine broods fed themselves regularly though not exclusively. Their captures of insects, including some on tree trunks and foliage, increased to adult-efficiency level with seven to nine weeks of experience, and they traveled up to 200 meters per night but tended to remain together inside parental home ranges like fledgling tawny owls do.[41]

At this time the essentially independent youngsters sometimes sang and hooted, albeit poorly, mantled prey on the ground if approached by siblings, and assumed the typical adult defensive display with erect feathers and raised wings in response to me. Female parents often accompanied the owlets, and males attended sometimes but only peripherally. Regardless of their increased territorial defense in July–September, the adults fed any begging youngster, so I call the whole time from fledging through dispersal the fledgling-dependency period. During natal dispersal, though, adults often chased owlets.

The nine broods from seven first and two replacement rests dispersed 9.8 ± 1.8 weeks after the last fledging in each, all siblings within a week of one another like the dispersal of seven Kentucky broods. Yet the latter dispersed an average of only 7.9 weeks after fledging (P = 0.02), though not significantly earlier in the summer (July 15.2 ± 3.3

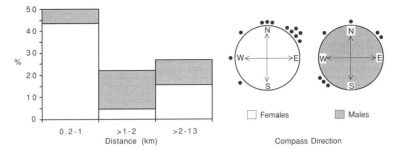

Figure 6.3.   Natal dispersal of seven males and twelve females recovered 10–14 months after fledging, 1977–91. Height of each histogram column is proportional to all movements of that distance; note that half of the dispersals are within 1 km, mostly by females (P = 0.06). The direction of each owlet's movement is indicated by a dot on the compasses and does not differ according to sex (NS); dispersal is 63 percent NNE in both sexes combined (Rayleigh's P < 0.10 > 0.05).

vs. July 31.3 ± 19.5 days; NS), possibly because they carried radio transmitters that impeded feeding and caused excessive movement (chapter 1).[42] The Texas owlets left earlier from larger broods (r = −0.65, P = 0.06) but generally about the time nymphal cicadas ceased emerging (July 24.0 ± 11.9 days, n = 10 years), so the scarcity of easy prey may combine with intraspecific conflict to trigger natal dispersal.[43]

Eighteen suburban fledglings and one from the rural plot were found as breeding yearlings 2.7 ± 3.3 (median 1.2) km from natal areas.[44] Twelve females dispersed about as far as seven males (medians 0.9, 1.6 km; NS), though males mostly moved beyond 1.0 km while females did not (figure 6.3). By contrast, females of other owls usually disperse farther than males, as do the females of many birds.[45] Perhaps my male owlets "flew the suburban gauntlet" of densely packed territorial males, and females were tolerated as potential mates, whereas sparse rural populations do not influence the dispersal of either sex (chapter 9). Nevertheless, despite a few long movements, short-distance natal dispersal characterizes my subjects as it does the Kentucky population.[46]

Population density clearly governed the average distance traveled by ten suburban cohorts, substantiating my gauntlet hypothesis (r^2 = 0.65, P = 0.005). Food supply and even average fledging size and date were not implicated (r < 0.31, NS), although they are important to local recruitment as breeding adults (chapter 8). Similarly, fledging date does not determine the dispersal distance of boreal owls, but food is an equivocal factor in that species.[47] Screech owlets moved farther when their population was denser, undoubtedly because vacant habitat was scarcer. Certainly recruitment as a local breeder is facilitated by a sparse population which enhances the likelihood of finding cavity space and food.

Natal dispersal was quite directional due to landscape constraints in my study area (figure 6.3). All but one owlet went north and northeast or west and southwest along the region's wooded corridor, the Balcones Escarpment (chapter 2). The exception dispersed northwestward away from this scarp but into ranchland with similar woods along major drainages of the region's northwest-to-southeast-flowing rivers. None traveled south or east into the tallgrass prairie region, now agricultural land and hence unsuitable except for its declining riparian vegetation. The directionality of my subjects contrasts with random dispersal by the species in Kentucky and Ohio, the heart of the eastern deciduous forest region, where there is more wooded habitat.[48]

The Essentials

Males usually roost within a few meters of active nests but move even closer when hatching begins. Also, they sit closest in the afternoon and select thermally sheltered sites. After brooding and during fledging, when females roost outside the nest cavity, males remain closer to nests than their mates, while the females stay nearest fledglings and are most prone to attack intruders. Males begin hunting earlier at hatching time, supplying all food through brooding and most of it afterward, while females dismember the items and feed chicks into their third week. Death of the female can result in most or all nestlings dying, if brooding and/or direct feeding are still necessary, because females are not replaced and males do not assume their role. Lost males are replaced, however, and associated brood loss is minimal.

Hatching occurs throughout the day and earlier in the season in suburbia than in the countryside. Most chicks hatch in staggered fashion, paralleling the asynchronous egg-laying, but delayed incubation in some nests permits coincidental hatching of the first two to three chicks. The oldest two come from larger eggs and are heavier than others. Hatching size relative to fledging size and adult sizes is intermediate among small cavity-nesting owls. Hatchlings are brooded for about ten days, or 38–40 percent of their nestling period, and longer in first nests because of cooler weather, although chicks alone or with their mother stabilize the nest-cavity microenvironment, keeping temperature and humidity at moderate levels compared to ambient conditions.

The owlets reach peach weights in 20–25 days but lose a few grams in the last days before fledging, partly because their parents withhold some food to induce fledging. Owlets average 28 days in the nest. Suburban nestlings grow faster than rural ones, and the oldest chicks in the smallest broods of oldest females grow fastest to the largest sizes. Food deliveries are not adjusted to brood size, so hatching interval influences the relative "runtiness" of youngest siblings but generally only during their first two weeks. After that, increasing sexual size dimorphism offsets size-age differences although youngest siblings starve, suffocate, or are killed and eaten in a quarter of the broods, usually in the largest, most crowded, and slowest-growing ones. Cannibalism is most frequent in the food-poor rural environment and in broods lacking cached food.

By contrast to these partial losses which are about the same in the suburban and rural populations, predation removes whole broods and is nearly ten times more severe in the countryside. Overall, proportionately fewer nestlings are lost in suburbia, especially where Texas blind snakes are symbionts in nests. These snakes are delivered as food but mostly uninjured, so they burrow in nest debris, eat ant and fly immatures, and thus reduce the numbers of these competitors for stored food. In broods with live-in blind snakes, siblings show less size disparity, grow faster, and suffer less mortality than in concurrent broods without the snakes. Yet there is no evidence that stocking live blind snakes in nests is anything more than accidental.

Rural chicks and those from wooded suburban sites have comparatively short nestling periods, seemingly because of the increased threat of predation; but all owlets fledge sooner from larger, faster-growing broods. Fledging occurs mostly in the half-hour after sunset and in order of age over several days depending on brood size. The youngsters simply climb into their nest tree or jump out on the ground or into vegetation and climb the nearest tree. Although only 69 percent of average adult size, hence with reduced wing loading compared to the larger flying fledglings of other owls, these screech owls cannot fly immediately. In two to three days, though, they fly weakly and in three to five days follow adults across gaps in the canopy.

Suburban fledglings are larger and more numerous than their rural counterparts and those from smaller broods are larger as well. Furthermore, first nests produce larger fledglings than replacement nests, primarily because of faster growth related to more nesting-season rain and food. The fledglings originate about equally from broods of all sizes. Fledging efficiency (fledglings/nestlings) is higher in suburbia, but the rural value is similar to those of other cavity-nesting owls. Replacement nests produce relatively more fledglings per hatchling than first nests, perhaps because of decreased predation, fratricide, and starvation later in the season, which may counteract the small size and hence lower survival potential of renest fledglings.

In their first two postfledging weeks, owlets tend to stay near each other but move progressively farther from the nest, averaging 30 m in the first week compared to 104 m in the second. Later they begin to catch insects on the ground regularly and may separate from each other but do not move outside their parents' home ranges until natal dispersal about ten weeks after fledging. Until that time they are still fed when they beg. Average natal dispersal is 2.7 km with males making more long movements than females. The distance traveled is longer if population density is high, probably because of competition for space; and it is directional, as essentially all owlets tend to follow woodland corridors.

7 Vocalizations
Clues to the Night

November 1, 1963—my first night as a suburbanite, temporary care-
taker of the land, and I am welcomed by a screech owl's autumn singing. Amidst the season's melancholy of falling leaves, musty woodland
odors, and a fading cricket orchestra, the notion of a suburban bird
appears, and I recall that long-ago time when a small boy on a bicycle
found a mystery. Twenty years later, almost to the day, I return from a
scientific meeting where I have made some left-brained pronounce-
ments about city and country screech owls, bringing that mystery
closer to solution. This night the singing seems less insistent.

In the exploratory years I listened closely to the eastern screen owl's
calls, because they were useful in locating the birds and their activities,
and I tried to record sounds for sonographic illustration but found the
proper paraphernalia so encumbering that it permitted little else to be
accomplished. I decided I might learn more if I used a cassette (replaced by microcassette) tape recorder for noting vocalizations together with events. Soon I found that the adult owls have five major
vocalizations and two nonvocal sounds with many variations. Youngsters add three more at least. Knowledge of each utterance helps im-
mensely to discern sexes, ages, nest and roost sites, and inter- versus
intraspecific contact.

Statements from the literature, mostly anecdotal, also stirred my interest, because they did not fit with my experience: for example,
"screech owls utter various sounds, not one of which can be called a
screech," and "besides the primary (territorial) and secondary (duet-
ting) songs there are calls given at dawn different from those at
dusk. . . ."[1] Contexts for the various published observations of hisses,
screeches, barks, yips, alarm notes, and food calls I found question-
able, because they were not backed up by information on who was
making what sound, where, and in response to what stimulus.

So I began to record the time and situation of voices during my nest
visits and watches, on nesting-density censuses, and in mobbing situations. All quantitative observations were in suburbia. The sounds of
territorial males, lower voiced than females, and responses to those
sounds were noted especially. A few hours each week at dusk and dawn
were devoted to listening for and recording vocalizations of the marked

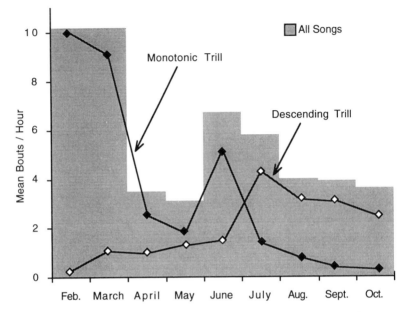

Figure 7.1. Seasonal shifts in singing with a comparison of monotonic and descending trills at one suburban nest site over three years (same pair of owls in 1980–81, new pair in 1982). Sample sizes are 10–18 monthly, equalled divided between dusk and dawn (there is no significant difference among years or between dawn and dusk in the frequency of either song, two-way ANOVA). Note that the two songs partially replace each other seasonally ($r_s = -0.83$, $P = 0.005$, n = 9 months) and the monotonic trill is bimodal with a peak during nest-cavity advertisement and courtship in February plus another during fledgling dependency in June. The peak of descending trills in July coincides with the beginning of fledging dispersal.

adults and young of 19 suburban pairs that used five different nest boxes and environs between late February and early October in the confirmatory period.

Songs

A mellow, quavering series of notes, mostly on one pitch, is what I call the monotonic trill.[2] Sometimes this song rises or drops slightly in pitch toward the end, and often it begins faintly and increases in volume. Monotonic trills are commonest in late winter as courtship begins but peak again in the early fledgling period (figure 7.1).[3] They

Table 7.1. Changes in timing of the first monotonic trills nearest
sunset in late winter to the nestling period. Data are mean ± one
standard deviation from ten samples per month each of two males
at the same suburban nest site (one 1980–81, the second 1982).
Note that trilling is shorter, more frequent, and begins closer to sunset as nesting progresses (b = −6.2, P < 0.001).

Feature	February 18–27 Courtship	March 17–26 Incubation	May 2–11 Nestlings	P
Minutes after (−)/ before (+) sunset	−109.6±13.6	−37.2±16.2	+2.0±1.8	=0.01
Trill duration (seconds)	5.0± 0.8	4.5± 0.6	3.8±0.4	NS
Interval between trills (seconds)	40.1±12.6	15.3± 5.2	14.5±5.4	=0.01

become shorter, more frequent, and commence closer to sunset as the
breeding season progresses (table 7.1). Similarly, the tawny owl begins
calling earlier in the evening from January to May, as it begins breeding.[4] Although given by both sexes throughout nesting, monotonic
trills are most characteristics of males who employ them primarily to
advertise nest cavities and nest-site territories and convey location to
family members (table 7.2).[5]

Males usually trill from specific singing perches and upon arriving
with food at a prey-delivery perch near incubating or brooding mates
(chapters 2, 3). They trill sporadically through the day, especially in
late afternoon and early morning, while roosting near their nesting
mates. The females may answer, and pairs normally engage in antiphonal trilling, whereas synchronous trills are given by neighboring males
at or near nests up to 300 m apart. After fledglings begin to feed themselves, by mid-July for most successful first nests, monotonic trills are
less frequent, probably because the functional necessity of family contact is reduced.

Loud trills apparently are reserved for longer distances as well as
out-of-sight family members, and I can hear them 75–150 m away,
depending on topography, neighborhood noise, and house and vegetation density. Males also trill inside potential nest cavities as do nesting
females and the males of boreal and elf owls.[6] Then they are hard to
hear as are muted trills given from tree perches close to family members. For instance, at 2115 hours one female trilled in muted fashion

Table 7.2. Sexual differences in average frequency of major vocal bouts per hour at 19 suburban nests, each observed for one to two hours at dusk, two to three times per week during the entire nestling period, 1976–89. Note that males give more monotonic trills (family contact signals, P = 0.02), while females utter more of the other vocalizations (predator- and competitor-recognition signals, P = 0.003). Male descending trills and female hoot-barks increase over time (b > 1.8, P < 0.05).

Nestling Weeks	Monotonic Trill		Descending Trill	
	Males	Females	Males	Females
1 (brooding)	8	1	0	4
2 (brooding)	11	0	3	18
3 (nonbrooding)	9	0	3	19
4 (fledging)	11	2	6	20
Mean±SD =	9.8±1.5	0.8±0.9	3.0±2.5	15.3±7.5

	Hoot-bark		Screech	
	Males	Females	Males	Females
1 (brooding)	2	4	0	0
2 (brooding)	4	10	0	1
3 (nonbrooding)	2	11	0	17
4 (fledgling)	3	21	0	17
Mean±SD =	2.8±0.9	11.5±7.0		4.8±8.2

2 m in front of her nest, whereupon her last owlet fledged. I have heard similar low-volume singing by western screech, elf, and flammulated owls and wonder if this is what has been deemed ventriloquistic by observers expecting a more distant singer.[7]

Two roosting males at one nest box in three successive years exemplify vocal behavior in the nest-cavity advertisement period of February to early March (figure 7.1). During 24 observation periods at dusk each year, each bird sat in the box entrance 9–56 minutes before leaving and delivered 4–35 song bouts of monotonic trilling. Then it flew or hopped to a short limb within a meter, sat 1–3 minutes more, and continued singing. First flights were to defecation perches within 30 m where trilling was heard or not; and, finally, the males flew to a creek or bird bath, drank, sometimes bathed, and departed out of contact. Thirty to 90 minutes later, they returned to the box and commenced monotonic trilling in it, on the nearest perch, or elsewhere within a 20-m radius for 20 minutes to three hours before leaving again (see also chapter 2). In the morning, singing stopped 20–44 minutes before sunrise.

The first of two principal variants, possibly a distinct song, is a paced series of notes on one pitch, a slow version of the monotonic trill. It is quite like the first part of the western screech or whiskered owls' territorial songs, though lacking the western's bouncing ball effect.[8] I hear this only in February–April from prenesting males inside or immediately outside cavities with females nearby. Is it an especially insistent form of cavity advertisement? On February 19, for example, a male sang the slow variant in seven bouts of 10–15 seconds each for five minutes at 1900 hours (dusk) within a few meters of a nest box as a silent owl flew about. On the 23rd he sang this variant at 1745 (daylight) inside the box, followed by the typical monotonic trill, and was answered with the same trill by a female roosting 45 m away. She flew into the box at 1825 (dusk).

"Took-took-took" describes this slow variant and also a second faster one. Both remind me of a Geiger counter's ticking, the first distant from radioactivity, the second much closer.[9] While the behavioral difference between slow and fast songs is unclear, it could have to do with offering just a nest cavity (slow variant) versus a cavity with food (fast variant). On February 9, for instance, the above-mentioned male gave the usual monotonic trill 5 m from the nest box at 1830, flew to it with prey, reappeared without the food item at the entrance, and sang the fast version. After he left, I found a freshly killed house sparrow in the box. No female was seen, although a pair nested there six weeks later.

On February 16 two other adults roosted side by side in a red cedar 10 m from a nest box but only 2 m from a natural cavity. I saw mutual preening at 0830 ad 1815 hours but heard no sounds. The male exited the roost at 1830 (dusk), flew into the nest box, and was quickly followed by the female who perched 0.5 m below the entrance. Then the male gave the fast song, flew out to a limb 2 m away, whereupon the female jumped into the entrance and gave the same song. After she finished, the male sang again as before and quickly flew down into a ravine, closely followed by the female. I could not tell if food was exchanged, but the box had been used for caching. No owls nested there that year.

Exceptions to the postnesting decline in length of monotonic trills involve replacement nesting or the late prospect of initial nesting. These males trill as long in April as in February and with increased

frequency expected of the late season. One renesting bird with an incubating mate on April 26 gave 5–7-second trills, 17–20 seconds apart,
in five bouts at dusk (cf. table 7.1). And unpaired males utter monotonic trills more often than descending trills in the summer but soon
switch to the normal fall routine. A lone male sang five monotonic
trills per descending trill in July but reversed the ratio in favor of descending trills by September (table 7.2).

I call the screech owl's quavering, down-the-scale series of notes the
descending trill. This song may rise slightly in pitch before descending
and is two to three seconds shorter than accompanying monotonic
trills.[10] Descending trills are rarely given in daylight or from habitual
perches by contrast to monotonic trills and are most frequent in the
fledgling-dispersal period when monotonic trills are comparatively infrequent. (figure 7.1).[11] They function in nest-site territorial enforce-
ment, particularly as regards adjacent pairs and dispersing owlets, but
also at the close approach of potential competitors like chuck-wills-
widows and large, presumably benign intruders like humans.

Females, primary defenders of the reproductive effort (chapters 5, 6)
give the most descending trills while nesting, but males sing this song
as often afterward (table 7.2). During fledgling dispersal male and female descending trills may be followed without break by lower-pitched
monotonic trills, or females give descending trills followed immediately by male monotonic trills. I believe this is nest-site defense in the
midst of mobile juveniles, coupled with mate signaling. Antiphonal descending trills are given by the pair and, like monotonic trills, are
muted when the two birds are in close proximity. Muted descending
trills are especially ventriloquistic to my ear, since I always expect the
singer to be at a distance proportional to the usual song.[12]

Antiphonal trilling must strengthen the territorial display, but muted
singing might not be as effective as full-volume trills. Is it possible that
the muted songs, descending or monotonic, confuse potential predators as to location of the singer in addition to or instead of being an
adjustment of intrapair contact? Muted songs could be as confusing to
natural predators as they are to me. By contrast, the relatively explosive
intruder and predator-recognition calls might startle and hence thwart
these animals or distract them from nests and fledglings, since such
sounds are readily located (see below).

The cadence of a descending trill is often shortened toward the end,
so it sounds like or grades into a type of screech during physical con-
frontations with other screech owls.[13] And rarely the trill is emitted
slowly or is a single short descending note. Whether the latter is aber-
rant, a type of screech, or another functionally different call is uncer-

tain, as I hear it too seldom for any reliable assessment. For instance on October 31 a resident male screeched, then quickly gave the single descending note, followed by three rapid bouts of typical descending trills. Upon seeing another silent screech owl of unknown provenance, closely followed (chased?) by the singer, I believe it was startled by an intruder hence screeched but, upon full perception, uttered the short descending note as an imperfect prelude to regular territorial trilling.

Of additional interest is persistent trilling, both descending and monotonic, during gibbous and full moons as in the western screech, boreal, and northern saw-whet owls.[14] I enumerated both songs from one nesting pair in the first hour after sunset and chose three nights around the peak of each moon phase during three monthly lunar cycles in March–May, 1986. Three song cycles were detected ($7°r^2$, P = 0.93) with an average of 14 singing bouts at the gibbous (waxing) peak, 17 during the full moon, 10 in the last half, and 7 per hour otherwise. Also, two neighboring males trilled monotonically every 25.6 ± 5.3 seconds per hour after sunset during the full moon on February 8 but only every 38.5 ± 3.7 seconds during the last-quarter moon eight days later (P < 0.001, n = 37, 25).

Finally, it seems likely that trilling is more persistent before stormy weather, though I have not verified this quantitatively. On three occasions I was careful not to disturb rapidly trilling males, as I attempted without success to find a song stimulus other than a drop in barometric pressure together with increased lightning, thunder, and sudden wind gusts. These incidents and many others with circumstantial evidence were in the nesting and fledgling-dispersal seasons. All singing declines as the year progresses (b = −0.69, P = 0.04; figure 7.1).[15] After October the birds are quietest, as great-horned and barred owls begin to reaffirm their territories, and they remain so until mid-January.

Hoots and Barks

One to seven, usually three or four, mild and rather soft notes on a single low pitch are difficult to mistake for anything other than hoots.[16] They differ in length and may descend slightly in pitch, particularly in the longer series, resembling a very slow beginning to the descending trill. But hoots are quite unlike the slow variant of the monotonic trill in being fewer, more forceful, and not heard during courtship. Hooting is common throughout nesting but especially so during the fourth week of nestling life and first two weeks of fledgling dependence (table 7.2). Also, surprised adults without young may hoot, although they usually screech and bill-clap. Hoots denote mild alarm at a potential predator.

Barks seem to be loud sharp single hoots associated with extreme agitation and may presage physical attack, particularly during fledging. I have been attacked by some barking females but not by any hooting screech owl. Sometimes barks precede or grade into a short descending trill. Another variant is the drawn-out, mournful "hoo," often a single note but rarely in descending series of two or three. This faint call comes from females that watch my handling of their chicks or are just released from inspection. One five-year-old female, handled innumerable times, gave a plaintive "hoo" 20 m away after her release and during my weighing of her three downy offspring. Hoos may be the mildest expression of concern about predation.

Both sexes hoot as do newly independent youngsters, which also trill, and the lower-pitched male voice is recognizable for the first time. Hand-held feathered nestlings hoot too but not commonly. One male two-hooted as I weighed his bill-clapping mate. But the postbrooding female hoots more often and at intruders apparently more threatening than those eliciting the descending trill—domestic cats and raccoons, for example (table 7.2). Vocalizations of parent owls are most different during the critical fledging period, when males mostly trill and females hoot, bark, and screech. Females are quite vocal then and prone to attack. Their predator-induced calls alone outnumber all monotonic trills 4.5 to 1.0 (table 7.2).[17]

Vocal and physical defense of nests increases as breeding progresses (table 7.2). Perhaps my repeated arrivals and departures cause loss of fear and reinforce defensive behavior. Alternatively, the owls have more energy invested in late-stage chicks, which are more vocal and hence potentially conspicuous to predators. Thus the parents have more to lose compared to earlier stages and are unlikely to replace lost chicks because of molt and time constraints, so they should defend older nestlings with greater vigor (chapters 4–6).[18] With this in mind I recorded parental vocalizations at five nests watched five nights each and compared them to five others observed ten nights each, one pair of both types per year in 1985–89. The nests belonged to yearlings and older individuals with broods of three or four, visited for two hours nightly beginning at sunset.

I found that pairs with the fewest experiences trilled (descending), hooted, barked, and screeched more per hour than those with more frequent exposure and hence better habituated to me. Their predator- and competitor-recognition calls averaged 19.6 ± 9.5 versus 2.1 ± 0.2 per hour, respectively (P = 0.02); whereas their family-contact songs (monotonic trills) were no different at 13.2 ± 3.3 versus 18.3 ± 7.5 per hour (NS). This does not confirm the hypothesis of reinforced defensive behavior. On the other hand, defensive signals increased weekly (b = 17.1, P = 0.05) while monotonic trilling did not (b = 1.1, NS), supporting the ideas of increased energy investment and molt-time constraints.

I also wanted to explain parent-age and brood-size variables if I could, because habituated older birds should tolerate me better than the less experienced yearlings and, as in the tawny owl, those with more reproductive investment (larger broods) ought to be more defensive.[19] So I found six yearling nests to compare with five contemporaneous nests of two- to six-year-olds, all with broods of three or four and watched for equal lengths of time in 1988. Predator-recognition calls were 14.2 ± 7.2 versus 1.9 ± 0.5 per hour, respectively (P < 0.001). Then I found four nests with one or two chicks to compare to five others with three or four, all of older adults watched the same amount of time in 1989, and recorded 0.2 ± 0.1 versus 3.5 ± 2.7 predator calls hourly (P = 0.02). My postulates were supported. Both learning and size of the reproductive "reward" seem to be adaptive factors in the effort given to defensive vocalization.

Screeches

This sound, surely defensive, befits the species' name, as it is common and difficult to mistake. Screeches are loud, often piercing or grating, single calls by agitated adults of both sexes, nestlings, and older owlets. The male voice is not recognizable. Near fledging time female parents are especially fractious hence prone to screech at nest-site intruders, and the sound is often accompanied by bill-clapping. Screeches may precede or accompany physical attack. The larger the predator or other interloper, the bolder its actions, and the more novel or sudden its appearance, the more likely owls are to screech, based on my experiences with adults at their nests.

Incubating females sometimes screech and bill-clap but more often are silent and behave cryptically, with or without an egg-kicking display, as I open nest boxes for examination (see also chapter 5). Never do they hoot or bark unless handled. One, for instance, kicked her four eggs from beneath her, lay on her back with talons open, and screeched (screamed) as I reached for her. The same day another of the same age (yearling) kicked her eggs too but then quietly hunkered down during the examination. I think that screeches, including scream and squawk variants, indicate personal fear compared to barks that signal anxiety and hoots that show mere apprehension towards intruders—a graded series decreasing in intensity of response to danger.

Screeches do sound like screams if drawn out or prolonged, as when irate females defend owlets. Between physical attacks these birds may perch with wide eyes, erect body feathers, and partially spread wings, conveying a large plus loud aggressive image. Or screeches can resemble squawks if short, as given by a surprised adult. The prolonged call sometimes increases in intensity, resembling a common barn owl's screech, whereas the short variant reminds me of a yellow-crowned night heron's call. Parent owls occasionally screech in a comparatively mild manner close to me, and feathered nestlings screech with much less than adult volume.

Bill-Claps and Hisses

Bill-claps or snaps are the nonvocal sounds of upper and lower beaks snapping together or perhaps tongue clicks as suggested for common barn owls.[20] They are not appreciably different from the bill-claps of other owls in my experience, typically numbering one to three in one or more bouts and being indistinguishable sexually. Bill-clapping is the most frequent response to individual disturbance and begins during nestling days 15–20 (appendix VII). Handling and the clapping of another screech owl almost invariably elicit this sound. The clapping of handled nestlings often causes postbrooding females to attack, and this sound from nesting females seems to be the only stimulus for male attack.

But stimuli to bill-clap may be inanimate as well, by contrast to those causing vocalizations. Once a dead limb hit the ground with a loud thud and caused a fledged brood to clap. The sound also differs from trills, hoots, and others in that it is common year-round, although the social context of nesting assures its greater frequency then. Moreover, bill-claps are equally frequent among large owlets and adults, whereas the youngsters vocalize uncommonly until they are independent. Perhaps bill-clapping conveys personal discontent, whereas hoots, barks, and screeches signal intrusion and potential predators.

Hisses, on the other hand, are nonfunctional, nonvocal sounds in my opinion. I have never heard them in a natural situation, only from adults and large juveniles being handled (appendix VII). They are mild expulsions of air, unaccompanied by any other behaviorism that I can see, and thus totally unlike the loud prolonged hisses of puffed-up and swaying barn owls visually confronted by potential predators. Of course I might not notice a naturally elicited hiss, if it is as quiet as hisses from handled birds, but I cannot imagine a natural context for this sound given the diverse vocal and nonvocal repertoire of eastern screech owls.

Juvenile Development

Peeps or cheeps, essentially like those of domestic chickens (chicks), are given by owlets a day or two before hatching and by the downy hatchlings throughout brooding (appendix VII). Peeping may occur up to about 50 g, the approximate start of feather development, but is rare after brooding ceases. Adult and sibling movements and my climbing to nests and subsequent handling elicit peeping, which may function in social facilitation. Hand-raised owlets peep until touched on the rictal bristles, which causes them to feed. Unfortunately, I lack observations on this call from owlets completely free of observational interventions, so my interpretations are provisional.

As peeping declines, chuckling or twittering increases, especially as eyes open during the second nestling week (appendix VII). Chuckles are usually three- to four-note calls, accented on the last note which may be higher pitched. Partially feathered owlets chuckle during handling and as they jockey with each other for defecational, feeding, and sleeping positions. This sound persists through fledging and could serve social-positional functions that are clearly different from food-begging by contrast to the more general function of peeping. Sometimes chuckling becomes chittering or rattling, as when about-to-fledge owlets jostle for position in the nest-cavity entrance, and sounds like the rattling of mobbed adults.

If mobbed intensely, especially by bluejays and northern mockingbirds, adults are liable to rattle, often grading into a high-pitched cackle before flying (chapter 3).[21] No sound is heard if only a few small birds mob and do not persist, particularly if the owl is ensconced in dense vegetation and does not fly. Incubating-brooding females twice gave this call as I inspected them for bands, but such birds are more likely to bill-clap, hoot, or screech mildly. Rattles and cackles during mobbing must indicate discomfort. The calling owls look about wide-eyed, seemingly with escape "in mind," rather than assuming the cryptic dead-wood pose or erecting feathers and spreading wings aggressively.

The rough, raspy, sometimes raucous vocalization of three- to four-week-old nestlings, fledglings, and courted adult females is a food-begging call (appendix VII). Its pitch is variable but usually drops toward the end, hence the sound has been called, "keerrr."[22] Mild renditions are much like the concomitant singing of round-winged katydids which may help to disguise the highly vocal youngsters from predators. I can hear fourth-week nestlings up to 30 m away on a still night and assume mammalian predators can too, but the possibility of katy-

Postbrooding female near her nest (*left*) in cryptic posture upon approach and (*right*) annoyed and giving the rattle-cackle call in response to mobbing.

did mimicry, together with the loud predator signals of adults and a guardian female, may mitigate the impact of predation at this time (chapter 6).

Juvenile food-begging is loudest at dusk within a week of fledging and for two to three weeks afterward, though owlets are silent during actual departure from the nest. Their raspy call is much louder and longer than the adult female rasp but tapers off in volume and persistence as satiation approaches. And rasps are not as loud before dawn, when katydids are silent, or during the actual feeding process. Katydid songs are also loudest soon after sunset and start to decline around 2200 hours, when the early-evening feeding of owlets drops off (chapter 3). The katydid chorus beings June 4.9 ± 5.5 days (n = 10 years) in the midst of fledging and ends July 19.7 ± 6.4 days (n = 4) as natal dispersal begins (chapter 6).

During their first two weeks of fledgling life in late May and early June, owlets from 14 broods began food-begging 15.0 ± 6.8 minutes before sunset, just as the first few katydids sang. Concurrently, chuck-will's-widows first sang 20.1 ± 15.3 minutes after sunset. The chuck's vocalizations and aerial hunting are coincident, so the young screech owls got a 35-minute head start in the possible competition between their parents and chucks for hunting space and insects. This is the same interspecific advantage they had as nestlings (chapter 3). For the first hour or two they keep up the clamor, even through light wind, rain, thunder, and lightning, undoubtedly because of their hunger, and are fed without interruption except during downpours.

The Essentials

Monotonic and descending trills are the screech owl's songs. The former is a contact signal employed to advertise nest cavities and coordinate family whereabouts, while the latter is a nest-site territorial defensive signal. Lower-voiced males sing the monotonic trill primarily, particularly during courtship and nesting, then switch to the descending trill during fledgling dispersal. This latter song is given mostly by females while nesting. Loud songs are uttered by individuals many meters apart, muted renditions with a ventriloquistic aspect by family members in close proximity. Both trills have several variants including slurred, slow or fast, and long or short versions, and both are often connected to each other or other vocalizations. For instance, monotonic trills are shorter, the bouts closer together and nearer sunset later in the nesting season when they may follow descending trills.

Among the variety of calls are hoots, barks, and screeches, a graded series of increasing intensity of response to predators. These too have variants and are given primarily by females during nesting. However, pairs habituate to my presence and reduce these warning signals accordingly. Older nesting adults give fewer such signals than yearlings, presumably because they have learned that I am little threat. Pairs with smaller broods also are less vocal, and all defensive signals increase as nesting progresses. This suggests that older chicks are defended with more vigor, because their parents have more energy invested in them and are less likely to be able to renest. Screech owls also utter a rattle or cackle if mobbed intensely and bill-clap like other owls when personally discomforted.

Hatchlings peep or cheep throughout the brooding phase and then begin to chuckle. Both are social facilitation signals, the former all-purpose, the latter relative to sharing nest-cavity space with siblings. Older chicks' chuckling becomes rattling like the sound of mobbed adults. The food-begging rasp, also given by courted adult females, develops soon after the chuckle in nestlings and may be loud and harsh at dusk when owlets are hungriest. Then, however, it is somewhat masked by the loud singing of round-winged katydids, whose song it seems to mimic. Owlets begin to beg a half-hour before chuck-wills-widows are active, giving them a head start on obtaining food, assuming the nightjar and screech owl compete for hunting space and food.

8 Lifetime Reproduction
Efforts of a Few

A female screech owl is sick with pesticide tremors, as are her fledglings. Her mate succumbed yesterday. Fourteen years and two months of avoiding cars, chainsaws, and inclement weather, only to die from eating poisoned insects, I suspect. Those who sprayed her pecan grove moved there ten years after she did. They are the environmentally unaware generation who inhabit constant-temperature brick cavities and for whom Monday night football speaks more loudly than trilling owls. But the four fledglings survive after two months of rehabilitation and reenter suburbia, perhaps armed with an inherited tendency for longevity. What will become of the closeted football fans?

One of the most startling revelations of long-term avian studies is that fewer than half the females of a population breed successfully and no more than a third of these contribute half or more of all offspring.[1] Corresponding values for my 80 female subjects were only 24 (rural) and 28 (suburban) percent breeding successfully with just 13 (rural) and 16 (suburban) percent of these producing half the fledged owlets (figure 8.1). Together with their short natal dispersal, this suggests that the owl's genetic variation could be very limited (chapter 6). Will this enhance their future in suburbia as that relatively stable environment, presumably selecting for less variation in the population, continues to encroach upon the more variable countryside?

Unfortunately, lifetime data are available for only three rural and 16 suburban males by contrast to the easier-to-catch females, so I must emphasize the females. Based on their four-year mean maximum lifespan in the nine exploratory years, I assumed that any female died or emigrated beyond the perimeter-survey zones, if I did not find it within four years. But only eight (10%) temporarily disappeared and then for only one to three years (e.g., appendix VIII). Surely I just overlooked those individuals, as none were known to forgo breeding in the manner of food- or site-restricted tawny, Ural, and long-eared owls.[2]

Surviving eastern screech owls are site-tenacious, if their previous nest was successful and hence readily rediscovered (chapter 2). Only 12 (24.5%) of 49 nests were in new locations but still within polyterritories after successes plus overwinter survival of the pair, and there was no significant difference between the two study sites in this regard. As

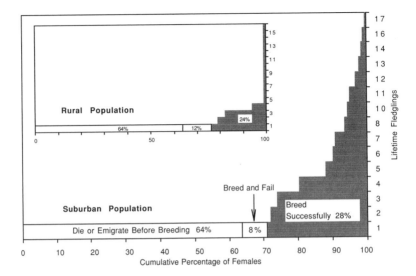

Figure 8.1. Lifetime fledglings produced by females in the two study populations, 1976–87 (n = 65 suburban, 15 rural). Note the remarkably skewed pattern wherein only about one-quarter of the females are productive, and just about one-sixth of these furnish more than half of all offspring. Proportions of successful versus unsuccessful females are no different in the two populations, and mean number of lifetime fledglings among successful breeders does not differ either (4.8 ± 2.9 suburban, 4.2 ± 4.1 rural; NS).

in the boreal owl, food scarcity was the likely reason for such switches, since the percentage of females changing cavities between years is negatively correlated with food supply the previous year, 1976–87 (r = −0.70, P = 0.01).[3] The percentage of switches is not related to population density (r = 0.25, NS), hence apparently not to competitive pressure.

Switches usually followed nest failures (chapter 5) and always followed divorces and mate deaths linked to unsuccessful nests. A confirmed divorce rate of six percent is within the 3–12 percent range represented by tawny and Ural owls.[4] For 27 long-lived suburban females, number of lifetime nest sites is correlated with number of mates (r = 0.88, P < 0.001), and year-to-year switches average 32.9 ± 27.4 percent over 1976–91 or somewhat higher than the 10–20 percent among tawny and Ural owls. Overall, just 44 percent of successful females returned to original nest cavities in their second year, mostly because of low yearling survival (chapter 9); but this fraction increased to 67 percent afterward with both suburban and rural study plots having statistically similar proportions of returnees in the two age categories.

Yearling females that nested or tried to and then vanished I call one-timers in order to compare their obviously limited lifetime productivity with that of other yearlings that became my group of long-lived breeders. The proportion of these survivors was about 17 percent higher in suburbia than in the countryside, an insignificant difference (chapter 9). In addition I noticed that a few females fledged more owlets than others with comparable lifespans and I postulated that production efficiency (fledglings/eggs) and lifespan contribute separately to lifetime reproduction. To me, the term production efficiency more accurately describes the fledglings/eggs relation than breeding success, which implies that total fitness (breeding offspring) is being measured.

Moreover, females ought to become better breeders as they gain experience with age, and large mass should be another advantage (chapters 4–6).[5] Of course their mates' abilities to furnish a safe nest site and sufficient food are other factors that might distinguish levels of lifetime reproduction. However, because large clutches and broods could be costly in terms of food requirements and susceptibility to predation, females might defer or limit reproduction in some manner. Most of these factors can be addressed in detail, but reproductive costs must be considered rather cursorily because of the nonexperimental nature of this study.

Since 85 percent of yearling males and 91 percent of the females try to nest, eastern screech owls generally do not defer breeding.[6] And because female reproductive effort does not differ between successive pairs of years over the four-year mean maximum lifespan, the owls must not limit their output (table 8.1). Thus I do not expect to find any reproductive costs, and none are indicated.[7] For example, the numbers of surviving versus disappearing first-year females per clutch or brood-size category are no different statistically. Also, there are no negative or significant relations between either parameter and longevity among all females. Similarly, reproductive costs are lacking in Finnish boreal owls.[8]

Age and Size

Between 1976 and 1987 yearlings comprised about half of all nesting females, and 52.6 ± 36.8 percent of them disappeared annually (see also chapter 9).[9] Values were similar at the two study sites (NS), but yearling performance was not. In suburbia most one-time females were unsuccessful (63% of 37) compared to survivors (20% of 20, P = 0.02), whereas on the rural plot the two types had similar degrees of

Table 8.1. Annual reproductive features of long-lived females in suburbia, 1976–90. Data are mean ± standard deviation (sample size in parentheses) and include nesting failures. In pair-wise comparisons of the same birds between years, means are no different statistically, but the increases in clutch size, number of fledglings, and fledglings/eggs over ages one through four are real (r_S = 1.0). Note also the apparent decline in reproductive output at age five despite continued high production efficiency (fledglings/eggs).

Features	Ages One (23)	Two (23)	Three (11)
Clutch size	3.8± 0.9	4.1± 0.8	4.2± 0.8
Number of fledglings	2.3± 1.5	2.6± 1.5	3.1± 1.6
Fledglings/eggs (%)	61.7±32.0	64.3±33.2	66.5±33.8
First egg date (March)	28.7±11.9	24.5± 5.3	21.5± 6.9
Incubation-brooding weight (g)	173.6±10.8	176.0± 8.5	180.0± 6.7

Features	Four (6)	Age Five (6)
Clutch size	4.5± 0.7	3.8± 0.9
Number of fledglings	3.2± 1.2	2.7± 1.4
Fledglings/eggs (%)	72.5±28.1	72.8±35.8
First egg date (March)	23.2± 5.4	24.6± 7.2
Incubation-brooding weight (g)	175.5± 6.3	175.0± 6.2

nest failure (56–61%) because of the high predation rate (chapters 5,6,9). Overall, though, it seems that a successful first-breeding attempt characterizes yearling females that become long-lived constituents of a screech owl population (P = 0.04).

Possibly some unsuccessful yearlings vanished because they emigrated, though none were ever recovered. Sixteen fruitless females even renested unsuccessfully and two tried and failed again in the next year before disappearing, but each follow-up was inside the same plot or its perimeter zone. Furthermore, dispersing female fledglings usually did not venture beyond the perimeter zones (chapter 6), and the great majority of immigrants were yearlings, not older birds that might have nested elsewhere (chapter 9). Even unsuccessful older owls remained on site where alternative nest cavities were available; so I believe that most one-timers died, leaving a tried and proven group of survivors.[10]

Nineteen one-time yearlings were successful, nonetheless, and I wonder about the degree of their accomplishments relative to 27 surviving yearlings that were successful too. In fact, 53 percent of those one-timers produced fledglings because they renested after failures compared to only 22 percent of the survivors that required a second attempt (P = 0.03). First-egg dates, clutch sizes, numbers of fledglings, and production efficiencies did not differ statistically. Why those particular one-timers disappeared is puzzling, especially when I consider that their nest sites were the same ones employed by survivors in other years (see below). Were they relatively unfit? Perhaps so, since they were smaller than the survivors (169.5 ± 10.6 g vs. 173.6 ± 9.5, P = 0.03).

Twenty-three of the suburban survivors and five rural counterparts furnished complete lifetime information with which to measure the possible influence of increasing age (experience). I illustrate only the suburban data set, since the rural birds were so few and heavily impacted by predation. Basically, three things are apparent (table 8.1). There is no year-to-year change in average productivity or in first-egg date and weight as supporting features, although productivity tends to increase through age four, and reproductive output declines in the fifth year without loss of efficiency. The lack of annual change also typifies female boreal and Ural owls, both of which display trends toward better breeding performance with age, as do most other birds.[11]

Aging screech owls might not produce larger clutches on average, because of flux in their food supplies (chapter 5), but they ought to hatch more eggs with increasing experience. Yet they do not. Mean egg mortality per nest actually increases from an average of 0.8 ± 0.9 to 1.0 ± 1.2 concomitant with the increase in mean clutch size over ages one to four (r_s = 1.0), although year-to-year differences are not significant (P > 0.5, NS). Instead, the added experience must allow older females to mitigate chick mortality, which drops from 0.4 ± 0.6 deaths per nest in the first year to 0.1 ± 0.3 at age four, coincident with the increasing mean number of fledglings (r_s = −1.0, cf. table 8.1). Again, however, annual differences are insignificant.

Improved chick rearing increases production efficiency, so I question whether efficiency accounts for more owlets aside from age. Apparently it does, for the two features are uncorrelated (r = 0.18, NS), with efficiency explaining 26 percent (P < 0.001) of the variation in lifetime fledglings beyond the 55 percent (P < 0.001) attributable to lifespan in a multiple stepwise regression (body mass and mean first-egg date explain nothing; $r^2 <$ o.o6, NS). In fact, just 13 of the long-lived suburban females fledged 53 percent of all the population's owlets from only 40 percent of its eggs. Not only were they more efficient than all other females (78% versus 46%; P = o.oo8), but they exceeded the 14 other long-lived individuals in this regard (52%, P = o.o5).

Despite the likely advantage of experience within increasing age, reproductive output declines soon after mean maximum longevity, and similar senescence is known in other birds, including perhaps the boreal and Ural owls.[11] My present subjects laid somewhat fewer eggs and fledged fewer owlets by age five but, unlike those of an earlier cross-sectional assessment, did not exhibit a simultaneous downturn in production efficiency (table 8.1).[12] Likewise, female Eurasian sparrowhawks but not Ural owls begin an absolute decline in egg output before their production efficiency drops, suggesting that physical senility may impair egg-laying, while experience permits the raising of proportionately more offspring.[13]

Age-related productivity is the rule among birds, regardless of the variety of environments they represent, and is no different in rural and suburban screech owls.[14] My females fledged additional owlets the longer they lived at an average rate of o.3 more per year. This is best illustrated by 12 suburban cohorts with complete life histories but also shows something surprising (figure 8.2). Population density in the year of hatching appears to have such a negative impact on a cohort's lifespan (r^2 = o.74, P < o.oo1) and hence its lifetime production (r^2 = o.29, P = o.o8), that cohorts from years with above-median densities have significantly fewer lifetime fledglings than do those from low-density years (figure 8.2).

On the other hand, population density during recruitment into the breeding population, the year after hatching, has no effect on lifespan or lifetime owlets (r < o.39, NS). Neither does food supply per se (r < o.21, NS), although the average incubation-brooding weight of female cohorts hatched at below-median densities exceeds the average of other cohorts (177.8 ± 3.8 g versus 169.5 ± 6.1 g, P = o.o5). Since all fledglings from low-density years were heavier (chapter 6), the females from those years probably had a weight advantage at a time when there was less competition for food during the nesting and fledgling-dispersal periods.

Earlier I found that large mass increased annual egg and fledgling numbers and suggested that it influenced lifetime reproduction as well (chapters 5, 6).[14] Now it is apparent that body mass does not add to my explanation of lifetime fledglings beyond that already explained by age and production efficiency. Instead, large mass may increase fitness

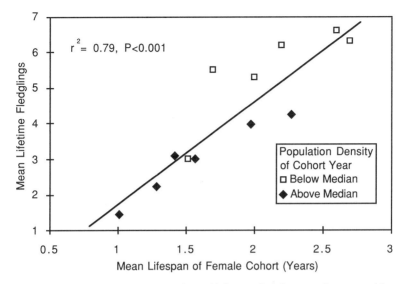

Figure 8.2.   Average number of lifetime fledglings as determined by average lifespan of 12 female cohorts in suburbia, 1975–86 (only owls no longer present by 1991 are depicted). Cohorts hatched in years of low density produced more fledglings per female than those hatched in high-density years (5.5 ± 1.3 versus 3.0 ± 1.0, P = 0.01).

by improving survival, for example during cold winters (chapter 4), and thus promote longevity with its consequent increases in experience and lifetime reproduction.[15] But mass and longevity are uncorrelated (chapter 4), so large mass must be most advantageous to survival in the first year as suggested earlier.

Among those females that do survive their first nesting year, I wonder if some are standouts for any reason. To find out I can compare reproductive parameters of the 27 suburban birds in successive pairs of years one through four with two-way analyses of variance and correlations. The ANOVAs confirm insignificant distinctions between years; but beginning with the year two versus three comparison, all attributes except clutch size differ significantly among the females (P < 0.05). In other words, after the birds have passed their yearling "test," individual performances are apparent, and some females may be better quality (better adapted) than others (e.g., compare 46039 with 87385 in appendix VIII).

Not surprisingly, then, correlations between attributes in the first versus second breeding years are insignificant (R < 0.25, NS), whereas all except those involving clutch size are positive and significant or nearly so thereafter ($r < 0.55$, $P < 0.07$). The yearling experience must be a major learning effort for survivors, as well as a "weeding out" of one-timers; and clutch size must be so influenced by environmental flux that learning cannot affect it greatly, at least not by comparison with effects on hatching and rearing owlets. But yearlings that survive that "gauntlet year" are surely consistent in addition to being individually distinctive performers.

Nest Sites and Mates

Since females select nesting cavities advertised by their mates and may switch sites, it seems likely that both their breeding place and provider influence lifetime productivity. I already know that especially productive sites are near houses or amidst sparse shrubbery (chapter 2) and that male weight positively determines female breeding condition (chapter 4). Yet mates and sites are potentially independent factors, because females choose among alternative sites offered by the same male. I might judge site quality by frequency of use, but most-used sites are not the most productive in suburbia ($r_s = 0.25$, NS) or the countryside ($r_s = -0.43$, NS; n = 20 each). Furthermore, successful females reuse certain sites year after year, so "good" ones may be confused with "good" females.

In trying to understand the influence of site versus owl on egg and fledgling production, I did repeatability analyses of 12 suburban females that used only one nest box in their lifetimes, 5 others that nested in two or more, and 13 suburban sites employed by two or more females over at least three generations (12 years). Results indicate the greater importance of owl quality. Repeatabilities of clutch size among females are 0.28 (same site) and 0.37 (different site), of fledglings 0.36 (same) and 0.20 (different). Conversely, the among-sites values are 0.02 for clutch size and 0.01 for fledglings; hence the contrast is quite similar to that given by repeatabilities of egg-laying date in the Eurasian sparrowhawk.[16]

Originally I suspected that surviving yearlings chose different (better?) nest cavities than one-timers, because that choice could promote their survival and, through repeated use, more lifetime fledglings. But they did not. At 13 suburban nest boxes employed over three generations, I recorded 1.8 ± 0.9 long-lived and 1.6 ± 0.9 one-time females (NS), and there were 1.3 females of each type in five similarly old rural boxes (natural cavities on each study plot were simply alternate sites for the same owls). This too suggests that female quality is at stake, although I do not discount the comparatively safe positions of certain boxes.

When I regress total fledglings from each of the 13 suburban sites on numbers of their long-lived versus one-time users, only long-lived females explain interbox differences ($r^2 = 0.52$, P = 0.001). And when I regress lifetime fledglings of the 27 suburban survivors on number of nests in their initial cavity, other nests, and number of mates, only the first site is explanatory ($r^2 = 0.55$, P < 0.001), undoubtedly because it is linked to longevity ($r = 0.53$, P = 0.01), the chief determinant of lifetime production. Simply put, long-lived females normally are successful in their first breeding experience, continue to use their first nest cavity, contribute the most to the site's output of owlets, and may be most productive with or without new mates.

Because an original female at an original nest site seems to be maximally productive, I want to know the ages of breedings pairs. Do females select same-age males as boreal owls and other birds do?[17] My sample of 19 males with complete life stories is meager yet suggests that mating is even more assortative than in boreal owls, as 68.4 percent had same-age mates compared to only 45.2 percent of 31 boreals (P = 0.09). Surely this is because my birds are residents and most (76%) form life-long pair bonds begun as yearlings. Female boreals are nomadic and form annual pairs. I have no record of a female screech owl choosing a younger male, also the rarest case among boreal owls and probably because younger males are poorer providers of food and nest cavities.

Five males of 64 in suburbia and none of 14 on the rural plot were polygynous (6.4% versus 11.7% of 529 male boreal owls, NS).[18] One supported two females with nestlings concurrently in nearest-neighbor sites, while a second fed one incubating female plus another with fledglings that also came from the closest alternate cavity. The other three males each supported two mates sequentially in the same nest box. Surprisingly, perhaps, the mean fledgling output of these five (3.2 ± 1.3) was no different from that of nine monogamous contemporaries (2.9 ± 1.6, NS), while the secondary mates only tended to be less successful than primary females (1.0 ± 1.5 versus 2.3 ± 1.4 fledglings, NS).

Again, residency and lifetime pairing by contrast to the temporariness of boreal owl pairs helps to explain the difference in frequency of polygny. Similarities are in the large populations of both species and ample foods that promote intersexual contact and the provisioning of secondary mates, respectively (all five of my cases occurred in years of above-average population densities and food supplies).[19] However, the lifetime productivity of male boreal owls is augmented by polygny, whereas that does not appear true of eastern screech owls. In the females of both species, productivity seems less influenced than for males but might be adversely affected.

Older or otherwise efficient males could attempt polygny in supportive environments, while younger and/or poorer hunters might not; so I seek answers among my few long-lived males with comparable life stories. Four suburban individuals were monogamous and contemporaneous during their first four years. Each had a polyterritory that housed both one-time and long-lived mates. Thus, special male prowess aside from age-related experience might appear in a two-way ANOVA of their four-year totals of fledglings by contrast to those of their mates. Yet, individuals of both sexes are distinguishable (P < 0.01), and the significant interaction between them (P = 0.03) suggests that male quality enhances female productivity synergistically.

Finally, home range or other habitat differences like those between Woodway and Harris Creek, open and wooded yards, or ridges and ravines might influence lifetime reproduction. If so, settlement in the "right place" after natal dispersal should be important. But the survival versus disappearance of 70 female yearlings in suburbia does not differ according to study sites or habitat; and, among the 27 long-lived suburban females, neither lifetime fledglings nor production efficiency does either (NS). I can only conclude that a few females and their mates are superior breeders (figure 8.1).

Recruitment and Inheritance

Of course the best estimate of a screech owl's fitness is its production of breeding offspring (population recruits) as they can perpetuate its genes. Therefore, I was excited to find 18 of 272 suburban fledglings plus 1 of 58 rural owlets nesting in suburbia or its perimeter zone, 1977–91. Recovery rates were no different considering environmental origin but significantly higher overall (5.7%) than rates for boreal owls (1.2%), tawnines (2.0%), and eastern screech owls in Ohio (0.8%; P < 0.001).[20] Sixteen recruits afford an opportunity to look for special features among them and their parents by contrast to siblings, other cohort members, and breeding adults.

Seven males and nine females comprise the sample, substantiating the population's 50:50 sex ratio I had predicted from fledgling body weights (chapter 6). All came from the annual first nests of ten long-lived females (nine suburban), one of whom produced four, another three, a third two, and the rest one recruit apiece (e.g., appendix VIII). This strongly skewed distribution (1.43) is further evidence that only

Posed broods of long-lived suburban females: (*top*) fledglings of one that produced three to four offspring per year over four years and two population recruits; (*bottom*) nestlings of another that produced five to six owlets per year over five years but no recruits.

a few females (12.5% of 80) are involved in maintaining the suburban population. At ages one through three the ten females collectively furnished five, six, and five recruits, respectively, hence breeding experience does not seem to matter. Also, number of recruits was unrelated to number of lifetime fledglings among the nine or all 27 long-lived suburban females (r < 0.37, NS).[21]

Table 8.2. Lifetime reproductive features of all recruit-producing and other long-lived females in suburbia, 1975–90. Data are mean ± standard deviation (sample size in parentheses). The two groups are distinct (MANOVA, P = 0.01). Note that recruit-producers are larger and nest earlier with greater production efficiency (fledglings/eggs).

Feature	Recruit-producers (9)	Others (18)	P
Lifespan (years)	4.2 ± 2.3	3.5 ± 2.0	NS
Incubation-brooding weight (g)	177.2 ± 7.8	171.1 ± 5.8	= 0.06
First-egg date (March)	20.4 ± 5.2	27.5 ± 7.9	= 0.01
Lifetime eggs	12.2 ± 3.8	11.6 ± 5.1	NS
Fledglings	8.3 ± 3.9	6.5 ± 4.4	NS
Fledglings/eggs (%)	74.2 ± 12.2	53.0 ± 25.4	= 0.04

The nine potentially influential females in suburbia used their initial nest sites, relative to alternatives, as faithfully as the 18 other survivors did (80% of nests vs. 72%; NS). And they were similar in other aspects of lifetime reproduction but with three important exceptions. Recruit-makers tended to be heavier, began nesting a week earlier, and were 21 percent more efficient at fledging owlets (table 8.2). In regressing recruit-making or not among the 27 females on the six reproductive attributes of table 8.2, early nesting (r^2 = 0.26, P = 0.01), then efficiency (r^2 added = 0.12, P = 0.02), and finally body mass (r^2 added = 0.09, P = 0.05) are significant positive factors. Among birds generally, recruits originate in early nests, although boreal owls may be an exception.[22]

My subjects are interesting in that early nesting does not influence fledgling output, which is uncorrelated with recruitment, and there is no apparent relation between early nests and fledgling-dispersal distance (chapter 6). But I remember another perhaps critical link to first nests of the season by contrast to replacement nests. First nests contain larger clutches with larger eggs from heavier females (chapter 5); in turn, heavier chicks hatch and they grow faster and fledge heavier (chapter 6). Thus, owlets from the beginning of the nesting season may have a size as well as time advantage for survival and subsequent recruitment.

Surely recruits come from early nests, because they permit early fledging and hence offer more time to learn self-sufficiency before dis-

Table 8.3. Features of nestlings from suburbia recruited into that breeding population by comparison with others in their cohorts aside from their siblings, 1977–90. Data are mean ± standard deviation and (sample size). Recruits are statistically like their siblings but distinct from other cohort members (MANOVA, P < 0.001).

Features	Recruits	Other Cohort Members	P[a]
Hatching order	2.3 ± 1.0 (13)	2.1 ± 1.1 (23)	NS
Brood size	3.1 ± 0.7 (14)	2.9 ± 1.2 (31)	NS
Growth rate (g/day)	4.5 ± 0.3 (12)	4.3 ± 0.6 (30)	= 0.07
Fledging weight (g)	125.5 ± 7.9 (14)	120.6 ± 9.7 (28)	= 0.05
Fledging date (May)	14.2 ± 5.5 (14)	28.6 ± 6.6 (28)	= 0.01

a. Between-group values from two-way ANOVAs in which all among-years values are insignificant except for brood size (P = 0.002).

persal, together with the potential for early settlement on a familiar home range before the rigors of winter.[23] That their mothers nest more efficiently suggests better nutrition leading to better parental care. Do recruits benefit by growing faster and heavier as nestlings? Yes indeed, but they do not differ from their siblings in these respects. Rather, there are major distinctions between recruits and nonsibling members of their cohorts (table 8.3). Both groups represent the same hatching order in same-size broods but recruits tend to grow faster and fledge two weeks earlier with a five-gram advantage in weight (table 8.3).[24]

Because low population density in the hatching year promotes female longevity, perhaps it or other environmental factors influence recruitment. So I regressed recruits from each of the ten recruit-producing years on annual density, food, precipitation, and average temperature; and found that population density ($r^2 = 0.50$, P = 0.02) plus food supply (r^2 added = 0.41, P = 0.08) explain almost everything. Density is a negative influent, while food is positive and independent of density (r = 0.12, NS). Neither factor nor any weather parameter explains differences among years in which recruits first nest. Thus, favorable conditions in the fledgling year, not the first breeding year, are most important to recruitment in a density-dependent fashion.

Owlets hatched in a sparse population amidst plentiful food are the most likely recruits, I believe, because they are larger at fledging (chapter 6), less likely to be driven away, and better able to find vacant cavities plus sufficient food. Since dispersal distance is directly related to population density, competitive pressure must be influential (chapter

6). While I also observed that dispersal does not relate to size of the food supply (chapter 6), density and food are unrelated, hence must operate independently on recruitment (chapter 9). Vacant roost and nest sites may induce young screech owls to stay near their natal areas, while abundant food insures their survival as it apparently does for fledgling boreal owls.[25]

Yet the environment may not "ease up" after the first year, for variation among the long-lived suburban females declines with increasing age, implying the existence of stabilizing selection (table 8.1). Aside from first-egg date, coefficients of variation of each reproductive feature drop dramatically in the four years before apparent senescence, and body mass continues to stabilize despite some reproductive flux at age five (b > −42.2, P < 0.03). Since they represent the first lifetime study in a relatively stable suburban setting, I am not surprised that female eastern screech owls are less variable than the females of eight other birds including the Eurasian sparrowhawk.[26]

Is it really feasible to attribute the decline in variation to natural selection, or is it an artifact of a progressively smaller sample of older owls due to old-age mortality? How much of each reproductive feature might be inherited and thus liable to selection? I can predict amounts with repeatability analyses which compare variation among females to that within each of them during their lifetimes. And I can judge the results against the heritabilities of my female recruits, derived by regressing their characteristics on those of their mothers. Both techniques provide estimates of the upper limits of inheritance but with a number of provisos about maternal and common environmental effects.[27]

Body mass, based on incubation-brooding weight, has significantly high repeatability (69% maximum), nearly matched by its heritability, although all heritability values are insignificant because of small sample sizes (table 8.4). Earlier I estimated that 40 percent of female nesting weight results from the feeding efforts of mates (chapter 4), and this is close enough to the present 31 percent of nonheritable variation, the obverse of repeatability, to underscore the importance of inherited body size. I can vouch for the fact that certain long-lived females are identifiably smaller or larger than others in a consistent manner year after year.

The four other reproductive features also have significant though smaller repeatability values and quite similar heritabilities except for production efficiency (table 8.4). As much as 26–37 percent of their variation may be inherited, similar to the extent of potential inheritance based on repeatability analyses in various nonraptorial birds. For

Table 8.4. Estimates of the maximum inheritance of reproductive features in 27 long-lived suburban females, 1976–90. To calculate repeatability (among females' variance/among + within females' variance), two to four consecutive years of data per individual are used. For heritability (twice the regression coefficient ± 2 standard errors of daughters' on mothers' values), five to eight pairs of first-year data are employed. Nest failures due to extraneous factors are not included in either analysis.

Feature	Repeatability	(P)	Heritability (all NS)
Incubation-brooding weight	0.69	($<$ 0.001)	0.68 ± 0.76
Fledglings	0.37	($=$ 0.002)	0.38 ± 1.51
Clutch size	0.35	($=$ 0.003)	0.30 ± 1.36
Efficiency (fledglings/eggs)	0.34	($=$ 0.01)	0.19 ± 0.78
First-egg date	0.26	($=$ 0.04)	0.22 ± 0.65

example, laying date and clutch size repeatabilities among female great tits, song sparrows, and snow geese are 23–49 percent. Conversely, other female raptors have lower repeatabilities of these two features. Values are 0–23 percent among boreal, tawny, and Ural owls, plus Eurasian sparrowhawks and kestrels, and are insignificant for the boreal owl.[28]

Of the five heritable attributes of my subjects, only production efficiency is suspect in that its heritability estimate does not closely approximate its repeatability (table 8.4). Since this character is important to recruit-making, if it is inherited, daughters ought to resemble their mothers (n = 6 pairs) rather than contemporaneous female immigrants (n = 11). When I make the three-group comparison with data from just the successful yearling nests, in an attempt to control environment and age as confounding variables, a difference exists. Mothers and daughters are alike statistically (P > 0.05) and each is more efficient than immigrants (76% and 80%, respectively, vs. 62%; P < 0.06).

Fourteen population recruits have incomplete life histories as of 1991, and two others bred but once, so it will take even more time to validate inheritance and the concept of quality lineages. Yet the evidence is compelling in my opinion. Production efficiency is a common thread, the only major determinant of both lifetime fledglings and recruits, although large mass, reflecting large size (skeletal proportions), is implicated in overall fitness. That recruitment is not a positive function of fledgling output is worth reiterating, because such a relationship could mean that recruitment is probabilistic—the more fledglings produced, the more likely one will become a breeding member of the population merely by chance.

Instead, I predict that recruitment involves selectively advantageous inherited features. Mothers that are successful breeders in being larger and more efficient, only partly because they are better fed by more efficient mates, nest earlier and raise more larger offspring per clutch of eggs; so owlets that fledge earlier at a larger size are more likely to survive their independence and find food and housing locally. In addition, a low-density population is very important in fostering survival and the local settling of owlets through reduced intraspecific competition for resources and in promoting the genes of recruits, which are proportionately more influential among fewer nesting individuals.

Is it possible that population cycles are advantageous genetically? Both the rural and suburban owls seem to have the same periodicity (chapter 9), and suburban adults apparently drive their offspring farther away during peak densities while allowing them to settle locally at population lows (chapter 6). Hence, genes advantageous in the local environment are fostered when the population "needs" them for recovery but dispersed when the recruitment of offspring is not so necessary, and inbreeding may be avoided in cyclic fashion.[29]

The Essentials

About half of all nesting females each year are yearlings, and half of them disappear from the population after their first session. These owls are smaller and usually unsuccessful, compared to the larger surviving yearlings that are successful, especially in suburbia; hence more body mass and a successful first nest are likely requisites for continuing in the population. The surviving females show no evidence of reproductive costs, only potential benefits in the form of more fledglings the longer they live in both suburban and rural environments. Their productivity increases through age four, primarily because they seem to gain experience in raising chicks, but declines with apparent senescence at age five.

Low population density in the year of hatching is associated with longevity and thus with increased lifetime reproduction. Also, the average body mass of female cohorts from low-density years is greater, but size does not promote number of lifetime fledglings over the combined influences of age (experience) and production efficiency (fledglings/ eggs). Body mass is uncorrelated with longevity, so it seems that large size is beneficial to survival primarily in the first year of life. Thereafter, long-lived females are distinguished by differences in reproductive output. Only about a quarter of all suburban and rural females nest successfully, and just one-sixth of these produce over half of all fledged owlets.

Long-lived breeders use the same nest sites as one-timers but more successfully and continue using initial sites as long as they are productive. Nest setting seems to make little difference in suburbia. Site usage and productivity are not correlated in either environment. Site switches are made mostly after failures, mate loss, and divorce, which are rare in suburbia, but failures are more common in the countryside because of the high predation rate. Life-long, monogamous, same-age pairs are the rule; but sequential and concurrent polygny occurs when food is plentiful and the nesting density is high, though it does not boost male productivity. As with certain "quality" females, particular males are more productive and mate with, indeed must enhance the productivity of, standout females (most aspects of lifetime reproduction in males are unknown, as few males were recaptured sufficiently often).

Six percent of the suburban and rural fledglings, both males and females, were recovered as population recruits. All originated from the yearly first nests of ten long-lived females, constituting only eight percent of all those that bred, and just three of these birds produced over half the recruits. Number of lifetime fledglings does not determine number of recruits per female, but a tendency to nest early with high efficiency and to be large are significant causative factors. Thus, recruits get an early start with more time to learn self-sufficiency, and they also fledge at a larger size than other cohort members except siblings, possibly because their mothers raise chicks more efficiently.

Recruitment is greatest in years of low population density and plentiful food. The recruits represent certain highly productive lineages that could restore population size most rapidly; whereas at high densities, offspring are dispersed more widely, reducing the potential of inbreeding. Recruits may inherit as much as 22–69 percent of each reproductive feature, with body mass as the most strongly determined trait and the one with the most general adaptive significance. All attributes of suburban females except first-egg date become less variable over time, suggesting that stabilizing selection operates in the relatively stable suburban setting.

9   Population Structure and Flux
Density Dependence in Action

The full moon was mysterious around the Halloweens of decades past and remains so today, especially on Indian summer evenings followed by fitful sleep, ambulance sirens, and unhappy headlines the next morning. Mice are hard to trap during full moons; and the owls seem skittish, flying quickly through the yard and out of sight, unlike their patient vigils on the perimeters of dark nights. They too may have a harder time trapping mice. Certainly they are more vocal, more apprehensive in this moon of falling leaves. I think we are all the moon's special children.

Habitats, foods, eggs, chicks, songs, and other features of life history are instruments in understanding the suburban and rural populations as symphonic wholes. Now the single lifetimes furnish perspectives wherein individuals are replaced by the collective effort. The survival and hence reproductive performance of age classes and cohorts becomes important. Peculiar factors like the heavy rural predation may be even more critical. And why were 1980–83 such poor years in suburbia? Are they part of a population cycle? Linked to what? Population productivity, the total fledgling output divided by total eggs laid, may be an important annual barometer.

Age Classes and Survival

The suburban and rural populations and even Harris Creek had similar age-class structures during their nine-year period of concurrent study (table 9.1). Yearlings comprised around half the breeding females but were less prominent in suburban Woodway; and, once more, Harris Creek was intermediate. Older females became progressively less common with increasing age in the expected curvilinear fashion, living 4.1 ± 2.8 (median 2.6) years in 1976–91. Nevertheless, the typical female survived only one year, including a single breeding season, though able to live at least 14 years, 2 months.[1]

Survival was significantly higher over ages one to five in suburbia, and the rural owls were much like ones in northern Ohio (figure 9.1). In those first five years, age-specific survival averaged 53.2 (rural) and 62.0 (suburban) percent, about like some populations of tawny (57.7–81.7%) and common barn (63.0–73.2%) owls but lower than great-

Table 9.1. Age-class structure of breeding females in three study
plots, 1979–87, and the entire regional population, 1976–91. The
proportions of yearlings and older females are similar statistically,
but note the increasing percentage of older individuals with suburban age and growth (Harris Creek is younger than Woodway).

Age (years)	Rural	Harris Creek	Woodway	Region (%)
1	9	7	15	40 (51.9)
2	2	1	9	13 (16.9)
3	1	0	4	9 (11.7)
4	1	2	2	4 (5.2)
5	1	1	0	4 (5.2)
6		0	1	0
7		1	1	3 (3.9)
8–14				4 (5.2)
Yearlings (%)	64.3	58.3	46.9	51.9
Older (%)	35.7	41.7	53.1	48.1

gray (84.1%) and Ural owls (89.6%).[2] I have no record of a rural female older than five and regrettably little data on suburban birds older
than that, as they make up only nine percent of the regional population
(table 9.1). For life-table construction, therefore, old-age values were
extrapolated and fledgling survival estimated as equal to average adult
mortality at ages one to five, in the stable suburban population (appendix IX).

While I am hesitant in presenting life tables because of the estimates,
they do provide additional population features suggesting that suburbia is more hospitable than the countryside (appendix IX). For instance, the fraction of surviving females increases steadily up to at least
age five in suburbia but only to age three in the country. Then the rural
output of fledglings drops 37 percent, while fledgling production continues to increase through age four in suburbia, after which it drops
only 16 percent (see also chapter 8). The net result of such differences
plus the lack of age classes older than five is a rural population that
did not maintain itself, while its suburban counterpart held steady in
1976–87.

Mortality was impossible to record accurately due to observability
biases but worth reporting, because the hierarchy of leading suburban
factors resembled those of two other areas, including one a half-
century removed in time.[3] Of 107 freshly killed individuals, most
(67.3%) were owlets between fledging and their first breeding season,

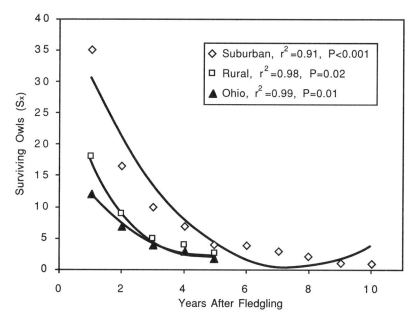

Figure 9.1. Survivorship curves for females in the suburban and rural populations, constructed from appendix IX data on all age classes in 1976–91, plus a curve for rural eastern screech owls in northern Ohio (data from Ricklefs, 1983). Over ages one to five the three survivorships are distinct (P = 0.01). Note that suburban owls survive better than either population of rural owls (P < 0.04).

and 55.1 percent of all were vehicle casualties. Most owlets were dispatched by cars in July–December (71.8% of 39), relative to the following six months when they are more experienced; whereas only 35.0 percent of 20 adults were killed on roads in July–December (P = 0.01).[4] Poisoning was the second greatest hazard (19.6%), then shooting and trapping (8.4%) and window-wall collisions (6.5%). Each year during 1976–91, as many breeders succumbed to cultural factors (1.6 ± 2.1) as were presumed dead or known to have died from natural causes (1.2 + 0.9, NS).

In suburbia the annual survival of all breeding females averaged 59.1 ± 15.8 percent from 1976 to 1987 and was increased by abundant winter foods ($r^2 = 0.24$, P = 0.05) and perhaps a sparse population (r^2 added = 0.11, P = 0.10). Winter temperature and precipitation had no influence by comparison (r^2 added < 0.05, NS; MSR). A similar but stronger density-dependent relation existed on the rural plot (r =

-0.58, $P = 0.05$), where the annual survival of all nesting females averaged 54.8 ± 31.6 percent concurrently (NS). Obviously, both populations relied heavily on immigrants to augment their numbers, as did a population of Eurasian sparrowhawks with similar survival values.[5]

The newcomers were almost all yearlings (91.2% of 80). Those hatched outside the study plots outnumbered local recruits 4.3 to 1.0 in suburbia, 1976–91, and comprised all first-year breeders in the country. Presumably because of density constraints, the suburban yearlings arrived in largest number when older females disappeared ($r^2 = 0.30$, $P = 0.03$), whereas that was not so on the sparsely populated rural plot ($r = 0.18$, NS). Another possible factor, but only in suburbia, was yearling availability as measured by greater productivity of that population the previous year (r^2 added $= 0.19$, $P = 0.10$; MSR).

Population density was bolstered by yearlings on both plots ($r > 0.61$, $P < 0.02$) and to a similar extent by surviving females on the rural plot ($r = 0.59$, $P = 0.04$), but the latter was not true in suburbia with its greater number of older females and hence stability ($r = 0.35$, NS). These suburban survivors may exclude immigrant yearlings, as population density increases to carrying capacity; for the yearlings-to-older-females ratio falls curvilinearly from 2.7:1.0 in the presence of only five older females to a stable 0.6:1.0 among ten older birds in 1976–91 ($2° r^2 = 0.76$, $P < 0.001$). The latter ratio equates with 16 females, six yearlings and ten older, in the average suburban population (see below).

Productivity

Since yearlings are inexperienced hence inefficient breeders, as among other species of birds (chapter 8), both study populations may decline when yearlings outnumber older females. This definitely obtains in suburbia, as the yearlings-to-older-females ratio in one year is inversely correlated with density the next year ($r = -0.55$, $P = 0.03$), partly because it is also inversely related to productivity ($r = -0.57$, $P = 0.02$). But there are no similar relationships in the rural population ($r < 0.16$, NS), where extreme predation adversely impacts breeders regardless of age (47% loss of 17 yearling nests contemporaneous with a 40% loss of 10 older-owl nests in 1976–87, NS).

As older suburban owls die, yearlings take their place and reproduction suffers; so the population declines until those yearlings that survive restore it by breeding more successfully as older individuals. But what causes the lower breeding success of yearling females? Besides inexperience it must be their smaller body mass hence poorer reproductive condition compared to older females, since small mass correlates with more weight, egg, and chick loss (chapters 4, 8). Behind all this is male provisioning, of course, and the yearling males of boreal owls make a bigger difference in breeding outcome than yearling females.[6] Among my screech owls, however, both sexes are about equally important, although males account for only 31–40 percent of female body mass (chapters 4, 8). Something else is necessary.

Female quality must be that critical factor, as the first-year productivity of ten suburban cohorts is strongly tied to low population density and more available food in the natal year ($r = -0.78$ and 0.65, respectively, $P < 0.04$) rather than in that first breeding year ($r < 0.25$, NS). Moreover, low natal-year density promotes longevity and hence lifetime productivity (chapter 8). The ten cohorts differ in egg and fledgling output plus percentage of successful nests as yearlings ($P < 0.04$). Those entering suburbia in 1980–83 were from a peak-density period, which helps to explain their poor reproduction in those years (chapters 5, 6).

If some cohorts are ill-prepared for full breeding potential, owing to a high demand for food (high density) but low supply during their natal development, what about the others? In fact, any yearling contribution to annual production, 1976–91, is proportionately small ($r^2 = 0.21$, $P = 0.005$). In only five of 16 years did the yearling output exceed that of any single older cohort. Among years it averaged 1.7 ± 0.8 owlets per female which is slightly less than the 1.8 needed for replacement of the pair based on age-specific survival.[7] Older cohorts were more productive at 2.4 ± 1.0 fledglings apiece ($P = 0.06$), which offset yearling inefficiency generally but was not compensatory on a year-to-year basis ($r_s = -0.17$, NS).[8]

Because yearlings tend to nest later than established females (chapter 8), their poor showing may be linked to some late-season factor in addition to nutrition. Yet I note that productivity does not decline over the whole nesting period as in other birds including the boreal and Ural owls.[9] First-nest output drops to be sure, but this trend is reversed in mid-April by replacement nesting, 75 percent of which is attributable to yearlings (table 9.2). Among all known causes of partial or complete nest failure, egg desertion tracks this curvilinear pattern most closely on both study plots ($3° r > 0.92$, $P < 0.001$), whereas predation and the sum of partial-loss factors like fratricide (siblicide) are less coincident ($3° r < 0.63$, $P > 0.09$). These two decline linearly after nesting peaks in late March ($r > 0.71$, $P < 0.10$).

Now I understand why screech owls lay replacement clutches, although the fledglings are disadvantaged by small size (chapter 6). Even if the time necessary to raise offspring is short, energy is limited by the

Table 9.2. Seasonality of reproductive output in the combined suburban and rural populations, 1976–87. Data are mean ± one standard deviation and percentages for all nests in the region, since the
two populations and six time periods are alike statistically (two-way
ANOVA). Note the decline in production through the first week of
April, the first-nest period, followed by increases during renesting.

1st Egg Dates	(n)	Fledglings/ Eggs (%)	Fledglings/ Pair	Succesful Nests (%)	Renests (%)
March 6–14	(12)	53.9 ± 32.4	1.9 ± 1.4	91.7	0
15–21	(27)	40.9 ± 39.3	1.7 ± 1.7	70.4	0
22–31	(53)	38.5 ± 42.1	1.6 ± 1.7	50.9	0
April 1–7	(15)	30.2 ± 42.9	1.2 ± 1.5	46.7	11
8–21	(19)	39.6 ± 41.1	1.3 ± 1.4	48.4	95
22–June 6	(15)	43.8 ± 44.9	1.9 ± 1.7	60.0	100

annual molt, and clutch size is reduced accordingly (chapters 4, 5), the
fledgling-benefit per egg-cost can equal or exceed that of first nests,
because predation and partial losses are reduced. When a pair loses
eggs after mid-March, it can relay in 1.5–3.5 weeks (partial-whole
clutch replacement) with nearly the same or greater production efficiency. This obtains for all except those few pairs that fail before mid-
March, when productivity is at a seasonal peak (table 9.2).

The seasonal changes notwithstanding, productivity increases with
increasing clutch size but only to four eggs. Among two- to six-egg
clutches, respective fledgling percentages are 25.0 (n = 20 suburban
plus rural eggs), 39.6 (192), 59.7 (324), 60.0 (120), and 61.1 (36);
the calculated asymptote is 60.3 percent.[10] Larger clutches would be
advantageous, if number of fledglings determined a breeder's chances
of passing on its genes; but that is not the case among my subjects
(chapter 8). While productivity remains at the same level for five- and
six-egg clutches, more offspring means smaller ones with less chance
of survival and thus wasted reproductive effort. Yet there is no apparent cost to future reproduction, perhaps because provisioning (cost) is
not adjusted to brood size (chapter 6).

Regardless of the asymptotic relationship, fledglings are only indirect indicators of fitness, as they are not necessarily indicative of breeding descendents. Recruits/eggs (per clutch size) is a quotient more appropriate to determining the adaptive significance of clutch-size
productivity. Four-egg clutches ought to provide proportionately more

recruits because of their maximum productivity when gauged against the lower outputs of smaller clutches and lower survival probability of owlets from larger clutches. That, in fact, is true. While recruits came from successful clutches of three (n = 2), four (14), five (2), and six (1), which totaled 69, 180, 75 and 24 eggs, four-egg clutches furnished 73.7 percent of them from only 51.7 percent of all eggs (P = 0.05).

That five- and six-egg clutches provide no insurance against partial egg or chick mortality is shown by ten long-lived females who averaged more than four eggs per clutch in their lifetimes but lost more eggs plus chicks than 16 others averaging fewer (1.9 ± 0.9 versus 1.1 ± 0.9, P = 0.03). Although they lost more reproductive potential, therefore, they lived just as long (3.1 ± 1.1 versus 2.9 ± 0.9 years, NS). Evidently, clutches larger than four contain superfluous eggs—overshoots of the optimal four-egg clutch, resulting from early food-rich conditions—and are neutral in terms of natural selection.[11]

In 1976–87 suburban productivity was 15 percent higher than on the rural plot (50.5% vs. 35.5%, P =0.03), and the suburban owls improved to 67.3 percent in 1988–91. Although the 54.1 percent value for all nests in all years is low compared to values for ten other cavity-nesting owls (62.3 ± 15.2%), it is no different statistically. Furthermore, all 11 owls resemble 12 cavity-nesting songbirds (66.6 ± 13.9%, NS) rather than 17 open nesters (49.2 ± 12.5%, P = 0.01).[12] Productivity among them is more strongly determined by hatching efficiency (r^2 = 0.69, P < 0.001) than fledging efficiency (r^2 added = 0.29, P < 0.001, MSR).

Year by year throughout the comparative study, suburban and rural screech owls had similar reproductive inputs per nest but very different outcomes (table 9.3). Suburbia was simply more productive.[13] Its success was mostly a matter of lower egg loss (r^2 = 0.70, P < 0.001) and chick loss (r^2 added = 0.19, P = 0.006). Conversely, greater chick mortality (r^2 = 0.76, P < 0.001) together with smaller broods (r^2 added = 0.10, P = 0.003) determined the poor rural showing in a second multiple stepwise regression. It would seem that the rural owls had as much potential per prospective breeder, but predation just overwhelmed them. Why didn't replacement nesting compensate for the losses?

Over all years rural nests failed most often in the nestling period (79.2% of 24) rather than during incubation, the period of greatest suburban failure (92.7% of 41, P = 0.004). This contrast is critical, since eastern screech owls always replace lost clutches but only rarely lost chicks (chapters 5, 6). In essence, then, the rural owls had at most a 20.8 percent chance of recouping losses by renesting. Thus, although

Table 9.3. Annual reproductive features of all nesting attempts in the suburban and rural populations in 1976–87. Data are mean ± one standard deviation with paired comparisons. Note that the two populations have similar potential, but the rural owls are less successful.

Feature	Suburban	Rural	Wilcoxon P
Per nesting attempt			
Clutch	3.6 ± 0.4	3.2 ± 0.7	> 0.10
Brood	2.0 ± 0.1	1.5 ± 1.3	> 0.10
Fledglings	1.8 ± 0.5	1.0 ± 0.8	= 0.04
Summed among nests (%)			
Hatchlings/eggs	56.5 ± 11.6	40.3 ± 34.0	> 0.10
Fledglings/chicks	86.3 ± 10.2	52.7 ± 44.9	= 0.08
Fledglings/eggs	49.3 ± 13.6	28.3 ± 24.6	= 0.04
Successful nests	61.2 ± 12.0	31.1 ± 24.4	= 0.02

completely successful nests were slightly more prevalent on the rural plot than in suburbia, their productivity could not offset the lack of replacement nesting. As a result, the picture of nesting success and failures is very different in the two study populations (figure 9.2).

What difference to productivity did the various suburban environments make? To begin with, the three sizes of nest boxes made none.[14] Twenty-eight sites in Woodway, classified as wooded or open and ridge or ravine, did not differ significantly either (NS, two-way ANOVA), although wooded ravines had the lowest and open ridges the highest average productivity as expected (50.3% vs. 61.4%, see chapter 2). Also, a comparison of population productivity in 1979–87 substantiates Harris Creek's intermediate nature (fledglings/eggs = 41.6 ± 24.1%, cf. table 9.3), further supporting my hypothesis that the urbanization of eastern screech owls is linked to city age and growth (chapter 6).

Still another study was conducted after a suggestion that life near high-power electric lines might be hazardous to human health because of electromagnetic fields around the lines. If humans, why not screech owls? During 1976–91 fourteen Woodway boxes remained at their original positions 10–1,200 m from a high-power line, but there are no significant correlations between distance and productivity, percent use, or turnover rates among users (r_s < 0.26). Therefore, I am not concerned that five pairs of owls and I have lived 180 m from this power line for 12 years.

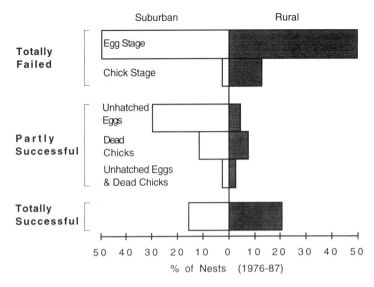

Figure 9.2. Nesting success and failure at different stages of the breeding cycle in the suburban and rural populations, 1976–87. Frequencies of failure, partial success, and total success differ (P = 0.005). In particular note fewer total failures involving chicks and the increased incidence of partial success in suburbia.

Finally, I want to look again at nesting-season food and weather, as they might have influenced annual productivity on both study plots in 1976–87. Although food supply affects clutches and hence brood sizes (chapters 5, 6), neither fledglings per egg nor fledglings per breeding pair are subject to it (r < 0.29, NS). Nor do maximum or minimum temperature exercise any "weight" (r < 0.36, NS). But heavy rainfall reduces the percentage of successful nests (r > −0.65, P < 0.01) because nests may flood, be usurped by shelter-seeking fox squirrels, or be deserted during incubation if male provisioning is impaired by rain (chapters 5, 6).[15]

Use of Space

During 1976–87 the suburban population numbered 12–20 (15.1 ± 2.6) nesting pairs at all box and natural-cavity sites, and 79–88 percent used the boxes. The mean through 1991 was 15.6 ± 2.4 pairs (nonnesting owls were not censused precisely so are not included in density figures). By contrast only two to six (3.1 ± 1.6) pairs nested on the rural plot, 69–80 percent in boxes. This suburban density is comparatively high as is year-to-year use of suburban nest boxes relative to tree cavities (P < 0.001), because all nest sites are comparatively scarce in suburbia (chapter 2). In the only other population study of a cavity-nesting owl, where box and natural-site use were investigated together, 33–75 percent of rural tawny owls nested in boxes.[16]

The population sizes suggest that, on average, each nesting pair of eastern screech owls had 17.9 ha of available space in suburbia compared to 87.1 ha in the rural environment. But, because green space amounts to only 25.9 percent of each suburban hectare (chapter 1), such space averaged only 4.6 ha per pair or just five percent of that available under the more natural rural circumstance. Thus, I am not surprised that screech owls are unconstrained by habitat area and can live in a culturally fragmented landscape—unlike so many native birds of the eastern deciduous forest.[17]

Nearest-neighbor analysis of used natural cavities plus nest boxes at each nesting density reveals that pairs were regularly dispersed over the suburban landscape (R = 1.4–1.7) but patchy in the countryside (R = 0.2–0.8).[18] Closest nests were only 30 m apart in suburbia, 190 m on the rural plot. Regular spacing could lead to the larger suburban population, also promoted by the species' small spatial requirement and tolerance of nearby pairs. Patchiness, however, probably contributes to the relative scarcity of rural owls and must be caused by nest-site competitors and especially predators; I never saw screech owls nesting within 300 m of barred or great-horned owls, although potential nest sites were regularly spaced on the rural study plot (R = 1.2).

Does a nesting pair's spatial allotment change according to population density? Probably not, as territorial males in suburbia command no more than about one-fifth of a hectare per nest cavity or half a hectare maximum in defending up to three neighboring cavities (chapter 2). Perhaps, though, home ranges are affected. Are they compressed or do they overlap more and thus impact hunting success at high densities (see chapter 6)? To find out I mapped the adjacent ranges of four males nesting in wooded yards during March–May, 1987–1989, as the entire suburban population grew from 12 to 17 pairs. Each season 21–36 nights were devoted to watching and mapping each hunting male for one to two hours per night at dusk and dawn.

Home ranges decreased from 7.1 ± 3.4 ha in 1987 to 5.8 ± 1.8 ha in 1989, an insignificant change, and overlap among them increased from 22.7 ± 5.3 to 27.9 ± 7.9 percent, likewise insignificant. Food could have been a factor, since it increased 1.2 times; but that would account only for a range-size decrease, not the added overlap more likely influenced by the pressures of increased density. Even so, at the maximum population density of 20 pairs, each home range could be 13.5 ha without overlap; and 13.2 ha was the largest range I found in any one year. The smallest was 4.0 ha.

In Connecticut, however, the home ranges of two suburban males in May–June were 9.9 ha and a surprising 95.3 ha. Even the smaller value exceeds my 6.3-ha mean (P = 0.05), perhaps because the Connecticut owls carried radio transmitters that reduced their foraging success and caused more widespread movements (chapter 1). Yet I computed 35.5 ± 16.2 ha for five radio-transmittered males in the nesting season of rural Kentucky, which is not significantly different than the 30-ha home range estimated from my itinerant observations of two rural males in 1985.[19] Thus, suburban ranges may average about one-fifth the size of rural ones, and suburban owls are about five-times denser than rural owls in my study area.

Densities and Cycles

Extrapolated to a standard area, population density was 4.4–7.4 pairs/ km^2 in suburbia and 0.7–2.2/km^2 on the rural plot during 1976–87. That the suburban owls were very concentrated can be underscored by looking at simultaneous nesting density in the suburban perimeter zone, most of which represents rural conditions (chapter 1). There, pairs numbered only 0.5–1.8/km^2, no different statistically from the rural plot or its own perimeter zone with 0.2–1.0 pairs/km^2. Density estimates from other rural populations (0.1–0.6 pairs/km^2) and even another suburban site (1.2 pairs/km^2) provide similar contrasts.[20]

Rural populations of boreal, flammulated, little, tawny, and Ural owls range from 0.1 to 2.5 pairs/km^2, hence are like the eastern screech owl's densities; but the rural tawnies studied with nest boxes numbered 3.3–6.1 pairs/km^2.[21] While it would appear that added nesting space increases population density, that cannot be true on my suburban plot where pairs had fewer nest sites than their rural counterparts (chapter 2). Abundant city food by itself may not explain increased density either, certainly not on an annual basis (r^2 = 0.17, NS). Even the rural tawny owls remained dense despite food scarcity that stopped their reproduction in some years.[22] Instead, besides regular spacing, I suggest that more operational space as opposed to potential nesting space fosters higher suburban densities.

By operational space I mean nest sites used successfully and hence constantly, because they are relatively free from interspecific competition and predation. When a pair's nest is destroyed, the owls usually move to renest, remaining where they are successful. If the negative impacts are reduced by human activity in suburban yards, nest sites continue to be profitable, and local density remains high and relatively stable (chapters 2, 5, 6). Use of the safer open-yard sites tracked population density more closely than did use of wooded-yard sites in 1976–91 (r = 0.72 versus 0.59, P = 0.02), as the number of successful nests was greater at more open sites (chapter 2).

The 1980–83 "debacle" in suburbia is illustrative, since competitor-predator displacement of breeding pairs averaged 64.7 percent compared with only 27.0–31.5 percent in any other four-year period through 1991. (P = 0.03). The population dropped to an average 13.2 pairs in 1984–87 compared to 15.7 in the previous four years and 17.2 afterward (P = 0.04). Obviously the population was density-dependent, but what controlled its flux? No primary relationships to food or weather were apparent (see below), just as in the Eurasian sparrowhawk; so I wondered about internal factors like age structure and its relation to productivity and nest-site turnover.[23]

Previous density determined the percentage of annual density change in both populations (r^2 > 0.52, P < 0.008). More owls one year meant proportionately fewer the next, because density increases hinge upon immigrant yearlings, about half of which vanish and thus reduce the density (see above). In multiple stepwise regressions more yearlings, not older females, precipitated population declines in subsequent years (r^2 > 0.31, P < 0.03); and, in suburbia, this was also caused by more unsuccessful nests (r^2 added = 0.11, P = 0.05) together with a greater turnover of females among nest sites (r^2 added = 0.10, P = 0.05). As with tawny owls and sparrowhawks, productivity was unaffected by density (r^2 < 0.19, NS).[24]

On the rural plot there were no significant influences besides yearlings and perhaps the heavy predation at all age levels (see below). Those owls experienced 2.6 times more annual flux than their suburban relatives; coefficients of density variation in 1976–87 were 44.9 and 17.3 percent, respectively. The rural value seems high compared with rural tawny owls (21.8%) but is no different from population flux among ten species of birds, including tawnies and the Eurasian sparrowhawk, while the suburban coefficient is significantly low.[25] Stability in suburbia is, of course, congruent with the stable climate and food supply, which promote stable reproductive performance (chapters 2, 3, 8).

Still, the suburban owls seemed to cycle in regular fashion (figure 9.3). My search for serial correlations between densities in one year and each of the following ten years, 1975–91, reveals two patterns: a four-year relation between population "peaks and valleys" (r = −0.57, P = 0.05) and a nine-year interval between successive peaks or

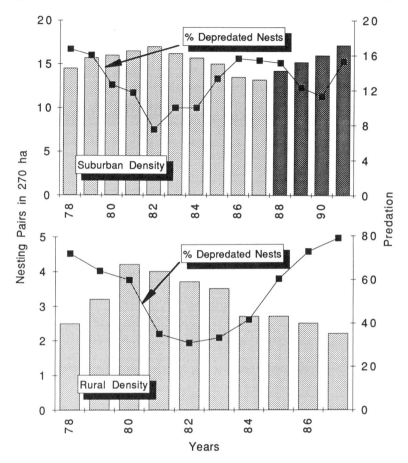

Figure 9.3.   Population and nest-depredation cycles on the suburban and rural study plots. Annual values are four-year running averages starting with 1975; those for suburban density in 1988–91 are
unmatched by rural data and hence darkly shaded. Note the concordant cycles and inverse relation between density and predation, especially on the rural plot.

valleys (r = 0.55, NS; but n = 7). By regressing four-year running-
mean densities on years, the nine-year periodicity is confirmed ($4° r^2 =$
0.87, P < 0.001). The owls reached 20 pairs in 1982 and 19 in 1991
with lows of 12 pairs in 1978 and 1986–87. Do they represent yet
another example of the wildlife's "ten-year" cycle, which actually has
an average periodicity between nine and ten years?[26]

Amazingly, the populations highs and lows coincide with lunar periodicity, wherein the lag in moonrise at the full moon nearest the vernal equinox reaches an extreme every 9.3 years.[26] Something about the monthly lunar cycle influences reproductive singing, so I might believe that consequent behavioral modulations of births and deaths could create the population cycle (chapter 7).[27] While many more years of data are needed even to figure average cycle time before there is any prospect of finding cause and effect, I am stimulated to continue recording densities; since other birds, including diurnal species, have nine-year cycles correlated with the lunar cycle.[28]

Of course the rural screech owls cannot vouch for any particular cycle, because their population declined (b = −0.20, P = 0.01 for the four-year running-mean density regressed on years). There were two pairs in 1976, six in 1980, and two again by 1984, suggesting the same four-year interval between highs and lows as in suburbia; but the population remained low thereafter (figure 9.3). Almost simultaneously, the percentage of depredated nests declined and then increased, suggesting that predators influenced density (r = −0.70, P = 0.02). When added to the yearling factor (r^2 = 0.31, P = 0.03) in a multiple stepwise regression, that may be true indeed (r^2 = 0.16, P = 0.08).

Predation in suburbia fluctuated more irregularly, undoubtedly modified by culture (figure 9.3), and averaged only 11.9 ± 6.0 percent of nests compared to 61.7 ± 31.6 percent on the rural plot in 1976–87 (P = 0.004). Suburban depredations offset density (r = −0.61, P = 0.03) but were so few as to be negligible in population control besides the yearlings:older-females factor (r^2 added = 0.02, NS; MSR). However, they were concordant with rural depredations (r = 0.59, P = 0.04), indicating similar cycles despite the different kinds of predators involved (chapters 5, 6), and reciprocal with both owl populations in a manner suggesting density-dependent regulation (figure 9.3). That suburban predation declined when the general food supply increased further supports this proposition (chapter 6).

Had I studied the rural owls longer I might have been able to confirm a visual impression that they rebounded during a post-1987 decline in predation. This was to be expected from the coincident rural and suburban population cycles in 1976–87 (r = 0.75, P = 0.001). Finally, because more breeders disappeared when winter food was scarce, I questioned a connection between food and population flux on both study plots but found only a marginal one in the countryside (r = 0.49, P = 0.10). And, because rufous-phase owls declined sharply in the hard winters of 1983–86 (chapter 4), I sought and found a population-cycle versus mean-minimum-temperature relation at both sites (r >

0.63, P < 0.01), although it said nothing about flux beyond the age-class explanation (r^2 < 0.06, NS).

Since there were several entangling correlations, I resorted to principal components analysis to sort them out by assembling new linear variables from the four-year running means of population density, yearlings:older-females, percent predation, food, and the minimum winter temperature during 1976–87 (n = 9). Density (r = −0.94) combined with the age-class ratio (r = 0.91) to explain the most suburban variation (61%), leaving the three environmental factors more strongly represented on a second linear variable (r > 0.67) that accounted for another 33 percent of variation in the data. In the rural setting, though, density (r = 0.97) joined with predation (r = −0.75), and then age-class ratio (−0.71), food (0.65), and temperature (0.62) on one linear variable that explained practically everything (97%).

Withal, I suggest that both populations are periodic due largely to the reproductive differences between novice and experienced breeders. Major instabilities are caused by severe environmental factors like predation that apparently damped the rural cycle in the late 1980s. Food and weather could act similarly but chiefly in the countryside, as there is abundant evidence that suburbia buffers environmental influents. Therefore, breeding experience can offset environmental impacts more easily in suburbia, where population maintenance is "finely tuned" to age-class structure.[29]

The Essentials

Although half of all breeding females are yearlings regionwide, proportionately more older females nest in suburbia, because survival is better there. In fact, no screech owl older than five years was found on the rural plot, whereas one female lived at least 14 years and another 11 years in suburbia. Generally, though, females live through only two breeding seasons. The survivorship curves for both populations are negatively curvilinear. Vehicle collisions, followed by poisonings, shootings plus trappings, and then window-wall collisions are the commonest types of mortality in suburbia.

Novice breeders are nearly all yearlings, mostly immigrants that arrive in largest numbers when more old females disappear during winters with low food supplies. In suburbia, older experienced females may exclude immigrants as shown by a yearling:older-female ratio that falls curvilinearly to a stable six yearling plus ten older females at the population's long-term mean density of 5.8 breeding pairs/km². This same ratio is inversely correlated with suburban population density the next year, partly because it is also inversely related to poor production efficiency by most yearlings who disappear. On the rural plot, however, such a pattern could not be found, since extreme predation impacted all breeders regardless of age.

First-year productivity of ten suburban cohorts was better for those hatched into low-density populations plus high-food conditions, rather than those immigrating into such an environment. Thus, initial female quality is important. Yet all yearlings average only 1.7 owlets per breeding attempt, less than the theoretical 1.8 needed for pair replacement, and the 2.4-owlet average of older females in suburbia. Although yearlings nest later than older owls and first-nest output drops as the season progresses, late nests (mostly replacements) are relatively productive, because of declining predation and partial-loss factors like fratricide.

Overall productivity, the total of fledglings per egg, increases rapidly up to 60 percent for the optimal four-egg clutch (the size producing the most population recruits). Five- and six-egg clutches are no more productive of fledglings or population recruits, although not an added cost to future reproduction. Suburban productivity exceeds the rural value; but, regionwide, is not unlike that of other cavity-nesting owls and songbirds compared to lower success among open nesters. While reproductive potentials are similar in both study populations, suburban nests fail more often during incubation, after which replacement nests are usual and potentially compensatory. Conversely, rural nests fail most frequently in the nestling period, too late for most renesting.

Suburban pairs are five times denser than rural pairs and more use nest boxes than cavities because of their greater shortage of nest space. Actual green space available to each suburban pair averages only 4.6 ha, but those owls are regularly distributed by contrast to the patchy rural population. Regular dispersion, small spatial requirement, and tolerance of nearby nesting pairs probably contributes to the unusually high suburban density. On the other hand, nest-site competitors and especially predators seem to influence the rural patchiness hence relative scarcity of those owls whose potential nest sites are regularly distributed. Rural density values are like those of other cavity-nesting owls.

Home ranges decrease slightly and overlap somewhat more as density increases in suburbia, although that population is exceptionally stable compared to the rural population which varies like those of other birds. Linked to stability is consistent use of nest sites. Nevertheless, the suburban owls exhibit a nine-year cycle like those of other birds and mammals and similarly coincident with the 9.3-year lunar cycle. The rural owls show a tendency for the same nine-year cycle based on visual observations and comparisons with suburbia. The ratio of novice to experienced breeders may determine population periodicity, which can be destabilized by unusually severe external factors like predation. However, cyclic upsets are less likely in suburbia, where predation, food, and weather are buffered by culture.

10 The Suburban Advantage

A Final Synthesis

I hesitate to bring any study to a close, even to a preliminary conclusion, because I like to anticipate investigations that confirm what I've been thinking or surprise me—that display repeated patterns or novelties. Either way, natural history is exciting work. Knowledge of repeated patterns is the essence of science and permits an assessment of planetary relations and responsibilities. I find comfort and utility in these things. And discovery provides the stimuli to keep going, when a few decades of human arrogance and ignorance threaten long-established patterns and my sense of well-being. I guess this endeavor is yet another journey without destination.

Although the eastern screech owl is quite like other cavity nesters, its reproductive strategy should be viewed in a broad spectrum of Holarctic owls. Therefore, relative clutch weights, incubation and nestling periods, and fledgling weights of this species and 19 other cavity and open nesters were submitted to principal components analysis. Small- and large-owl reproductive modes were verified by multiple analysis of variance on one component defined by body mass, which explained 74 percent of variation in the data (P < 0.001, figure 10.1).

This picture suggests that the eastern screech owl is intermediate in reproductive effort (figure 10.1).[1] Its short incubation and nestling periods, a departure from the small-owl mode, could mean less likelihood of reproductive failure due to storms and predators; while the small-owl feature of producing proportionately larger eggs can result in larger fledglings that survive better. Also, the large-owl attribute of fledging at a relatively small size is potentially advantageous in that screech owlets experience their major environment earlier and can follow parents to food and safety.

By contrast, the threatened spotted owl typifies the large-owl group that expends relatively less egg energy and requires a long time for incubation and chick development (figure 10.1). This species relies on large body size, associated longevity, and habitat constancy to persist, rather than on rapid reproduction, which allows for replacement nests and is especially adaptive in a disturbed environment like suburbia. Of course the eastern screech owl thrives in fragmented landscapes, while the spotted owl does not. A major point of contrast is that the screech

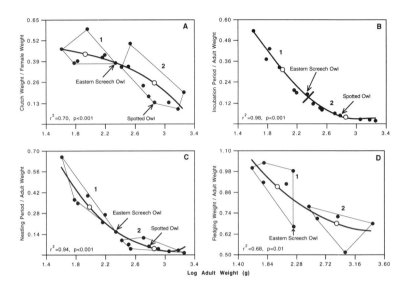

Figure 10.1. Four major reproductive features among owls. Based on species clusters in a PCA of features A through D among the following species, there are two distinct groups verified by MANOVA: (1) boreal, burrowing, eastern screech, elf, flammulated, little, northern pygmy, and Eurasian pygmy; (2) barn, barred, eagle, great-gray, great-horned, hawk, long-eared, short-eared, snowy, spotted, tawny, and Ural. Group means are the circles (data on all species not available for each graph). Note the rapid change in reproductive effort with increasing body size. Also, observe that the eastern screech owl, well adapted to suburbia, is intermediate between small- and large-owl modes; while the threatened spotted owl, dependent on mature coniferous-forest habitat, is a typical large species.

owl's lifestyle is geared to environmental flux, while the spotted's is consistent with stability.[2]

Large owls, especially open nesters, are simply too conspicuous in suburbia. Even if tolerant of patchy habitat, they are less readily habituated and hence less tolerated by humans, because they often try to repulse intruders instead of hiding from them. Also, they require considerable space for hunting large, wide-ranging prey which brings them into greater human contact and potential conflict. Among large species only the tawny owl seems to be a frequent city dweller, probably because it uses tree cavities, has a broad food niche, and is a sit-and-wait (inconspicuous) forager.

Though small species are more secretive cavity users by virtue of their size, my experience suggests that only the little and western screech owls seem to tolerate patchy habitat and human activity like the eastern screech owl. The western screech owl is enough like its sister species to be truly preadapted to suburbia, although it appears to be more narrowly focused in wooded parks and green belts, based on my viewing in the Southwest and Pacific Northwest. This species may simply lack the eastern's centuries of expanding urban contact, not its preadaptations.

Cultural contact and adjustment processes can be appreciated by listing suburban amenities and the eastern screech owl's preadaptive traits, followed by an overview of the city-owl connection that results in such high productivity. I am mindful that during the same 12-year period the suburban study population produced 1.5 times more fledglings from its egg-laying effort than the rural owls did and, on average, sustained five times more individuals per unit area than in the countryside.

Suburban Amenities

Suburbia's largess includes a relatively moderate climate due to the buffering influence of the urban heat island. Temperature extremes and droughts are moderated, and certain food items like June bugs, cicadas, earthworms, and small snakes are promoted though also enhanced by watered and fertilized lawns. The city climate permits early nesting, in turn allowing the owls to precede nest-site competitors and produce independent owlets early enough to gain survival experience before facing the stress of dispersal and winter.

The comparatively open ground of suburbia, including pavement and park-like trees, makes hunting easier and discloses or deters predators so that nesting is more successful. Of course, eastern screech owls benefit because they mostly hunt the ground stratum. I can think of two stipulations, however. Injured or otherwise "unsightly" trees are pruned or removed, which opens the habitat but eliminates natural cavities, and vehicles kill owls flying low across streets or hunting on the pavement.

On the other hand, suburbia often contains a more evergreen and mature canopy, a more protective tree stratum than the countryside, and the owls select tree cavities or evergreen foliage as winter and early nesting-season roosts for thermoregulatory reasons. Natural cavities prevail in the larger, older trees preferred by suburbanites unless the cavities are sealed to prevent rotting and further damage to the trees or are in unsightly limbs that are cut off.

Permanent water for drinking and bathing at lawn sprinklers, bird-baths, and fish ponds is readily available in suburbia but often more than a home-range distance away in the rural landscape. Moreover, there are large numbers of avian, rodent, and invertebrate prey, propagated by the watering and artificial feeding and concentrated at other sources of supply like bird feeders and patio lights. But biocides are widely used to control insects and rodents in suburbia, and they kill the owls secondarily.

Another suburban advantage is the absence or scarcity of certain other predators and competitors like the larger raptors. There is less opportunity for predation and contention anyway because of nest cavities near houses with ongoing human and pet activity in the relatively open landscape. As always, however, there are provisos. In suburbia there may be more adversaries of other kinds like raccoons, squirrels, and European starlings.

The interplay of amenities could foster large, stable, screech owl populations, reducing genetic drift and increasing variability, which affords more adaptive opportunity for a species with potential in suburbia. On the other hand, small semi-isolated populations may result from the landscape fragmentation that characterizes cities. Then variation would be limited by the restricted gene flow, although a relatively homozygous gene pool might be advantageous in the environmentally buffered setting.

Preadaptations of Eastern Screech Owls

Among beneficial traits is the species' small spatial requirement, primarily because of its small body size, polyterritoriality, and catholic food habits. Therefore, its needs are satisfied in the patchy suburban landscape of interspersed buildings, yards, and parks. Additional aspects include the screech owl's preference for park-like habitat that facilitates its arc-type flying and sit-and-wait hunting for ground dwellers. Nevertheless, some predators like barred owls and competitors like European starlings also select such habitat.

Catholic food habits linked to body size, together with crepuscular periodicity and frequent food-caching, mean that suburban food supplies generally are not limiting. In this regard, the owl is "plastic" behaviorally in caching large items while eating small ones and in the seasonal switching of hunting times and among prey types. Even so, clutch size, recruitment, breeding success, and overwinter survival are influenced by reductions in food supply though not as drastically as in the countryside.

The species is easily habituated to most everyday human and pet activity, except the constant presence of house cats, and especially to man-made nesting structures in lieu of natural ones. While the owls prefer deep cavities with small entrances, they readily accept a variety of cavity types and nest-box sizes. Their residential nature affords an increased opportunity to learn as shown by yearling females that shift from active to passive defensive behavior with increased suburban nesting experience.

Moreover, screech owl behavior is inconspicuous and generally innocuous. Attributes include a seemingly ventriloqual voice, the mimicry of katydid songs by fledglings, secluded roost and nest sites, arc-type flights, sit-and wait foraging, usually unaggressive males, and secreted (nesting) females. On the other hand, with late-stage nestlings and early fledglings, screech owls may attack close intruders, and I have known a few that became so habituated as to be incautious about humans and their pets.

Surely the screech owl's balanced color dimorphism is advantageous in "weathering" natural cool-dry and warm-wet climatic cycles, hence the rufous morph is preadapted to living in the suburban heat island. Interestingly, among the 19 other species of owls I surveyed, the tawny is the only common city dweller with similar colormorphism; but no one knows if its rufous phase is relatively abundant in cities, and there is no information about adaptive significance of its color phases.

Rapid and persistent reproduction is still another preadaptive feature of eastern screech owls. Most yearlings breed, and all nesting starts early in the spring. The first few eggs are laid at almost daily intervals, incubation usually is immediate, and there is multiple replacement of lost clutches and infertile eggs with no season decline in productivity. Owlets fledge quickly; and, while their inability to fly may limit an immediate escape to safety, they climb readily and follow their parents within a few days to one week.

The short-distance natal dispersal of these fledglings facilitates settlement in suburban habitat, so suburban populations are restocked with adaptive characteristics. This, however, limits genetic variability with the potential for inbreeding depression, although periodic high-population densities disperse the owlets relatively farther from their natal areas. Population flux could counteract inbreeding in this manner.

Connections

Implicit in the blending of suburban amenities and screech owl preadaptations is the rural contrast and my belief that both of my study populations typify the species. Certainly, fundamental habits and seasonality appear to be much the same everywhere, despite local ecological peculiarities like types of food and day-night cycles.[3] Intermediate features of the developing suburban population at Harris Creek support my postulate that age and size of a city determine the extent of screech owl suburbanization.

Experience with new suburban habitat that developed in former cropland at one edge of my Woodway study plot suggests that 20 percent wooded green space with an average of 53 mature trees per hectare (average 30 cm diameter) and one suitable nest cavity or box are minimum requirements for nesting.[4] But, because of their polygyny and indulgence of nearby nesting pairs, social facilitation could play a role in establishing screech owl populations. If the habitat is suitably large, suburban owls may be quite dense, since they respond positively to suburban munificence, demand little space, and are not easily deterred by humans.

The warm-wet suburban setting stimulates early nesting, and more eggs survive the incubation period because of less predation and more mild weather. While partial clutches may be deserted due to cultural disturbance, the eggs are replaced; and disturbed clutches are not so prevalent later in the season, when predation and nest-site competition decline, and the experience of incubating females improves. The larger fraction of long-lived suburban females assures a quicker, larger hatch, since these birds have learned to adjust to culture.

Compared to their rural cousins, suburban chicks stay longer in the nest, due to fewer threats from predation and less stressful weather, so they fledge at a larger size which enhances their survival. More food and experienced females also mean faster growth to a larger size and less nestling mortality. Too, more first nests are successful in suburbia, and first-nest chicks grow faster and larger, fledge earlier, and thus are more likely to become local breeders.

Owlets inherit some components of their body size and breeding potential, so those recruited locally in place of missing older owls help to maintain genetic continuity as well as population size. Predation, food, and weather can limit reproduction and thus population density but are minor influents compared to the territorial pressure of older owls in effecting an age-class ratio of about one yearling pair for every two older pairs at average breeding density. Thus, suburban populations are quite stable.

With these substantial changes in lifestyle and population consequences, do suburban owls alter our knowledge of avian ecology?[5] For instance, breeding is believed to start when food is sufficiently abundant and stop early enough to raise independent offspring plus complete the adult molt before winter. But food is less limiting in suburbia, where nest starts are most responsive to temperature (although egg number and size are determined by food supply). Nesting begins earlier but is not concluded earlier, though quickly enough for first-nest chicks to become successful breeders and for a complete summer molt.

Also, clutches are thought to be larger earlier in the season and laid by larger, older or better-nourished females. While true of the suburban owls, this is partly because later replacement clutches are smaller than first clutches. Time and molt constraints force renesting at below-optimum weight, even though food becomes increasingly abundant. Since there is no seasonal decline within first-nest or replacement clutches, which have other distinctions like smaller renest fledglings less likely to survive, it is wise to discern the two clutch-types, not just look at an overall seasonal trend.

Furthermore, to understand why suburban eggs survive so much better than their rural counterparts, one must separate the dynamics of egg survivability (those that withstand external environmental threats like predation long enough to hatch) from those of hatchability (the surviving fraction that actually hatch, subject to mostly different impacts like infertility). When this is accomplished, survivability turns out to be higher in safer suburbia, whereas hatchability is essentially the same in both suburban and rural environments.

There are additional hypotheses that clutches are either as large as possible or optimized to the most productive size for raising offspring. Clearly, the owls attain their highest fledging efficiency from the modal first-nest clutch of four eggs but maintain that efficiency with even larger clutches. However, they do not produce more breeding offspring from larger clutches, because the additional fledglings are smaller with less survival potential. Rather, they produce the most population recruits from optimal four-egg clutches.

Supposedly, hatching asynchrony is adaptive in speeding up the development of oldest chicks and, by mortality of the youngest chicks, in reducing brood size to that supported by the food supply. But many owlets hatch coincidentally, experienced females reduce their mortality, and youngest siblings often catch up to older ones despite feeding rates unadjusted to brood size. Hence, asynchrony simply permits feeding entire broods adequately, as younger, smaller chicks do not require as much food. Even so it is of little consequence in suburbia, where relatively few chicks die because of the abundant food.

Still another hypothesis is the advantage of reproducing quickly, because more breeding years mean more fledged offspring, even though there may be a cost to future reproduction or survival. Yet more fledglings do not mean greater fitness (more recruits) among the suburban owls, and there are no apparent reproductive costs. Breeding yearlings certainly characterize the species but are fewer in suburbia, since survival is better there, allowing established (older) birds to predominate.

Besides the connection to suburban environmental stability, survival is linked to large size which promotes greater breeding success, further promoted by learning. The size-related suite of adaptive features leads to larger nestlings produced earlier in the season, and eventually to more recruited owlets. Among birds generally, yearlings are thought to be comparatively poor breeders because of their inexperience; but, among screech owls, they also suffer from being smaller. The smallest ones are least successful and most likely to disappear from the breeding population.

Food as a major limiting factor outside the breeding season is yet another general postulate but not so critical for eastern screech owls due to their broad food niche. In addition, food appears to be of little importance in suburbia because of its large supply and the small number of interspecific competitors. Nonetheless, abundant food determines the recruitment of owlets by fostering their natal-year survival and lessens the winter emigration and mortality of adults, contributing to population stability.

Nest sites are also said to limit bird populations, especially secondary cavity nesters, but suitable tree cavities are more numerous than breeding pairs of suburban screech owls. Further, the requisite cavities are regularly dispersed, because they are commonly made by storms and enlarged by squirrels and decay if not drilled by large woodpeckers. This is why the owls are polyterritorial and nest close to one another, and why territoriality in the traditional sense of one defended area does not regulate their numbers. Although the proximity of breeding avian predators disperses pairs and reduces density, this factor is important only in rural habitat where predators are more numerous.

Thus nest sites per se do not limit screech-owl density, but the "ownership" of two or three cavities per established pair does. Suburban density changes only after the death or breeding dispersal of long-lived owners, allowing yearlings to occupy the vacated cavities. Of course temporary food limitations are implicated in some vacancies, but human factors may contribute equally, because as many experienced breeders are lost each year from cultural impacts like vehicle collisions as from all other factors combined.

Perhaps I should reiterate the three major conclusions of this synthesis, because they are so important in understanding the reciprocity between owls and people. First, by virtue of its history of cultural contact and size-related reproductive strategy, the eastern screech owl is especially well suited for coexistence with humans. Second, modern suburbia is quite munificent toward this species and the few other natives that can utilize its resources. And, third, the amenity-preadaptation connections certainly modify some of our ideas about avian ecology.

Above all, the suburban owls feature high productivity and density together with population stability, a unique ecological combination. In nature, however, the first two traits typify organisms in simplistic, highly productive and dynamic, young communities, whereas population stability is more common in complex, less productive, and less fluctuating, older communities. Thus, in the urbanization of the eastern screech owl, we have created a new ecology for an old native species.[6]

Prescription for the Future

Certainly, eastern screech owls are potentially good environmental predictors—living "barometers"—and other native species successful in cities and the countryside may serve as well.[7] The Eurasian tawny and little owls have similar potential; and, worldwide, the common barn owl may be the best environmental indicator among raptors, perhaps among all birds, in having the broadest nesting niche in both time and space.[8]

A network of investigators could obtain a wealth of coordinated information studying these species. Political, geographical, and temporal variations of urbanization could be assessed and used in decision making that refines cultural development to include natural values. Aspects of environmental safety could be checked, for example toxic contaminants in screech owls eggs.[9] Related educational goals could be served by student involvement in the field work and data analysis, including computerized data storage and communication among workers in distant places.

Such studies require long-term commitments, as screech owls in my study area suggest that nine years or three generations are minimal, and 28 years (three 9.3-year population cycles) optimal for understanding population ecology. But the need for exploration beyond one year can be obviated by my experience. Thus, I offer some tactical suggestions for investigating eastern screech owls in special support of education and environmental monitoring.

First, though, I must advise that there are physical risks. If one has qualms about climbing ladders and trees or about the owl's physical defenses, I recommend against studying this species in the manner suggested. Also, be aware that bird banding and other handling require federal and state permits which have their own protocol for use. And

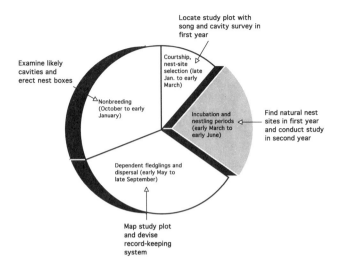

Figure 10.2. Annual cycle of the eastern screech owl and a calendar of coordinated investigations. Dimensions of the "pie slices" are proportional to number of weeks; nesting, the heart of the breeding season, is emphasized by the shading.

may I recommend that all field work be approved by home owners and police patrols at the start of each season.

Getting Started (figure 10.2): Accomplish as much habitat reconnaissance as possible and erect nest boxes in your first or exploratory year. Remember: (1) reproduction begins with nest-site advertisement and courtship in late January–early March, (2) incubation lasts about 30 days in early March–late May, (3) the nestling period of approximately 28 days is in early April–early June; and (4) fledglings remain in their natal area about 10 weeks before dispersing in early July–late September.

On several evenings in February to early March, at dusk and for one to two hours afterward, establish a 200–300-ha plot in a suburban screech owl population by listening for and mapping the locations of monotonic trills (given within 40 m of potential nest cavities). Moonlit nights without precipitation and no more than a breeze are best. Listen every 100 m or so along public streets and paths in potential habitat, using five minutes of taped trills or your imitations to elicit the song if nothing is heard. Then search for nests in the ensuing spring and erect nest boxes after breeding is finished for the year.

Watch for feeding flights to and from particular places and known cavities in the April–June nestling period. Owls peering from holes near dusk indicate roosting and nesting sites, and males roosting consistently within 12 m of a suitable cavity are certain evidence of a nest. After fledglings disperse, climb to and examine likely cavities, looking for signs of previous or current use such as eggshell fragments, feathers, and pellets. Natural nest and roost sites should be mapped along with all nest boxes.

The boxes should be in place before February of the second year, 30 m apart or more and similarly spaced from natural nesting cavities. Put three handfuls of dry broadleaf litter in them to simulate the squirrel or bird nests usually found in natural cavities and position the boxes about 3 m above ground (easily reached with a 1.8 m stepladder) in shady spots free of obstacles to flight. Nest boxes may face in any direction; but I recommend one with easy viewing from a house window or other "hiding place," to obviate the need for habituation, and illuminated by porch, patio, or street lights for nighttime watching.

Their size and material makes little difference to nest-site selection or degree of nesting success, so I suggest using outdoor plywood, painted dark brown outside, 18 × 18 cm bottoms with 0.5-cm drain holes at each corner, a 7-cm entrance hole centered 30 cm above the floor, and sloping lid 5 cm above the entrance, hinged at the back and with a screen-door hook at the side. I use a 5-cm extension at the top of the back panel with two screw holes, through which boxes are readily fastened to and removed from trees. For stability and security, they also sit on a 10-cm nail.

Basic Techniques: Nest checks should be in early to midafternoon when screech owls sleep, never at night. Minimize the intrusion—no large groups, loud talk, bright clothes, shiny jewelry, or nervous or clumsy behavior. A wooden ladder is quietest, and familiar background noise (passing vehicles, lawnmowers) helps disguise climbing. Quickly put a hand over the entrance hole when within arm's length to prevent an owl from exiting, and keep it plugged or blocked by your body. This reduces changes of desertion and lets you check identity. Rarely, owls fly from the opened box top, right in your face, so always wear glasses.

When handling an adult, hold it firmly with one hand around midbody, palm on the back, fingers posterior of the sternum to pin the legs straight backward. This confines the talons, allows you to read a band and estimate physical condition, and frees your other hand for manipulations like banding. The owl's defensive power is in its feet, not its beak. Eastern screech owls seldom bite and then not hard, but their claws easily penetrate human skin, so you may wish to wear gloves.

The birds often attack intruders, including human investigators, especially in the last nestling week and first two fledgling weeks. At those times, I recommend wearing a hat that protects ears and neck, a long-sleeved shirt, and gloves in addition to glasses, for the birds aim at the head and hands and their raking talons draw blood. During nest checks, people standing close sometimes divert attacks and should be warned. Barks and screeches, accompanied by bill claps, signal the physical aggression.

If they are unbanded, do not handle incubating females, indicated by their laterally spread breast feathers, for they may be yearlings that readily desert eggs unlike older, learned females. Initially band and weight females only during brooding, within a week after first hatch, as healthy chicks attended by at least one parent are never deserted. Brooding is indicated by males moving to tree roosts closer to their nests. Try to replace females on eggs and chicks and leave the area quickly if the bird flies. This will facilitate its quick return and lessen chances of egg and chick mortality due to chilling.

To ascertain eggs or small nestlings and female identity, gently feel under incubating-brooding individuals and move the banded leg later-ally for reading (band males and females on different legs to expedite identification). Aggressive birds expose and may damage eggs and chicks, so make determinations and exit expeditiously. If a particular female cannot be caught by hand, put a long-handled, tapered net over the nest entrance during brooding. After she flies into it, twist, and bring her to the ground for handling but replace her on the chicks, blocking her exit until she calms down.

For assessing body mass and growth, I suggest using a preweighed, dark sack and hand-held spring scales in the early to midafternoon to minimize disturbance, facilitate habituation, and negate a periodicity bias. Weigh chicks every five days, if you wish to record growth, and band them only after a week of age—at 50 g or larger. Females can be weighed while recording final clutch size (standardized as three weeks after the first egg), brood size (10 days after the first hatch), and num-ber of potential fledglings (14 days after counting chicks).

Nightly observations should begin by sunset but are valid only after a nesting pair is habituated to you. Wear dark clothing and sit quietly against a backdrop like a house, tree, or fence to help disguise and protect you from attacks, especially in that fourth nestling week. Ha-bituation requires about two hours per night over two weeks for owls already familiar with other human activity. Use a microcassette tape recorder for note-taking in order to stay focused on events.

Record Keeping (see, for example, the field notes in appendix I): Location, date, identity, and breeding success of each nesting female

Author replacing two-week-old chick in nest box. (Rod Aydelotte
photo)

constitute the necessary minimum for understanding long-term population dynamics and annual productivity. Males add much to the picture, of course, but must be specially trapped; and I think a meaningful study is possible without data on their individual identities.[9] I suggest computerized record keeping of each nesting attempt, defined as at least one egg, accessed by female identity as well as date, site, and nesting efficiency (fledglings/eggs).

One should try to record laying date of the first egg and always note the completed clutch size. First-hatch and first-fledge dates are useful but not necessary, although brood size is important, and number of fledglings crucial to understanding productivity. During nest checks, other observations such as stored food, symbionts, and evidence of cannibalism can be obtained. At night I usually note female departure and return, vocalizations and their context, number and duration of feeding visits, and types of prey.

The first of two useful notebook or computer files is an annual summary of nests from which data can be retrieved by nest site and breeding adult. For each nesting attempt (row), are columns for site, female and male identities (band number, age, weight), first egg, hatch, and fledge dates, clutch and brood sizes, number of fledglings, and special comments like replacement nest or cannibalism. From this I can compute totals, averages, ratios, and percentages such as number of nests, mean clutch size, yearling:older females, and fledglings/eggs.

The second file, an among-years summary of the population, has columns for successive nesting seasons (years) and rows for population density, yearling:older females, mean age of females, total eggs, chicks, fledglings, fledglings per egg and per nesting pair, mean clutch and brood, mean egg and chick losses per pair, total food supply, mean minimum and maximum temperature, and total rainfall. This information can be retrieved in many ways to understand population dynamics.

A parallel investigation of suburbia is necessary, because the screech owl's population flux and attendant changes in reproductive dynamics are related to cultural change. House and human density, traffic patterns, biocide use, yard space, size and dispersion of parks, surface-water supplies, bird feeders, and artificial lights are exemplary census items that will provide the background for a better understanding of the unnatural history of urbanization.

Epilogue

I have learned much about and perhaps even more from eastern screech owls; but long-term events like population cycles need more time, and

Adult eastern screech owl in repose.

I continue to monitor the suburban population. Field experiments are possible now that I know the "rules of the game," so the final phase of investigation begins. Studies of wildness must begin with learning what to do and how to do it, proceed over a reasonable number of generations, and end with experimentation to verify the findings.

During the next few years, my prescription for the future will be given a trial run by another observer in another city in a study designed around the development of an educational curriculum for school children. Of course the youngsters will learn about the owls. But will they also learn from them? Will they discover their intangible meaning, the necessity of maintaining wildness to understand our place among living creatures? As adults, will they promote an urban blend of nature and culture?

Appendix I
Field Notes

To provide specific examples of the main topics of chapters 2–7 on life history, I have paraphrased selected field notes from 1976 to 1991. Observations are presented chronologically by chapter, although in some cases originally separate entries about one owl, nest site, etc., are combined to give a meaningful sequence of events. For a more thorough perspective, on one nesting event, "Fisher" includes edited versions of every written and taped observation made in 1986 at this typical suburban site.

Chapter 2. Landscape: The Owls Select Habitat

January 9, 12, 1985, at 13SC: on 9th resident male is 2.5 m high in red cedar by open-top hollow Shumard oak (low temperature 1°C); on 12th owl moves to nest box 7 m away (1 cm snow and −3 to −6°C).

January 24, 1979, at Baylor (natural cavity): gray male in rotted, squirrel-enlarged hole facing southwest, 6 m high (cavity is old limb scar); rufous female is 0.5 m higher in second, south-facing cavity between major trunk forks where a third fork apparently was lost and its base rotted. Tree is cedar elm, 66 cm diameter, 19 m high, and 14 m from street.

February 17, 1986, at 13SC: male in red cedar, 6 m from box and 3 m high in A.M.; by 1600, when sunny and 26°C, he moves 0.5 m deeper into tree and is joined by female; both fly into box at 1835 (dusk).

March 10, 1977, at 7717: female leaves box roost at 1845; her mate is 25 m away in a red cedar; both fly around (disturbed by me?), then copulate on open cedar limb 2 m from box at 1850 for about five seconds (note: female has occupied box every day since February 14).

April 1, 1990, at 13SC: male sings monotonic trills for nearly an hour at 2025 hr in and around nest box, then returns to his natural-cavity nest and incubating mate 106 m away where he gives a few more trills before flying off; did he feed mate before advertising second nest site? (Note: no nest in 13SC this year.)

April 12, 1980, at Bush: pair side by side in nest box with female incubating single egg; cold front drops temperature 27° to 3°C in 24 hrs, which could have forced the male inside, as the deciduous foliage is not fully mature.

April 14, 1987, at Bice: storm knocks over hollow, 23-cm diameter Shumard oak with 16-cm diameter nest cavity 1.5 m above ground; female broods four downy chicks in open-top cavity but flies as chainsaws begin to work on down timber. (Note: I inverted a plastic bucket over nest, leaving open slot below bucket rim, and brood fledged May 3–7.).

April 18, 1982, at 13SC: showed neighbors roosting owl, 3 m high next to trunk in Shumard oak; they used chainsaw on dead tree within 3 m of the bird without flushing it in late P.M.

April 30, 1989, at Wise: four downy chicks in live oak cavity 4 m high 30 m from nest box used successfully the past three years by same pair. Why the switch? (Note: oak is dead and cut down March, 1990, whereupon pair nests again successfully in the box.)

May 15, 1985 at Davis: six feeding visits by male cross street at 2102–2121 hours; he flies 2 m above ground with 1.0 m rises to food-delivery perch in live oak 2 m in front of the 3.9-m-high box.

May 27, 1981, at Prachar (rural): nestlings in badly weathered, squirrel-chewed, martin box on utility pole at pasture fenceline 400 m from nearest woods. Only nearby trees are small mimosas in yard and 2.5-m red cedar with roosting adult, 15 m from nest. (Note: female from this brood nested in Harris Creek, 1.5 km away, March 23, 1985.)

June 9, 1979, at Wise: female no longer brooding is 4.5 m from nest box and 1.5 m from male, 3 m from box, who sits on abandoned fox squirrel nest 5 m high in live oak 9 m high.

October 23, 1985, at Fisher: cannot get box vegetation data today because police have drug bust in progress across street, one of the more unusual vicissitudes of research on suburban "wildlife."

October 29, 1985, near Davis: mobbing Carolina wrens find roosting gray adult, crouched and fluffed in dense greenbriar tangle 2.5 m high in white ash grove away from woods (0800, 14°C); standing in dead-stick pose at 1600 (23°C).

December 6, 1985, at NESC: unbanded gray adult in day roost 1.5 m high in 2.5 m deciduous holly with leaves beside trail at 0730; scolded by hermit thrush, drops from perch, and flies 1 m above ground into thicker woods as I approach within 2m.

December 16, 24, 1989, at 13SC: on 16th resident rufous female eating bluejay at 0730 in hollow, open-top Shumard oak trunk 3.5 m above ground (cavity is 43 cm deep); on 24th her gray mate is there at 0800 but flies as I climb; returns about 1230. (Note: this is same cavity noted January 9, 1985.)

December 25, 1983, at 13SC: longest subfreezing streak I remember; five days so far. Max./min. at house reads −3/−15°C, same on ground, but ravine reads −1/−20 for air and 7/−4 on ground under 3 cm leaf litter. Roosting owl looks out at 10:00 A.M., suns, as I head out at −7°C to check other boxes.

Chapter 3. Food Supplies and Predation: Why Owls Are Mobbed

January 12, 1979, at Gordon-1: banding Harris sparrows and cardinals at 1800 (dusk); distress scream of male cardinal brings gray owl to ground 3 m away; while I am banding this cardinal, the owl strikes my hand. I walk 30 m away to thicket to release cardinal, followed by the owl overhead, but it does not pursue the released bird, which hides in the thicket. Owl then returns to banding trap and hops around, apparently looking for the cardinal. I throw a dead house sparrow to it, which it looks at intently for perhaps 10 seconds before pouncing and flying swiftly away with it.

January 13–17, 1982, at 13SC: an Inca dove banded on the 9th plus a black rat are cached and frozen; 20 cm snow on 14th and Inca dove partly eaten but not black rat (both carcasses frozen at −11°C tonight); on 17th Inca dove is completely gone and only the rat tail remains (temperature range has been −11 to 6°C since the 14th, but no owl roosting here since the 5th).

February 2–6, 1985, at 13SC: after 14 cm snow and −15°C night, headless American goldfinch, and headless dark-eyed junco but no owl in box; junco originally banded here December 18, 1983, retrapped January 28, 1985; only junco left on 3rd, gone on 6th.

March 22–23, 1981, at 13SC: on 22nd watched resident male at 2130 during full moon with partial cloud cover at 14°C, as he caught small moths from lighted bedroom window after moving to the balcony railing, where he watched for them between catches; on 23rd at 1849, he brings white-throated sparrow to incubating female who now sits in box entrance and backs inside for delivery.

April 15, 1989, at 13SC: two male cardinals and a female mob male owl in his deciduous holly roost, surrounded by dozens of yellow-rumped warblers and cedar waxwings that pay no attention whatsoever (1130 hours); repeat performance at 1400 and still no participation by migrants which now include a Swainson's thrush, several kinglets and Nashville warblers.

April 17–26, 1989, at 13SC: male leaves roost 10 minutes before sunset on 17th (female incubating), jays and cardinals mob vacant roost; on 20th roosting male mobbed by jays 18 minutes before sunset, all but one depart and that one mobs nest box and then male again until he departs 7 minutes before sunset (many passage migrants in vicinity quiet by 30 minutes before sunset); on 26th, 3 minutes before sunset, single jay flies toward male catching insect on ground and the owl flies at the jay a meter away, driving it off without a sound.

April 20, 1980, at 13SC: at 1215 the resident male silently watches tufted titmice and Carolina chickadees mob 80-cm rat snake on the patio; the owl simply stares wide-eyed 3 m away, as the parids scold both the snake and owl (note: his mate incubates in a box 12 m away); after 5 minutes the owl flies 30 m into a Shumard oak roost, whereupon four bluejays discover him and drive him 60 m further into a natural cavity roost.

April 25–May 3, 1990, at Holmes; last nestling week (first fledge May 4); 12 of 14 observed catches 2–15 m from nest on ground (1 tree trunk, 1 dogwood flower) using 1–3-m high perches including balcony railing and picnic table; 5–10-m flights; female hunts mostly at patio bug "zapper" 45 m from nest and makes 89 of 151 deliveries in 5.4 hours, including transfers from male; identified prey is 4 small snakes, 15 beetles, 21 moths.

April 29, 1979, at Gordon-1: cloudy, 15°C afternoon; rufous male brings in small bird a 1300 and another at 1700; this is the first day of a notably large songbird migration, coincident with a cool front (*fide* Ann Gordon).

May 3, 1979, at Gordon-2: four 12–38 g chicks and one egg hatching; cached food includes two whole crawdads and three rough earth snakes; as I leave at 1500 rufous male returns to the box with what appears to be an earthworm. Today is only partly cloudy.

May 5–10, 1983, at Baldridge: four chicks are 58–97 g on 5th when one quarter of a bluejay is stored; no stored food on the 6th, but half of a headless Inca dove on the 7th and a similar portion of another bluejay on the 8th; no food on the 9th or the 10th, when the chicks have grown to 94–127 g (*fide* Bob Baldridge, in part).

May 8, 1976, at Davis: four nestlings are 56–96 g, but one has lost two grams in the past five days despite excess food; four headless house sparrows (2 males, 2 females, 1 fledgling) plus one 25-cm lined snake in box at 1630 (both adults roosting outside).

May 9–10, 1980, at 13SC: male delivers small songbird to nestlings at 0845 which causes migrants, bluejays, and cardinals to fuss; as I walk under box, nestlings are calling loudly. At 1030–1130, male catches earthworms in front yard after rain; on 10th, box debris messy with earthworm-laden feces and bands on nestlings occluded with this material; Nashville warbler feathers in box.

May 10, 17, 1979, at Gordon-2: on 10th three nestlings are 66–93 g, while the fourth (new hatchling) is 19 g (a fifth that died shortly after May 3 is gone); 2 black crickets and 5 June bugs plus the rear end of a rusty lizard are cached; on 17th the late hatchling apparently has been cannibalized, regardless of headless bluejay, hind quarters of a rat, and another small rusty lizard in the cache.

May 30, 1979, at Middle Bosque-2 (rural): chicks have fledged; in nest debris is a Texas horned lizard head, the first evidence of predation on this spiny and increasingly rare species; unusual observation because the owls often decapitate prey before bringing it to the nest (note: this is my last observation of a Texas horned lizard in the Waco area through the 1991 field season).

June 2, 1981, at Fisher: 37- and 52-g chicks, third one missing; box piled 3–4 cm deep with uneaten nymph and adult cicadas, walkingsticks, katydids, underwing moths, and 14-cm DeKay's (brown) snake, all quite maggot-ridden. Female seems to be missing and apparently the male is just dropping whole food items into the box.

December 21–24, 1982, at 13SC: on 21st, as I band distress-calling white-throat at 1600, owl looks from box 10 m away, is immediately mobbed, backs inside quickly, but looks out again about 5 minutes after mobbers disappear and studies the area the white-throat and I were in intently before looking around; on the 24th the same bird is in a cedar tree when discovered by the same assemblage of mobbers (chickadees, titmice, kinglets, bluejays, and single mockingbird) which drive it into the box within a few minutes.

Chapter 4. Adult Size, Coloration, and Molt: Basic Contraints

January 6, 1982, at Gordon-1: rufous male, 815–46047, banded at 172 g (note: has gray mate with four eggs May 3, but only one gray nestling is produced; see April 29, 1983, below).

February 6, 1981, at 13SC: gray male (escaped) and brown female (187 g) in box together; 2–7°C with rain. (Note: female was 191 g four days ago at Schlecte.)

February 12, 1979, near Davis: 685–64472 is dead on the road, freshly killed at 0815 hr; bird is 175 g male, fledged May 26, 1978, at about 110 g.

February 18–April 4, 1985, at Davis-2: 154-g male and 180-g female banded in box on February 18; male killed in street 12 m from box on 20th. A 165-g male killed by car in almost same spot March 13, and female lays first egg on 14th which she deserts about the 19th. Female renests April 4; she is 170 g and has 167-g mate (heaviest of three and her certain second if not third mate of year).

March 13, 1975, at Graves: rufous female is 685–64415; she was 224 g when banded here March 18, 1974, five days prior to laying first egg. (Note: bird never reweighed as both the 1974 and 1975 nests were destroyed by ring-tails.)

April 7, 1983, at Schlecte: gray male is 141 g; was 145 g on January 25 and 173 g on December 29,1982, at this box; his gray mate was 197 g on March 10 but is not disturbed today, as she incubates three eggs. Nest abandoned about April 10, and she is not recaptured.

April 10–May 3, 1986, at Keelen: rufous female, 835–87344, is 191 g with 14- and 27-g downy chicks plus two eggs; she is 178 g on April 20, the chicks are 98 g (gray) and 117 g (rufous), and they fledge at 123 g and 139 g, respectively. (Note: she weighed 194 g with 14–36-g chicks on April 23, 1985; these four were 62-g gray, 97-g rufous, 113-g rufous, and 122-g gray on May 7, 1985; her mate was gray both years.)

April 22, 1979, at Gordon-1: rufous female at 186 g has 17- and 21-g hatchlings plus three eggs; her mate is rufous but uncaught; at 115–127 g on May 10, all chicks are rufous.

April 26, 1979–May 25, 1985, at Gordon and Keating (composite): gray female, 595–14814, is 183 g with five eggs on April 26, 1979; 170 g with one 20-g chick and two eggs on May 8, 1982; 176 g with 12–28-g chicks on April 25, 1984; and 187 g with two 16-g hatchlings and two eggs on May 21, 1985. (Note: she is at least 7.5 years old in 1985.)

April 27, 1983, at Graves: gray female, 685–64468, is 192 g and broods three 15–16-g chicks. (Note: she was 196 g while brooding 17–29-g chicks April 22, 1979 and 178 g while brooding 33–85-g nestlings May 5, 1978; she is at least 6.5 years old in 1983.)

April 27–May 12, 1985, at Graves: new gray female is 168 g with 14-g hatchling (wet) and two eggs at 1530; she is 179 g with 27–47-g, brooded nestlings on May 2 and 170 g with 67–91-g, unbrooded nestlings on May 7.

April 29–May 7, 1983, at Gordon-1: same rufous male as last year (815–46047, escaped weighing) has same gray mate (815–46039) at 172 g (was 213 g on March 20 before laying); chicks are 60–105 g and their color is uncertain on May 4, but on May 7 they are: 60 g (rufous and dead, apparently suffocated) 118 g (gray), and 127 g (rufous).

May 1, 1982, at 13SC: gray female is 164 g and incubates five eggs (note: she was 197 g on February 14 and 233 g on January 3 before nesting).

May 2–21, 1978, at Lewis: rufous female is 180 g with 71–93-g chicks; the chicks fledge May 18–21 at 121 (gray), 125 (gray), 128 (rufous), and 138 (rufous) g. Her mate is gray, uncaught; she is the same bird that lost a clutch in this box last year, is very flighty, and hence is handled only once.

July 6, 1984, at 13SC: adult bathes and drinks at 2150; A.M. examination reveals molted primaries and contour feathers (another primary July 8; note no nest here this year).

July 16, 1989, at Bush: chicks banded today; two primary feathers in yard (note: this is latest suburban nest; chicks fledged July 20–24.)

November 23, 1979, at Wise: gray resident male is 157 g; banded as 71 g nestling May 6, 1978 at 7717, 700 m SW of Wise, and fledged May 24.

Chapter 5. Eggs and Incubation: Perilous Times

February 19–April 22, 1983, at 13SC; fox squirrel with young February 19; first owl use by male on March 13; female with three eggs April 13; on April

22 mammalian predator destroys clutch. (Note: this female abandoned her first clutch on April 2, renested here April 12.)

March 7, 1981, at 13SC: heavy morning rain causes fox squirrel to fill box with leaves burying cached, headless hermit thrush; on March 15 gray male reoccupies box.

March 13, 1979 at Wise: unbanded gray female incubating single egg; on 18th egg cracked with adhering squirrel hairs, and nest litter plus fresh leaves indicate temporary squirrel occupation; we have had three days of stormy weather. (Note: on 30th cold egg is removed; no more signs of owls or squirrels.)

March 19–May 18, 1982, at Gordon-2: starling nest without eggs March 19; owl without eggs on 26th, flies as I open box; no owl on 28th; same female without eggs on April 2; owl egg on ground, starling nest with five starling eggs on 9th (no adult); on 26th owl incubates two eggs with five starling eggs pushed to one side; on May 18, five cold, unattended owl eggs (these removed on May 28, all fertile).

March 28–May 20, 1980, at Lewis: gray owl leaves as I climb, one egg on March 28; incubating four eggs on April 20, only three on 30th and May 6; only one egg plus one hatchling (11 g) on May 11; infertile egg remains, nestling gone on 20th.

March 20, 1988, at Vodopich: female is 835–87315 in her fifth year and sits quietly as I pull her left leg out slightly, rotate the band to read the number; no eggs; she has two eggs on April 8 and stays quiet. (Note: this female is 10 years old and has four eggs on May 8, 1993; she has nested here six of the past ten years.)

March 24–26, 1988, at Graves: no owl on 24th; 835–87316 is back for 5th year but no egg; nest checks at dusk indicate she is in box on the 25th-29th before laying first egg, either the 29th or 30th.

April 1–5, 1979, at Echelle: last year's 2-year-old female (number 58) has three eggs on 1st: the fourth arrives April 3; a 5th egg on April 5.

April 5–10, 1979, at Bush: at 1300 on 5th, female sits beside two eggs, (air 30°C); on 7th at 1300 she sits beside three eggs (air 31°C); on the 10th she incubates four eggs but air is 24°C at 1400.

April 7–May 5, 1983, at Davis: on April 7 835–87302 flies as I climb tree, leaving single cold egg; on April 18 she flies again as I climb, but four eggs are warm, and she reenters box from a perch about 10 m away as I leave yard; on May 5, female kicks the eggs aside, erects body feathers and partially spreads wings as I open box lid, then flies but returns from 10 m away, as I take ladder down; on 17th, female in box but only three eggs, all cold, and Dub and Claudia say squirrels have been looking in box off and on for over a month; on 25th, only two rotten eggs remain.

April 11, 1989, at 13SC: male in usual holly roost, 4 m from nest box, flies at 1953; cardinals scold at 2007, as he returns; tries to catch moths from foliage within 5–6 m of box, as female looks out; she leaves at 2016, returns 2039.

April 22–May 2, 1980, at Rolf-1 (rural): four cold eggs on April 22, no sign of owls, much mud and raccoon tracks on box front and top, so perhaps attempted predation frightened female away; nothing here on 27th, but same female 685–64487 incubates two new eggs on May 2.

April 23–May 4, 1981, at Gordon-2: 595–14814 female incubates two starling eggs plus two of her own on April 22; (fox squirrel had box in March, but squirrel nest removed by starlings and present debris is starling nest); by May 3 owl has three eggs and only one starling egg remains: on 4th squirrel apparently evicts owl and dumps eggs on ground during heavy rain.

April 27, 1983, at Graves: female is 685–64468 banded here May 5, 1978; her three newly hatched chicks, 15, 15, and 16 grams, indicate 29-day incubation period for the first egg, and 27 days for the second and third (female didn't begin incubation until the second egg, and cold weather may have forced her to sit tighter, hence the short incubation).

May 1–June 23, 1982, at Wise: female still incubating six eggs on May 1; on 3rd, female incubates but snaps bill and kicks eggs; on 7th she incubates and kicks all eggs aside as I investigate (39 days since first egg laid); on May 11 only incubates two of the six eggs; on 19th she has only four eggs; on 22nd still four (56 days since first egg laid); on 9 June female still incubates four eggs but has molted a primary; female finally left three infertile eggs June 23; incubation at least 78 days.

Chapter 6. Chicks and Fledglings: Greater Investments

February 6, 1980, at Burleson (natural cavity): three large chicks sunning at 1500 hr (air 16°C) in west-facing cavity; female in south-facing cavity of same cedar elm tree. (Note: chicks fledge February 11–13, the earliest record of completed nesting in eastern screech owls.)

April 23, 1987, at Deaver: dry 15-g hatchling, and two eggs at 1530 hrs; female broods quietly though snaps bill; cedar waxwing and two inland silversides cached, but acrobat ants carrying out bits of the fish.

May 1, 1986, at Bush: yearling female has only a 21-g chick plus two of her four eggs, but also the hind end and legs of another downy hatchling which she must have killed and eaten or fed to the 21-g chick; the single live chick is too small for fratricide; no male and no cached food in the nest. (Note: new male on May 6.)

May 2–5, 1980, at 13SC: male on Shumard oak perch 5.5 m from nest at 0600–1400 hr; and moves between two other perches 5–7 m from nest (one only 1 m above ground) when hassled by blue jays and cardinals; finally flies

away at 1940; on 3rd and 4th he is in same Shumard oak roost between
dawn and noon but gone in the afternoon; female ceases brooding on the
4th; on the 5th he is 6 m away while the female is 9 m farther; he flies to another perch 9 m from nest at 1600 hr and is mobbed by the jays and mockingbirds who don't see or ignore female.

May 2–15, 1978, at Graves: on 2nd, female broods 23–49-g chicks at
18°C (1600 hrs); on 7th at 29.5°C female peers from box entrance at 1300
hrs; on 11th she broods 58–114-g chicks; but on the 16th she is out of the
box, as the 97–119-g chicks pant at 34°C (1430 hrs).

May 3–17, 1979, at Gordon-2: on 3rd I find a freshly dead 12-g chick,
three 24–38-g siblings, and a hatching egg plus cached food (two crayfish
and three rough earth snakes); as I leave yard at 1500 hrs, the rufous male returns with an earthworm; on the 10th female sits beside four 19–93-g chicks
and the hind end of a Texas spiny lizard; the dead chick is gone, surely cannibalized; on the 17th, the 19-g runt is also missing, despite lots of bluejay
feathers, the hind quarters of a half-grown brown rat, and a whole spiny lizard (mean sibling weight is 81.7 g).

May 7–18, 1982, at 13SC: female broods four 14–52-g chicks with 5th egg
on the 7th; four days later she and the unhatched egg are missing; severe
storm on the 11th does not flush male from his roost; on the 12th chicks are
34–91 g and a female cardinal is stashed but, again, no female owl; on the
13th female is back, wet and standing over wet chicks beneath entrance hole
as very heavy wind gusts blow rain into box; the smallest chick is dead on
the 15th, and larger chicks are 78–98 g, one with a maggot-infested leg in-
jury; on the 18th, chicks are 94–115 g and no sign of female, but 11 live and
1 dead blind snakes are in the nest debris, and the chick's injured leg is
healing.

May 9–June 3, 1991, at Bush: on 9th as female broods four chicks, male is
killed on the street, and the smallest chick is cannibalized next day; by the
17th, female acquires a new mate or helper-male; on 24th I recover 12 live
blind snakes in the nest; two chicks fledge on May 26–28, the last on June 3.

May 10–20, 1987, at Davis: live blind snake with three 109–132-g chicks
on 10–15th but snake gone on 20th, when all three fledge together. (Note:
this is first record of entire brood fledging simultaneously, but the older ones
apparently had been put off by five consecutive windy rainy nights.)

May 12–June 10, 1980, at Bush: four eggs at noon on 12th but wet 15-g
hatchling at 1600 hrs; on 13th wet 11- and 12-g hatchlings at 1315 hrs; female does not brood at nest temperature of 32°C; on 16th three nestlings are
21–31-g with unhatched egg, female does not brood or incubate at 1400 hrs
and nest temperature of 28°C; on 18th nestlings are 30–40 g with unhatched
egg and nonbrooding female at noon, nest temperature of 31°C; on 23rd female is gone at 1300 hrs and nest temperature is 35°C, chicks are 55–79 g (fe-

male removed unhatched egg about the 20th); on 28th live blind snake crawls amongst 87–106-g chicks, lying on east side of 34°C box at 1600 hrs; on June 2, 103–122-g nestlings lay prone at 1700 hrs but occasionally pant at 34°C; first-hatched chick fledges on the 9th; on 10th next chick looks from hole at 1845 hrs and climbs out and up over box top into tree at 2020 (dusk); then female sings low monotonic trill in front of hole and the last owlet, looking out at 2110, jump-flaps to a lower limb of the nest tree.

May 13–15, 1990, at Vodopich: new 12–14-g hatchling each day; Darrell and Donna see broadwing hawk perched on stub 2 m in front of box at 2015 hrs on 13th, peering intently at box, presumably hearing the hatching activity; headless baby cottontail in box on 15th.

May 20–30, 1979, at Gordon-1: number 95 owlet fledges at 2045 hrs on 20th, whereupon female comes by with lizard but does not deliver it (she was seen taking lizard hind quarters out of box yesterday by Ann); 96 fledges on 21st at 1630 hrs; female is killed in a severe storm at 0900 on 22nd; on 30th number 96 is found dead under its roost tree, 5 m from nest box, apparently drowned in last night's 5.7-cm downpour. (Note: this fledgling had gained 2 g above its 96 g low, relative to its 118-g fledging weight, and had flown up to at least 50 m away from the nest; its daytime fledging is a unique event.)

June 4, 1989, at Moes: brooding female death-feigns as I lift her from 36–59-g chicks (5–8 days old); Pam holds her in an open hand for several minutes, while I weigh chicks; suddenly she flies away, quickly and with obvious direction; male roosting 9 m away in ash foliage follows her.

June 9–10, 1979, at Wise: female with 39- and 41-g nestlings roosts 4.5 m from box at 1540 hrs and 32°C air temperature; she is 1.5 m from her mate who sits on abandoned squirrel nest but flies during my weigh of the nestlings; cold front during night and female broods nestlings next 0930 at 16°C air temperature.

June 30, 1990, at Holmes: four fledglings still together, without adults, are feeding themselves on ground insects tonight (they fledged May 4–8); occasionally one goes back into the box, apparently out of curiosity, but does not stay long (note: natal dispersal is July 8–14.)

July 16–20, 1989, at Bush: chicks lying prone and apparently not panting despite high nest temperature in box at 35.2°C; these fledge on the 20th.

August 9, 1989, at Graves: chick fledged between May 18 and 22 found dead 182 m east of birth place hence still within its natal area 11.5 weeks after fledging. (Note: contrast with another from here that fledged May 17, 1991, recovered dazed but well on September 25, 1.4 km SW of birth place.)

August 18–22, 1979 at Graves: two banded owlets that fledged May 21–23, roost on window sill at about 0530 and are gone by dark (2100 hr) each day; no evidence of their parents.

Chapter 7. Vocalizations: Clues to the Night

January 22, 1977, at Davis: first rigorous monotonic trilling of season; bouts 2–3 minutes apart, beginning about 1800 in live oaks 10–30 m from box.

February 8, 12, 1976, at 7717: beginning 1730 on 8th, resident male gives a monotonic trill every 25 second for five seconds. On 12th at 2100 he sings in box for three minutes and then yard. Another male trills about 100 m south toward Graves, and he flies 30 m toward the second singer. The two sing synchronously at 25–60-second intervals for about five seconds each at 2100–2135.

April 13, 1982, at 13SC: first summer-resident chuck-wills-widow of year sings 30 m from incubating female at 1925–2015 and 2135–2215. Within a minute at 1925, male begins monotonic trilling around nest box and keeps it up until 2030 but does not resume during second chuck serenade.

April 25–May 20, 1984, at Keating: on April 25, male roosts 2.5 m from box, bill-claps, stares wide-eyed, then flies as I inspect brooding female and chicks; on 30th female is at former male roost mobbed by mockingbird pair as I weigh 29–75-g chicks; she flies away but comes back, stares round-eyed and hoots during weighing. On May 5, female is 2 m from box, swoops twice as I weigh chicks but no vocalizations (male not seen); on 12th chicks are 116–122 g and all bill-clap during weighing, which attracts parents who swoop and bill-clap; then female perches and gives plaintive hoo while male trills monotonically; and finally both provide several bouts of hooting. On 20th last chick fledges, as I place ladder on tree at 1600; females attacks though mobbed by mockingbirds, cardinals, and a common grackle; when perched she rasps and rattles during mobbing.

May 8, 12, 1981, at 13SC; while weighing 96–120-g owlets at 1300 on 8th, both adults hit me on the head, the female first after screeching, while chicks bill-clap; no sound from male. On 12th a nestling looks out at 1920, and female flies by bill-clapping and screeching, while male remains until 2015, seemingly unperturbed in his day roost, 3 m from box and 8 m from my observation post.

May 15, 1980, at 13SC: 94–120-g owlets food-begging a 2030; parents very vocal with bill-claps and screeches at my approach to nest; at 2130 female gives four hoots in each of three bouts from oak by patio, as our cat comes to the screened doorway; owl stops hooting when cat moves away at 2135.

May 20, 1982, at 13SC: feeding visit to 112–121-g owlets at 2151, one of which looks from the hole; immediately three hoots 3 m behind me as I sit at my usual observation station 9 m from box; neighbors' company leaves their porch 20m from nest box; female flies past me to perch and gives two hoots, a very short descending trill, and then four more hoots. Males gives a faint descending trill about 2 m from box. Female flies to perch 3 m from him and utters descending trills antiphonally for about a minute; now a monotonic trill from male, and female flies off.

May 21, 1981, at 13SC: female hoots for five minutes at dusk; some of the hoots are descending. Is she aggravated at our white towels drying on the balcony railing? I remove towels, and she flies toward fledgling, 90 m away in ravine, without additional vocalizations.

June 9, 1976, at 7717: largest hand-raised fledgling (141 g, 27 days old) "fledges"; it climbs pecan trunk to branch 2 m above ground, rasps, and is looked over by resident female, who trills monotonically for three minutes without apparent response from youngster, who nibbles pecan leaflets; when she flies by him, the owlet gives four imperfect hoots.

June 12, 23, 1980, at Rolf-1 (rural): 99–105-g nestlings bill-clap during weighing at 1430, which brings hooting female to perches 4–8 m away; she leaves when mobbed by titmouse family. On 23rd, the female is 3 m from me, as I inspect nestlings, and delivers several hoots and barks without billclapping; no sign of male either time.

July 12, 1980, at 13SC: single fledgling and parents use bird bath each evening this week, accompanied by descending trills and an occasional monotonic trill and hoot or bark (bird bath is 18 m from nest box).

July 13, 1979, at 7717: two independent juveniles from Graves 200 m away (fledged May 16–19) come to bird bath at 2050. One hoots and then gives a monotonic trill; they stay about ten minutes but fly off without drinking, apparently frightened by my presence on the patio 5 m away. No adults seen.

August 13, 1984, at 13SC: descending trill by resident bachelor male at 2015–2030 (still very light) during thunderstorm that skirts area. Storm passes and owl is quiet (no nest here this year).

August 19–30, 1980, at 13SC: between 2050 and 2130 on 19th, male has four descending trill stations 15–100 m from nest box; at 2025 on 25th, his independent youngster (fledged May 25) drinks at bird bath amid many antiphonal descending trills from both parents about 30 m away but seems unperturbed. At 2315 male drinks, perches 3 m from bird bath, catches insect on ground, gives descending trill from eating perch, then again 15 m away, and again 30–40 m further away at 2338 (juvenile gone from natal area by 30th).

September 16, 1984, at 13SC: bark, then descending trill (at first lacking vibrato) at 2145 from resident male; continues four minutes; five minutes later great-horned owl flies across his calling position over house, and screech owl is quiet.

October 10, 1983, at 13SC: migrating chuck-will's-widows and whip-poor-wills fly-catching at dusk (1915) give frequent chuck calls coincident with descending trills from resident male owl; descending trills quickly followed by lower-pitched monotonic trills. (On 12th a churring brown trasher, about to roost, appears to cause the same response—descending trills with associated monotonic trills.)

Fisher

Nothing in the box except an old fox squirrel nest on January 18—no evidence of screech owls nearby, nor can I find any on February 23. On March 8, however, I notice a banded gray owl sitting in an English ivy vine tangle, 3 m high, and next to a tree trunk only 2 m from the box. On the 11th, the bird is in exactly the same position, so I catch it with a net and rediscover the male from this nest site last year. He weighs 155 g. On the 15th he occupies the same roost, and the box remains empty.

But on March 22, his grayish brown mate incubates a single egg in the box, while he continues to use the ivy roost. The female seems placid, so I gently rotate the band on her leg, as she leans away from my hand. She remains in concealment posture with ear tufts raised, eyes squinted, and body feathers clamped down. Like the male, she was first banded here last spring during a probable renesting (she laid two eggs and fledged one youngster). I do not revisit the nest until the expected hatching date, 30 days later, and on April 20 find 20- and 25-g chicks, shell fragments, and two eggs under the quiet, 172-g female. Twenty-eight days is the likely incubation period for the largest, two-day-old nestling. I also record a fresh, headless black rat in the box and dye the female's tail tip yellow for identification at night.

On April 22 at 1900 (CST) bluejays and cardinals scold, as the male flies to a food-delivery perch 3.5 m in front of the nest box. He brings a large sphinx moth (the area is illuminated by a street light 5 m away). At 1943 the female sits in the entrance for three minutes and then leaves but returns in 11 minutes, flying first to the food-delivery perch and then into the box. Two minutes later the male returns, carrying a small bird, gives a faint monotonic trill at the food perch, flies to the box entrance, and then back to another perch. There he works on an apparent Nashville warbler and finally delivers it, headless and slightly plucked, to the box.

At 2030 he brings an item to the delivery perch, gives a monotonic trill, delivers, flies to a bare limb 2.5 m above my head, trills again, watches my dictating, then preens. Another delivery by the male occurs at 2043, one at 2050, and still another at 2056; the owl is catching insects at a porch light about 30 m west of the box. At 2100 I leave, as the same house cat that walked by the box an hour ago, without any apparent recognition by the owls, returns in the direction he came from (air 17°C).

Two nights later, again during the full moon, I resume the watch at 1900.

A lawn sprinkler runs 5 m from the nest box. The male arrives at 1920, flies to the box entrance with an unknown item, back to his usual food-delivery perch, and again to the box apparently for the actual delivery. (Was he startled by the sprinkler spray?) Subsequent deliveries are at 1924 and 1926, neither item identifiable. His mate looks out at 1927, leaves two minutes later, and I hear the first chuck-wills-widow at 1930, about 90 m to the east, together with the male's monotonic trill about 10 m in that direction.

Four cars pass between 1937 and 1959, and both adults owls perch over my head and watch me during this time. At 2005 the female returns to the box but looks out two minutes later, flies to a perch 6 m away, then back into the box at 2010 and out again. She does not deliver food. At 2012, however, she catches a cricket on the ground about 6 m to my right, only 2.5 m from still another passing car, eats it on a perch, and returns to the box. Within a few seconds the male flies to the delivery perch, the female looks out, he gives a low monotonic trill, and she flies to the perch above my head with a muted descending trill. He flies to her, apparently with food, and she quickly returns to the nest. She does not leave again while I watch.

At 2015, the male catches something on the ground only 6 m from the box and makes a delivery. Then he flies 15 m south, behind some trees, but is back in a minute with an unknown item. Two more cars, and at 2047 the male makes a delivery. At 2050 Elmer is out with his dog and turns off the lawn sprinkler. Then I notice the male watching him. Three minutes afterward the owl catches something on the ground, goes to the delivery perch, trills, and then flies to the nest, going all the way inside this time. He sits in the entrance for five seconds before flying to a perch and trilling. Two more cars pass, and I depart (air 17°C).

Next night, the sprinkler is on again and hits the nest tree 0.5 m below the box. A car passes at 1915. The male trills montonically from 15 m east of the box at 1920, and the female comes to the entrance. Her mate flies up to the entrance with insect food but does not deliver. (Is he trying to bring his mate out?) A minute later, though, he does transfer a June bug to the sitting female and is back in 40 seconds with another. Meanwhile, the female has backed into the box but reappears for a 1925 delivery, preceded by her mate's trilling. A soon as he leaves, she does also. The evening's first chuck-will's-widow calls.

At 1926 she is back with food and again at 1930 when a car passes. This time she remains inside the box, looking out, and the male gives her a June bug after trilling from the delivery perch. At 1934 she flies out, then back and out a minute later; back inside, out again at 1937, out, back, and out once more as two cars pass (can she be agitated at the sprinkler hitting the tree?). She perches over my head but does not vocalize and flies north out of sight at 1939, returning to the box at 1941. She leaves and returns at 1942 and then out a minute later when she utters muted descending trills over my head. A cat yowls 15 m away, and she continues to trill with new meaning to me.

Just after a car at 1950, the male returns to a different perch, trills monotonically, and transfers a caterpillar to the female who has flown over to him. She gives descending trills again, delivers to the box (goes inside), and flies back to the same perch with more trilling. She still trills at 1954, when the male returns with a small moth, but I notice a cat walking about 10 m behind the nest box. The descending trills cease and both parents fly off at 1957, as the cat moves about 20 m away. (Interestingly, the male shows no recognition of the cat.)

The female returns to the box at 2021, not to leave again before my departure at 2100. Two more cars have passed. The males arrives at 2034 and at 2038 with food, trilling monotonically each time before delivering to the box entrance. The female does not look out. Another cat crosses 10 m behind the box to the south, but there is no apparent cognizance of the fact from either parent owl.

On April 26 the downy owlets are 58 and 75 g, large enough for banding, and their mother is 169 g. She does not brood, though it is not particularly hot (air 25°C). The two remaining eggs are gone. (Apparently unhatched, they were taken from the nest, because I cannot find shell fragments.) Now the male is in his cedar elm roost of last year, 3 m east and 3 m above the nest box which is 3 m above ground. The owlets are 92 and 113 grams on May 1, again brooded by the female who has lost another four grams. On the 6th, she has regained two grams and sits beside her well-feathered chicks; they are 112 and 127 g. Her mate shows little response to her bill-clapping and a muffled screech or the bill-claps of both owlets as I weight them. He just opens his eyes wider.

A storm is brewing in the west, the sky is partly cloudy, and the south wind strong as I arrive at 2010, April 29. The female is looking out but retreats inside the nest box. A Carolina wren sings about 50 m to the south. At 2016 the male flies from his English ivy roost, and a chuck-wills-widow sings. The female reappears at 2020 and accepts 2026 and 2028 food deliveries from her mate at the box entrance. The wind is so strong and the highway noise so loud that I may not be hearing vocalizations. At 2038 the female flies from the nest, over my head, and across the road eastward.

At 2044 the male make a delivery, sits in the entrance for ten seconds and then strikes something on a tree trunk 10 m in front of the box. He delivers the second item at 2045; both visits involve straight flights into the box. Two minutes later I hear descending trills 12 m south and then a monotonic trill, all apparently from the male. I see no stimulus. At 2048 the female flies straight into the box, as the male delivers prey. So far tonight all food is so small that I cannot see what it is. The female sits a few seconds in the entrance at 2057, then flies to a stump 3 m in front of the box, catches a black cricket, and flies to the bare limb over my head where she eats it.

Her mate flies to her at 2102, gives two muted monotonic trills, transfers food, and disappears. She flies to another perch out of my sight and at 2104 back to the box after giving one descending trill. At 2106 the male returns, catches something on the ground beneath the street light, flies to the delivery perch, then inside the box, and finally sits in the entrance a few seconds before flying. At 2112 the female reappears, the male catches something else beneath the street light, flies to the food-delivery perch, whereupon the female flies to him, accepts the item, and eats it there.

At 2115 I see a male delivery, closely followed by a female delivery to the nestlings. She remains inside, and the male comes back at 2116 and goes inside too. He flies out within five seconds, though, and the female then sits in the entrance . She quickly leaves for the food-delivery perch. At 2128 the male catches something on the ground at the light, flies up to the female, feeds her, and flies off toward the north. She sits quietly, so I shall dictate some general impressions before departing early because of the poor viewing conditions (air 22°C).

First, it is apparent that there are a number of function-specific perches and precise flight lines among them, all beneath the canopy or in its lower half. It seems the birds have chosen convenient aerial paths like mammal trails on the ground. They usually swoop between about 1 and 3 m above ground. Secondly, the male is doing the major share of provisioning and revisits spots with multiple prey like porch and street lights instead of bringing several small items at once. Unlike the female, he seems unconcerned with nest protection, whereas she is relatively uninvolved with feeding, an interesting division of labor. The male hunts primarily if not exclusively within 60 m of the nest box.

The stormy weather has passed by May 2; the sky is partly cloudy, no wind, the air is 18° at 2015 tonight. We have had two nights and a day of rain, 7 cm altogether. The female appears in the entrance at 2026, as a cat walks down a path 12 m south of the box. She ducks inside. The cat disappears, and the first chuck-will's-widow calls at 2029. The male decapitates a ground skink (lizard) on the plucking perch and delivers the body at 2030. His mate reappears at 2040 and flies eastward, as he arrives at the food perch with a monotonic trill and a moth at 2043. He delivers to the box entrance himself.

The yellow cat repeats its walk by the nest box without notice by the owls and heads for me, so I shoo it away. A third car at 2056, and the female arrives at the delivery perch. At 2100 another car passes, as the male comes to another perch with a caterpillar and trills monotonically. His mate flies over to him, takes the prey, and flies across the street with it. At 2104 he brings another caterpillar to the nestlings at the entrance, while the female gives descending trills toward the cat, who sits about 25 m from the box across the street. Now the male flies northward, seemingly uninvolved with the feline encounter. The female continues to trill for three minutes.

Feeding visit to the nest at 2115 by the female, then by the male, while his mate commences trilling again 10 m southeast of the box. At 2117 he flies to her, apparently gives her food, whereupon she quits vocalizing and feeds her two nestlings. Another feeding visit at 2125 by the male, who flies in from behind the box and, in a landing maneuver on the delivery perch, turns around to face the nest. Then he perches near the street light, catches a moth in the air (?), and makes another delivery at 2126. He delivers again at 2128, 2133, and 2145, flying to and from a street light about 60 m south of the box. Meanwhile, the female has reentered the box but leaves at 2138 just as a neighbor stops to talk, and I end this night's watch (air 17°C).

On May 5 another cold front approaches; the sky is partly cloudy, the air 23°C, and a strong south wind blows as I begin observations at 2015. The nestlings are already active and food-begging at 2020, when the male leaves his day roost in the ivy tangle. He drops abruptly to about 1 m above ground, flies 20 m, then rises to a 2.5 m perch. His mate appears in the entrance at 2022 and is fed at 2029; she then leaves quickly. The male feeds the nestlings at 2032. Two cars pass, and there is unsexed feeding visit at 2051. A high-pitched, faint descending trill from the female to my right suggests the male made the last delivery. A car at 2054; then the female flies to the food perch, a beetle is transferred to her, and she retreats inside the box at 2057.

At 2059 the female looks out as the male flies by, catches something from the leaves of a shrub in front of the box, and delivers it to her. She then leaves for a perch by the street light, where she looks about until her mate arrives at 2108. He give a monotonic trill, but I cannot see him. She flies in his direction at 2111. Five minutes later, she catches something on the ground beneath the light, delivers it to the nestlings at the box entrance, flies to the plucking perch and utters a descending trill. (This is the first certain indication that the female catches her own prey for delivery to the nestlings: she had started to feed herself on April 24.)

The male passes an insect to his mate at 2124 but then flies to the box. (Is this a nest check or feeding visit?) The female catches a black cricket on the ground near me at 2126 and delivers it immediately to the nestlings, whereupon the male makes another food delivery. Still another set of deliveries at 2131. A male-to-female-to-nest transfer sequence occurs at 2136, employing the food-delivery perch followed by a female-only delivery at 2144, also using this perch. At 2153 the female begins three bouts of muted descending trills from this perch but then sits quietly until food is transferred by her mate at 2200. She takes the unknown item to the box.

When I weigh the owlets on May 11 (124 and 139 g) I cannot locate either parent, but in the afternoon of May 16 the male is on his usual cedar elm roost. The remaining nestling weighs 127 g on the 16th; it is the younger, smaller one (the older one fledged May 15).

At 2015 on May 11, it is a muggy 26°C as I begin my nightwatch. The female flies in from the south, perches in the box entrance a few seconds and leaves at 2018. (This is just a nest check, familiar nightly behavior after females stop spending their days with nestlings.) I can see the youngsters stretching and looking at me from within the box. I talk with Elmer Fisher a few minutes at 2025, which may put the adults off somewhat. The first food delivery is at 2036, sex unknown.

The female feeds at 2045 and the male at 2046, while the nestlings look out but do not perch in the entrance. A car passes at 2054, male deliveries happen at 2057 and 2058, followed by the male's monotonic trilling behind me. More male deliveries take place at 2110, 2121, and 2140, but none by the female until 2136 (then only one more by her at 2146 during this evening's watch). I hear a mild screech about 15 m south of the nest at 2142 but cannot see the stimulus or the bird. (Screeches alone cannot be sexed.)

At 2144 the male arrives at the delivery perch with a large moth, sits 20 seconds, goes inside the box with the moth, then sits in the entrance with it a few seconds, in a tree 3 m in front of the box ten seconds more, and finally flies away with the moth intact. This inducement to fledge is the first such for the brood. (Considering the nestling looking-out behavior and the apparent reduced rate of feeding, I think fledging will take place this week.) The male catches a moth on a tree trunk at 2155 and eats it himself, as I leave for the evening (air 22°).

It is 2015 on May 12 and songbirds plus chuck-will's-widows are active as I begin my watch. The last common grackle flock moves out at 2025, and the male owl begins monotonic trilling 15 m north of the nest. Within the minute he comes by, looks in the box, and departs, as does the female a few seconds later. A nestling looks out at 2037, and the female delivers a beetle, while the male resumes trilling in his original position. The first car passes at 2038, then feeding visits by the female at 2040 and male at 2042.

I hear descending trills from the female, perhaps 50 m southwest of the nest at 2047, and a minute later she flies to the plucking perch, looks at me for a few seconds, turns around to face the nest and direction she came from, and begins muted trilling again. (If I had not seen her, I would be confused about her location, thinking it much farther away, and about her intent, thinking it directed toward me, the territorial intruder.) Folks in the house,

14 m from the nest box, are doing something on their patio southwest of the
box, and they may be the cause of her singing. At 2048, she begins to follow
each fourth or fifth descending trill with a monotonic trill.

A car at 2057 and trumpet practice in an adjacent house at 2115 bracket
the female's next food delivery at 2106. At 2120 and 2122 are more feeding
visits by her, the last after a June bug transfer from the male on the plucking
perch. At 2123, on the trunk of a pecan, she catches something she eats herself, and the male delivers insects to the nestlings at 2125, 2126, and 2127,
following flights from the same spot about 25 m east of the box. One nestling actually perches in the entrance for the first time at 2126, and it bobs
and weaves looking around at its environment. The male feeds again at 2134,
then trills monotonically for six minutes, and I depart (air 22°C).

Again it is stormy weather with gusty south winds and lightning but no
rain on May 14. I begin watching at 2015. One nestling is already looking
out, perched in the entrance, but ducks inside as I arrive. When I sit down,
the nestling reappears. At 2016, the female flies in to a perch 6 m in front of
the box, and the quiet nestling looks at her for four minutes before retreating
inside. The male arrives on the food-delivery perch at 2036 and sits, as the female flies directly inside the box at 2040, knocking the nestling from the entrance. I cannot tell if she brought food.

An adult flies directly into the box at 2052, 2111, and 2115, (such direct
flights may obviate problems perching in the wind, also observed under similar conditions April 29). It is impossible to tell which adult and whether food
is involved; the action is too quick. At 2126 the male catches a 14-cm snake,
seemingly a rough earth snake, on the bare ground only 3 m from me and
flies back up to the plucking perch. Upon arriving he faces away from the
box but turns toward it before working on the snake. He spends five seconds
on the ground but 72 seconds to dispatch the snake, then sits 27 seconds
with it dangling straight down from his beak, flies to the delivery perch for
ten seconds, and then to the box.

Another car and another feeding visit by an adult at 2127, again a direct
flight into the box. (By direct I only mean no food-delivery perch; the adults
still employ the shallow U-flight maneuver.) Still another car and another
visit at 2142, but this one employs the food perch, so I can see the female
with a beetle. Also, I note an alert nestling watches her intently the five seconds she sits on the perch but does not vocalize. She flies inside the box but
leaves quickly without sitting in the entrance, the case with all other food-
delivery flights tonight, and the nestling reappears in the entrance. I leave at
2200 (air 23°C).

As I arrive May 15, a nestling is perched in the box entrance, and its closest human neighbor pets a cat on a patio 14 m to the west. It is partly cloudy
and 24° with a light south breeze at 2115. The female parent flies from her

ivy tangle roost at 2017, and the nestling ducks inside. At 2024 the male trills monotonically 45 m north of the nest, while the female delivers a wood roach to the nestling in the entrance. The male continues singing until 2034, and I continue talking with Elmer Fisher until another feeding visit at 2044. I do not notice who or what is involved.

The female flies to the delivery perch with a large moth at 2045, goes to the box entrance, sits there facing inward a few seconds, then flies back to the delivery perch for a few more seconds—looking toward the box—and finally departs out of sight to the south (another apparent instance of fledging inducement). At 2050 both adults fly to the delivery perch almost simultaneously, the male transfers a black cricket to the female, and she makes the delivery. I lose track of the male, but the female flies past me with a slight descending trill. Now I hear the two nestlings chittering as they jockey for position in the entrance.

At 2054 a car passes and two dogs bark at a cat that walks behind the nest box. Both nestlings continue to chitter and take turns perching in the entrance. I hear no food-begging rasps. The first chuck-will's-widow of the evening calls a moment later; whereupon both nestlings disappear into the box, though one reappears within a minute. At 2056 the female flies directly to the entrance with another large moth, then quickly to a tree trunk 2 m in front of the entrance. As the alert nestling watches and food-begs, she flies about 3 m further away into the lower canopy. (Her enticement behavior is very obvious.)

After 14 minutes of adult inactivity, the female visits the box, but I cannot tell about a food delivery. She goes inside and leaves promptly. At 2114 a nestling reappears in the entrance and within two minutes comes all the way out, clinging to the entrance for a minute before climbing up on the roof with the aid of its beak and flapping wings. Immediately its sibling perches in the entrance. After a minute's rest the fledgling begins climbing the nest tree with beak, feet, and flapping wings and by 2120 is 2 m above the box, perched on a small limb. By 2123 it is out of sight, at least 3 m above the box or about 6 m above ground in the lowermost dense canopy.

Two more cars pass, the remaining nestling continues to look out, but the adult owls do not revisit until 2125. Then one of them comes to the fledgling. At 2144 is another fledgling visit. I am unable to see who is involved or what food is delivered because of the dense canopy, but I note that the nestling is unattended through at least 2200 when I leave (air 22°C).

On May 16 at 2015 the air is 24°, and the south breeze has picked up. At 2028 a family walks by on the road; at 2030 a car passes. Then at 2035 the second nestling looks out, coincidentally with the first chuck-will's-widow song of the night. At 2038 the male gives one monotonic trill 10 m south, and at 2041 the female catches something from a tree trunk 15 m to the north. She feeds the nestling then flies back to the delivery perch, gives a monotonic trill, followed by a much fainter descending trill, and flies directly over my head, so close that I can feel the wing beats.

At 2044 the male makes a 20-m, 45°-angle flight from a perch about 3 m in front of me and near the box, across the street, and catches a small rodent on the far side. He spends only about ten seconds on the ground, then flies to the plucking perch, works on the catch for 80 seconds, flies directly to the box with it, pauses in the entrance a few seconds, and then exits to another perch where he begins to eat. At 2046 he returns directly to the box with a piece of the rodent, knocks the nestling out of the entrance, and quickly flies back to the plucking perch. (Second and third instances of inducement of fledge, employing the same prey item—interesting!)

As a car approaches at 2047, the male flies across the street with the remaining piece of food (perhaps to feed his mate, since that is the direction she flew.) And the nestling reappears in the box entrance. At 2052 the male flies back to the delivery perch and is immediately seen by the nestling, who starts to beg. He flies to another perch, closer to the nestling, but I cannot see if he carries anything. At 2055 he flies southward, and the nestling stops food-begging and begins to peer intently at the ground. I hear monotonic trilling by the male 3 m south of the box at 2100.

The female flies to the delivery perch at 2107 and in 30 second flies to a large pecan tree about 3 m behind the nest tree, apparently catches something on the lower leaves and flies into the canopy above the delivery perch. No notice by the nestling. At 2122 a nearly repeat performance by the female, which causes the nestling to look up, but I hear no begging. At 2126, however, the female flutters in front of the nestling and makes an aerial transfer of some insect. This is the last visit I notice before leaving at 2145 (air 22°) and I believe the nestling will not fledge tonight. I do not locate the first fledgling again this evening, but think it is in the canopy above the delivery perch, based on adult flight patterns.

On the morning of May 17 I check the box to discover I was wrong last night. The younger nestling fledged after I left. None of the screech owls is in the immediate vicinity, but I do not spend much time looking because a storm is brewing (we receive 3.5 cm of rain and mothball-size hail for about eight minutes soon after I depart). The nest debris is too sparse to collect for analysis of pellets, food remains, and decomposer insects.

I arrive at 2030 P.M. May 17 and station myself 12 m north of the box, rather than by the street. I seek a different angle. The male calls monotonically in his usual spot 15 m north of the box. Some cardinals scold. Within three minutes I locate both fledglings about 28 m northeast of the box in the top of a red cedar amongst live oaks. They are about 10 m above ground, 2 m apart but immediately move together. At 2035 the male flies into the cedar and gives a muffled descending trill. Then the female appears and utters several bouts of three and four hoots, followed by one of seven hoots. (A mockingbird also scolds me, so my walking around to find the fledglings may evoke these alarm vocalizations.)

Just as the fist chuck-will's-widow sings at 2044, 27 m away, the female in the cedar with the fledglings screeches (gives a prolonged scream actually). Meanwhile the male, back at his original song post, commences monotonic trilling again. Three more bouts of hoots from the female at 2046 as she flies about the area. (I have returned to my usual seat, so she may be perturbed about the chuck-will's-widow.) I see one fledgling walking around on limbs in the canopy at 2047, silhouetted against the sky, and change my position again to see better.

The female flies to a bare limb 6 m in front of me, gives a couple of descending trills, apparently spots something on the ground, and makes a beeline for it. She is back with a descending trill by 2054 and feeds a fledgling. The male still gives his monotonic trill. One fledgling walks, hops, and flaps through short canopy spaces, as it moves about 2 m back toward the nest box. At 2102 is another feeding visit, and I hear the food-begging call. Then I see one youngster has moved 2 m toward the north, while the other has moved southward toward the box. At 2108 an adult visits the northward-moving owlet. I cannot see anything well, since it is quite dark, and leave at 2115 (air 15°C).

At 2015 on May 18 the air is 15°C, and the sky is clear with a light north breeze. I easily locate the male owl, roosting in a red cedar, 5 m from the female in a live oak, herself 1 m from both fledglings who are about 0.3 m apart. This is almost the same position they were in last night. The youngsters are 7 m above ground, 2 m from the top of the oak and 0.5 m above their mother. At 2027 the male flies north. The female does likewise at 2030, while the owlets remain unmoving.

The male returns at 2033 and carries a large beetle in his beak to a perch 3 m from me. He loudly cracks the beetle for a few seconds, gives one monotonic trill, and the female flies up beside him. She utters a faints food-begging twitter and he transfer the beetle, which she eats quickly. The male then flies to another bare limb, wipes his beak, and gives several faint descending trills before flying 12 m northward. At 2035 the female is finished eating and flies eastward. (By now I am certain that prey may be immobilized when caught but is not ready for consumption until after it is returned to a food-processing perch, seemingly a much safer place than the ground or other unfamiliar site.)

At 2037 the female flies in over my head with another beetle, which she cracks for five seconds before flying up to feed a fledgling. The unfed sibling then jumps and flaps across about 1 m of open space toward the fed one. At

2040 the male returns with a large caterpillar and a monotonic trill. The female flies to him, to a limb over my head, then 6 m away and eats the caterpillar. By 2043 both fledglings are actively food-begging and flapping about in a 2-m radius of their day roost. At 2045 an adult flies to within 3 m of them, and the begging is louder. The other parent comes closer, and one fledgling flaps across 1.5 m of space to it and is fed.

The preceding pattern is repeated at 2048 with both fledglings flapping another several meters northward some 10 m above ground. I hear four hoots in a bout and then five near the owlets. At 2055 the youngsters continue to beg at their "mobile feast," but I must give up watching for tonight. (Surely the adults are enticing the owlets with food to follow them away from a roost, just as they induced fledging.) The air is 14°C but the leaf litter feels much warmer to my touch; it is the source of tonight's June bugs that are emerging all around me.

On May 19 at 2020, both parent owls roost in a dense clump of cedar elm trees 8 m above ground and 17 m north of last night's position. They are 6 m apart, and the female is 0.5 m from the side-by-side fledglings. The male leaves at 2025, whereupon the female shifts her perch 2 m. She departs at 2034 with the reappearance of her mate, who catches something from a tree trunk and delivers it immediately to a fledgling. He flies 3 m into a neighboring tree, and the fed youngster tries to follow, though his father flies again. The owlet very actively flap-hops from perch to perch in the canopy.

This fledgling sustains a level, 3-m flight across an opening at 2036. (If the older youngster, its first real flight comes four nights after fledging.) An adult flies in and feeds it immediately, and its sibling suddenly appears only 0.5 m away (did it too fly across the gap?). Both are 10 m high in a pecan. Another food visit to the first youngster comes at 2038, and I am still unable to see which adult is involved. This owlet moves 7 m from the other and again gets fed. After the adult departs, the young bird obviously tries to follow, flapping across a 2 m canopy gap.

Two feeding visits happen in rapid succession at 2043. The second begging owlet has closed the gap, and I cannot see who gets what. Again two rapid visits at 2045 and at 2047. A moment later food-begging ceases, and I note the owlets are about 12 m east of their day roost. The first chuck-will's-widow sings at 2050. I also hear one hoot from an adult. Then someone calls a cat (the possible stimulus). I see additional deliveries at 2052 and 2057, but it is too dark for good observations and I depart. There is a gibbous moon (another potential stimulus for increased vocalizing the past few nights).

At 2015 on May 20 the family is not over 10 m from their previous roost position. They are in the same pecan as last night, but I do not see everyone until the female stretches at 2020 and a fledgling flaps over to her from 1 m away. Just as the second youngster flies 1 m to her roost, she leaves at 2025.

By 2030 both owlets have climbed down a limb about 3 m. Both give loud begging rasps. At 2032 the male flies 6 m, catches something from foliage, and feeds an owlet, 3 m below its roost position. Immediately both youngsters try to follow their departing father and make 5-m slightly downward flights in tandem.

At 2033 the female returns, feeds one owlet, and leaves to the east in the direction of the male. A minute later he returns to within 6 m of the brood, whereupon the quiet fledgling quickly flies 3 m toward him, although he flies in to feed the food-begging sibling almost simultaneously. Both intently watch their parents, now flying about beneath the canopy, 4 m below them. At 2040 the unfed owlet flies 1.5 m up to a limb, while the fed bird flies nearly 6 m on the level close to today's roost site. They still do much bobbing and weaving.

One youngster flies 3 m on the level, and the other flies up perhaps 0.5 m, covering 2 m at 2042. Elmer Fisher comes by for brief conversation at 2044, as both fly 1.5 m further and nearly together. Then there is a feeding visit by the male and another at 2045 by the female, and I hear some bill-clapping by the owlets. Another visit at 2050, and two more at 2052 accompanied by additional bill-clapping. Then the owlets are quiet to at least 2100 when I leave. (I am impressed that both young birds fly more frequently tonight and well though not strongly; their wing beats are much slower than those of their parents.)

On May 21 I do not find the family until I see the male catch something near the nest box and deliver it to the female, 40 m from yesterday's position. It is 2040. Then I note both owlets together in a red cedar, only 5 m above ground but 20 m east of last night's position. They are 3 m from their mother, but this may not be the day roost. I sit and watch them fly deeper into the cedar break. One makes a 8-m level movement across open space at 2058 and is clearly a proficient flyer save for its comparatively slow wing beats.

I walk as far as I can without "busting brush," thus scaring the birds, and see a youngster perched on a telephone wire. Within a few seconds it flies 5 m into a live oak on adjacent property at least 60 m from the nest box (that property, a fishing club, is out of bounds to me). Apparently the rest of the family has already flown in that eastward direction, because until 2130 there is no further activity in the original 0.5-ha core hunting area. On May 22 and again on the 28th I do not find the owls in their original range.

Appendix II
Climate

Comparisons of the three study sites (Part A) and four microthermal stations in Woodway (Part B), 1985–87, are given below. Data are averages and percent coefficients of variation, derived from concurrent weekly readings of maximum-minimum thermometers—1.5 m high, sheltered, and 1 m from the east sides of houses (Woodway, Harris Creek) or large trees (rural, ridge, ravine)—plus 12.5-cm rain gauges with mineral oil to prevent evaporation and placed in the open at each site (Part A). Microthermal assessments employ additional maximum-minimum thermometers on the soil surface beneath 1–3 cm of leaf litter (Part B). The ridge station is 15 m from the Woodway site and 22 m above the ravine station.

In one-way ANOVAs of each parameter in each screech owl season during the three-year period (N = 48 per site or station), Woodway is significantly warmer and wetter than the other two sites (P < 0.04), which do not differ statistically from one another, and all four microthermal stations differ (P < 0.05). Also, CVs of the three sites and four stations show different patterns of flux (P < 0.01).

	Nesting March–June	Fledgling Dispersal July–October	Winter November–February
Part A			
Mean maximum air temperature (°C)			
Woodway	27.8 (7%)	32.5 (6%)	21.1 (11%)
Harris Creek	25.9 (7%)	29.7 (7%)	19.8 (13%)
Rural	26.4 (8%)	30.2 (8%)	20.3 (15%)
Mean minimum air temperature (°C)			
Woodway	10.1 (24%)	15.9 (16%)	0.2 (27%)
Harris Creek	8.8 (25%)	14.1 (20%)	−0.5 (27%)
Rural	9.1 (30%)	14.6 (20%)	−1.2 (33%)
Total precipitation (cm)			
Woodway	44.9 (77%)	31.7 (86%)	30.5 (91%)
Harris Creek	37.9 (100%)	30.5 (107%)	25.4 (128%)
Rural	37.4 (102%)	29.1 (109%)	24.8 (136%)

	Nesting March–June	Fledgling Dispersal July–October	Winter November–February
		Part B	
Mean maximum temperature (°C)			
Air			
Ridge	29.2 (6%)	33.1 (7%)	21.3 (9%)
Ravine	27.4 (4%)	31.2 (7%)	20.6 (8%)
Ground Ridge	26.1 (6%)	28.4 (7%)	18.0 (10%)
Ravine	23.4 (4%)	27.7 (5%)	17.6 (9%)
Mean minimum temperature (°C)			
Air			
Ridge	9.5 (27%)	16.3 (17%)	−2.8 (31%)
Ravine	6.5 (22%)	13.9 (15%)	−6.4 (25%)
Ground Ridge	11.9 (18%)	18.3 (12%)	−0.7 (27%)
Ravine	14.0 (15%)	20.2 (9%)	4.3 (15%)

Appendix III
Habitat Features

These are arranged in order of decreasing levels of significance (F) from ANOVAs, following significant MANOVAs for vegetation, dominant trees, and physical structures (asterisks = P < 0.05 in LSD tests). Features were measured at nests or in point-quarter transects centered on used natural or nest-box sites. Importance value (IV) is % density + % diameter + % frequency.

Analyses Features	F	Nesting Environment Open Yard (16)
Vegetation structure		
Shrub density (n/ha)	48.1	195.0 ± 87.0*
Tree canopy coverage (%)	42.9	71.1 ± 9.3*
Shrub height (m)	29.2	0.7 ± 0.1*
Tree density (n/ha)	9.7	327.3 ± 238.0*
Tree diameter at 1.4 m (cm)	4.2	28.4 ± 7.1*
Shrub diversity (H'log₂)	3.5	2.0 ± 0.2
Tree diversity (H'log₂)	2.3 (NS)	1.9 ± 0.5
Evergreens in canopy (%)	2.1 (NS)	35.2 ± 18.8
Tree height (m)	0.1 (NS)	10.4 ± 1.2
Dominant trees (IV)		
Cedar elm	7.3	33.0 ± 40.4*
Shumard oak	6.9	52.8 ± 35.6*
Scalybark oak	3.7	20.8 ± 31.5*
Live oak	2.6	102.6 ± 33.9*
Red cedar/Ashe juniper	2.3 (NS)	33.0 ± 47.9
White ash	1.2 (NS)	10.8 ± 15.0
Sugarberry	1.0 (NS)	33.4 ± 26.9
Physical structure		
Distance to house (m)	40.9	13.3 ± 8.1
Distance to water (m)	9.1	55.3 ± 34.8*
Distance to nearest cavity (m)	7.2	109.3 ± 89.1*
Nest tree diameter (cm)	4.2	40.6 ± 18.0*
Nest height (m)	3.4 (NS)	3.3 ± 0.5
Nest floor area (cm²)	0.8 (NS)	392.6 ± 189.0

Analyses Features	Nesting Environment	
	Wooded Yard (15)	Rural (17)
Vegetation structure		
Shrub density (n/ha)	1923.0 ± 492.0*	4807.0 ± 862.0*
Tree canopy coverage (%)	96.5 ± 1.6	96.3 ± 3.7
Shrub height (m)	1.4 ± 0.2*	1.9 ± 0.3*
Tree density (n/ha)	1504.0 ± 697.0*	1082.0 ± 502.0*
Tree diameter at 1.4 m (cm)	23.4 ± 4.3	23.1 ± 4.1
Shrub diversity (H'log₂)	2.3 ± 0.4*	1.8 ± 0.3*
Tree diversity (H'log₂)	2.1 ± 0.3	1.5 ± 0.5
Evergreens in canopy (%)	24.0 ± 19.3	14.4 ± 19.2
Tree height (m)	10.6 ± 2.1	10.5 ± 1.8
Dominant trees (IV)		
Cedar elm	53.4 ± 29.2*	156.0 ± 37.5*
Shumard oak	88.0 ± 41.8*	< 10*
Scalybark oak	47.4 ± 38.2*	< 10*
Live oak	32.0 ± 47.8*	53.8 ± 49.8*
Red cedar/Ashe juniper	53.4 ± 52.8	36.4 ± 14.3
White ash	55.0 ± 32.0	17.6 ± 26.0
Sugarberry	29.2 ± 33.2	46.4 ± 9.0
Physical structure		
Distance to house (m)	28.7 ± 14.7*	252.7 ± 52.8*
Distance to water (m)	20.4 ± 18.6*	129.4 ± 60.0*
Distance to nearest cavity (m)	77.5 ± 39.6	80.1 ± 36.7
Nest tree diameter (cm)	26.7 ± 4.8*	32.2 ± 5.8*
Nest height (m)	3.0 ± 0.4	2.9 ± 0.2
Nest floor area (cm²)	368.4 ± 151.6	351.6 ± 148.4

Appendix IV
Stored Foods

Whole items or body parts cached in nest boxes and natural cavities in the winter and nesting seasons, 1976–87, with a few suburban additions through 1991. The latter are not figured into the summary calculations or data syntheses in the text. Species are arranged by abundance and then biomass (g) within and among major taxa; the summary is arranged by biomass (mean live weight × individuals per species if more than one). Percentage of winter records is in parentheses after individuals; otherwise, only the nesting season is represented.

Status of birds is: PR, permanent resident; WR, winter resident; SR, summer resident; M, passage migrant, following F. R. Gehlbach et al., "Checklist of birds in McLennan County, Texas," *Centrl. Texas Audubon Soc. Publ.* II (1988).

All items were dead except for 39 live blind snakes (91%). All were adults except for 29 nestlings and fledglings of the birds marked with asterisks (20%), 14 of the brown and black rats (78% juveniles, estimated on the basis of size), the five eastern cottontails (recent nestlings), two recently transformed frogs, and those invertebrates indicated as immature stages.

Taxon (x̄ Weight), Status	Suburban Individuals (% Winter)	Biomass	Rural Individuals (% Winter)	Biomass
	BIRDS			
House sparrow (27) PR*	53 (35)	1,431	4	108
Inca dove (55) PR*	31 (48)	1,705		
Northern cardinal (44) PR*	30 (41)	1,320	5 (40)	220
Cedar waxwing (35) WR	30 (15)	1,050	1	
Blue jay (90) PR*	27 (12)	2,430	3 (33)	270
Northern mockingbird (50) PR*	18 (29)	900	2	100
Common grackle (95) PR, M	16	1,520		
Dark-eyed junco (20) WR	8	160	1	
Brown thrasher (70) WR, PR	6 (67)	420	1	
White-throated sparrow (30) WR	6 (83)	180	3 (100)	90
Carolina wren (20) PR*	6 (67)	120		
	5 (67)	400		
Swainson's thrush (35) M	5	175	1	
Mourning dove (120) PR, M*	4 (25)	480	2 (50)	220
Hermit thrush (35) WR	4 (75)	140	1	

229

Taxon (x̄ Weight), Status	Suburban Individuals (% Winter)	Biomass	Rural Individuals (% Winter)	Biomass
Brown-headed cowbird (35) PR, M	3	105		
Purple finch (25) WR	3 (100)	75		
American goldfinch (15) WR	3 (75)	45	1	
Nashville warbler (10) M	3	30	1	
Northern flicker (127) WR	3	381		
Tufted titmouse (22), PR	3 (33)	66	1	
Red-winged blackbird (68) PR, M	2	136		
Ladder-backed woodpecker (50), PR	2 (100)	100	1	
Purple martin (45), SR	2	90	1	
Painted bunting (30) SR	2	60	1	
Great-tailed grackle (159), PR, M	1			
Killdeer (80), PR	1			
European starling (67), PR, WR	1			
Yellow-billed cuckoo (56), SR	1		1	
Great-crested flycatcher (35), SR	1		1	
Scissor-tailed flycatcher (40), SR			1	
Rufous-sided towhee (40), WR	1			
Gray catbird (36), M	1			
Northern oriole (33), M, SR	1			
White-crowned sparrow (28), WR			1	
Downy woodpecker (25), PR	1			
Field sparrow (15), PR, M	1			
Chipping sparrow (15), SR, M	1			
Pine siskin (15), WR	1			
Yellow-rumped warbler (12), WR, M	1			
Yellow warbler (10), M	1			
Bewick's wren (10), PR	1		1	

	MAMMALS			
Black/brown rats (110)	17 (62)	1,870	1	
Hispid cotton rat (80)	5 (80)	400	11 (73)	880
White-footed mouse (20)	4 (75)	80	1	
House mouse (15)	4 (100)	60	1	
Eastern cottontail (52)	4 (67)	156	1	

Taxon (x̄ Weight), Status	Suburban Individuals (% Winter)	Biomass	Rural Individuals (% Winter)	Biomass
Fulvous harvest mouse (15)	1			
Northern pygmy mouse (10)	1			
Least shrew (10)	1		1	
	REPTILES			
Texas blind snake (3)	64	192	5	15
Rough earth snake (5)	34 (3)	170	2	10
Texas spiny lizard (30)	7	210	1	30
Lined snake (14)	4	56		
Flathead snake (2)	4	8		
Brown snake (10)	2	20		
Green anole (3)	2	6		
Ground skink (2)	2	4	2	4
Mediterranean gecko (3)	2	6		
Texas horned lizard (20)			1	
Rough green snake (15)	1			
Common garter snake (18)	1			
Western ribbon snake (14)	1			
Ground snake (7)	1		1	
	INVERTEBRATES			
Crayfish (6)	41 (8)	246	8 (12)	48
Scarab beetle (0.7)	27	19	15	10
Moth (mostly noctuids) (0.2)	23 (4)	5	10	2
Cicada (including nymphs)	18			
Black field cricket	14		8	
Katydid	14		10	
Earthworm	10			
Grasshopper	4		1	
Wood roach	4		1	
Carabid beetle	3			
Camel cricket	3		2	
Oriental roach	3			
Centipede	2			
Sphinx moth	2			
Moth/Butterfly caterpiller	2			
Walkingstick	2			
Cerambycid beetle	1			
Millipede	1			
Dragonfly naiad	1			
Hackberry butterfly	1			

Taxon (x̄ Weight), Status	Suburban Individuals (% Winter)	Biomass	Rural Individuals (% Winter)	Biomass
Reduviid bug	1			
Dobson fly	1		1	
	AMPHIBIANS			
Rio Grande leopard frog (18)	7 (28)	126	2 (50)	36
Bullfrog (12)			1	
Narrow-mouth salamander (8)	1			
	FISHES			
Longear sunfish (7)	6	42	5 (20)	35
Inland silverside (3)	5	15		
Red shiner (3)	2	6		
Green sunfish (5)	1			
Gizzard shad (5)	1 (100)			
	SUMMARY			
Birds (41 species)	269	12,963	34	1,589
Mmmals (9 species)	36	2,527	15	1,035
Reptiles (14 species)	87	584	12	86
Invertebrates (18 taxa)	169	ca. 270	55	ca. 60
Amphibians (3 species)	8	134	3	48
Fishes (5 species)	12	56	7	35

Appendix V
Food Supplies

Annual availability of terrestrial vertebrates eaten by eastern screech owls, based on population censuses in 1976–87.

Values for the birds are mean number of adults per 6.1 ha and coefficient of annual variation (CV %) in November–June. Primarily winter species[a] and nesting-season species[b] are distinguished. Passage migrants are not included. Means marked by asterisks are significantly different (P < 0.05). Note that same-size, ecologically similar species are lumped and also the two woodpeckers, since the downy replaced the ladder-backed in the suburban plot during the 1980s.

There are significant differences in abundance among 15 (68%) of the 22 bird species in common between the suburban and rural census plots; 14 of these are more numerous in suburbia, and the suburban birds are more numerous overall. CVs of the 15 species in common are no different statistically in the two plots.

Mean number of individuals and annual CVs for the mammals are from November, February, and June and those for the small snakes March–June, all per 6.1 ha. Species are listed from most (top) to least (bottom) abundant within classes and suburbia.

Mean density and biomass in kilograms differ among the rural birds, mammals, and small snakes (P < 0.02). Birds are least abundant; mammals and snakes the same; and the birds represent less biomass than the mammals, but not snakes (LSD tests, P < 0.05).

Species	Suburban Mean	CV (%)	Rural Mean	CV (%)
BIRDS				
Purple finch[a]	119.4*	180	4.8	232
American goldfinch/Pine Siskin[a]	67.3*	140	24.3	178
Dark-eyed junco[a]	39.2*	71	22.9	102
Common grackle[b]	31.6*	91	9.1	216
American robin[a]	19.5*	210	11.2	200
White-throated sparrow[a]	15.4	89	6.5	64
Northern cardinal	10.1*	33	6.1	42
Cedar waxwing[a]	9.8*	76	5.7	141
Chipping/Field sparrow[a]	8.6	233	3.4	106
Brown-headed cowbird[b]	7.8	126	20.5*	90
Inca dove	7.5*	111	0.4	200

Species	Suburban Mean	CV (%)	Rural Mean	CV (%)
Carolina wren	6.0*	30	2.1	42
Bluejay	5.6*	39	1.7	89
Yellow-rumped warbler[a]	5.4*	75	0.8	105
Tufted titmouse	5.2*	35	2.7	39
Mourning dove	5.1*	41	1.5	56
Yellow-billed cuckoo[b]	4.2	38	4.0	45
House sparrow	4.2	69	0	
Northern mockingbird	3.6	42	3.4	36
Brown thrasher[a]	2.2*	55	0.4	119
Painted bunting[b]	2.1	110	1.3	64
Downy/ladder-backed woodpecker	1.8	44	2.3	31
Hermit thrush[a]	1.7	58	0.4	97
Bewick's wren	0		4.1	38
White-crowned sparrow	0		7.8	111

MAMMALS

Hispid cotton rat			346.5	81
Pygmy mouse			230.6	67
Fulvous harvest mouse			85.4	65
House mouse			7.3	99
Eastern cottontail			3.0	—
White-footed mouse			<1.0	—
Brown rat			<1.0	—

SMALL SNAKES

Rough earth snake			161.6	37
Ground snake			117.1	20
Texas blind snake			71.4	42
Lined snake			43.9	86
Flathead snake			31.7	71
Brown snake			6.0	—

SUMMARY

Birds				
Mean density ($\bar{x}$ CV)	16.7*	(87)	6.1	(102)
Mean biomass	0.6*		0.2	
Total biomass	15.5		5.9	
Mammals				
Mean density ($\bar{x}$ CV)			112.1	(78)
Mean biomass			6.3	
Total biomass			31.7	

Species	Suburban		Rural	
	Mean	CV (%)	Mean	CV (%)
Small snakes				
Mean density ($\bar{x}$ CV)			71.9	(51)
Mean biomass			0.4	
Total biomass			2.6	

Mobbing Birds

Species are listed according to their residential status and mobbing frequency each season in suburbia, 1976–89. See appendix IV for frequency in the screech owl's diet, and appendix V for local abundance.

	Number of Mobs in:		
Group/Species	November–February	March–June	July–October
Permanent residents			
Bluejay	10	25	3
Tufted titmouse	9	7	3
Carolina chickadee	9	7	2
Northern cardinal	2	9	1
Carolina wren	2	6	2
Northern mockingbird	1	6	1
Common grackle		4	
American robin	1	2	
European starling	1	2	
American crow	1	1	
Bewick's wren	2		
House sparrow		2	
Downy woodpecker		1	
Winter residents			
Ruby-crowned kinglet	6	3	1
Brown thrasher	3	2	
Yellow-rumped warbler	1	2	
Hermit thrush	2	1	
Golden-crowned kinglet	1		
Dark-eyed junco	1		
White-throated sparrow	1		
Winter wren	1		
Migrants–seasonal residents			
Swainson's thrush		3	
Nashville warbler		1	1
White-eyed vireo		1	
Warbling vireo			1
Eastern wood pewee			1
Empidonax flycatcher			1
Chestnut-sided warbler		1	
Yellow warbler		1	
Gray catbird		1	
Archilochus hummingbird		1	

Group/Species	Number of Mobs in:		
	November–February	March–June	July–October
Median frequency			
Permanent residents	2.0	5.0	2.0
Winter residents	1.0	2.0	
Migrants–seasonal residents		1.0	1.0
All groups combined	1.0	2.0	1.0

Appendix VII
Nestling Development

Althea (A), in recognition of Althea Sherman who made the first detailed study of nestling development in the eastern screech owl, and Lowell (L), in recognition of Lowell Sumner who made the first similar study of the western screech owl, were raised from eggs taken from an abandoned suburban clutch in 1976.[a] They were kept in a 15 × 15 × 30-cm-high box at 20–28°C in a dark room except at midday and fed to satiation on venison and natural foods at sunset, 2300 hr, sunrise, and occasionally at midday. Behavioral development was noted at these times. Their weight is compared to the mean ± standard deviation of suburban nestlings of approximately the same age (sample size in parentheses); statistically significant departures are indicated by asterisks.

	Weight (g)			
Day	A	L	Suburban (n)	Behavior, Development
−1 (eggs)	18	17	18.0 ± 1.1 (92)	Cheeping inside piped eggs when rolled
1	14	13	13.2 ± 1.1 (61)	A hatches at 1500 hr May 13, L at 1700 hr May 15
2	15	—	20.1 ± 6.7 (7)	A barely able to sit up, much cheeping
3	17	—	20.7 ± 1.5 (6)	—
4–5	—	19*	38.2 ± 8.4 (50)	L cheeps and shivers (needs brooding)
6	28*	24*	40.5 ± 2.9 (4)	A sits well on tarsi, still shivers
7	33*	—	47.5 ± 2.4 (5)	A's back and wing-feather tracts appear
8	39*	—	57.6 ± 7.8 (7)	A's toes turn pink to brown, cannot grasp, eyes barely open and looks around
9–10	—	37*	74.5 ± 9.5 (49)	L's eyes barely open, feather tracts appear, sits unsteadily
11	63*	43*	78.7 ± 1.9 (4)	A mostly stands, grasps with feet, feathers appear, shivering stops; L sits well on tarsi, stops shivering

			Weight (g)	
Day	A	L	Suburban (n)	Behavior, Development
12	—	—	80.6 ± 3.0 (5)	—
13	71	56*	89.6 ± 10.9 (5)	A's egg tooth gone, eyes wide open, primaries 2–3 mm, chuckles; L cannot stand or grasp
14	—	—	104.1 ± 7.9 (16)	Five pellets avg. 8.3 × 10.6 mm (0.28 g dry)
15	88	72*	101.1 ± 11.5 (29)	A perches, chuckles, rasps, and head bobs; L's egg tooth gone, scratches head under wing
16	—	84*	106.2 ± 7.0 (6)	L stands poorly, head bobs
17	105	—	107.7 ± 14.1 (3)	Both owlets back into corner to defecate, pick up food pieces, wipe bill on box; A's primaries 5–10 mm, sheaths 30–40 mm, hisses when handled only
18	116	102	107.4 ± 7.5 (8)	A bill-claps, "ear" tufts appear; L grasps well but does not stand flat-footed
19	—	104	116.7 ± 9.2 (15)	No clear dominance-subordinance relations though L is feistier with me
20	128	107	108.8 ± 9.9 (28)	A has adult-size pellets, wing stretches and flaps; L seeks body contact with A for prone sleeping; both owlets well feathered
21	125	—	105.7 ± 11.2 (3)	Six pellets avg. 10.8 × 19.7 mm (0.54 g dry)
22	128	114	115.4 ± 11.8 (5)	A partly defeathers, dismembers and consumes whole house sparrow (together owlets eat 90–110 g/ 24 hrs (e.g. 3 house sparrows and 3 venison pieces)
23	—	114	112.2 ± 12.2 (6)	L dismembers house sparrow, bill-claps, wing stretches and flaps, has adult-size pellets
24	132	—	116.5 ± 11.0 (18)	A's food-begging rasps very loud, reluctant to take food from hand, pounces on food

Day	A	L	Weight (g) Suburban (n)	Behavior, Development
25	134	118	115.5 ± 12.3 (19)	1 pellet every 1–2 days by both owlets; A hops out of the nest box (fledges), pounces on live scarab beetles; L does the same; primaries erupted 45–50 mm.
26	—	—	115.9 ± 10.0 (8)	—
27	141	126	132 (1)	A makes 0.5–1.5 m flights without lift; L assumes first "dead stick" posture by either owlet; both climb trees easily
28	—	130	106 (2)	Ten pellets avg. 13.3 × 25.6 mm (0.68 g dry)[b]
29	142	—	126 (2)	A has 0.5-m lift in 2–3 m flights, 20–25-mm tail feathers
30–35	145	130	136 (1)	A's weight flux is 140–145 g, L's is 123–130; A holds prey in one foot while plucking or eating; L makes 2–3-m flights[c]

a. Sherman (1911), Sumner (1928).
b. These resemble 28 adult pellets averaging 14.3 × 29.8 mm (1.10 g dry weight).
c. Both owlets readily capture June bugs on the ground two weeks after fledging (up to 61 per owlet in 90 minutes at dusk) and visit patio feeding station for dead house sparrows most nights until 45 days after fledging. They remain within about 200 m for 70 days, then disperse without apparent pressure about August 15 in the midst of their first body-feather molt. One is seen 450 m SW 22 days later.

Lifetime Reproduction

Ten long-lived females selected from all study sites to show the kinds of variation inherent in lifetime reproductive features, 1976–90, and arranged from least to most lifetime fledglings within longevity classes. Missing years suggest that I missed those particular females or they did not breed. March 23/April 12, for example, means unsuccessful first nest/replacement nest. Weight (g) is an average of three or more incubation-brooding weights. Efficiency is fledglings/eggs (%). Question marks indicate that I could not obtain accurate information or touchy individuals required noninterference to insure an unbiased nesting attempt. Number 835-87344 is the only rufous owl represented.

Age	Weight	Egg Date(s)	Clutch	Fledglings (Recruits)	Efficiency	Nest Site	Mate
			Three Years				
685-64473 (rural)—4 fledglings, 0 recruits							
1	161	April 6	3	predation	0	—	—
2	157	April 4	4	1	25	1st	1st
3	171	March 17	4	3	75	1st	2nd
685-64458 (Woodway)—12 fledglings, 0 recruits							
1	182	April 17	5	3	60	—	—
2	186	March 28	6	4	80	1st	1st
3	185	March 25	5	5	100	1st	1st
			Four Years				
595-14838 (rural)—0 fledglings, 0 recruits							
1	181	March 21	5	predation	0	—	—
3	?	April 1	4	predation	0	1st	?
4	?	March 28	5	predation	0	1st	?
815-46039 (Harris Creek)—7 fledglings, 0 recruits							
1	165	March 23/ April 12	4	2	50	—	—
2	?	?	5	0	0	2nd	1st
3	172	March 18	3	2	67	1st	1st
4	174	March 22	4	3	75	2nd	1st
835-87385 (Woodway)—14 fledglings, 2 recruits							
1	182	March 16	4	3 (1)	75	—	—
2	?	March 24	4	4	100	1st	1st
3	?	March 24	3	3 (1)	100	1st	1st
4	?	?	4	4	100	2nd	?

Age	Weight	Egg Date(s)	Clutch	Fledglings (Recruits)	Efficiency	Nest Site	Mate

Five Years

835-87344 (Harris Creek)—11 fledglings, 3 recruits

Age	Weight	Egg Date(s)	Clutch	Fledglings (Recruits)	Efficiency	Nest Site	Mate
1	?	?	4— abandoned	0	0	—	—
2	191	April 2	3	3 (2)	100	2nd	2nd
3	194	March 23	4	3 (1)	75	2nd	2nd
4	185	March 7	4	2	50	2nd	2nd
5	?	March 14	4	3	75	2nd	2nd

685-64487 (rural)—16 fledglings, 0 recruits

Age	Weight	Egg Date(s)	Clutch	Fledglings (Recruits)	Efficiency	Nest Site	Mate
1	188	March 18	5	5	100	—	—
2	?	March 27/ April 30	8	4	50	1st	?
3	184	March 25	4	4	100	1st	?
4	?	April 1	4	3	75	1st	?
5	?	April 1	predation	0	0	1st	?

Seven Years

685-64468 (Woodway)—11 fledglings, 4 recruits

Age	Weight	Egg Date(s)	Clutch	Fledglings (Recruits)	Efficiency	Nest Site	Mate
1	176	March 21	4	3 (1)	75	—	—
2	178	March 30	4	4 (2)	100	1st	1st
3	187	March 22	5	4 (1)	80	1st	1st
6	?	March 29	1— abandoned	0	0	1st	2nd
7	?	March 29	4	predation	0	1st	2nd

595-14814 (Harris Creek)—11 fledglings, 0 recruits

Age	Weight	Egg Date(s)	Clutch	Fledglings (Recruits)	Efficiency	Nest Site	Mate
1	183	March 29	5	3	60	—	—
2	178	March 26	3	1	33	1st	1st
3	?	March 20	3— abandoned	0	0	1st	1st
4	?	March 26	4	1	25	2nd	2nd
6	176	March 22	5	3	60	2nd	2nd
7	187	?	4	3	75	2nd	2nd

835-87316 (Woodway)—17 fledglings, 0 recruits

Age	Weight	Egg Date(s)	Clutch	Fledglings (Recruits)	Efficiency	Nest Site	Mate
1	172	March 29	3	3	100	—	—
4	?	March 22	4	4	100	1st	2nd
5	?	March 29	4	4	100	1st	2nd
6	?	March 25	4	4	100	1st	2nd
7	?	March 24/ May 19	7— predation	2	28	1st/2nd	?

Appendix IX
Life Tables

Time-specific life tables for female eastern screech owls including all age classes present on each study area during 1976–91. S_x = survivorship, L_x = probability of further survival ($S_x \cdot L_x$), B_x = female offspring based on known 1:1 sex ratio, R_0 = population replacement rate, G = generation time. As survivorship and especially fecundity data are scarce for owls older than five, these data are extrapolated. Note the calculated stability (R_0 = 0.97) for the suburban population compared to the prospect of a rural decline (R_0 = 0.52) and the 2.6-fold difference in generation times, owing to lower survival in the rural situation.

Age Classes		S_x	L_x	$\bar{x}$ Fledglings	B_x	L_xB_x	Age (L_xB_x)
Fledglings		0.36	1.00	0.0	0.0	0.00	0.00
Adults	1	0.49	0.49	0.36	1.8	0.9	0.32
	2	0.58	0.18	2.6	1.3	0.23	0.47
	3	0.61	0.10	3.1	1.5	0.15	0.45
	4	0.67	0.06	3.2	1.6	0.10	0.38
	5	0.75	0.04	2.7	1.3	0.05	0.26
	6	0.75	0.03	2.7	1.3	0.04	0.23
	7	0.75	0.02	2.7	1.3	0.03	0.18
	8	0.75	0.02	2.7	1.3	0.03	0.21
	9	0.75	0.01	2.7	1.3	0.01	0.12
	10	0.75	0.01	2.7	1.3	0.01	0.13
						$R_0 = \overline{0.97}$	$G = \overline{2.75}$
				Rural			
Fledglings		0.30	1.00	0.0	0.0	0.00	0.00
Adults	1	0.36	0.30	1.6	0.8	0.24	0.24
	2	0.60	0.11	2.3	1.1	0.12	0.24
	3	0.67	0.06	3.2	1.6	0.10	0.30
	4	0.53	0.04	2.0	1.0	0.04	0.16
	5	0.50	0.02	2.0	1.0	0.02	0.10
						$R_0 = \overline{0.52}$	$G = \overline{1.04}$

Common and Scientific Names

Acrobat ant	*Crematogaster lineolata*
American crow	*Corvus brachyrhynchos*
American elm	*Ulmus americana*
American goldfinch	*Carduelis tristis*
American kestrel	*Falco sparverius*
American robin	*Turdus migratorius*
American sycamore	*Platanus occidentalis*
Arizona ash	*Fraxinus* (cultivar)
Army ant	*Neivamyrmex* sp.
Ashe juniper	*Juniperus ashei*
Asian privet	*Ligstrum* sp.
Barred owl	*Strix varia*
Bewick's swan	*Cygnus columbianus (bewickii)*
Bewick's wren	*Thryomanes bewickii*
Black-chinned hummingbird	*Archilochus alexandri*
Black field cricket	Orthoptera: Gryllidae
Black (roof) rat	*Rattus rattus*
Black ratsnake	*Elaphe obsoleta*
Black vulture	*Coragyps atratus*
Black walnut	*Juglans nigra*
Bluejay	*Cyanocitta cristata*
Boreal (Tengmalm's) owl	*Aegolius funereus*
Boxwood	*Buxus* sp.
Broad-winged hawk	*Buteo platypterus*
Brown (Dekay's) snake	*Storeria dekayi*
Brown (Norway) rat	*Rattus norvegicus*
Brown thrasher	*Toxostoma rufum*
Brown-headed cowbird	*Molothrus ater*
Bullfrog	*Rana catesbeiana*
Bur oak	*Quercus macrocarpa*
Camel cricket	Orthoptera: Gryllacrididae
Carabid beetle	Coleoptera: Carabidae
Carolina chickadee	*Parus carolinensis*
Carolina wren	*Thryothorus ludovicianus*
Cedar elm	*Ulmus crassifolia*
Cedar waxwing	*Bombycilla cedrorum*
Centipede	Chilopoda

Cerambycid beetle	Coleoptera: Cerambycidae
Chestnut-sided warbler	*Dendroica pensylvanica*
Chipping sparrow	*Spizella passerina*
Chuck-will's-widow	*Caprimulgus carolinensis*
Cicada	Homoptera: Cicadidae
Common barn owl	*Tyto alba*
Common garter snake	*Thamnophis sirtalis*
Common grackle	*Quiscalus quiscula*
Cooper's hawk	*Accipiter cooperi*
Coralberry	*Symphoricarpos orbiculatus*
Coturnix quail	*Coturnix coturnix*
Crayfish	Crustacea: Decopoda
Dark-eyed junco	*Junco hyemalis*
Deciduous holly	*Ilex decidua*
Dobson fly	Neuroptera: Corydalidae
Downy woodpecker	*Picoides pubescens*
Dragonfly naiad	Odonata: Anisoptera
Eagle owl	*Bubo bubo*
Earthworm	Annelida: Oligochaeta
Eastern bluebird	*Sialia sialis*
Eastern cottontail	*Sylvilagus floridanus*
Eastern red cedar	*Juniperus virginiana*
Eastern wood pewee	*Contopus virens*
Elf owl	*Micrathene whitneyi*
Eurasian kestrel	*Falco tinniculus*
Eurasian pygmy owl	*Glaucidium passerinum*
Eurasian sparrowhawk	*Accipiter nisus*
European starling	*Sturnus vulgaris*
Ferruginous pygmy owl	*Glaucidium brasilianum*
Field sparrow	*Spizella pusilla*
Fire ant	*Solenopsis* sp.
Flammulated owl	*Otus flammeolus*
Flathead snake	*Tantilla gracilis*
Florida scrub jay	*Aphelocoma coerulescens*
Fox squirrel	*Sciurus niger*
Fulmar	*Fulmaris glacialis*
Fulvous harvest mouse	*Reithrodontomys fulvescens*
Geometrid caterpillar	Lepidoptera: Geometridae
Gizzard shad	*Dorosoma cepedianum*
Golden-crowned kinglet	*Regulus satrapa*
Grasshopper	Orthoptera: Acrididae
Gray catbird	*Dumetella carolinensis*

Great gray owl	*Strix nebulosa*
Great tit	*Parus major*
Great-crested flycatcher	*Myiarchus crinitus*
Great-horned owl	*Bubo virginianus*
Great-tailed grackle	*Quiscalus mexicanus*
Green anole	*Anolis carolinensis*
Green ash	*Fraxinus pennsylvanica*
Green sunfish	*Lepomis cyanellus*
Ground skink	*Scincella lateralis*
Ground snake	*Sonora semiannulata*
Hackberry butterfly	*Asterocampa celtis*
Harris' sparrow	*Zonotrichia querula*
Hawk owl	*Sturnia ulula*
Hermit thrush	*Catharus guttatus*
Hispid cotton rat	*Sigmodon hispidus*
Holly	*Ilex* sp.
Honey bee	*Apis mellifera*
House martin	*Delichon urbica*
House mouse	*Mus musculus*
House sparrow	*Passer domesticus*
House wren	*Troglodytes aedon*
Inca dove	*Columbina inca*
Inland silversides	*Menidia beryllina*
June bug	*Phyllophaga* sp.
Killdeer	*Charadrius vociferus*
Kittiwake	*Rissa tridactyla*
Ladder-backed woodpecker	*Picoides scalaris*
Least shrew	*Cryptotis parva*
Lined snake	*Tropidoclonion lineatum*
Live oak	*Quercus virginiana (fusiformis)*
Long-eared owl	*Asio otus*
Longear sunfish	*Lepomis megalotis*
Magpie	*Pica pica*
Mediterranean gecko	*Hemidactylus turcicus*
Merlin	*Falco columbarius*
Millipede	Diplodopa
Moth/butterfly caterpiller	Lepidoptera
Mourning dove	*Zenaida macroura*
Narrow-mouth salamander	*Ambystoma texanum*
Nashville warbler	*Vermivora ruficapilla*
Noctuid moth	Lepidoptera: Noctuidae
Northern bobwhite	*Colinus virginianus*

Northern cardinal	*Cardinalis cardinalis*
Northern flicker	*Colaptes auratus*
Northern mockingbird	*Mimus polyglottos*
Northern oriole	*Icterus galbula*
Northern pygmy mouse	*Baiomys taylori*
Northern pygmy owl	*Glaucidium gnoma*
Northern saw-whet owl	*Aegolius acadicus*
Orchard oriole	*Icterus spurius*
Oriental roach	Orthoptera: Blattidae
Painted bunting	*Passerina ciris*
Paper wasp	*Polistes exclamans*
Pecan	*Carya illinoensis*
Pine marten	*Martes martes (americana)*
Pine siskin	*Carduelis pinus*
Polyphemus moth	*Antheraea polyphemus*
Purple finch	*Carpodacus purpureus*
Purple martin	*Progne subis*
Raccoon	*Procyon lotor*
Red mulberry	*Morus rubra*
Red Shiner	*Notropis lutrensis*
Red-bellied woodpecker	*Melanerpes carolinus*
Red-shouldered hawk	*Buteo lineatus*
Red-tailed hawk	*Buteo jamaicensis*
Red-winged blackbird	*Agelaius phoeniceus*
Reduviid bug	Hemiptera: Reduviidae
Ringtail	*Bassariscus astutus*
Rio Grande leopard frog	*Rana berlandieri*
Rough earth snake	*Virginia striatula*
Rough green snake	*Opheodrys aestivus*
Roughleaf dogwood	*Cornus drummondii*
Round-winged katydid	*Amblycorypha rotundifolia*
Ruby-crowned kinglet	*Regulus calendula*
Ruby-throated hummingbird	*Archilochus colubris*
Ruffed grouse	*Bonasa umbellus*
Rufous-sided towhee	*Pipilo erythrophthalmus*
Scalybark oak	*Quercus sinuata (breviloba)*
Scarab beetle	Coleoptera: Scarabaeidae
Scissor-tailed flycatcher	*Tyrannus forficatus*
Scops owl	*Otus scops*
Sharp-shinned hawk	*Accipiter striatus*
Short-eared owl	*Asio flammeus*
Shumard oak	*Quercus shumardii (texana)*

Skunkbush	*Rhus aromatica*
Snow goose	*Anser caerulescens*
Snowy owl	*Nyctea scandiaca*
Song sparrow	*Melospiza melodia*
Sphinx moth	Lepidoptera: Sphingidae
Spotted owl	*Strix occidentalis*
Sugarberry	*Celtis laevigata*
Summer tanager	*Piranga rubra*
Swainson's thrush	*Catharus ustulatus*
Tawny owl	*Strix aluco*
Texas blind snake	*Leptotyphlops dulcis*
Texas horned lizard	*Phrynosoma cornutum*
Texas spiny lizard	*Sceloporus olivaceus*
Tufted titmouse	*Parus bicolor*
Ural owl	*Strix uralensis*
Virginia oppossum	*Didelphis virginiana*
Walkingstick	Orthoptera: Phasmatidae
Warbling vireo	*Vireo gilvus*
Western ribbon snake	*Thamnophis proximus*
Western screech owl	*Otus kennicottii*
Whiskered (screech) owl	*Otus trichopsis*
White ash	*Fraxinus americana* (*texensis*)
White mulberry	*Morus alba* (cultivar)
White-crowned sparrow	*Zonotrichia leucophrys*
White-eyed vireo	*Vireo griseus*
White-footed mouse	*Peromyscus leucopus*
White-throated sparrow	*Zonotrichia albicollis*
Winter wren	*Troglodytes troglodytes*
Wood ant	*Camponotus* sp.
Wood roach	Orthoptera: Blatellidae
Yellow warbler	*Dendroica petechia*
Yellow-billed cuckoo	*Coccyzus americanus*
Yellow-crowned night-heron	*Nycticorax violaceus*
Yellow-rumped warbler	*Dendroica coronata*

Notes

Chapter 1. On Studying Screech Owls: An Introduction

1. See Marshall (1967) for a description and the taxonomy of screech owls. I do not hyphenate screech owl in the interest of simplicity and correct English.

2. The long-term study is Van Camp and Henny (1975), stemming from an investigation of wood duck nest boxes. In 1950–51 I briefly participated in field work that led to this publication, many aspects of which are based on assumptions and estimations, because data were lacking and the data analyzer and writer was not the field worker. Clark et al. (1978) list 143 articles with screech owl or its equivalent in the title, 127 (89%) of which are anecdotal in my judgment.

3. For examples of urban-rural comparative studies and extensive bibliography, mostly about European birds, see Tomialojc and Gehlbach (1988).

4. Gehlbach (1994b) validates the nest-box method, obviating Moller's (1989, 1992) criticisms insofar as the present study is concerned.

5. An admirably admitted example of observer bias is in Pietiainen (1989).

6. I find no comments on the value of enlightening exploration prior to data-collecting better than Niko Tinbergen's succinct, "Each time I study a new species I am amazed to find how much more I see after I have become thoroughly acquainted with it," quoted in Kilham (1989), p. 183.

7. Compare Korpimaki (1984, 1987c), Gauthier (1988), and Robertson and Rendell (1990), and Gehlbach (1994b).

8. See Gehlbach (1994b).

9. Examples of intensive (29–43 boxes) and extensive (355, 500–621 boxes) owl studies are Southern (1970) versus Korpimaki (1981, 1987c) and Carlsson et al. (1987), respectively.

10. For instance, see the various estimates including back-dating in Korpimaki (1981), Van Camp and Henny (1975) and Carlsson et al. (1987).

11.   Taylor (1991) obtained similar results, but no other student of owls
        seems to have tested techniques before using them.
12.   I cannot find controls on the possibility of a transmitter-antenna
        bias in Merson et al. (1983), Smith and Gilbert (1984), or Belthoff
        and Ritchison (1989, 1990b). Korpimaki (1990a) records weight
        loss in transmitted male boreal owls. Lately, adequate controls have
        been used and serious transmitter biases reported by Patton et al.
        (1991) but not Taylor (1991) for other owls.
13.   Inefficiency of the tape-playback method is shown in Smith et al.
        (1987).
14.   This and the rural plot were incorrectly given as 135 ha, the size of
        my exploratory plot, in Gehlbach (1989).
15.   The 2-km wide perimeter is based on four of five natal dispersals be-
        tween 0.2 and 2.0 km in the exploratory period (see also chapter 6).
        Knowledge of natural nest sites derives from a plot of the cumula-
        tive number found versus cumulative time spent searching; the sub-
        urban asymptote was reached in 1976, the rural asymptote in 1981.
16.   See table 10–4 in Landsberg (1981).
17.   Particularly in multivariate analyses, I made Bonferroni adjustments
        to probability levels, but my attitude about probability and other as-
        pects of statistics is pretty much like Toft's (1990). With Southern
        and Lowe (1968) I must agree that statistics are no substitute for
        knowledgeable observations, but unlike them think statistics can
        contribute findings that might be missed otherwise.
18.   This is briefly put in Tukey (1980) and well described in James and
        McCulloch (1985).
19.   Data revealing adaptation versus natural selection are discussed in
        Grafen (1988).
20.   My field experience includes one or more nest studies of the great-
        horned, barred, burrowing, elf, ferruginous pygmy, flammulated,
        little, spotted, tawny, western screech, and whiskered owls. I have
        seen all but the ferruginous pygmy and spotted nesting in suburbia.
        Most work on the flammulated owl has been in collaboration with
        D. A. McCallum.
21.   Read, for example, the introduction to Kilham (1989).

Chapter 2. Landscapes: The Owls Select Habitat

1.   Regional biogeography is analyzed in Gehlbach (1991).
2.   On the heat-island phenomenon, see Landsborg (1981).
3.   More rain means more evapotranspiration in plants, hence more pri-
        mary and secondary productivity (Rosenzweig, 1968).

4.   Graber and Graber (1983) document the rural-urban contrast very
      nicely.
5.   Regional woody vegetation is described in Gehlbach (1988a).
6.   I have not surveyed habitat fragments generally, but Robbins et al.
      (1989) found eastern screech owls in Maryland-area forest patches
      as small as 0.8 ha (C. Robbins, pers. comm.). In seven Ohio forest
      preserves, screech owls were positively influenced by young-forest
      area ($r^2 = 0.57$, $P = 0.05$), not area per se or amount of old
      growth, probably because they avoided larger raptors ($r = -0.65$,
      $P = 0.11$) that were more abundant in larger preserves ($r = 0.88$,
      $P = 0.002$; calculated from data in Mutter et al., 1984). The small-
      est successful natural nest site I know of is a dead Shumard oak, 20-
      cm diameter, with a 14-cm wide, 47-cm deep cavity in its hollow
      trunk, broken off 3 m above ground. The largest is a 12-cm diame-
      ter knot hole 4.2 m above ground in a 1.5-m diameter live oak with
      a completely hollow trunk to ground level (apparently the owls nest
      at ground level). The smallest cultural equivalent is a $15 \times 15 \times$
      18-cm high hanging nest box intended for a wren but with an ap-
      proximately 6×6-cm entrance enlarged by a fox squirrel. The
      largest is a 0.5-m diameter, 2.5-m high, hollow porch column,
      opened about 8×15 cm at the top by a northern flicker and fox
      squirrels, in which the owls nest at ground level (several nestlings
      died inside but at least some fledged).
7.   Woodway contained mixed evergreen-deciduous woodland and ri-
      parian deciduous forest historically, while Harris Creek was entirely
      riparian deciduous forest, and they remain quite different today.
      Woodway has more taller trees with more canopy, more shrubs, and
      greater tree and shrub diversity.
8.   Compare McComb and Noble (1981a), Forsman et al. (1984), and
      McCallum and Gehlbach (1988), though nest and roost sites are
      not separated in the first reference.
9.   All vegetational and physical features were chosen as potentially
      meaningful to screech owls during exploratory-period observations;
      for example, nest boxes closest to alternative cavity sites were used
      most often ($r_s = 0.71$, $P < 0.001$, $n = 17$), so closest cavities were
      deemed important. On methods of vegetational data synthesis see
      Gehlbach (1988).
10.   Solheim (1983), Carlsson et al. (1987).
11.   Alternative nest sites must be vacant concurrently, but used for-
      merly or be usable on the basis of exploratory observations, so I
      know they are suitable for comparison with chosen sites. Selectivity
      cannot be studied otherwise; contrast McCallum and Gehlbach

(1988) with Belthoff and Ritchison (1990b) and see Gehlbach (1994b).

12. These use rates are much higher than the 4–13 percent previously reported for eastern screech owls by Van Camp and Henny (1975), McComb and Noble (1981a), and Fowler and Dimmick (1983), and the 31 percent box use by boreal owls (Korpimaki, 1987c). Perhaps this is because I sited and censused my boxes with the advantage of exploratory experience. Turnover is 0.5 $(S_1/N_1 + S_2/N_2) \times 100$, where S = sites occupied only in year 1 or 2 and N = total sites available in those years (cf. Erwin et al., 1981).

13. Korpimaki (1987c), Pitts (1988), Gehlbach (1994b).

14. Two exemplary studies among many are Osborne and Osborne (1980) and Tomialojc (1980).

15. Dow and Fredga (1985), Sonerud (1985a), Korpimaki (1987c), and Gauthier (1988).

16. Apparent habituation to people by roosting screech owls is described in Smith et al. (1987).

17. Reduced shrub density also typifies eastern screech owl habitat in Maryland (Robbins et al., 1989) and Kentucky (Belthoff and Ritchison, 1990b). Openness characterizes the habitat in New Jersey (Bosakowski et al., 1987) and Wisconsin (Swengel and Swengel, 1987) by contrast to that of coexisting owls.

18. See Norberg (1970) and McCallum and Gehlbach (1988). Open subcanopy space is important to the spotted owl as well (Gould, 1977). Cryptic aspects of the U-flight are noted in Newton (1986).

19. Less predation on owls in sparse vegetation is shown in Sonerud (1985b), while more predation by them in such cover is noted in Southern and Lowe (1968) and suggested by Wendland (1980).

20. Elsewhere it is claimed that the two colormorphs roost differently (Johnsgard, 1988), perhaps based on the scops owl (Mikkola, 1983).

21. Swengel and Swengel (1987).

22. Merson, et al. (1983).

23. Barrows and Barrows (1978), Forsman et al. (1984). For general background see Kendeigh (1961).

24. This is similar to the 48–58 percent frequency of sunning reported by Smith et al. (1987).

25. Schantz and Nilsson (1981).

26. This hypothesis only resembles that of Korpimaki (1985b), because female boreal (Tengmalm's) owls do not usually return to the same mate and nest cavity already used successfully, whereas eastern screech owls do.

27.   Lundberg (1979) and Korpimaki and Hongell (1986) suggest nest-
        site scarcity and hence nomadism but do not demonstrate it, and
        Korpimaki (1988c) denies it. The scarcity paradigm is questionable,
        certainly in North America. It does not obtain for songbirds or
        screech owls in my study area and elsewhere (e.g., McComb and
        Noble, 1981a; Waters et al., 1990); and, where applicable, de-
        scribes only successional habitats and particular species (e.g., Brawn
        and Balda, 1988; East and Perrins, 1988).
28.   Hayward and Garton (1988).

Chapter 3. Food Supplies and Predation: Why Owls Are Mobbed

1.   The eating of small and storing of large prey are mentioned in
        Turner and Dimmick (1981), Forsman et al. (1984), and Korpimaki
        (1987b). The latter reviews theories of food storage as do Smith
        and Riechman (1984).
2.   The pioneering study of bird-eating is Allen's (1924). See also the
        extensive list of stored birds in Van Camp and Henny (1975).
        Ritchison and Cavanagh (1992) review screech owl food.
3.   Harrison (1960), Wendland (1980), Wijnandts (1984).
4.   Data from tables 1 and 2 in Van Camp and Henny (1975) on migra-
        tory versus seasonal-resident birds. Ohio screech owls cache more
        mammals than birds compared to my subjects generally (41 vs.
        14%, P < 0.001), whereas those in Tennessee do not (Turner and
        Dimmick, 1981). Cities furnish more avian food for tawny owls as
        well (e.g., Wendland, 1980).
5.   Orians and Pearson (1979); also see Bull et al. (1989a).
6.   Korpimaki (1981) and see, for example, Halle (1988) and Kotler et
        al. (1988). The literature on prey-size selection by screech owls is
        conflicting; for example, compare Marti and Hogue (1979) with
        Postler and Barrett (1982), and these experiments neglect selection
        for storage versus immediate use.
7.   I used the selectivity index $S-A/S+A$, where S = proportion stored
        and A = proportion available, from Ivlev (1961).
8.   See also Geer (1982), Korpimaki (1987b), Breitwisch and Hudak
        (1989). Jill Leverett and I (unpubl.) found that male northern
        cardinals mob eastern screech owl songs more often than females
        do.
9.   Southern and Lowe (1968), Korpimaki (1988b). Despite relatively
        few young birds in the general larder of my eastern screech owls,
        when fledglings of permanent residents are available for the first

time in mid-late April, they may comprise most avian prey (e.g. four of five items in three nests one afternoon).

10. Ross (1989).
11. Gehlbach and Baldridge (1987).
12. Allen (1924).
13. My observations are like those of Prescott (1985). The owls hop from shore or fly from a sit-and-wait perch into water up to at least 10 cm deep, feet outstretched, wings held back, but hit the water with their wings in taking off. They do not seem to float.
14. Watkins et al. (1969).
15. Korpimaki (1988b).
16. Lundberg (1981), Solheim (1984b), Wendland (1984), Korpimaki and Sulkava (1987), Korpimaki (1988b), Korpimaki et al. (1990).
17. Niche metrics use density data and are $1/\Sigma p_i^2$ for niche width, where P_i is the proportion of each prey species or other taxon; and $\Sigma P_{ij} P_{ik}/\sqrt{\Sigma P_{ij}^2 \Sigma P_{ik}^2}$ for niche overlap, where j and k are the two entities being compared.
18. Wendland (1980), Wijnandts (1984).
19. Van Camp and Henny (1975); my calculations are from their tables 1 and 2.
20. My computations are from Korpimaki (1988b, table 1), although the boreal owl's food niche is broader southward in its range (Korpimaki, 1986a) like the eastern screech owl's.
21. Korpimaki (1987b).
22. Van Camp and Henny (1975), Turner and Dimmick (1981).
23. Van Camp and Henny (1975) suggest that nesting in northern Ohio screech owls is timed to utilize migrants, but their breeding chronology closely matches the Central Texas schedule, so I disagree. (cf. p. 25 in Van Camp and Henny with figure 1.1, this volume). My field experience in Ohio indicates that migrants tend to concentrate on the south shore of Lake Erie before crossing and are eaten in response to their temporary abundance by that lakeside population of screech owls. While my Central Texas subjects eat few neotropical migrants, their caches reveal a decline in numbers of these birds over 1976–91 ($b = -0.21$, $p < 0.06$), particularly strong since the mid-1980s, and corroborated by my census data of nesting individuals ($b = -0.82$, $P < 0.001$). Thus, eastern screech owls substantiate a potentially serious problem reviewed by Askins et al. (1990).
24. See the theoretical characterization by Jaksic and Carothers (1985). I estimated hunting distances to the nearest meter and perch heights to the nearest half-meter, when actual measurements were impossible.

25.   For the boreal owl, data on delivery rates and prey size related to sex are in Korpimaki (1981). Examples of males catching small prey relative to that of females are Poole and Boag (1987) and Longland (1988).

26.   Norberg's (1970) data on boreal owl foraging are used in all comparisons.

27.   Sutton (1929) and Ligon (1968) discuss fly-catching and hovering. Little owls also fly-catch and hover, using both bill and feet to capture insects; and tawny, common barn, and short-eared owls hover as well (Haverschmidt, 1946). Screech, elf, little, and tawny owls are sit-and-wait predators, though, while the common barn and short-eared are active-search predators. Hovering by other owls is mentioned in Haverschmidt (1946). Wing-beat flushing of prey by barn owls is noted in Bunn et al. (1982).

28.   See Craig et al. (1988) about long-eared owls.

29.   Data on the flammulated owl are mine from 31 unpublished observations, on the American kestrel from Rudolph (1982) and Toland (1987).

30.   Nishimura and Abe (1988), Bull et al. (1989a), and table 14 in Curio (1976). Also see Griffiths (1980).

31.   This was first seen by Allard (1937), who also noted the longer activity time of nesting males compared to their mates, which I attribute to the demands of hunting.

32.   I looked through a 5-cm-diameter tube to judge the overhead cloud cover, pointing it through the nearest leaf gap during nesting (no clouds = clear; half or less cloud cover = partly cloudy; more than half cloud cover = cloudy). Light readings were the average of straight up and down foci, converted to foot candles. The winter data were subjected to a three-way ANOVA of sunset versus departure values under the three different sky conditions during winter versus nesting.

33.   Data from Korpimaki (1981).

34.   Deduced from Allen (1924) and based on my six-year experience with eastern screech owls around Ithaca, New York.

35.   See Mikkola (1983), in particular figures 14, 15, 17, 18, and 31–33 on activity periods and tables 5, 20–22, 34, 42, and 49 on food niches. Also see Korpimaki and Huhtala (1986), but Hayward and Garton (1988) note bimodal hunting in boreal owls in Idaho.

36.   For historical background, see Altmann (1956). My operational definition of mobbing is a bird or birds oriented toward a screech owl or its nest or roost within 3 m and calling with alarm.

37.   Shedd (1982, 1983).

38.   Mobbers attracted to the screech owl's voice orient to formerly occu-
      pied sites rather than speakers, according to Mcpherson and Brown
      (1982).
39.   See also Chandler and Rose (1988).
40.   On learned mobbing, see Curio et al. (1978) and Vieth et al.
      (1980).

Chapter 4. Adult Weight, Coloration, and Molt: Basic Constraints

1.   On use and misuse of body weight see Clark (1979) and on the pri-
      macy of weight as a criterion of sexual size dimorphism see Smith
      and Wiemeyer (1992). I controlled for diel flux by weighing only at
      1300–1600 hours but did not evaluate other cycles (e.g., see Kelso,
      1942).
2.   According to Marti (1990), there is no pattern in the first-year ver-
      sus older-bird weight relationship among raptors (cf. Gehlbach,
      1989).
3.   Korpimaki (1990a).
4.   Gehlbach (1989) compared to Korpimaki (1988d).
5.   Newton (1989), Saurola (1989b), Korpimaki (1990a).
6.   Both sexes are heavier in northern Ohio than Central Texas by an
      average of 9 g each (P < 0.001), comparing my annual means with
      data from table 1 in Henny and Van Camp (1979). On larger east-
      ern screech owls in colder and/or dryer climates, see Owen (1963b)
      and James (1970). Other data on size dimorphism are reduced from
      table 1 in Snyder and Wiley (1976).
7.   Two exceptions are the long-term studies by Ian Newton and associ-
      ates on the Eurasian sparrowhawk, collated in Newton (1986), and
      by Erkki Korpimaki and coworkers on the boreal (Tengmalm's)
      owl, especially Korpimaki (1986b, 1987d) and Hakkarainen and
      Korpimaki (1991) in the present context.
8.   Compare with Lundberg (1986), Mendelsohn (1986), and Mueller
      (1986).
9.   That smaller male raptors use less energy than larger females of the
      same species is shown by Mosher and Matray (1974) and Kaiser
      and Bucher (1985). That their maintenance of polyterritory and
      hunting for family offset anisogamy is my opinion (cf. Beissinger,
      1987; Rosenfield and Bielefeldt, 1991).
10.   See Earhart and Johnson (1970) and Schantz and Nilsson (1981).
11.   Some indication that large female raptors choose small males is in
      Korpimaki (1986b) but not Bowman (1987) or Marti (1990), and

the finding is refuted by Hakkarainen and Korpimaki (1991). See also Safina (1984) and Mueller (1989).

12. Advantages of female owls storing emergency fat are discussed in Wijnandts (1984) and Hirons (1985b). See also Newton et al. (1983).

13. Female great-gray (Hoglund and Lansgren, 1968), spotted (Forsman et al., 1984), tawny (Wallin, 1987) and Ural (Saurola, 1989b) owls are also primary nest defenders, but perhaps not female snowy owls (Wiklund and Stigh, 1983) and boreal and hawk owls (E. Korpimaki, pers. comm.). The larger-female-defender role may be secondary to the others, therefore.

14. See figure 18 in Balgooyen (1976).

15. Variation of the boreal owls is estimated from figure 4B (perhaps not all females) in Korpimaki and Hongell (1986).

16. Similar insignificant annual but significant seasonal variation occurs in the boreal owl (Korpimaki, 1990a), and male Eurasian sparrowhawks lose weight feeding their mates and fledglings (Newton et al., 1983). Norberg (1981) gives the theoretical argument for flying-feeding efficiency and see Andersson and Norberg (1981).

17. Ohio data from table 2 in Henny and Van Camp (1979). Captive eastern screech owls lost 16% according to Wiemeyer (1987).

18. Among 16 females with 10 or more weight records in one year, weight loss from late winter to incubation averages 11.1% or 5.3 ± 2.4 g/day, exceeding that from incubation through brooding (7.6% or 0.6 ± 0.2 g/day; P < 0.01). The total loss of 19% is like that (15.2 ± 4.1%) of five species of breeding raptors including boreal, little, and tawny owls (Korpimaki, 1990a). For background see Moreno (1989).

19. Similarly, Hakkarainen and Korpimaki (1991) find that sexual size differences in pairs of boreal owls do not influence breeding success.

20. Wing area, measured by tracing around each flattened wing and computing total area with a polar planimeter, averages 406.8 ± 11.0 cm^2 among the males and 463.3 ± 13.5 cm^2 in their mates (P < 0.001). These means are smaller than the uncontrolled (unpaired) values reported by Poole (1938).

21. Hoglund and Lansgren (1968), Southern (1970), Marti and Wagner (1985).

22. Cold intolerance of the rufous morph is noted in Mosher and Henny (1976), but their birds were not segregated by sex.

23. The predominance of rufous females over males, relative to gray birds of each sex, is also shown by a Fisher's Exact P < 0.001 for data on p. 646 in Hasbrouck (1893) but not by Van Camp and

Henny (1975). Bent (1938, p. 245) also noticed "that it has always been the red bird, in a mixed pair, that I have found sitting on the eggs, or brooding the young."

24. See Hrubant (1955) and table 26 in Van Camp and Henny (1975).

25. Calculations are categories 5 + 6/n of each sample in table 1 from Owen (1963b); Minnesota to Connecticut ($\bar{x}$ = 27% rufous, n = 9), New York to Arkansas ($\bar{x}$ = 65% rufous, n = 9), and Texas to Florida ($\bar{x}$ = 19% rufous, n = 10) are distinct (P < 0.001).

26. Climatic data are from U.S. Dept. Commerce, NOAA (1979).

27. First suggested in Gehlbach (1988b). For background see Lythgoe (1979).

28. Mean maximum relative humidity at 0700 hours is 86.6 ± 2.4% in the southern sample compared to 78.6 ± 2.9% in the mid-latitudinal and northern samples in note 24 (P < 0.001).

29. See explanations in Burtt (1986).

30. From north to south, mean annual precipitation is 27.4 ± 7.4, 47.2 ± 3.9, and 44.2 ± 15.5 inches (P = 0.01) and mean daily sky cover is 5.7 ± 0.6, 5.6 ± 0.3, and 5.3 ± 0.3 tenths (NS). Respective mean monthly CVs are 41.0, 22.6, and 37.0 for precipitation (P < 0.001) and 14.1, 8.5, and 11.5 for sky cover (P = 0.01); only the mid-latitudinal sample is distinct (P < 0.001).

31. The midwestern population is in Schorger (1954). From my MSR of this and relevant NOAA data, r^2 = 0.43 for January temperature and r^2 = 0.15 added for annual precipitation. In the Waco area, 1976–89, r^2 = 0.74 for the previous year's annual precipitation with 0.14 added for current January temperature (all P < 0.05).

32. Comparing the Austin and Waco percentages of rufous, 1979–86, r_s = 0.74 (P = 0.03), although rufous averages only 4.6% around Austin (data on 53–87 owls/year, recovered for rehabilitation by Jane Lyons).

33. Computed from table 19 data in Van Camp and Henny (1975).

34. Hasbrouck (1893) first noticed the predominance of rufous females and rufous birds generally at mid-latitudes with mild temperatures versus gray birds in the northern cold and southern humid regions. He did not deserve Allen's (1893) diatribe.

35. My observations corroborate Kelso's (1950).

36. Reduced flying ability due to plucked feathers, presumably similar to molted feathers, is shown in Slagsvold and Lifjeld (1988). See also Wijnandts (1984) whose explanation for the timing of molt in the long-eared owl differs from mine.

37. Hirons et al. (1984), Pietiainen et al. (1984), Wijnandts (1984). A few contour feathers shed in September–early October belonged to

young of the year; by November they were in fresh body plumage (see also Kelso, 1950).

Chapter 5. Eggs and Incubation; Perilous Times

1. Ligon (1968), Korpimaki (1981), Forsman et al. (1984).
2. Examples are Dhondt et al. (1984), Eden (1985), Luniak and Mulsow (1988), and Wendland (1980).
3. Newton and Marquiss (1981), Dijkstra et al. (1982), Korpimaki (1987e, 1989a), and Hornfeldt and Eklund (1990).
4. Southern (1970), Hirons et al. (1984), Korpimaki and Hakkarainen (1991). Despite considerable differences in latitude and hence climate, eastern screech owls in northern Ohio (Van Camp and Henny, 1975), tawny owls in England (Southern, 1970), boreal owls in Finland (Korpimaki, 1981), and Eurasian pygmy owls in Norway (Solheim, 1984a) also begin egg laying in late March–early April.
5. Tawny owls also show this tendency (Southern, 1970). My very earliest nest was in a suburban natural cavity about mid-December, 1979, based on two chicks that fledged February 11–13, 1980. Also in 1979 a suburban pair laid in late January, based on two freshly broken eggs beneath the nest box on January 30 (both nests outside study plots).
6. Perrins (1970), Klomp (1970), Pietiainen (1988a).
7. Similarly, tawny owls usually move to lay replacement clutches (Southern, 1970), although raptors in general are not reported to do so (Morrison and Walton, 1980). My experience suggests that secondary-site users like cavity-nesting owls usually move, probably because predators that check nest cavities regularly select against those that don't (chapter 2).
8. Southern (1970), Lundberg (1981), Hirons (1985b).
9. See, for example, Newton and Marquiss (1984) and Korpimaki and Lagerstrom (1988).
10. This partial clutch mean resembles that for boreal owls (12.5 days; Sonerud 1985a) and American kestrels (11.1 days; Bowman and Bird, 1985), while the full-clutch mean is like the one for great gray owls (25.5 days; Bull et al., 1989b) and tawny owls (27.8 days; Southern; 1970). See also Slagsvold (1984).
11. Egg loss in both suburban and rural populations was caused by 36 mammals (67%), 9 European starlings (17%), 3 black ratsnakes (5%), 3 males killed away from the nest (5%), 2 presumed cases of insufficient feeding during unusually cold or rainy weather (4%), and 1 instance of intraspecific competition (2%). Fox squirrels also

displace the owls in southern Michigan (Craighead and Craighead, 1969). That starlings displace screech owls is substantiated by Fowler and Dimmick (1983) and contrary with Van Camp and Henny (1975).

12. Compare with 3.6–3.8 eggs per average clutch (Van Camp and Henny, 1975; Murray, 1976). That my rural owls produce the same size clutches as suburban owls, despite their less stable environment, contradicts Cody (1966).

13. Using mean clutch size for two owls and nine hawks with N > 1 in table 1 of Morrison and Walton (1980), plus present data for the eastern screech owl and like data for the black vulture (Gehlbach, unpubl.), first clutches average 3.4 ± 1.2 eggs compared to 3.0 ± 1.4 eggs in replacement clutches (P ± 0.001). This kind of variation and others usually are not assessed in determining the seasonality of clutch size (Klomp, 1970, Daan et al., 1988; but see Meijer et al., 1988).

14. Newton and Marquiss (1984) note that weather 2–3 months before egg laying is influential in the Eurasian sparrowhawk. Clutch size should respond to resource seasonality according to Hussell (1985); also see Korpimaki and Hakkarainen (1991).

15. Newton and Marquiss (1981), Village (1981), Pietiainen et al. (1986), Korpimaki (1987a), Hornfeldt et al. (1990), Korpimaki and Hakkarainen (1991).

16. Newton and Marquiss (1976) and Korpimaki (1988d) indicate that "territory" (nest-site) quality influences clutch size and other aspects of breeding but they determine site quality by number of times a site is occupied. This can confound site with bird quality, if individuals reuse successful sites as boreal, eastern screech, and Ural owls do (see also Saurola, 1989b). Nevertheless, mean clutch size is unrelated to number of site occupancies in my study (r = −0.17, NS, n = 20), and site does not influence egg and fledgling production compared to owl quality (chapter 8).

17. Korpimaki (1988c) and Newton (1979), but see note 6 above, especially Pietiainen (1988a).

18. Karlsson and Nilsson (1977), Eriksson (1979), Korpimaki (1985a), Alatalo et al. (1988).

19. Pietiainen et al. (1986), Hakkarainen and Korpimaki (unpubl.).

20. Twenty-seven historic eggs from Central Texas in the Strecker Museum, Baylor University, Waco, Texas, average 34.8 × 30.0 mm, hence are no different from all my 1976–87 eggs. See also p. 280 in Bent (1938).

21. This suggests that last eggs are not sacrificeable which does not sup-

port the brood reduction hypothesis so commonly attributed to raptors (e.g., Slagsvold et al., 1984; Pietiainen et al., 1986) but perhaps
erroneous (Clark and Wilson, 1981; see also chapter 6).

22. Data synthesized from several sources: Bent (1938), Korpimaki
(1981, 1990a), Mikkola (1983), Solheim (1984a), Cannings
(1987), Johnsgard (1988), Green and Anthony (1989), and Gehlbach (unpubl. on flammulated owls). Surely small cavity-nesting
owls invest more egg energy in reproduction than large open nesters, because they have a more sheltered nest site and must make the
reproductive effort "count," inasmuch as they are more vulnerable
hence shorter lived as adults.

23. Astheimer (1985), Johnsgard (1988).

24. Newton and Marquiss (1981), DeLaet and Dhondt (1989).

25. See also Wijnandts (1984), Pietiainen (1988b).

26. Perhaps 26 days originated with Sherman (1911), but I figure 27.7
± 0.9 incubation days from Sherman's own data, although 28.6 ±
2.9 days is what I consider accurate from her observations. The boreal owl data are from Korpimaki (1981), the saw-whet data from
Cannings (1987); see also 29.7 days as the tawny owl average
(Southern, 1970). Among abnormally long unsuccessful incubation
periods in owls, 78 days in one of my suburban birds is the record
(cf. Marks, 1983).

27. Egg kicking could divert predators from the female and/or startle
them by its suddeness and light-egg-in-dark-cavity contrast (see also
Bloom and Hawks, 1983). Egg defense is generally like that of the
neotropical screech owl (Thomas, 1977).

28. This age-related shift in behavior is also reported by Reid (1988),
while Sonerud (1985b) notes a correlation between alarm behavior
and nest predation rate in the boreal and hawk owls, postulating
that alarm behavior is learned. Behavioral shifts adaptive to successful nesting in suburbia are known in other birds (e.g., Knight et
al. 1987).

29. Elf owls may be an exception (Ligon, 1968), but my experience
with elf, flammulated, western screech, and whiskered owls is that
females usually appear at the nest hole upon disturbance at their
tree and fly as I climb it (see also Sonerud, 1985b).

30. Southern (1970), Hirons (1985). Female elf owls exhibit similar behavior but may feed themselves during the recess (Ligon, 1968).

31. Data are from Ligon (1968), Southern (1970), Korpimaki (1981),
Lundberg and Westman (1984), Bunn et al., (1982), Cannings
(1987), Pietiainen (1989), Exo (1992), Johnson (1994) and my 83.3
percent clutch efficiency for 14 flammulated-owl nests. The average

for all nine owls (72.0%) is like the 75.9 ± 13.9 percent efficiency for 23 populations of 11 songbirds (data from table 1 in Nice, 1957) and the 69.8 percent value for captive screech owls (Wiemeyer, 1987).

32.   Despite its similarity, that in Lundberg (1985) is not the same approach.

33.   Using data in Southern (1970), Sonerud (1985a, 1985b), and Korpimaki (1987c), plus mine on flammulated owls.

34.   Koenig (1982) is the review, Korpimaki (1987a) the source for the boreal owl, and my unpublished data is used for flammulateds.

Chapter 6. Chicks and Fledglings: Greater Investments

1.   Ligon (1968), Southern (1970), Richmond et al. (1980), and Korpimaki (1981) plus my unpublished notes on flammulated owls. Delayed incubation and coincident hatching was first seen by Sherman (1911) and is known also in hawks (e.g., Village, 1990).

2.   Aspects of hatching asynchrony are reviewed and tested by Nilsson (1993a, 1993b).

3.   Southern (1970), Korpimaki (1981).

4.   Boreal owl hatching size is from Korpimaki (1981), adult size from Korpimaki (1990a); data on the flammulated owl is mine (unpubl.) and on the hawk owl from Huhtala et al. (1987).

5.   Data calculated from table 10 in Skutch (1976). Brooding lasts 15 days (48%) of the 31-day nestling period in the tawny owl (Southern, 1970; Hirons, 1985) compared to 14 of 22 days (64%) in the long-eared owl (Wijnandts, 1984) and perhaps 21.1 of 31.7 days (66%) in the boreal owl (Korpimaki, 1981).

6.   See also Lohrer (1985).

7.   For background read Ligon (1969). Spotted owls are also heat stressed at 32–33°C (Forsman et al., 1984). My only nest mortality, linked to heat stress but seemingly caused by suffocation, happened to a 106-g chick among four, 93–106 g, in a 36°C nest box (air 31°C) on May 18, as the surviving chicks panted heavily.

8.   Equipment and logistic constraints prevented my getting a large sample, hence the strict controls on brood size and vegetative environment. Humidity as a nest-cavity factor is noted by McComb and Noble (1981c) who also indicate that natural cavities are more stable thermally than nest boxes (1981b) but do not control for differences in cavity and box volumes.

9.   For example, read Newton (1979) and Johnsgard (1988).

10.   I have not seen helping behavior as reported by Smith and Hiestand

(1990) but could have missed it, since most males were not color marked.

11. Similar comments abut other raptors are, for example, in Newton (1979) and Bunn et al. (1982); but in some species like the Eurasian kestrel, widowed males may assume female roles (Village, 1990).

12. This is true in some other raptors (Snyder and Snyder, 1973; Newton, 1986; Geer, 1981), including perhaps the boreal owl for which the present evidence is equivocal (Korpimaki 1981, 1988a), but is not the case in all species (Dijkstra et al., 1990).

13. Korpimaki (1981), Wijnandts (1984), Hayward (1986), Korpimaki and Huhtala (1986), Reynolds and Linkhart (1987b), plus my personal observations of flammulated owls.

14. Contrast, for example, Ligon (1968), Hayward (1986), and Reynolds and Linkart (1987) with Wijnandts (1984) and Korpimaki and Sulkava (1987).

15. Data from Sumner (1928) for the western screech owl, Korpimaki (1981) for the boreal, and Cannings (1987) for the saw-whet owl. I followed Ricklefs (1968a), who determined the asymptote for the western screech owl using the logistic-growth model. Prefledging weight loss in owls is contrary to Ricklefs (1968b); see Sumner (1929) for such weight loss in hawks and owls.

16. Southern (1970).

17. Among sexually dimorphic chicks of several species, there is little evidence that the smaller sex is prejudiced against, and motor development may be faster in the smaller males, obviating any disadvantage (Drummond et al., 1991). On sibling competition compare Werschkul and Jackson (1979) with Ricklefs (1982).

18. I cannot sex nestlings externally except possibly by size at and near fledging and I made no attempt to sex them internally.

19. My data on 11 broods of flammulated owls plus Ligon (1968), Southern (1970), Village (1981), Hirons (1985b), and Pietiainen (1989) for the other species.

20. Compare, for example, cavity-nesting Eurasian kestrels (Village, 1990) with open-nesting Eurasian sparrowhawks (Newton, 1986) in the same region.

21. Hirons (1985b).

22. Mock (1984) provides terminology and a general review of fratricide and infanticide in birds, while Ricklefs (1969) summarizes nestling mortality from all causes, which is comparatively low among raptors. I never saw one chick kill another as did Allen (1924) but saw physical aggression and cannibalism by chicks and cannibalism by adult females.

23.   Background references include Ingram (1959), Stinson (1979), Magrath (1990), and Nilsson (1993a). Owl students usually endorse the brood reduction hypothesis (e.g., Southern, 1970; Hornfeldt and Eklund, 1990), though there are objections to it, both empirical (Bunn et al., 1982) and theoretical (Clark and Wilson, 1981).

24.   An apparently accidental case of fratricide is recounted by Allen (1924).

25.   While my nest boxes had drain holes, one became plugged during a heavy, blowing rain and filled with water, drowning three of four 5–10-day old nestlings at the same time as a natural-cavity nest with three chicks had only 2 cm of standing water. Seemingly acceptable natural cavities that occasionally filled with water had no roosting or nesting screen owls. One downy hatchling and a 21-day-old chick fell from boxes to their deaths on the ground, apparently from exposure (I did not determine if they were fed after falling).

26.   Calculated from data in appendix table 1 of Southern (1970).

27.   Data from Lundberg (1981), Lundberg and Westman (1984), Korpimaki (1988a), Pietiainen (1989), and Gehlbach (unpubl. for flammulateds). A 44.2 percent loss reported by Cannings (1987) for the saw-whet owl is based on only seven nests and so deviant as to be suspect.

28.   Basic information is in Gehlbach and Baldridge (1987). The present account covers an additional five years including 24 more live-in blind snakes from 13 more nests but presents essentially the same conclusions. See also Gehlbach et al. (1968).

29.   Exotic fire ants kill cavity-nesting birds, including at least one case of nestling eastern screech owls near Belton, Texas, 1990, but one of my open-yard sites in suburbia had a heavy fire-ant infestation while fledging owlets in 1987–90 (no nest in 1991). Twice fire ants invaded this nest box in late May but only after fledging (on ants nesting in bird boxes see Davis et al., 1984). Similarly, honey bees and paper wasps used nest boxes after fledging, and when a box had no active nest, but were gone the following year.

30.   References for the other owls include Ligon (1968), Southern (1970), Clark (1975), Thomas (1977), Korpimaki (1981), Reynolds and Linkhart (1987b), Cannings (1987), and Bull et al. (1989b). See especially figure 61 in Wijnandts (1984) and the contrast between open- and cavity-nesting spotted owls in Forsman et al. (1984).

31.   Korpimaki (1981).

32.   Ricklefs (1968b).

33. Data from Ligon (1968), Southern (1970), Korpimaki (1981), and
     Huhtala et al. (1987). Only once in 29 fledges did I see a screech
     owlet fly weakly about 2 m slightly down to a tree limb.
34. Korpimaki (1981).
35. Nestling and fledgling data averaged per species or percentages are
     from Ligon (1968), Southern (1970), Bunn et al. (1982), Lundberg
     and Westman (1984), Cannings (1987), Korpimaki (1988a), Pieti-
     ainen (1989), Exo (1992), and Johnson (1994), and include my
     80.0 percent efficiency value for flammulated owls. Ligon's data
     modified by humans is omitted, resulting in different values com-
     pared to Johnsgard (1988). Fledging efficiency for captive eastern
     screech owls is 94.4 percent (Wiemeyer, 1987).
36. Even figured biweekly there is no seasonal decline in fledgling pro-
     duction (b = −0.13, NS). Van Camp and Henny (1975) report a
     seasonal decline for eastern screech owl fledglings in Ohio, but their
     several calculations (table 12 and pp. 30–32) are based on assump-
     tions and results so incompatible as to be problematic.
37. For hawks see Newton (1979). Pietiainen (1989) indicates no sea-
     sonal difference in the production of fledgling Ural owls but does
     not specify first versus replacement nests.
38. Southern (1970), Korpimaki (1981). Rain adversely impacts open-
     and cavity-nesting hawks too (Newton, 1986; Village, 1990; but see
     Kostrzewa and Kostrzewa, 1990).
39. Even the Woodway mean is significantly lower (P < 0.004) than an
     estimated mean of 2.5 fledglings/pair in rural northern Ohio (Van
     Camp and Henny, 1975), but mortality is higher in that population
     and may offset the higher production (chapter 9).
40. Belthoff and Ritchison (1990b). These authors used radio-
     transmittered subjects without controls, which may explain why
     their owls generally moved farther than mine (chapter 1). Alterna-
     tively, their rural subjects may have been less densely packed than
     my suburban ones, hence less restricted in movements.
41. Southern et al. (1954).
42. Belthoff and Ritchison (1989).
43. Ritchison et al. (1992) suggest that dispersal follows innate restless-
     ness based on laboratory fledglings toting 30-g pedometers, who in-
     creased activity up to five weeks after fledging and then were less ac-
     tive. Instead, I think those owlets may have exhibited conditioning
     stress because of their 30-g burdens, despite possible innate dis-
     persal tendencies (see appendix VII).
44. In calculating a root mean square dispersal of 2.9 km, I follow
     Payne's (1990) advice by including extraplot dispersals. Of course

there is always a bias against the recovery of long-distance dispersers, especially if they are few, but my perimeter survey zones, auxiliary nest-box area, and 25 years of study "soften" that bias.

45. Korpimaki and Lagerstrom (1988), Sonerud et al. (1988), Newton and Marquiss (1983), and see the general review of avian dispersal by Greenwood and Harvey (1982).

46. In startling contrast to my data and the 2.3-km median distance in Kentucky (Belthoff and Ritchison, 1989), Van Camp and Henny (1975) record average natal dispersal as 32 km (median ca. 25 km) in an Ohio population of the eastern screech owl. Unfortunately, they used 23,500-ha areas to record movements, each one of which could encompass hundreds to thousands of home ranges (see chapter 9). Despite this inaccuracy, a few Ohio individuals do move farther, triggered I think by occasionally severe winters that do not affect southern populations in the same manner. This could suggest, erroneously, that some individuals are short-and others long-distance dispersers (Van Camp and Henny, 1975).

47. Korpimaki and Lagerstrom (1988) indicate no relation between food and natal dispersal distance. Sonerud et al. (1988) suggest shorter dispersal when food is more abundant but do not consider density. Newton and Marquiss (1983) cannot relate density to natal dispersal in Eurasian sparrowhawks.

48. Van Camp and Henny (1975), Belthoff and Ritchison (1989). I am quite familiar with eastern screech owls and their habitat in Ohio, Michigan, and New York (chapter 1).

Chapter 7. Vocalizations: Clues to the Night

1. Respective quotes from Oberholser (1974), p. 444, and Marshall (1967), p. 7. Also see the denial of screeching and other errors on pp. 256–57 in Bent (1938), corrected by Allen (1951).

2. Also called the tremolo, for example, by Kelso (1941) who notes 4–6 second trills, 5–30 seconds apart, hence like those I recorded. Called the bounce song by Cavanagh and Ritchison (1987), who provide two short sonograms and also note the lower-voiced male. Another sonogram of this song is the so-called secondary song of *Otus asio* (*asio* group) in figure 10 of Marshall (1967).

3. Also shown in a Kentucky population by Ritchison et al. (1988).

4. Mikkola (1983).

5. Note the definition of such acoustic contact signals, which apply to all screech owl songs and calls, in Helverson (1980).

6. Ligon (1968), Korpimaki (1981). Also see Kelso (1941).

7. Karalus and Eckert (1974), p. 102. Ligon (1968) observes that elf owls also seem to call their nestlings from cavities (stimulate fledging?).

8. It is like the first second of the sonogram of *Otus asio* (*kennicottii* group) in Marshall (1967), figure 10. See also Kelso (1941).

9. Can these be the "wuh-wuh-wuh notes like rubbing sandpaper with a stick" described by Kelso (1941)?

10. This is the so-called primary song of *Otus asio* (*asio* group) in Marshall (1967), figure 10, although the illustrated sonogram is about half the usual length I recorded. Descending trills are also called whinnies, for example by Cavanagh and Ritchison (1987), who provide short sonograms of this and the monotonic trill (see their figure 1, and tables 2, 3).

11. Similar seasonality was reported by Hough (1960), Smith et al. (1987), and Ritchison et al. (1988).

12. I disagree with Ritchison et al. (1988) that descending trills are responses to distant screech owls, while monotonic trills are to nearby ones.

13. Compare with Rea (1968).

14. Johnson et al. (1981) and Palmer (1987), but note the contrary evidence for eastern screech owls in Smith et al. (1987). Also see Mills (1986). Kelso (1942) describes lunar cycle–related weight and behavioral changes in eastern screech owls.

15. Based particularly on sequential resident pairs at two suburban nest-box sites. This contrasts with the late-summer to early fall peak of song responses to tape recordings (e.g., Smith et al., 1987; Ritchison et al., 1988); because, as these authors note, newly dispersed juveniles augment the responsive population. Juveniles do not ordinarily sing at this time, however.

16. Bent (1938), p. 257, describes what I presume to be this call as "Ho-ho-ho-ho."

17. Sproat and Ritchison (1993) say that males are primary nest defenders, despite the functional similarity of vocalizations in both of our studies. Did they misidentify sexes? If not, perhaps their birds were vexed by the radio transmitters they carried and unfamiliar lights set up for observations, as no habituation time is indicated. Even so, males do become more defensive with increasing parental investment in the reproductive effort (chapter 6).

18. Defense reinforcement is promoted by Knight and Temple (1986), who contend that birds' call rates do not differ relative to human exposure though defense is more aggressive toward familiar humans (Knight and Temple, 1981). Conversely, see Biermann and Robert-

son (1981), Wallin (1987), and Montgomerie and Weatherhead (1988). Regarding eastern screech owls, Sproat and Ritchison (1993) mention defense reinforcement but did not test it, as they combined data from birds exposed once to humans with that from repeatedly exposed individuals and did not account for age-related experience. Their results support hypotheses of increasing parental investment and/or molt-time constraints.

19.   Wallin (1987). Similarly, Eurasian sparrowhawks tend to be more defensive with chicks than with eggs (Newton, 1986).
20.   Bunn et al. (1982), p. 52.
21.   Also see Karalus and Eckert (1974), p. 103. This may be the sound described by Kelso (1940), apparently first noticed in 60-day-old owlets.
22.   Bent (1938), p. 257. Similar calling behavior is known in many owls; for example read Muir (1954).

Chapter 8. Lifetime Reproduction: Efforts of a Few

1.   Newton (1989).
2.   Southern (1970), Village (1981), Hirons (1982), Lundberg and Westman (1984).
3.   Korpimaki (1987c).
4.   Saurola (1987).
5.   Clutch size varies independently of age more often than do egg size, fledgling output, and reproductive timing among the variety of birds reviewed by Saether (1990). However, among 10 suburban females with known first-egg dates and clutch sizes each year of their 3–10-year lifespans, earlier layers produced larger clutches on average ($r = -0.73$, $P = 0.01$).
6.   My value of 85% resembles the 77–83% reported by Van Camp and Henny (1975). I censused nonbreeding males rather accurately by their singing but not nonbreeding females, which I estimate as 9%, based on 91% of first-time breeders being yearlings (chapter 9). For background on deferred breeding see Curio (1983).
7.   On measuring reproductive cost read Reznick (1985) and Nur (1988).
8.   Korpimaki (1988a).
9.   The nearly 50% of breeding yearlings contrasts with 30% for boreal and 20% for Ural owls, calculated from data in Korpimaki (1988c) and Pietiainen (1988a); and the 53% disappearance rate is lower than that (76%) for yearling Ural owls (Saurola, 1989b).
10.   Causes of mortality are listed in chapter 9. Among 80 breeding fe-

males only two (2.5%), one long-lived and a one-timer, were debil-
tated in any obvious manner; both were blind in one eye but nested
successfully. I never saw a debilitated male. As more active foragers,
impaired males may be eliminated more quickly than females.

11. Korpimaki (1988c), Pietiainen (1988a), Newton (1989).

12. A cross-sectional analysis compares all known-age individuals
among age classes as in Gehlbach (1989), whereas a longitudinal
analysis compares only the same individuals between sequential age
classes employing pairwise analyses as in table 8.1.

13. Based on my appraisal of mean data in figure 58 of Newton (1986)
and figure 1 of Pietiainen (1988a).

14. Gehlbach (1989).

15. This hypothesis and others about age-improved breeding are stated
by Nol and Smith (1987) and reviewed by Clutton-Brock (1988).
See also Newton (1989).

16. I follow the repeatability technique of Lessells and Boag (1987),
whose sparrowhawk recalculations are the ones referenced. The
same approach by Goodburn (1991) and Kennedy and White
(1991) produces the same contrasting pattern of low-site versus
high-bird repeatability in magpies and house wrens, respectively.

17. I employed only the first year's data from Korpimaki (1989b). Flammulated owls may be an exception based on my assessment of data
from table 3 in Reynolds and Linkhart (1987).

18. Combined data from table 1 in Korpimaki (1991b) and table 1 in
Carlsson et al. (1987).

19. Besides Korpimaki (1989b), see Solheim (1983) and Korpimaki
(1988e).

20. Recovery rates calculated from data in Southern (1970), Van Camp
and Henny (1975), and Korpimaki and Lagerstrom (1988). Adding
two additional suburban owlets that bred outside my study plots
(chapter 6) brings the recovery rate up to 6.1 percent (Gehlbach,
1994c).

21. A small but significant correlation (r = 0.43, P = 0.04) between
fledgling and recruit numbers was reported by Gehlbach (1989) and
the general relationship holds for some other birds (Newton, 1989)
but cannot be substantiated in the present data set. This relation is
even weaker (r_s = 0.31) in boreal owls (Korpimaki, 1991a).

22. See chapters on individual birds in the books edited by Clutton-
Brock (1988) and Newton (1989), especially Saurola (1989b), plus
read Korpimaki and Lagerstrom (1988).

23. A similar idea is in Newton and Marquiss (1984) and Saurola
(1989b).

24. Early fledging and large size enhance fledgling survival for some
     birds but not others; not the Eurasian sparrowhawk, for example
     (Newton and Moss, 1986).
25. Korpimaki and Lagerstrom (1988).
26. Average CVs for female eastern screech owls are 47% (age), 27%
     (eggs), and 69% (fledglings) compared to 58%, 30%, and 86%, re-
     spectively, derived by averaging square roots of the standardized
     variances reported for female Eurasian sparrowhawks, great tits,
     Florida scrub jays, fulmars, house martins, song sparrows, Bewick's
     swans, and kittiwakes in the book edited by Clutton-Brock (1988).
     Of the 18 individual CVs available for these eight species, only four
     are lower than the comparable screech owl value.
27. Again, my repeatability analyses follow Lessells and Boag (1987),
     and heritability is estimated by doubling the regression coefficients;
     see Boag and van Noordwijk (1987) and Hailman (1987).
28. Cooke (1987), Lessells and Boag (1987), van Noordwijk (1987),
     Korpimaki (1990b).
29. Krebs (1978) reviews hypotheses about such "alternating genetic
     currents." Following Rockwell and Barrowclough (1987), Koenig
     (1988), and Payne (1990), I estimate effective population size as
     488 for the suburban screech owls, which average 11.5/km², and
     2,440 for the rural owls, which average 2.3/km². Theoretically, there-
     fore, areas of 42–212 km² are needed to maintain populations
     across the spectrum of known densities (chapter 9). The effective
     population size of 4,310 in Barrowclough and Coats (1985) is too
     large, based as it is on supposition and some questionable dispersal
     data (chapter 6).

Chapter 9. Population Structure and Flux: Density
Dependence in Action

1. This oldest individual, a female from my Lake Air survey area, is
    the oldest known eastern screech owl (cf. Clapp et al., 1983). My
    second oldest, also a female, was 11 years, 11 months upon death
    and nested in the suburban perimeter zone. On human-related mor-
    tality in birds see Banks (1979). Values for suburban versus rural
    survival were reversed in Gehlbach (1988b).
2. Data on females or unspecified adults are averaged from Henny
    (1969), Southern (1970), Lundberg and Westman (1984), and Bull
    et al. (1989b). See Botkin and Miller (1974) for a review of age-
    specific survival in birds.

3.   Data from Sutton (1927) and Jane Lyons (pers. comm.) for Austin, Texas, 1979–83. An apparaisal of nine leading causes of mortality in these and my studies shows their statistical similarity. Similar data but of unspecified provenance is in table 16 of Van Camp and Henny (1975).

4.   Juveniles of tawny, barn, and little owls suffer the most mortality in July–October of their fledging year (Glue, 1973; Hirons, 1985a). In Connecticut the most road-killed eastern screech owls are in found in October–March (Devine and Smith 1985).

5.   Newton and Marquiss (1986), Newton et al. (1993). With data from the latter reference and those cited in note 2 above, I calculate the annual survival of breeders as $61.7 \pm 8.2\%$ (n = 12 populations) in the eastern screech owl and three hawks of less than 300-g adult size by contrast to $74.1 \pm 10.1\%$ (10) in four owls and four hawks larger than 300 g (P = 0.008).

6.   Korpimaki (1988c).

7.   Fledgling output per female required for population stability is estimated with survival data from appendix IX and the equation on p. 58 in Van Camp and Henny (1975). My value of 1.8 contrasts with Van Camp and Henny's 2.2, but their rural population had lower adult survival.

8.   Offspring production per yearling or older female, not total production of each type as in Gehlbach (1989), is the information necessary to understand replacement rate because of different numbers in each age class.

9.   Korpimaki and Lagerstrom (1988), Pietiainen (1989). On hawks see Newton and Marquiss (1984), and Village (1990), for example.

10. For the curvilinear pattern, 2^0 r^2 = 0.97, P = 0.03; and, similarly, the asymptote is 61.1 percent at seven eggs in the boreal owl (2^0 r^2 = 0.99, P < 0.001; computed with data from table 4 in Korpimaki, 1987a). But see table 5 in Ligon (1968) and table 13 in Bunn et al. (1982) for other possible patterns.

11. Optimal-clutch theory is reviewed by Cody (1966), Klomp (1970), Drent and Daan (1980), Murphy and Haukioja (1986), and Vanderwerf (1992). In the last paper, four of the five references employing recruitment as a test of clutch-size optimization versus maximization favor the optimum compared to only nine of 36 references using fledgling number (P = 0.02).

12. Productivity values for owls are from Ligon (1968), Southern (1970), Solheim (1984a), Cannings (1987), Johnson (1987), Korpimaki (1988a), Pietiainen (1989), Exo (1992), Johnson (1994), and

Gehlbach for flammulateds (67.6%, unpubl.). The 66.6 and 49.2 percent averages are from data on the named species in tables 1 and 2 of Nice (1957) and like Lack's (1954) 67 and 45 percent values. Captive eastern screech owls were 65.9 percent productive (Wiemeyer, 1987).

13.   Most birds reproduce better in cities (Tomialojc and Gehlbach, 1988). The only other data on urban versus rural raptors suggest that merlins (Warkentin and James, 1988) and tawny owls (Wendland, 1980) are most productive in cities (also see Gehlbach, 1994a).

14.   Nest-box size makes no difference to eastern bluebirds either (Pitts, 1988), but larger boxes produce more boreal owlets (Korpimaki, 1985a).

15.   In concluding this section I am mindful that productivity should be the product of survivability, hatchability, and fledgeability; since they are independent events (chapters 5, 6). Presently, however, the results for suburbia ($70 \times 84 \times 85 = 50\%$) and the rural plot ($45 \times 87 \times 71 = 28\%$) are no different from fledglings/eggs values in table 9.3).

16.   Southern (1970).

17.   Interestingly, 15 of 23 forest species nesting on my suburban plot are also unaffected by habitat area. This is based on table 3 of Robbins et al. (1989), applied to species listed in appendix V plus the chuck-wills-widow, black-chinned and ruby-throated hummingbirds, red-bellied woodpecker, great-crested flycatcher, American crow, Carolina chickadee, white-eyed vireo, orchard oriole, and summer tanager.

18.   Using the method of Clark and Evans (1954).

19.   Data from Smith and Gilbert (1984) for Connecticut and table 1 in Belthoff et al. (1993) for Kentucky.

20.   Data are from Craighead and Craighead (1969), Nowicki (1974), Allaire and Landrum (1975), Cink (1975), Lynch and Smith (1984), Mutter et al. (1984), Swengel and Swengel (1987), and DeGeus and Bowles (1991) but represent estimates for different seasons obtained by various methods not necessarily comparable to my exact counts. Johnson et al. (1981) report the astonishingly high density of nine pairs of western screech owls per four rural hectares, which I cannot substantiate.

21.   Calculated from data in Southern (1970), Wendland (1980), Lundberg (1981), Korpimaki (1981), Hirons (1985a), McCallum and Gehlbach (1988), Galeotti (1990), and Exo (1992). Galeotti refers

to one other rural group of tawny owls exceeding the 0.1–2.5/km²
span and believes the data to be in error (pers. comm.). Swengel
and Swengel (1987) claim 5.0–12.9 singing saw-whet owls/km²,
though their mapped information suggests fewer than 1.0/km².

22. Southern (1970).

23. Newton and Marquiss (1986) and Newton (1988).

24. Newton (1988) and Southern (1970), but see Hirons (1985a). Out
of curiosity I did a key-factor analysis of the suburban population
in 1976–87. The maximum-possible-eggs factor (k_1) was successful
nests $\times$ 6 (largest clutch) − actual eggs, and fledglings lost to recruitment (k_5) was nesting females one year − those next year $\times$
mean adult female survivorship (0.62). There were no significant
correlations of any key factor with density one year or the next; K
was correlated only with k_1 ($r = 0.67$, $P = 0.01$) and perhaps k_5
($r = 0.53$, $P = 0.07$), much as in the tawny owl and Eurasian sparrowhawk.

25. For comparisons, standard deviations of $\log_{10}$-transformed densities
were computed from appendix table 1 in Southern (1970), table 1
in Newton and Marquiss (1986), or taken from Connell and Sousa
(1983). The suburban owls are more stable ($P = 0.03$), the rural
owls no different than populations of ten other species including
tawny owls, sparrowhawks, grouse, and songbirds. Certain other
raptors may be equally stable, however (Newton, 1991).

26. Archibald (1977) and also see Keith (1963).

27. Kelso (1942) notes monthly weight and activity rhythms that seem
to be correlated with lunar rhythms, though the data are minimal
and only suggestive.

28. Archibald (1977), Roseberry and Klimstra (1984), plus my preliminary assessment of population data from table 1 in Newton and
Marquiss (1986). See also Lack (1954).

29. Similar theories of population regulation are reviewed by Krebs
(1978).

Chapter 10. The Suburban Advantage: A Final Synthesis

1. Members of the small- and large-owl groups are in figure 10.1.
Data were averaged from many studies, including one or more populations per species, cited in the endnotes of preceding chapters deal-
ing with comparative reproductive features (summarized in Mikkola, 1983, and Johnsgard, 1988). For weight I mostly used Snyder
and Wiley (1976, table 1).

2. Forsman et al. (1984) provide life history background on the spotted owl in Oregon, and Perrins (1991) contrasts the demographies of endangered and nonendangered birds.

3. Pertinent here is an explicit comparison with Van Camp and Henny's (1975) 20-point summary of eastern screech owls in northern Ohio: (1) 30 years of Ohio data, 25 in Texas; (2) similar diets; (3) same nonmigratory status; (4) natal dispersal farther in Ohio; (5) short- versus long-distance dispersal groups in Ohio, not in Texas, (6) dispersal random in Ohio, directional in Texas, but on apparent differences in dispersal see Chapter 6; (7) similar nesting phenology, (8) similar clutch size, fledgling production, and nesting success; (9) similar annual flux in fledglings per successful nest; (10) predatory influence unmeasured in Ohio; (11) same 50:50 sex ratio; (12) similar age-specific mortality; (13) similar proportions of nesting yearlings; (14) eggshell thinning and toxin residues unstudied in Texas; (15) similar intermediate colormorphs; (16) similar poor cold adaptation of rufous owls; (17) no sex-colormorph connection in Ohio as in Texas; (18) same dominance of the rufous allele; (19) same lack of a brood size-colormoph relation; and (20) both populations stable but cyclic.

4. Beginning in the early 1950s suburbia expanded 350 m from the northeastern edge of the Woodway study plot. Forty years later the 10 ha area (2 ha green space) was quite wooded in aspect, though 30 percent of its trees, all planted, were exotics. In 1993 a nest box was deployed 800 m from the closest previously nesting screech owls and used successfully by immigrant yearlings. No natural cavities could be found.

5. Reviewed, for example, by Lack (1954, 1966) and Perrins and Birkhead (1983). Also see Newton (1979, 1989, 1991).

6. Gehlbach (1994a) offers a model of raptor urbanization.

7. Morrison (1986) and Temple and Wiens (1989) conclude that birds are poor indicators of environmental change but do not mention urbanization, well documented by changes in the breeding biology of birds in Europe if not North America (Tomialojc and Gehlbach, 1988).

8. See Burton (1984). In Central Texas, for instance, the barn owl's nesting niche includes a variety of cultural structures (hunting blinds, childrens' tree houses, and grain silos besides the "traditional" building attics and natural cliff and tree hollows) employed in producing 2–3 broods/year in all seasons except mid-winter.

9. DDE-connected eggshell thinning has not been found in free-living screech owls though induced in the laboratory (Van Camp and

Henny, 1975; Klaas and Swineford, 1976). Other toxic residues are present in wild eggs and have adverse consequences for the birds in lab tests (references in Wiemeyer, 1987).

10.   Nesting males are caught by netting or noosing at a day roost (poorest methods), at dusk on a bal-chatri trap baited with a live mouse or house sparrow or in a baited mist net (better), or by "night fishing" (best). Night fishing involves casting a small rubber frog, mouse, or snake without hooks toward a hunting male, reeling in slowly to allow him to follow closely, and popping a net over him when within reach.

References

Alatalo, R. V., A. Carlson, and A. Lundberg. 1988. Nest cavity size and clutch size of pied flycatchers *Ficedula hypoleuca* breeding in natural tree holes. *Ornis Scand.* 19:317–19.

Allaire, P. N., and D. F. Landrum. 1975. Summer census of screech owls in Breathitt County. *Kentucky Warbler* 51:23–29.

Allard, H. A. 1937. Activity of the screech owl. *Auk* 54:300–303.

Allen, A. A. 1924. A contribution to the life history and economic status of the screech owl (*Otus asio*). *Auk* 41:1–16.

Allen, F. H. 1951. Notes of the eastern screech owl *Otus asio naevius:* a correction. *Auk* 68:241–42.

Allen, J. A. 1893. Hasbrouck on evolution and dichromatism in the genus *Megascops*. *Auk* 10:347–51.

Altmann, S. A. 1956. Avian mobbing behavior and predator recognition. *Condor* 58:241–53.

Andersson, M., and R. A. Norberg. 1981. Evolution of reversed sexual size dimorphism and role partitioning among predatory birds, with a size scaling of flight performance. *Biol. J. Linn. Soc.* (1981):105–30.

Archibald, H. L. 1977. Is the 10-year wildlife cycle induced by a lunar cycle? *Wildl. Soc. Bull.* 5:126–29.

Askins, R. A., J. F. Lynch, and R. Greenberg. 1990. Population declines in migratory birds in eastern North America. Pp. 1–57 in *Current Ornithology*, vol. 7. D. M. Power, ed. New York: Plenum Press.

Astheimer, L. B. 1985. Long laying intervals: a possible mechanism and its implications. *Auk* 102:401–409.

Balgooyen, T. G. 1976. Behavior and ecology of the American kestrel (*Falco sparvarius* L.) in the Sierra Nevada of California. *Univ. Calif. Publ. Zool.* 103:1–85.

Banks, R. C. 1979. Human related mortality of birds in the United States. *U.S. Fish and Wildl. Serv., Spec. Sci. Rept.* 215.

Barrowclough, G. F., and S. L. Coats. 1985. The demography and population genetics of owls with special reference to the conservation of the spotted owl (*Strix occidentalis*). Pp. 74–85 in *Ecology and Management of the Spotted Owl in the Pacific Northwest*. R. J. Gutierrez and A. B. Cary, eds. USDA Forest Service Genl. Tech. Rept. PNW-185.

Barrows, C., and K. Barrows. 1978. Roost characteristics and behavioral thermoregulation in the spotted owl. *Western Birds* 9:1–8.

Beissinger, S. R. 1987. Anisogamy overcome: female strategies in snail kites. *Amer. Natur.* 129:486–500.

Belthoff, J. R., and G. Ritchison. 1989. Natal dispersal of eastern screech owls. *Condor* 91:254–65.

———. 1990a. Nest-site selection by eastern screech-owls in central Kentucky. *Condor* 92:982–990.

———. 1990b. Roosting behavior of postfledging eastern screech owls. *Auk* 107:567–79.

Belthoff, J. R., E. J. Sparks, and G. Ritchison. 1993. Home ranges of adult and juvenile eastern screech owls: size, seasonal variation, and extent of overlap. *J. Raptor Res.* 27:8–15.

Bent, A. C. 1938. Life histories of North American birds of prey (part 2). *U. S. Natl. Mus. Bull.* 170.

Biermann, G. C., and R. J. Robertson. 1981. An increase in parental investment during the breeding season. *Animal Behav.* 29:487–89.

Bloom, P. H., and S. J. Hawks. 1983. Nest box use and reproductive biology of the American kestrel in Lassen County, California. *J. Raptor Res.* 17:9–14.

Boag, P. T., and A. J. van Noordwijk. 1987. Quantitative genetics. Pp. 45–47 in *Avian Genetics: A Population and Ecological Approach*. F. Cooke and P. A. Buckley, eds. London: Academic Press.

Bosakowski, T., R. Speiser, and J. Benzinger. 1987. Distribution, density, and habitat relations of the barred owl in New Jersey. Pp. 135–44 in *Biology and Conservation of Northern Forest Owls*. R. W. Nero, R. J. Clark, R. J. Knapton, and R. H. Hamre, eds. USDA Forest Service, Genl. Tech. Rept. RM-142.

Botkin, D. B., and R. S. Miller. 1974. Mortality rates and survival of birds. *Amer. Natur.* 108:181–92.

Bowman, R. 1987. Size dimorphism in mated pairs of American kestrels. *Wilson Bull.* 99:465–67.

Bowman, R., and D. M. Bird. 1985. Reproductive performance of American kestrels laying replacement clutches. *Canadian J. Zool.* 63:2,590–93.

Brawn, J. D., and R. P. Balda. 1988. Population biology of cavity nesters in northern Arizona: do nest sites limit breeding densities? *Condor* 90:61–71.

Breitwisch, R., and J. Hudak. 1989. Sex differences in risk-taking behavior in foraging flocks of house sparrows. *Auk* 106:150–53.

Bull, E. L., M. G. Henjum, and R. S. Rohweder. 1989a. Diet and optimal foraging of great gray owls. *J. Wildl. Mgmt.* 53:47–50.

———. 1989b. Reproduction and mortality of great gray owls in Oregon. *Northwest Sci.* 63:38–43.

Bunn, D. S., A. B. Warburton, and R. D. S. Wilson. 1982. *The Barn Owl.* London: T. & A. D. Poyser Ltd.

Burton, J. A. 1984. *Owls of the World: Their Evolution, Structure, and Ecology.* Dover: Tanager Books.

Burtt, E. H., Jr. 1986. An analysis of physical, physiological, and optional aspects of avian coloration with emphasis on wood-warblers. *Ornithol. Monogr.* 38.

Cannings, R. J. 1987. The breeding biology of northern saw-whet owls in southern British Columbia. Pp. 193–98 in *Biology and Conservation of Northern Forest Owls.* R. W. Nero, R. J. Clark, R. J. Knapton, and R. H. Hamre, eds. USDA Forest Service, Genl. Tech. Rept. RM-142.

Carlsson, B. G., B. Hornfeldt, and O. Lofgren. 1987. Bigyny in Tengmalm's owl *Aegolius funereus:* effect of mating strategy on breeding success. *Ornis Scand.* 18:237–43.

Carpenter, T. W. 1987. Effects of environmental variables on responses of eastern screech owls to playback. Pp. 277–80 in *Biology and Conservation of Northern Forest Owls.* R. W. Nero, R. J. Clark, R. J. Knapton, and R. H. Hamre, eds. USDA Forest Service, Genl. Tech. Rept. RM-142.

Cavanagh, P. M., and C. R. Ritchison. 1987. Variation in the bounce and whinny songs of the eastern screech owl. *Wilson Bull.* 99:620–27.

Chandler, C. R., and R. K. Rose. 1988. Comparative analysis of the effects of visual and auditory stimuli on avian mobbing behavior. *J. Field Ornithol.* 59:269–77.

Cink, C. L. 1975. Population densities of screech owls in northeastern Kansas. *Kansas Ornithol. Soc. Bull.* 26:13–16.

Clapp, R. B., M. K. Klimkiewicz, and A. G. Futcher. 1983. Longevity records of North American birds: Columbidae through Paridae. *J. Field Ornithol.* 54:123–237.

Clark, A. B., and D. S. Wilson. 1981. Avian breeding adaptations: hatching asynchrony, brood reduction, and nest failure. *Quart. Rev. Biol.* 56:253–77.

Clark, G. A., Jr. 1979. Body weights of birds: a review. *Condor* 81:193–202.

Clark, P. J., and F. C. Evans. 1954. Distance to nearest neighbor as a measure of spatial relationships in populations. *Ecology* 35:445–53.

Clark, R. J. 1975. A field study of the short-eared owl, *Asio flammeus (Pontoppidan) in North America. Wild. Monogr.* 47.

Clark, R. J., D. G. Smith, and L. H. Kelso. 1978. *Working Bibliography of Owls of the World,* Natl. Wildl. Fed. Sci./Tech. Ser. 1.

Clutton-Brock, T. H. 1988. Introduction. Pp. 1–6 in *Reproductive Success: Studies of Individual Variation in Contrasting Breeding Systems.* T. H. Clutton-Brock, ed. Chicago: University of Chicago Press.

Cody, M. L. 1966. A general theory of clutch size. *Evolution* 20:174–84.

Connell, J. H., and W. P. Sousa. 1983. On the evidence needed to judge ecological stability or persistence. *Amer. Natur.* 121:789–824.

Cooke, F. 1987. Lesser snow goose: a long-term population study. Pp. 407–32 in *Avian Genetics: A Population and Ecological Approach.* F. Cooke and P. A. Buckley, eds. London: Academic Press.

Craig, E. H., T. H. Craig, and L. R. Powers. 1988. Activity patterns and home-range use of nesting long-eared owls. *Wilson Bull.* 100:204–13.

Craighead, J. J., and F. C. Craighead Jr. 1969. *Hawks, Owls, and Wildlife.* New York: Dover Publ. Inc.

Curio, E. 1976. *The Ethology of Predation.* Berlin: Springer-Verlag. Publ. Co.

———. 1983. Why do young birds reproduce less well? *Ibis* 125:400–404.

Curio, E., U. Ernst, and W. Vieth, 1978. Cultural transmission of enemy recognition; one function of mobbing. *Science* 202:899–901.

Daan, S., C. Dijkstra, R. Drent, and T. Meijer. 1988. Food supply and the annual timing of avian reproduction. *Acta XIX Congr. Internatl. Ornithol.* vol. 1:392–407.

Davis, W. H., W. C. McComb, and P. Allaire. 1984. Ants (*Crematogaster clara* Mayr) nesting in bird boxes (Hymenoptera: Formicidae). *Entomol. News* 95:29–30.

DeGeus, D. W., and J. B. Bowles. 1991. Relative abundance of eastern screech-owls in a south-central Iowa township. *J. Iowa Acad. Sci.* 98:91–92.

DeLaet, J. F., and A. A. Dhondt. 1989. Weight loss of the female during the first brood as a factor influencing second brood initiation in great tits, *Parus major,* and blue tits, *P. caeruleus. Ibis* 131:281–89.

Devine, A., and D. G. Smith, 1985. Eastern screech owl (*Otus asio*) mortality in southern Connecticut. *Connecticut Warbler* 5:47–48.

Dhondt, A. A., R. Eyckerman, R. Moermans, and J. Huble. 1984. Habitat and laying date of great and blue tits, *Parus major* and *P. coeruleus. Ibis* 126:388–97.

Dijkstra, C., A. Bult, S. Bijlsma, S. Daan, T. Meijer, and M. Zijlstra. 1990. Brood size manipulations in the kestrel (*Falco tinnunculus*): effects on offspring and parent survival. *J. Animal Ecol.* 59:269–85.

Dijkstra, C., L. Vuursteen, S. Daan, and D. Masman. 1982. Clutch size and laying date in the kestrel *Falco tinnunculus:* effect of supplementary food. *Ibis* 124:210–13.

Dow, H., and S. Fredga. 1985. Selection of nest sites by a hole-nesting duck, the goldeneye, *Bucephala clangula. Ibis* 127:16–30.

Drent, R. H., and S. Daan. 1980. The prudent parent: energetic adjustment in avian breeding. *Ardea* 68:225–52.

Drummond, H., J. L. Osorno, R. Torres, C. G. Chavelas, and H. M. Larios. 1991. Sexual size dimorphism and sibling competition: implications for avian sex ratios. *Amer. Natur.* 138:623–41.

Earhart, C. M., and N. K. Johnson. 1970. Size dimorphism and food habits of North American owls. *Condor* 72:251–64.

East, M. L., and C. M. Perrins. 1988. The effect of nestboxes on breeding populations of birds in broadleaved temperate woodlands. *Ibis* 130:393–401.

Eden, S. F. 1985. The comparative breeding biology of magpies *Pica pica* in an urban and a rural habitat (Aves: Corvidae). *J. Zool. London* 205:325–34.

Eriksson, M. O. G. 1979. Clutch size and incubation efficiency in relation to nest-box size among goldeneyes *Bucephala clangula. Ibis* 121:107–109.

Erwin, R. M., J. Galli, and J. Burger. 1981. Colony site dynamics and habit use in Atlantic Coast seabirds. *Auk* 98:550–61.

Exo, K. M. 1992. Population ecology of little owls in central Europe: a review. Pp. 64–75 in *The Ecology and Conservation of European Owls.* C. A. Galbraith, I. R. Taylor, and S. Percival, eds. Peterborough: U.K. Nature Conserv. 5.

Forsman, E. C., E. C. Meslow, and H. M. Wight. 1984. Distribution and biology of the spotted owl in Oregon. *Wildl. Monogr.* 87.

Fowler, L. J., and R. D. Dimmick. 1983. Wildlife use of nest boxes in eastern Tennessee. *Wildl. Soc. Bull* 11:178–81.

Franklin, A. B. 1988. Breeding biology of the great-gray owl in southeastern Idaho and northwestern Wyoming. *Condor* 90:689–96.

Galeotti, P. 1990. Territorial behaviour and habitat selection in an urban population of the tawny owl *Strix aluco* L. *Boll. Zool.* 57:59–66.

Gauthier, G. 1988. Factors affecting nest-box use by buffleheads and other cavity-nesting birds. *Wildl. Soc. Bull.* 16:132–41.

Geer, T. 1981. Factors affecting the delivery of prey to nestling sparrowhawks (*Accipiter nisus*). *J. Zool. London* 15:71–80.

———. 1982. The selection of tits *Parus* sp. by sparrowhawks *Accipiter nisus. Ibis* 124:159–67

Gehlbach, F. R. 1988a. Forests and woodlands of the northeastern Balcones Escarpment. Pp. 57–77 in *Edwards Plateau Vegetation: Plant Ecological Studies in Central Texas,* B. B. Amos and F. R. Gehlbach, eds. Waco: Baylor University Press.

———. 1988b. Population and environmental features that promote adaptation to urban ecosystems: the case of eastern screech owls (*Otus asio*) is Texas. *Acta XIX Congr. Internatl. Ornithol.* vol. 2:1809–1813.

———. 1989. Screech owl. Pp. 315–26 in *Lifetime Reproduction in Birds.* I. Newton, ed. London: Academic Press.

———. 1991. The east-west transition zone of terrestrial vertebrates in central Texas: a biogeographic analysis. *Texas J. Sci.* 43:415–27.

———. 1994a. Eastern screech owls in suburbia: a model of raptor urbanization. In *Raptors Adapting in Human-altered Environments.* D. M. Bird, P. Varland, and J. J. Negro, eds. Proceedings Symp. Raptor Res. Fndtn., Charlotte, N. Car.

———. 1994b. Nest-box versus natural-cavity nests of the eastern screech owl: an exploratory study. *J. Raptor Res.* 28 (in press).

———. 1994c. Recruitment in an eastern screech owl populations: on components of fitness and inheritance. In *Raptors in the Modern World,* R. D. Chancellor, ed. Berlin: IV World Conference on Birds of Prey (in press).

Gehlbach, F. R., and R. S. Baldridge. 1987. Live blind snakes (*Leptotyphlops dulcis*) in eastern screech owl (*Otus asio*) nests: a novel commensalism. *Oecologia* 71:560–63.

Gehlbach, F. R., J. F. Watkins, and H. W. Reno. 1968. Blind snake defensive behavior elicited by ant attacks. *Bioscience* 18:784–85.

Glue, D. 1973. Seasonal mortality in four small birds of prey. *Ornis Scand.* 4:97–102.

Goodburn, S. F. 1991. Territory quality or bird quality? Factors determining breeding success in the magpie *Pica pica. Ibis* 133:85–90.

Gould, G. I., Jr., 1977. Distribution of the spotted owl in California. *Western Birds* 8:131–46.

Graber, J. W., and R. W. Graber. 1983. Expectable decline of forest bird populations in severe and mild winters. *Wilson Bull.* 95:682–90.

Grafen, A. 1988. On the uses of data on lifetime reproductive success. Pp. 454–71 in *Reproductive Success,* T. H. Clutton-Brock, ed. Chicago: Univ. of Chicago Press.

Green, G. A., and R. G. Anthony. 1989. Nesting success and habitat relationships of burrowing owls in the Columbia Basin, Oregon. *Condor* 71:347–54.

Greenwood, P. J., and P. H. Harvey. 1982. The natal and breeding dispersal of birds. *Ann. Rev. Ecol. Syst.* 13:1–21.

Griffiths, D. 1980. Foraging costs and relative prey size. *Amer. Natur.* 116:743–52.

Hailman, J. P. 1987. The heritability concept applied to wild birds. Pp. 71–95 in *Current Ornithology,* vol. 4, R. F. Johnston, ed. New York: Plenum Press.

Hakkarainen, H., and E. Korpimaki. 1991. Reversed sexual size dimorphism in Tengmalm's owl: is small male size adaptive? *Oikos* 61:337–46.

Halle, S. 1988. Avian predation upon a mixed community of common voles (*Microtus arvalis*) and woodmice (*Apodeum sylvaticus*). *Oecologia* 75:451–55.

Harrison, C. J. O. 1960. The food of some urban tawny owls. *Bird Study* 7:236–40.

Hasbrouck, E. M. 1893. Evolution and dichromatism in the genus *Megascops. Amer. Natur.* 27:521–33, 638–49.

Haverschmidt, F. 1946. Observations on the breeding habits of the little owl. *Ardea* 34:214–46.

Hayward, G. 1986. Activity pattern of a pair of nesting flammulated owls (*Otus flammeolus*) in Idaho. *Northwest Sci.* 60:141–44.

Hayward, G. D., and E. O. Garton. 1988. Resource partitioning among forest owls in the River of No Return Wilderness, Idaho. *Oecologia* 75:253–65.

Helverson, D. V. 1980. Structure and function of antiphonal duets. *Acta XVII Congr. Internatl. Ornithol.* 1:682–88.

Henny, C. J. 1969. Geographical variation in mortality rates and production requirements of the barn owl (*Tyto alba* ssp.). *Bird-Banding* 40:277–90.

Henny, C. J., and L. F. Van Camp. 1979. Annual weight cycle in wild screech owls. *Auk* 96:795–96.

Hirons, G. J. M. 1982. The effects of fluctuation in rodent numbers on breeding success in the tawny owl *Strix aluco. Mammal Rev.* 12:155–57.

———. 1985a. The effects of territorial behaviour on the stability and dispersion of a tawny owl (*Strix aluco*) population. *J. Zool. London (B)* 1:21–48.

———. 1985b. The importance of body reserves for successful reproduction in the tawny owl (*Strix aluco*). *J. Zool. London (B)* 1:1–20.

Hirons, G. J. M., A. R. Hardy, and P. I. Stanley. 1984. Body weight, gonad development and molt in the tawny owl (*Strix aluco*). *J. Zool. London* 202:145–64.

Hoglund, N. H., and E. Lansgren. 1968. The great gray owl and its prey in Sweden," *Viltrevy* 5:363–421.

Hornfeldt, B., B. G. Carlsson, O. Lofgren, and U. Eklund. 1990. Effects of cyclic food supply on breeding performance in Tengmalm's owl (*Aegolius funereus*). *Canadian J. Zool.* 68:522–30.

Hornfeldt, B., and U. Eklund. 1990. The effect of food on laying date and clutch-size in Tengmalm's owl *Aegolius funereus. Ibis* 132:95–406.

Hough, F. 1960. Two significant calling periods of the screech owl. *Auk* 77:227–28.

Hrubant, H. E. 1955. An analysis of the color phases of the eastern screech owl, *Otus asio,* by the gene frequency method. *Amer. Natur.* 89:223–30.

Huhtala, K., E. Korpimaki, and E. Pulliainen. 1987. Foraging activity and growth of nestlings in the hawk owl: adapative strategies under northern conditions. Pp. 152–56 in *Biology and Conservation of Northern Forest Owls,* R. W. Nero, R. J. Clark, R. J. Knapton, and R. H. Hamre, eds. USDA Forest Service, Genl. Tech. Rept. RM-142.

Hussell, D. J. T. 1985. Clutch size, day length, and seasonality of resources: comments on Ashmole's hypothesis. *Auk* 102:632–34.

Ingram, C. 1959. The importance of juvenile cannibalism in the breeding biology of certain birds of prey. *Auk* 76:218–26.

Ivlev, V. S. 1961. *Experiment Ecology of the Feeding of Fishes.* New Haven: Yale Univ. Press.

Jaksic, F. M., and J. H. Carothers. 1985. Ecological, morphological, and bioenergetic correlates of hunting mode in hawks and owls. *Ornis Scand.* 16:165–72.

James, F. C. 1970. Geographic variation in birds and its relationship to climate. *Ecology* 51:365–90.

James, F. C., and C. E. McCulloch. 1985. Data analysis and the design of experiments in ornithology. Pp. 1–63 in *Current Ornithology,* vol. 2, R. F. Johnston, ed. New York: Plenum Press.

Johnsgard, P. A. 1988. *North American Owls; Biology and Natural History.* Washington, D.C.: Smithsonian Inst. Press.

Johnson, D. H. 1987. Barred owls and nest boxes, results of a five year study in Minnesota. Pp. 129–34 in *Biology and Conservation of Northern Forest Owls.* R. W. Nero, R. J. Clark, R. J. Knapton, and R. H. Hamre, eds. USDA Forest Service Genl. Tech. Rept. RM-142.

Johnson, P. N. 1994. Barn owl (*Tyto alba*) selection and use of natural and nest-box nesting sites in an agricultural landscape. *J. Raptor Res.* 28 (in press).

Johnson, R. R., B. T. Brown, L. T. Haight, and J. M. Simpson. 1981. Playback recordings as a special avian censusing technique. *Studies in Avian Biology* 6:68–75.

Kaiser, T. J., and T. L. Bucher. 1985. The consequences of reverse sexual size dimorphism for oxygen consumption, ventilation, and water loss in relation to ambient temperature in the prairie falcon, *Falco mexi-canus*. *Physiol. Zool.* 58:749–58.

Karalus, K. E., and A. W. Eckert. 1974. *The Owls of North America*. New York: Doubleday.

Karlsson, J., and S. G. Nilsson. 1977. The influence of nest-box area on clutch size in some hole-nesting passerines. *Ibis* 119:207–11.

Keith, L. B. 1963. *Wildlife's Ten-Year Cycle*. Madison: Univ. of Wisconsin Press.

Kelso, L. 1940. Antipathy in the screech owl. *Auk* 57:252–53.

———. 1941. Behavior of the eastern screech owl (*Otus asio naevius*). *Biol. Leaflet* 23.

———. 1942. Weight variation in *Otus asio*. *Biol. Leaflet* 18.

———. 1950. The post juvenal molt of the northeastern screech owl. *Biol. Leaflet* 50.

Kendeigh, S. C. 1961. Energy of birds conserved by roosting in cavities. *Wilson Bull.* 73:140–47.

Kennedy, E. D., and D. W. White. 1991. Repeatability of clutch size in house wrens. *Wilson Bull.* 103:552–58.

Kilham, L. 1989. *The American Crow and Common Raven*. College Station: Texas A&M Univ. Press.

Klaas, E. E., and D. M. Swineford. 1976. Chemical residue content and hatchability of screech owl eggs. *Wilson Bull.* 88:421–26.

Klomp, H. 1970. The determination of clutch-size in birds: a review. *Ardea* 58:1–124.

Knight, R. L., D. J. Grout, and S. A. Temple. 1987. Nest-defense behavior of the American crow in urban and rural areas. *Condor* 89:175–77.

Knight, R. L., and S. A. Temple. 1981. Methodological problems in studies of avian nest defense. *Animal Behav.* 29:561–66.

———. 1986. Why does intensity of avian nest defense increase during the nesting cycle? *Auk* 103:318–27.

Koenig, W. D. 1982. Ecological and social factors affecting hatchability of eggs. *Auk* 99:526–36.

———. 1988. On determination of viable population size in birds and mammals. *Wildl. Soc. Bull.* 16:230–34.

Korpimaki, E. 1981. On the ecology and biology of Tengmalm's owl (*Aegolius funereus*). *Acta Univ. Ouluensis, Ser. A. Biol. 13*.

———. 1984. Clutch size and breeding success of Tengmalm's owl *Aegolius funereus* in natural cavities and nest-boxes. *Ornis Fennica* 61:80–83.

———. 1985a. Clutch size and breeding success in relation to nest-box size in Tengmalm's owl *Aegolius funereus*. *Holarctic Ecol.* 8:175–80.

————. 1985b. Wintering strategies of Tengmalm's owl *Aegolius funereus.* *Aquilo Ser. Zool.* 24:55–63.

————. 1986a. Gradients in population fluctuation of Tengmalm's owl *Aegolius funereus* in Europe. *Oecologia* 69:195–201.

————. 1986b. Reversed size dimorphism in birds of prey, especially Tengmalm's owls *Aegolius funereus:* a test of the "starvation hypothesis," Ornis Scand. 17:326–33.

————. 1987a. Clutch size, breeding success, and brood experiments in Tengmalm's owl *Aegolius funereus:* a test of hypotheses. *Ornis Scand.* 18:277–84.

————. 1987b. Prey caching of breeding Tengmalm's owl *Aegolius funereus* as a buffer against temporary food shortage. *Ibis* 129:499–510.

————. 1987c. Selection for nest-hole shift and tactics of breeding dispersal in Tengmalm's owl *Aegolius funereus.* *J. Animal Ecol.* 56:185–96.

————. 1987d. Sexual size dimorphism and life history traits of Tengmalm's owl: a review. Pp. 157–61 in *Biology and Conservation of Northern Forest Owls,* R. W. Nero, R. J. Clark, R. J. Knapton, and R. H. Hamre, eds. USDA Forest Service, Genl. Tech. Rept. RM-142.

————. 1987e. Timing of breeding of Tengmalm's owl *Aegolius funereus.* *Ibis* 129:58–68.

————. 1988a. Costs of reproduction and success of manipulated broods under varying food conditions in Tengmalm's owl. *J. Animal Ecol.* 57:1,027–1,039.

————. 1988b. Diet of breeding Tengmalm's owls *Aegolius funereus:* long-term changes and year-to-year variation under cyclic food conditions. *Ornis Fennica* 65:21–30.

————. 1988c. Effects of age on breeding performance of Tengmalm's owl *Aegolius funereus* in western Finland. *Ornis Scand.* 19:21–26.

————. 1988d. Effects of territory quality on occupancy, breeding performance and breeding dispersal in Tengmalm's owl. *J. Animal Ecol.* 57:97–108.

————. 1988e. Factors promoting polygny in European birds of prey: a hypothesis. *Oecologia* 77:278–85.

————. 1989a. Breeding performance of Tengmalm's owl *Aegolius funereus:* effects of supplementary feeding in a peak vole year. *Ibis* 131:51–56.

————. 1989b. Mating system and mate choice of Tengmalm's owls *Aegolius funereus.* *Ibis* 131:41–50.

————. 1990a. Body mass of breeding Tengmalm's owl (*Aegolius funereus*): seasonal, between-year, site, and age-related variation. *Ornis Scand.* 21:169–78.

———. 1990b. Low repeatability of laying date and clutch size in Tengmalm's owl: an adaptation to fluctuating food conditions. *Ornis Scand.* 21:282–86.

———. 1991a. Lifetime reproductive success of male Tengmalm's owls. *Acta XX Congr. Internatl. Ornithol.* 3:1,528–1,541.

———. 1991b. Poor reproductive success of polygynously mated female Tengmalm's owl: are better options available? *Animal Behav.* 41:37–47.

Korpimaki, E., and H. Hakkarainen. 1991. Fluctuating food supply affects clutch size of Tengmalm's owl independent of laying date. *Oecologia* 85:543–52.

Korpimaki, E., and H. Hongell. 1986. Partial migration as an adaptation to nest-site scarcity and vole cycles in Tengmalm's owl *Aegolius funereus. Var. Fagelv. Supp.* 11:85–92.

Korpimaki, E., and K. Huhtala. 1986. Nest visit frequencies and activity patterns of Ural Owls *Strix uralensis. Ornis Fennica* 63:42–46.

Korpimaki, E. Huhtala, and S. Sulkava. 1990. Does the year-to-year variation in the diet of eagle and Ural owls support the alternative prey hypothesis? *Oikos* 58:47–54.

Korpimaki, E., and M. Lagerstrom. 1988. Survival and natal dispersal of fledglings of Tengmalm's owl in relation to fluctuating food conditions and hatching date. *J. Animal Ecol.* 57:433–41.

Korpimaki, E., and S. Sulkava. 1987. Diet and breeding performance of Ural owls *Strix uralensis* under fluctuating food conditions. *Ornis Fennica* 64:57–66.

Kostrzewa, A., and R. Kostrzewa. 1990. The relationship of spring and summer weather with density and breeding performance of the buzzard *Buteo buteo,* goshawk *Accipiter gentilis,* and kestrel *Falco tunniculus. Ibis* 132:550–59.

Kotler, B. P., J. S. Brown, R. J. Smith, and W. O. Wirtz II. 1988. The effects of morphology and body size on rates of owl predation on desert rodents. *Oikos* 53:145–52.

Krebs, C. J. 1978. A review of the Chitty hypothesis of population regulation. *Canadian J. Zool.* 56:2,463–80.

Lack, D. 1954. *The Natural Regulation of Animal Numbers.* London: Oxford Univ. Press.

———. 1966. *Population Studies of Birds.* London: Oxford Univ. Press.

Landsberg, H. E. 1981. *The Urban Climate.* London: Academic Press.

Lessells, C. M., and P. T. Boag. 1987. Unrepeatable repeatabilities: a common mistake. *Auk* 104:116–21.

Ligon, J. D. 1968. The biology of the elf owl, *Micrathene whitneyi. Misc. Publ. Zool. Univ. Michigan* 136.

———. 1969. Some aspects of temperature relations in small owls. *Auk* 86:458–72.

Lohrer, F. E. 1985. Ontogeny of thermoregulation in the eastern screech owl. *J. Field Ornithol.* 56:65–66.

Longland, W. S. 1989. Reversed sexual size dimorphism: its effects on prey selection by the great-horned owl, *Bubo virginianus*. *Oikos* 54:395–98.

Lundberg, A. 1979. Residency, migration and a compromise: adaptation to nest-site scarcity and food specilization in three Fennoscandian owl species. *Oecologia* 41:273–81.

———. 1981. Population ecology of the Ural owl *Strix uralensis* in central Sweden. *Ornis Scand.* 12:111–19.

———. 1986. Adaptive advantages of reversed sexual size dimorphism in European owls. *Ornis Scand.* 17:133–40.

Lundberg, A., and B. Westman. 1984. Reproductive success, mortality and nest site requirements of the Ural owl *Strix uralensis* in central Sweden. *Ann. Zool. Fennici* 21:265–69.

Lundberg, S. 1985. The importance of egg hatchability and nest predation in clutch size evolution in altricial birds. *Oikos* 45:110–17.

Luniak, M., and R. Mulsow. 1988. Ecological parameters in urbanization of the European blackbird. *Acta XIX Congr. Internatl. Ornithol.* 2:1,787–93.

Lynch, P. J., and D. G. Smith. 1984. Census of eastern screech-owls (*Otus asio*) in urban open-space areas using tape-recorded song. *Amer. Birds* 38:388–91.

Lythgoe, J. N. 1979. *The Ecology of Vision.* Oxford: Clarendon Press.

Magrath, R. D. 1990. Hatching asynchrony in altricial birds. *Biol. Rev.* 65:587–622.

Marks, J. S. 1983. Prolonged incubation by a long-eared owl. *J. Field Ornithol.* 54:199–200.

Marshall, J. T., Jr. 1967. Parallel variation in North and Middle American screech-owls. *Western Found. Vert Zool. Monogr.* 1.

Marti, C. D. 1990. Sex and age dimorphism in the barn owl and a test of mate choice. *Auk* 107:246–54.

Marti, C. D., and J. C. Hogue. 1979. Selection of prey size in screech owls. *Auk* 96:319–27.

Marti, C. D., and P. W. Wagner. 1985. Winter mortality in common barn owls and its effect on population density and reproduction. *Condor* 87:111–15.

McAtee, W. L. 1980. *An Evaluation of the Short and Long-term Impacts Along an Escarpment Landform.* B. S. thesis, Baylor Univ., Waco, Texas.

McCallum, D. A., and F. R. Gehlbach. 1988. Nest-site preferences of flammulated owls in western New Mexico. *Condor* 90:653–61.
McComb, W. C., and R. E. Noble. 1981a. Nest-box and natural cavity use in
three mid-south forest habitats. *J. Wildl. Mgmt.* 45:93–101.
———. 1981b. Microclimates of nest boxes and natural cavities in bot-
tomland hardwoods. *J. Wildl. Mgmt.* 45:284–89.
———. 1981c. The effect of screech owl presence upon relative humidity inside a nest box. *Kentucky Warbler* 57:63–64.
McPherson, R. J., and R. D. Brown. 1982. Mobbing responses of some passerines to the calls and location of the screech owl. *J. Raptor Res.*
15:23–30.
Meijer, T., S. Daan, and C. Dijkstra. 1988. Female condition and reproduction: effects of food manipulation in free-living and captive kestrels.
Ardea 76:141–54.
Mendelsohn, J. M. 1986. Sexual size dimorphism and roles in raptors—fat females, agile males. *Durban Mus. Novitates* 13:321–36.
Merson, M. H., L. D. Leta, and R. E. Byers. 1983. Observations on roosting
sites of screech-owls. *J. Field Ornithol.* 54:419–21.
Mikkola, H. 1983. *Owls of Europe.* London: T. and A. D. Poyser Ltd.
Mills, A. M. 1986. The influence of moonlight on the behavior of goatsuck-
ers (Caprimulgidae). *Auk* 103:370–78.
Mock, D. W. 1984. Infanticide, siblicide, and avian nestling mortality. Pp. 3–
30 in *Infanticide: Comparative and Evolutionary Perspectives,* G.
Hausfater and S. B. Hrdy, eds. New York: Aldine.
Moller, A. P. 1989. Parasites, predators and nest boxes: facts and artifacts in
nest box studies of birds? *Oikos* 56:421–23.
———. 1992. Nest boxes and the scientific rigour of experimental studies.
Oikos 63:309–11.
Montgomerie, R. D., and P. J. Weatherhead. 1988. Risks and rewards of nest
defence by parent birds. *Quart. Rev. Biol.* 63:167–87.
Moreno, J. 1989. Strategies of mass change in breeding birds. *Biol. J. Linn.
Soc.* 37:297–310.
Morrison, M. L. 1986. Bird populations as indicators of environmental
change. Pp. 429–51 in *Current Ornithology,* vol. 3. R. F. Johnson,
ed. New York: Plenum Press.
Morrison, M. L., and B. J. Walton. 1980. The laying of replacement clutches
by falconiforms and strigiforms in North America. *J. Raptor Res.*
14:79–85.
Mosher, J. A., and C. J. Henny. 1976. Thermal adaptiveness of plumage
color in screech owls. *Auk* 93:614–19.
Mosher, J. A., and P. F. Matray. 1974. Size dimorphism: a factor in energy
savings for broad-winged hawks. *Auk* 91:325–41.

Mueller, H. C. 1986. The evolution of reversed sexual dimorphism in owls: an empirical analysis of possible selective forces. *Wilson Bull.* 98:387–406.

———. 1989. Evolution of reversed sexual size dimorphism: sex or starvation? *Ornis Scand.* 20:265–72.

Muir, R. C. 1954. Calling and feeding rates of fledged tawny owls. *Bird Study* 1:111–17.

Murphy, E. C., and E. Haukioja. 1986. Clutch size in nidicolous birds. Pp. 141–80 in *Current Ornithology,* vol. 3, R. F. Johnston, ed. New York: Plenum Press.

Murray, G. A. 1976. Geographic variation in the clutch sizes of eleven owl species. *Auk* 93:602–13.

Mutter, D., D. Nolin, and A. Shartle. 1984. Raptor populations on selected park preserves in Montgomery County, Ohio. *Ohio J. Sci.* 84:29–32.

Newton, I. 1979. *Population Ecology of Raptors.* London: T. and A. D. Poyser Ltd.

———. 1985. Lifetime reproductive output of female sparrowhawks. *J. Animal Ecol.* 54:241–53.

———. 1986. *The Sparrowhawk.* London: T. and A. D. Poyser Ltd.

———. 1988. A key factor analysis of a sparrowhawk population. *Oecologia* 76:588–96.

———. 1989. Synthesis. Pp. 441–69 in *Lifetime Reproduction in Birds,* I. Newton, ed. London: Academic Press.

———. 1991. Population limitation in birds of prey: a comparative approach. Pp. 3–21 in *Bird Population Studies: Relevance to Conservation and Management.* C. M. Perrins, J. D. Lebreton, and G. J. M. Hirons, eds. New York: Oxford Univ. Press.

Newton, I., and M. Marquiss. 1976. Occupancy and success of nesting territories in the European sparrowhawk. *J. Raptor Res.* 10:65–71.

———. 1981. Effect of additional food on laying dates and clutch sizes of sparrowhawks. *Ornis Scand.* 12:224–29.

———. 1983. Dispersal of sparrowhawks between birthplace and breeding place. *J. Animal Ecol.* 52:463–77.

———. 1984. Seasonal trend in the breeding performance of sparrowhawks. *J. Animal Ecol.* 53:809–29.

———. 1986. Population regulation in sparrowhawks. *J. Animal Ecol.* 55:463–80.

Newton, I., M. Marquiss, and A. Village. 1983. Weights, breeding, and survival in European sparrowhawks. *Auk* 100:344–54.

Newton, I., and D. Moss. 1986. Post-fledging survival of sparrowhawks *Ae-*

cipiter nisus in relation to mass, brood size and brood composition at fledging. *Ibis* 128:73–80.

Newton, I., I. Wyllie, and P. Rothery. 1993. Annual survival of sparrowhawks *Accipiter nisus* breeding in three areas of Britain. *Ibis* 135:49–60.

Nice, M. M. 1957. Nesting success in altricial birds. *Auk* 74:305–21.

Nilsson, J. A. 1993a. Energetic constraints on hatching asychrony. *Amer. Natur.* 141:158–66.

———. 1993b. Energy constraints and ultimate decisions during egg-laying in the blue tit. *Ecology* 74:244–57.

Nishimura, K., and M. T. Abe. 1988. Prey susceptibilities, prey utilization and variable attack efficiencies of Ural owls. *Oecologia* 77:414–33.

Nol, E., and J. N. M. Smith. 1987. Effects of age and breeding experience on seasonal reproductive success in the song sparrow. *J. Animal Ecol.* 56:301–13.

Norberg, R. A. 1970. Hunting technique of Tengmalm's owl *Aegoius funereus* L. *Ornis Scand.* 1:51–64.

———. 1981. Temporary weight decrease in breeding birds may result in more fledged young. *Amer. Natur.* 118:838–50.

Nowicki, T. 1974. A census of screech owls (*Otus asio*) using tape-recorded calls. *Jack-Pine Warbler* 52:98–101.

Nur, N. 1988. The cost of reproduction in birds: an examination of the evidence. *Ardea* 76:155–69.

Oberholser, H. C. 1974. *The Bird Life of Texas,* vol. 1. E. B. Kincaid, ed. Austin: Univ. of Texas Press.

Orians, G. H., and N. E. Pearson. 1979. On the theory of central place foraging. Pp. 155–77 in *Analysis of Ecological Systems.* D. J. Horn, R. D. Mitchell, and G. R. Stairs, eds. Columbus: Ohio State Univ. Press.

Osborne, P., and L. Osborne. 1980. The contribution of nest-site characteristics to breeding success among blackbirds *Turdus meruula. Ibis* 122:512–17.

Owen, D. F. 1963a. Polymorphism in the screech owl in eastern North America. *Wilson Bull.* 75:183–90.

———. 1963b. Variation in North American screech owls and the subspecies concept. *Syst. Zool.* 12:8–14.

Palmer, D. A. 1987. Annual, seasonal, and nightly variation in calling activity of boreal and northern saw-whet owls. Pp. 162–68 in *Biology and Conservation of Northern Forest Owls.* R. W. Nero, R. J. Clark, R. J. Knapton, and R. H. Hamre, eds. USDA Forest Service, Genl. Tech. Rept. RM-142.

Patton, P. W. C., C. J. Zabell, P. L. Neal, G. N. Steger, N. G. Tilghman, and
  B. R. Noon. 1991. Effects of ratio tags on spotted owls. *J. Wildl.
  Mgmt.* 55:617–22.
Payne, R. B. 1990. Natal dispersal, area effects, and effective population size.
  J. Field Ornithol. 61:396–403.
Perrins, C. M. 1970. The timing of birds' breeding season. *Ibis* 112:242–55.
———. 1991. Constraints on the demographic parameters of bird popula-
  tions. Pp. 190–206 in *Bird Population Studies: Relevance to Conser-
  vation and Management.* C. M. Perrins, J. D. Lebreton, and
  G. J. M. Hirons, eds. New York: Oxford Univ. Press.
Perrins, C. M., and T. R. Birkhead. 1983. *Avian Ecology.* London: Blackie.
Pietiainen, H. 1988a. Breeding season quality, age, and the effect of experience on the reproductive success of the Ural owl (*Strix uralensis*).
  Auk 105:316–24.
———. 1988b. Reproductive tactics of the Ural owl *Strix uralensis* depending on cyclic vole populations. Ph.D. diss., Univ. of Helsinki,
  Finland.
———. 1989. Seasonal and individual variation in the production of offspring in the Ural owl, *Strix uralensis. J. Anim. Ecol.* 58:905–20.
Pietiainen, H., P. Saurola, and H. Kolunen. 1984. The reproductive constraints on moult in the Ural owl *Strix uralensis. Ann. Zool. Fennici.* 21:277–81.
Pietiainen, H., P. Saurola, and R. A. Vaisanen. 1986. Parental investment in
  clutch size and egg size in the Ural owl *Strix uralensis. Ornis Scand.*
  17:309–25.
Pitts, T. D. 1988. Effects of nest-box size on eastern bluebird nests. *J. Field
  Ornithol.* 59:309–13.
Poole, E. L. 1938. Weights and wing areas in North American birds. *Auk*
  55:511–17.
Poole, K. G., and D. A. Boag. 1988. Ecology of gyrfalcons, *Falco rusticolus,*
  in the central Canadian Artic: diet and feeding behavior. *Canadian
  J. Zool.* 66:334–44.
Postler, J. L., and G. W. Barrett. 1982. Prey selection and bioenergetics of cap-
  tive screech owls. *Ohio J. Sci.* 82:55–58.
Prescott, K. W. 1985. Eastern screech-owl captures goldfish in patio pond.
  Wilson Bull. 97:572–73.
Rea, S. C. 1968. A territorial encounter between screech owls. *Wilso Bull.*
  80:107.
Reid, W. V. 1988. Age-specific patterns of reproduction in the glaucous-
  winged gull: increased effort with age? *Ecology* 69:1,454–65.
Reynolds, R. T., and B. D. Linkhart. 1987a. Fidelity to territory and mate in
  flammulated owls. Pp. 234–38 in *Biology and Conservation of*

Northern Forest Owls. R. W. Nero, R. J. Clark, R. J. Knapton, and R. H. Hamre, eds. USDA Forest Service, Genl. Tech. Rept. RM-142.

———. 1987b. The nesting biology of flammulated owls in Colorado. Pp. 239–48 in *Biology and Conservation of Northern Forest Owls.* R. W. Nero, R. J. Clark, R. J. Knapton, and R. H. Hamre, eds. USDA Forest Service, Genl. Tech. Rept. RM-142.

Reznick, D. 1985. Cost of reproduction: an evaluation of the empirical evidence. *Oikos* 44:257–67.

Richmond, M. L., L. R. Deweese, and R. E. Fillmore. 1980. Brief observations on the breeding biology of the flammulated owl in Colorado. *Western Birds* 11:35–46.

Ricklefs, R. E. 1968a. Patterns of growth in birds. *Ibis* 110:419–51.

———. 1968b. Weight recession in nestling birds. *Auk* 85:30–35.

———. 1969. An analysis of nesting mortality in birds. *Smithsonian Contrib. Zool.* 9.

———. 1982. Some considerations on sibling competition and avian growth rates. *Auk* 99:141–47.

———. 1983. Comparative avian demography. Pp. 1–32 in *Current Ornithology,* vol. 7. R. F. Johnston, ed. New York: Plenum Press.

Ritchison, G., J. R. Belthoff, and E. J. Sparks. 1992. Dispersal restlessness: evidence for innate dispersal by juvenile eastern screech-owls. *Animal Behav.* 43:57–65.

Ritchison, G., and P. M. Cavanaugh. 1992. Prey use by eastern screech-owls: seasonal variation in eastern Kentucky and a review of previous studies. *J. Raptor Res.* 26:66–73.

Ritchison, G., P. M. Cavanagh, J. R. Belthoff, and E. J. Sparks. 1988. The singing behavior of eastern screech owls: seasonal timing and response to playback of conspecific song. *Condor* 90:648–52.

Robbins, C. S., D. K. Dawson, and B. A. Dowell. 1989. Habitat area requirements of breeding forest birds of the middle Atlantic states. *Wildl. Monogr.* 103.

Robertson, R. J., and W. B. Rendell. 1990. A comparison of the breeding ecology of a secondary cavity-nesting bird, the tree swallow (*Tachycineta bicolor*) in nest-boxes and natural cavities. *Canadian J. Zool.* 68:1,046–52.

Rockwell, R. F., and G. F. Barrowclough. 1987. Gene flow and the genetic structure of populations. Pp. 223–55 in *Avian Genetics: A Population and Ecological Approach.* F. Cooke and P. A. Buckley, eds. London: Academic Press.

Roseberry, J. L., and W. D. Klimstra. 1984. *Population Ecology of the Bobwhite.* Carbondale: Southern Illinois Univ. Press.

Rosenfield, R. N., and J. Bielefeldt. 1991. Reproductive investment and anti-predator behavior in Cooper's hawks during the pre-laying period. *J. Raptor Res.* 25:113–15.

Rosenzweig, M. L. 1968. Net primary productivity of terrestrial communities: prediction from climatological data. *Amer. Natur.* 102:67–74.

Ross, D. A. 1989. Amphibians and reptiles in the diets of North American raptors. *Wisconsin Endangered Species Rept.* 59.

Rudolph, S. G. 1982. Foraging strategies of American kestrels during breeding. *Ecology* 63:1,268–76.

Saether, B. E. 1990. Age-specific variation in reproductive performance of birds. Pp. 251–83 in *Current Ornithology,* vol. 7. D. M. Power, ed. New York: Plenum Press.

Safina, C. 1984. Selection for reduced male size in raptorial birds: the possible roles of female choice and mate guarding. *Oikos* 43:159–64.

Saurola, P. 1987. Mate and nest-site fidelity in Ural and tawny owls. Pp. 81–86 in *Biology and Conservation of Northern Forest Owls.* R. W. Nero, R. J. Clark, R. J. Knapton, and R. H. Hamre, eds. USDA Forest Service, Genl. Tech. Rept. RM-142.

———. 1989a. Breeding strategy of the Ural owl, *Strix uralensis.* Pp. 235–40 in *Raptors in the Modern World.* B. U. Meyburg and R. D. Chancellor, eds. Berlin: World Working Group on Birds of Prey.

———. 1989b. Ural owl. Pp. 327–45 in *Lifetime Reproduction in Birds.* I. Newton, ed. London: Academic Press.

Schantz, T. von, and I. N. Nilsson. 1981. The reversed size dimorphism in birds of prey: a new hypothesis. *Oikos* 36:129–32.

Schorger, A. H. 1954. Color phases of the screech owl between Madison, Wisconsin, and Freeport, Illinois. *Auk* 71:105.

Shedd, D. H. 1982. Seasonal variation and function of mobbing and related antipredator behaviors of the American robin (*Turdue migratorius*). *Auk* 99:342–46.

———. 1983. Seasonal variation in mobbing intensity in the black capped chickadee. *Wilson Bull.* 95:343–48.

Sherman, A. R. 1911. Nest life of the screech owl. *Auk* 18:155–68.

Skutch, A. F. 1976. *Parent Birds and Their Young.* Austin: Univ. of Texas Press.

Slagsvold, T. 1984. Clutch size variation of birds in relation to nest predation: on the cost of reproduction. *J. Animal Ecol.* 53:945–53.

Slagsvold, T., and J. T. Lifjeld. 1988. Ultimate adjustment of clutch size to parental feeding capacity in a passerine bird. *Ecology* 69:1918–22.

Slagsvold, T., J. Sandvik, G. Rofstad, O. Lorentsen, and M. Husby. 1984. On the adaptive value of intraclutch egg-size variation in birds. *Auk* 101:685–97.

Smith, C. C., and O. J. Riechman. 1984. The evolution of food caching by birds and mammals. *Ann. Rev. Ecol. Syst.* 15:329–51.

Smith, D. G., A. Devine, and D. Walsh. 1987. Censusing screech owls in southern Connecticut. Pp. 255–67 in *Biology and Conservation of Northern Forest Owls.* R. W. Nero, R. J. Clark, R. J. Knapton, and R. H. Hamre, eds. USDA Forest Service, Genl. Tech. Rept. RM-142.

Smith, D. G., and R. Gilbert. 1984. Eastern screech-owl home range and use of suburban habitats in southern Connecticut. *J. Field Ornithol.* 55:322–29.

Smith, D. G., and E. Hiestand. 1990. Alloparenting at an eastern screech-owl nest. *Condor* 92:246–47.

Smith, D. G., and S. N. Wiemeyer. 1992. Determining sex of eastern screech owls using discriminant function analysis. *J. Raptor Res.* 26:24–26.

Snyder, N. F. R., and H. A. Snyder. 1973. Experimental study of feeding rates of nesting Cooper's hawks. *Condor* 75:461–63.

Snyder, N. F. R., and J. W. Wiley. 1976. Sexual size dimorphism in hawks and owls of North America. *Ornithol. Monogr.* 20.

Solheim, R. 1983. Bigyny and biandry in the Tengmalm's owl *Aegolius Funereus. Ornis Scand.* 14:51–57.

———. 1984a. Breeding biology of the pygmy owl *Glaucidium passerinum* in two biogeographical zones in southeastern Norway. *Ann. Zool. Fennici* 21:295–300.

———. 1984b. Caching behavior, prey choice and surplus killing by pygmy owls *Glaucidium passerinum* during winter, a functional response of a generalist predator. *Ann. Zool. Fennici* 21:301–308.

Sonerud, G. 1985a. Nest hole shift in Tengmalm's owl *Aegolius funereus* as defense against nest predation involving long-term memory in the predator. *J. Animal Ecol.* 54:179–92.

———. 1985b. Risk of nest predation in three species of hole-nesting owls: influence on choice of nesting habitat and incubation behavior. *Ornis Scand.* 16:261–69.

Sonerud, G. A., R. Solheim, and K. Prestrud. 1988. Dispersal of Tengmalm's owl Aegolius *funereus* in relation to prey availability and nesting success. *Ornis Scand.* 19:175–81.

Southern, H. N. 1970. The natural control of a population of tawny owls (*Strix aluco*). *J. Zool. London* 162:197–285.

Southern, H. N., and V. P. Lowe. 1968. The pattern of distribution of prey and predation in tawny owl territories. *J. Animal Ecol.* 37:5–97.

Southern, H. N., R. Vaughan, and R. C. Muir. 1954. The behaviour of young tawny owls after fledging. *Bird Study* 1:101–10.

Sproat, T. M., and G. Ritchison. 1993. The nest defense behavior of eastern screech-owls: effects of nest stage, sex, nest type and predator location. *Condor* 95: 288–96.

Stinson, C. H. 1979. On the selective advantage of fratricide in raptors. *Evolution* 33:1,219–25.

Sumner, E. L., Jr. 1928. Notes on the development of young screech owls. *Condor* 30:333–38.

———. 1929. Comparative studies on the growth of young raptors. *Condor* 31:85–111.

Sutton, G. M. 1927. Mortality among screech owls of Pennsylvania. *Auk* 44:563–64.

———. 1929. Insect catching tactics of the screech owl (*Otus asio*). *Auk* 46:545–46.

Swengel, S. R., and A. B. Swengel. 1987. Study of a saw-whet owl population in Sauk County, Wisconsin. Pp. 199–208 in *Biology and Conservation of Northern Forest Owls.* R. W. Nero, R. J. Clark, R. J. Knapton, and R. H. Hamre, eds. USDA Forest Service, Genl. Tech. Rept. RM-142.

Taylor, I. R. 1991. Effects of nest inspections and ration tagging on barn owl breeding success. *J. Wildl. Mgmt.* 55:312–15.

Temple, S. A., and J. A. Wiens. 1989. Bird populations and environmental changes: can birds be bioindicators? *Amer. Birds* 45:260–70.

Thomas, B. T. 1977. Tropical screech owl nest defense behavior and nestling growth rate. *Wilson Bull.* 89:609–12.

Toland, B. R. 1987. The effect of vegetative cover on foraging strategies, hunting success and nesting distribution of American kestrels in central Missouri. *J. Raptor Res.* 21:14–20.

Tomialojc, L. 1980. The impact of predation on urban and rural woodpigeon (*Columbia palumbus* L.) populations. *Polish Ecol. Studies* 5:141–220.

Tomialojc, L., and F. R. Gehlbach (ed.). 1988. Avian population responses to man-made environments. *Acta XIX Congr. Interntl. Ornithol.* vol. 2:1,777–1,830.

Toft, C. A. 1990. Reply to Seaman and Jaeger: an appeal to common sense. *Herpetologica* 46:357–61.

Tukey, J. W. 1980. We need both exploratory and confirmatory [statistics]. *Amer. Statistician* 34:23–25.

Turner, L. J., and R. W. Dimmick. 1981. Seasonal prey capture by the screech owl in Tennessee. *J. Tennessee Acad. Sci.* 56:56–59.

U.S. Dept. Commerce, NOAA. 1979. *Climatic Atlas of the United States.*

Vanderwerf, E. 1992. Lack's clutch-size hypothesis: an examination of the evidence using meta-analysis. *Ecology* 73:1,699–1,705.

Van Camp, L. F., and C. J. Henny. 1975. The screech owl: its life history and population ecology in northern Ohio. *N. Amer. Fauna* 71.

van Noordwijk, A. J. 1987. Quantitative ecological genetics of great tits. Pp. 363–80 in *Avian Genetics: A Population and Ecological Approach.* F. Cooke and P. A. Buckley, eds. London: Academic Press.

Vieth, W., E. Curio, and U. Ernst. 1980. The adaptive significance of avian mobbing. Part III, Cultural transmission of enemy recognition in blackbirds: cross-species tutoring and properties of learning. *Animal Behav.* 28:1,217–29.

Village, A. 1981. The diet and breeding of long-eared owls in relation to vole numbers. *Bird Study* 28:215–24.

———. 1990. *The Kestrel.* London: T. and A. D. Poyser Ltd.

Wallin, K. 1987. Defence as parental care in tawny owls (*Strix aluco*). *Behaviour* 102:213–30.

Warkentin, I. G., and P. C. James. 1988. Nest-site selection by urban merlins. *Condor* 90:734–38.

Waters, J. R., B. R. Noon, and J. Verner. 1990. Lack of nest site limitation in a cavity-nesting bird community. *J. Wildl. Mgmt.* 54:239–45.

Watkins, J. F., II, F. R. Gehlbach, and J. C. Kroll. 1969. Attractant-repellant secretions in blind snakes (*Leptotyphlops dulcis*) and army ants (*Neivamyrmex Nigrescens*). *Ecology* 50:1,098–1,102.

Wendland, V. 1980. Der waldkauz (*Strix aluco*) im bebaüten Stedtgebiet von Berlin (West). *Beitr. Vogelkd. Jena* 26:157–71.

———. 1984. The influence of prey fluctuations on breeding success of the tawny owl *Strix aluco. Ibis* 126:284–95

Werschkul, D. F., and J. A. Jackson. 1979. Sibling competition and avian growth rates. *Ibis* 121:97–102.

Wiemeyer, S. N. 1987. Propagation of captive eastern screech-owls. *J. Raptor Res.* 21:49–56.

Wijnandts, H. 1984. Ecological energetics of the long-eared owl, *Asio otus. Ardea* 72:1–92.

Wiklund C. G., and J. Stigh. 1983. Nest defence and evolution of reversed sexual size dimorphism in snowy owls *Nyctea scandiaca. Ornis Scand.* 14:58–62.

Index

accidents. *See* mortality

adoption, of chicks, 6

age: and breeding success, 83, 116, 151–54, 156–57, 171, 173; classes of, 167–68; and clutches, 89; and density flux, 178; and fratricide mediation, 116, 153; and juvenile development, 114; and population cycles, 170–71, 181

ant: as commensal, 120–22; as predator, 122

behavior: allopreening, 6, 139; bathing, 57, 96, 138; copulation, 81; courtship, 6, 68, 136–37, 139, 194; daytime, 57; defecation, 96, 138; defensive, 8, 53, 78, 95–96, 129, 142–44, 189, 195–96; feeding-foraging, 53–56, 186, 188–89; fledgling, 129–30; flying, 31–32, 53–54, 129, 188–89; guarding, 34, 36, 68; habituation, 8, 31, 142–43, 188–89; hunting, 6, 52–53, 67, 111–12, 130, 189; individual, 8; learned, 96; mantling, 130; mimicry, 71; mobbing, 13, 58–61, 145; perching, 55, 68; secretive, 187, 189; sex differences in, 8, 52–53, 95, 111–12, 129–30; thermoregulatory, 33–37, 67, 107, 109, 111. *See also specific behaviors*

bill clap, 142, 144

biomass, 51–52, 187; and food, 40, 42, 51–52, 54

birds: as cavity excavators, 57; cavity-nesting, 44, 73; flocks of, 43, 49; foliage-feeding, 43; as food, 42–44, 49, 54, 57, 59, 69, 71, 112, 139; ground-feeding, 43, 49; migrant, 40, 47–48, 50, 59–60; as mobbers, 58–61; nest box-using, 4–5, 34, 81, 82; open-nesting, 44, 116, 173, 186; permanent-resident, 40, 47–49, 83; winter-resident, 47, 49, 83

body size. *See* weight

breeding (nesting): costs/benefits of, 151, 172–73, 191–92; effort of, 92–93; lifetime, 149–53, 158; at replacement nests, 171–72; seasonality of, 47–48, 171; senescence and, 154; strategies for, 185–86; suburban versus rural, 168, 173–74, 178–81; success of, 4, 30–31, 70, 121–22, 151–52, 157, 185; of superior individuals, 155–56, 158–60

brooding: period for, 61, 70, 107–108, 112; period after (post-brooding), 61, 109, 112; temperature for, 108–10. *See also* behavior; periodicity

brood size, 125. *See also* chick; incubation

cache. *See* food

cannibalism, 116–19

cavity, tree: destruction of, 10, 28–29, 187; dimensions of, 5, 22, 27, 68; discovery of, 10; environment and, 23–28; location of, 4, 175–76; making, 27, 192; number of, 10, 12, 192; and preferences, 5, 189; surrogates and, 3; types of, 27. *See also* nest box

chick (nestling): cannibalism of, 116–19; coincidental hatch of, 105; downy-wet, 106; fledging, 125–29; fratricide (siblicide) of, 117–19, 127, 171; growth of, 114–15, 119, 122, 190–91; hand-raised, 8; mortality of, 116–20, 173, 190–91; replacement of, 84; weight of, 106–107. *See also* cohort; fledgling; food; hatching; survival

climate. *See* weather

clutch: environmental influences on, 88–90, 190; hatchability and, 97–99, 191; inheritance of, 162–63; loss of, 8, 84; optimal, 172–73, 191; replacement of, 84, 88, 173–74, 191; seasonal decline in, 87, 191; size of, 8, 87–90, 171–73, 191; survivability of, 97–98, 191; weight of, 93. *See also* cohort; egg

vocalizations (*cont.*)
as, 28, 81, 124, 136–43, 194; muted
(ventriloquistic), 137–38, 140, 189;
screech as, 135, 140–44; sex differences
in, 137, 140, 142

weather: and cavity use, 81; cold front
as, 21; extreme, 21, 71; and hatching
date, 99; and laying date, 83, 191; microclimate and, 21–22; and nest desertion, 87, 175; and population cycles,
180–81, 190
weight (body mass): age-related, 65–66,

162; breeding, 69–71; and breeding success, 67–71, 170–71; and color morphs,
76; flux of, 68–69; inheritance of,
162–63; and longevity, 154–55; loss of,
69–71; and mortality, 71, 153, 192;
and renesting, 92–93; seasonal change
in, 65–67; selective advantage of, 153–
54, 160–64, 185, 188, 192; and sexual
dimorphism 6, 34–36, 66–68; surface
area/volume ratio of, 36, 67; and
weather, 68–69. *See also* biomass
wing-loading: adult, 71; fledgling, 124–
25. *See also* dimorphism, sexual